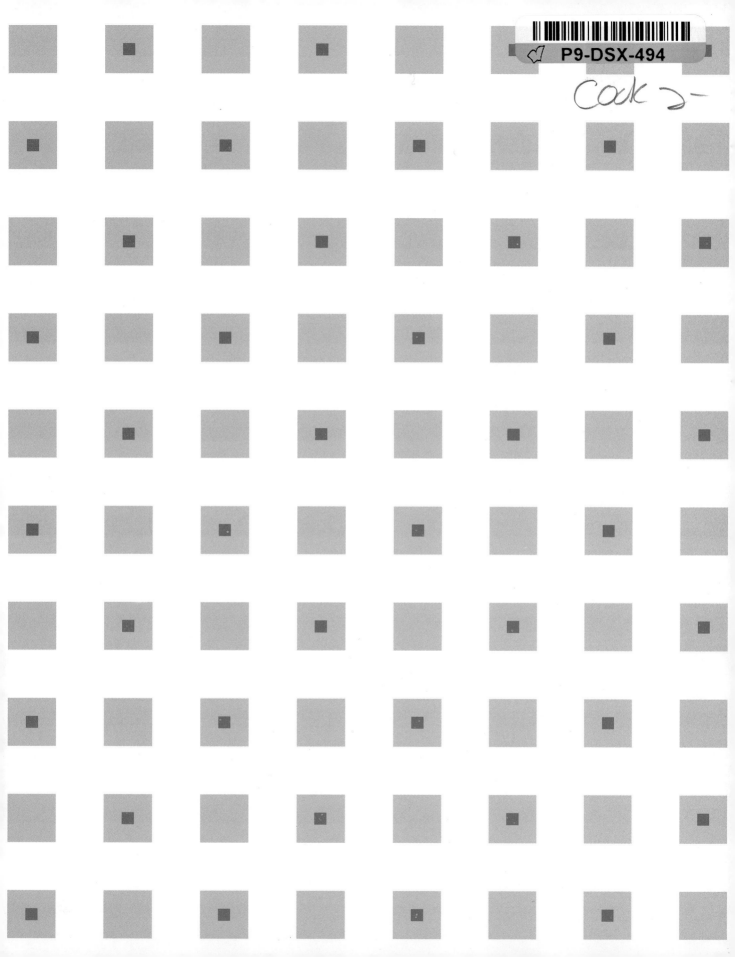

Cook 2-

Michel Richard's

Home Cooking

with a French Accent

Michel Richard's
Home Cooking
with a
French Accent

Michel Richard

with Judy Zeidler and Jan Weimer

William Morrow and Company, Inc.

NEW YORK

It is the policy of William Morrow and Company, Inc., and its
imprints and affiliates, recoginizing the importance of preserving
what has been written, to print the books we publish on acid-free
paper, and we exert our best efforts to that end.

Library of Congress Cataloging-in-Publication Data

Richard, Michel.
    Michel Richard's home cooking with a French accent / by
Michel Richard with Judy Zeidler and Jan Weimer.
        p.   cm.
    Includes index.
    ISBN 0-688-08494-X
    1. Cookery, French. 2. Cookery, American—California style.
I. Ziedler, Judy. II. Weimer, Jan. III. Title.
TX719.R448   1993
641.5944—dc20   92-25344
                                                        CIP

Printed in the United States of America

First Edition

1 2 3 4 5 6 7 8 9 10

BOOK DESIGN BY RICHARD ORIOLO

To André,
my best friend, my brother,
who left us too early

Contents

Preface

I first met Michel Richard in his Los Angeles pastry shop in 1980. I walked in for a croissant and walked out with the beginning of an extraordinary friendship. I was enamored with this exuberant and talented young chef.

Soon Michel, my husband Marvin, and I became close friends. We would roll up our sleeves and spend hours in the kitchen, sharing cooking secrets and experimenting with novel recipes.

Marvin and I were captivated by Michel's stories about growing up in France and his dreams for his future. He didn't want to spend his career bound by the limitations of being a pastry chef, even though he was considered the best in his field. Michel longed to open a restaurant, a place where he could excite diners with savory and sweet dishes that excited him.

Between marathon cooking sessions, we talked at length about opening a restaurant called Citrus together. Michel drew sketches of an exhibition kitchen—he wanted to be able to see his patrons as he cooked and to allow them to share in his joy of cooking. This exhibition kitchen became one of the first in Los Angeles; now they are almost standard in every new restaurant.

Before we could open Citrus, we needed investors. To assist in the process, Michel would prepare a bevy of phenomenal dishes for sampling—raviolis made from mozzarella cheese instead of pasta, snails presented in pastry shells, fish encrusted with paper-thin slices of potatoes. I'll never forget how Michel would shyly stand by his dishes, while potential investors marveled at his food, mesmerized with every bite.

Michel's dream came true in 1987 when Citrus opened and he began serving his distinctive interpretation of California/French cuisine. Michel was so dedicated to the restaurant that he almost never went home; we often found him asleep on the banquette in the dining room the following morning.

Michel is tireless. It's not uncommon for him to work eighteen-hour days Monday through Saturday. On Sunday, his idea of relaxation is to cook a sumptuous family dinner in the wood-burning oven on his home patio. He enjoys preparing rustic, comforting dishes of his native Brittany—chicken with garlic, shallots and potatoes or rack of lamb with tomato crust.

No matter how busy Michel is, he always finds time for his friends. He's there to celebrate every occasion, from birthdays to weddings. In fact, he usually insists on baking friends' wedding cakes, beginning work at 4:00 A.M. to painstakingly create the most intricate designs.

Michel loves giving parties as much as attending them. When we celebrated my husband's birthday at Citrus with a Middle Eastern theme, Michel arranged for a camel to greet guests at the door. He unabashedly joined the belly dancers in their gyrations, much to everyone's great amusement.

It's hard not to be swept up in Michel's *joie de vivre*—even when he wears the guise of practical joker. At his own wedding, he staged an "accident," letting a prop cake crash to the floor in a creamy mess. While all the guests shrieked in dismay, he whisked in the real wedding cake.

Michel may love to laugh, but he is also the rare chef who cares deeply and passionately about the quality of his cuisine. In the six years since Citrus has been open, Michel has never let us eat the same dish twice. Whenever we're about to order, he snatches the menu away and dashes back into the kitchen. He always returns to our table as we sample the first bite of his newest creation, anxious to see if we really like it.

When Michel opened the Broadway Deli in Santa Monica in 1990, he was eager to create a new style of deli—one that stretched the definition to incorporate how we eat today.

Just a few days before the Broadway Deli opened, Michel spotted a shiny new stockpot and immediately went to work preparing a head cheese terrine like he used to make in France. I took one peek in that stockpot and knew that thanks to Michel, the Broadway Deli would be unlike any deli in the country.

When I think about Michel today, I remember the young pastry chef I met in 1980. Michel may have achieved an enormous amount of international recognition, but little else has changed; he's still the same enthusiastic, compassionate man.

The warmth, exuberance, charm, and talent of the real Michel Richard is captured in these pages. I know you will delight in his recipes and anecdotes as much as I have.

—Judy Zeidler

Foreword

Meet Michel Richard

The tears roll down Michel Richard's cheeks when he speaks about his life: the difficulty of growing up as one of five children in a poor matriarchal household in northern France; the jeering he endured at school when he announced he wanted to be a chef; the sadness and loneliness of a young apprentice working from 5:00 A.M. until 10:00 P.M. in a foreign town, afraid that nobody would help him. After winning the "Best Young Apprentice Pastry Chef in Champagne," his first job brought a garret with rats. His wages barely covered its rent and were garnisheed for every sandwich he ate and vanilla bottle he shattered. His poverty was so extreme, he was tossed out of a café in Paris, mistakenly identified as a bum because of his used greatcoat and the holes in his shoes.

There was little pride in being a chef in those years when conventional wisdom said, "He's an idiot? Well, send him to chef's school." One's mentors were poor, unhygienic and alcoholic. For Michel Richard, there was no choice. "You either are or are not a chef inside of you," he believes.

He has been a chef *inside* since age four, when he first pulled a stool up to the counter where his mother was cooking. By age nine, he was the man of the house slaughtering chickens and rabbits while his older brother cowered in a corner. His first visit to a restaurant was through the back door of a bistro owned by the family of a school chum. The flames, white heat, and steam were mesmerizing. He left the restaurant knowing he wanted to return through the back door. He wanted to be a chef.

At fourteen the time had come for him to be on his own. He had also thought of being an artist, but he had no money for school, and the children laughed even more at that guarantee-to-pennilessness idea. His passage to manhood was marked by the donning of the apprentice's jacket and a very, very small cap. It was a very, very big moment.

Michel Richard's life changed in 1971 when Gaston Lenôtre hired him to be a pastry chef. Mr. Lenôtre, the first person Michel met who treated his employees with respect, taught him the art and dignity of their profession. Michel had come from shops where there was no equipment, where cans substituted for bowls, and margarine for butter, where alcohol was cheap and chocolate inferior. With Mr. Lenôtre, only the best was accepted. "What a feeling it was to work with good ingredients," Michel remembers. With only a nine-hour workday, there was plenty of time to perfect his skills. He practiced at home with toothpaste, patiently copying the scrolls and script he'd observed at the patisserie. When the sugar man got sick, he was ready to stand-in.

In 1974, Mr. Lenôtre sent him to New York to oversee a pastry shop. That shop closed, but his horizons opened. When a man phoned to ask if he knew of a pastry chef for a bakery in Santa Fe, Michel answered "me." "I was ready for America and it was ready for me," he recalls. "It was too soon to go back to France. It would have been like stopping sex before the end." With no green card and *sans parlant Anglais*, this young man headed West with his girlfriend, eventually opening his own pastry shop in Los Angeles.

After moving to California, Michel got the "disease of the restaurateur." After ten years of treating his friends as guinea pigs, Michel Richard opened Citrus on Melrose Avenue in 1987. The restaurant is acclaimed not only for its food but also for its stunning glassed-in kitchen, which the health inspector labeled "the cleanest he has ever seen." Michel's mission is to "create a serious restaurant with serious food and serious service that is fun." The kitchen is "the heart" of this restaurant. "I want to open it to my guests and let them see how we function," Michel says. "I want to change people's opinions of chefs."

The young man who didn't want to leave his country has stayed in America long enough for his beard to turn white. Citrus has begat Citronelle in Santa Barbara and a high-stepping chorus line of successful Broadway Delis, an international-style brasserie. This man may not be a mogul, but he's an unmitigated success, well loved for his generosity and warm, impish personality.

There are two Michel Richards. There is the chef who sits in the restaurant at the end of the evening smugly puffing self-satisfied smoke rings of braggadocio on his cigar. And there is the sensitive, man-boy, slumped in a chair at his birthday party that ended sooner than he wanted. For Michel, a restaurant is a party. If a guest doesn't have a good time, it is a personal affront. He is hurt when he sends out a piece of cheese or a gift that isn't touched. If something comes back, he doesn't sleep. In his cuisine, he says, "the main ingredients are a caring and willingness to serve the customer."

An emotional link between customer and chef dictates the food here, but it is fashioned with a genius that emanates from the soul. Michel builds magnificent architectural structures that depend on his ability to wield a knife, not froufrou garnishes.

In this constructionist's hands, curlicues of house-dried duck *ham* intertwine to form a giant lotus blossom hiding apples diced smaller than a pin. Slices of mozzarella are ground, bound lightly with gelatin and molded into a sausage that can be evenly sliced and stacked without leaning like the Tower of Pisa. Cantilevered over pools of *Crème Anglaise* and caramel, blocks of chocolate are balanced more intricately than the modern sculptures that grace the restaurant's entrance. Who else peels spring peas because he doesn't like the skin? The perfectionist is a detail man.

Stark drama is softened by whimsey. He forms *trompe l'oeil frites* out of ground beans and spins spirals of pimiento potatoes around a feisty chili sauce and the plumpest, sweetest, briniest scallop that bristles with kataifi (the shredded wheat used in Middle Eastern desserts) on a black and white triangular plate. Classically trained, he has dipped into the melting pot of his adopted country, adding spice from the Southwest and colors of the California sunset. Everything he values is on that plate. "What is the most important thing about a dish, Michel?" His mouth and hands open and close in tandem. No words come out. He grinds his teeth, demonstrating a bite and crisp crunch. "Texture!" The response never varies.

To emulate the expertise of Michel Richard, you have to be an architect, engineer, philosopher-poet, explorer, inventor and comedian with the wonderment of a child. You must possess the fine dexterity of three-year-olds who weave Persian carpets and the balance of the Flying Wallendas. Quite a tall order for a short-order cook feeding family and friends. So why would Michel Richard write a cookbook? Wouldn't it be better for home cooks just to make a pilgrimage to Citrus when they do Disneyland?

The answer lies in one additional characteristic that distinguishes Michel's vision. As he describes it, his food is *"bien propre,"* or clean and pure, simple and straightforward. This is the access key for the home cook. "I like very few ingredients in each recipe," Michel explains. "You don't have to use a ton of things for a dish to taste good. That is a California sickness. You have to know where to stop."

Lengthy, time-consuming *bien propre* restaurant recipes such as a Tobacco of Mushrooms that takes five days to reduce are not included here, but the principles and logical structure of good cooking behind them are. Michel claims to be "profoundly challenged" to share his knowledge in a manner that will enhance home-style meals within the context of today's lifestyle. His passion for both lusty, earthy peasant dishes and elegant, modern offerings are here for the taking. Wearing his teaching toque, he has pruned his approach, addressing the needs of people who must juggle jobs, family and fun with such basics as getting dinner on the table. I think he has done a marvelous job, and I hope others will enjoy these recipes and find them as easy to work with and incorporate into a busy schedule as I have.

—Jan Weimer

Acknowledgments

I want to thank the following people for their hands-on help with this book: Sara J. Mitchell, Kathie Alex, Alain Giraud, Jean-Jacques Retourné, Cal Stamenov, Michel Blanchet, Julio Iturbe, Linda Dooner, Anthony d'Onofrio, Kora Gail, Pierre Sauvaget, Michel Ohayon, Tony Pels, Anita Turkel, Robert Curry, Diane Mohilef, Russ Parsons and Joan Bram. Thank you to the entire Citrus staff for being such a great help.

I am particularly grateful to Fred Hill, my agent, and to Harriet Bell and Ann Bramson, my editors at William Morrow, for their exactitude and attention to detail in shepherding this project. And to Dominique Guillemot for his beautiful photographs.

There are many other friends who have been extremely supportive throughout my career whom I would also like to thank:

Jean-Louis Palladin for his great inspiration.

Jean-Louis De Mori and Silvio De Mori for showing me the Italian way.

Robert Robaire for his invaluable wisdom over the years.

Mona Robaire for teaching me how to cook couscous and use North African spices.

To Marvin, my friend, partner, and guinea pig, who managed to stay thin over the years. To my two partners, Larry Shupnick and Bruce Marder. Without them, Citrus and the Broadway Deli would not have been possible.

To all my Citrus and Broadway Deli partners for all your continued support and Paul Whetsell for your help with all the Citronelles.

Laurence Richard for being such a wonderful wife and mother to our children.

To Christophe, Chloe, Christel, and our newborn Clement, to whom I owe a lot of recipes while cooking with them on Sunday afternoons. To Michael, my oldest son, who followed my footsteps, and Sebastien, who loves to spend his vacations with me in the kitchen.

I am indebted to Gaston Lenôtre for sending me to the United States and for commanding respect for our profession. I owe a great deal as well to Jack Sauvage, who pushed me into this field with lots of energy when I was his apprentice at age fourteen.

Thank you to all the chefs in the world who respect our profession and to our guests who make the restaurant industry such a unique business.

A special thank you to my mother who worked so hard to raise five children by herself. *À ma mère, merci pour tout.*

Acknowledgments

Michel Richard's

Home Cooking

with a French Accent

Introduction

At Citrus I strive to create magic on the plate, to provide that unexpected twist or surprise that brings a smile. I want to do things for my patrons that they can't do for themselves. To achieve the fantastic, I merely apply the same methods and principles I use to throw together a makeshift meal at home. The difference between restaurant cooking and home cooking for me is but one of degree. Restaurant cooking is the refinement of an obsessed chef. It is using bottled mineral water in a soup or crêpe batter to eliminate chlorine and hand chopping meat or fish for an airier texture than can be obtained from a machine. Niceties—but not necessities—for producing a delicious meal.

I worked as an apprentice for three years before I knew how to properly scrape a bowl, but there is no way most home cooks can—or care to—invest this kind of time in learning to cook. Regardless, the more that is understood about the fundamentals of cooking and the more restaurant rules described in this book are adopted at home, the easier it will be to prepare a successful casual meal without being overwhelmed. Eventually, these rules will become second nature as you cook.

Train Your Palate

Learn what good, well-prepared food tastes like. When you are eating in a restaurant or in someone else's home, pay attention to what you like and don't like, and analyze the dish to understand why. Is the fish or chicken unusually moist and cooked *à point?* Question the chef or your friend about the preparation method so you'll know how to reproduce the result.

Understand Basic Principles and Generalize

Before I trained as a chef, I thought puff pastry was a gift from God. When I finally understood that steam made the layers rise, it helped me perfect not only my puff pastry technique but also my method for cream puffs. Knowing ''why'' is a ticket to a shortcut. When you make a dish, pay attention to tips, technical explanations and procedures that work. Keep your eyes and mouth open. Collect information that can be applied to other preparations. Learn what a lamb chop feels like when cooked to your desired degree of doneness, then look for that sensation every time you cook a lamb chop. Use this same knowledge when preparing a steak. If Grand Marnier works for you with chocolate, substitute it for the liquid in another chocolate recipe. If you like my onion crust with salmon, try it with chicken. Recipes change and get made like children. The difference is you've got ingredients moving around and recombining, not DNA. Good principles, on the other hand, never vary.

Respect Your Ingredients, Equipment and Audience

I'm 100 percent chef. It's a religion and I'm a priest of food. I never made a dish without loving it. That's how I think. That's what I do. ''Yes,'' I recognize that I am possessed and, ''no,'' I don't expect you to be. Yet, in my experience, the more respectful the cook, the better the dish. Twenty years ago, if a chef dropped a mold into the garbage, he would rummage through the entire barrel until he found it. The dishwasher would immediately wash and dry it so it wouldn't rust. Today I lose hundreds of molds a year. People don't seem to care anymore. I continually have to let workers go because the disregard they have for my equipment is expressed in everything they do. Sloppiness, a bad attitude and lack of respect translate into terrible food.

Purchase Good Quality Foodstuffs

To stock my restaurant larder, I search for the world's finest ingredients, always seeking unusual items neither I nor my customers have encountered before. I airfreight my Belon oysters from Maine and purchase baby lettuces at the farm of a boutique grower in Malibu. Home cooks may not be as interested in these exotic ingredients as chefs are, but everyone has the right to affordable ingredients of impeccable quality. This applies to snowy white button mushrooms with closed gills as much as it does to expensive truffles.

Food can taste only as good as the ingredients used to prepare it. With dishes increasingly simplified and pared down to their hearts like artichokes, each component must have maximum flavor for a dish to be delectable. If the salmon you were planning to buy doesn't look shiny and fresh, choose something else. Superior foodstuffs, like superior equipment, make you feel good. Whenever possible, go to the market with no menu in mind so you can take advantage of whatever is freshest and best that day.

Ready Your *Mise en Place*

Be organized. *Mise en place* ("put in place") everything you will need for the preparation of a dish. Good chefs aren't caught with floury hands when they need to get an egg out of the refrigerator. *Mise en place* also means premeasuring, peeling, cutting, and prepping ingredients in advance so when it comes time to cook, everything is ready on trays. I start this process as soon as food arrives from the market, and go so far as to arrange a cold first course on plates.

I hesitate to mention this in today's climate of *quick*, but my fervent wish is that all of you would include the making of good base stocks as part of your *mise en place*. Stocks can be prepared at night or during the weekend, and stopped and started at your convenience. They can be frozen in small quantities and pulled out as needed. Nothing enhances or transforms a dish as much as a few tablespoons of reduced stock. Unfortunately, homemade stock seems to be going the way of the beret.

Be Creative

I have a definite advantage at the restaurant. I can mix a sauce from one pot with a sauce from another pot, take several different vegetables and meat or fish and play with them until I like what I have created. I know you don't have pots of prepared sauces on the back burner, but if you build upon the techniques you know already, you should be able to put together a wonderful meal with whatever is in your refrigerator. It may take some time to know instinctively what goes with what, but if you cook enough, it will happen. Don't give up. The main thing is not to be afraid to try something new. Feel free to make risky combinations. How else can you reach the sublime? If an experiment is inedible, order a pizza.

Present Food Simply

Beautiful food is its own best garnish. What makes a plate successful is the look. You have to know where to stop. Food must be presented as simply as it is conceived. Extras such as parsley or fruit slices have no spiritual connection with the food. They are rarely eaten and they don't belong on a plate. Most fussy little touches end up in the garbage.

The plate itself is an important statement. When choosing tableware, look for dramatic oversize platters. Choose white or black or another dark tone that will contrast with the food. Before bringing plates to the table, check to see that edges are clean and the food is neatly arranged.

Of course, there is a practical issue. I have thirty people assisting me with each plate; you have only yourself. Unless you get help, the first plate will be cold by the time the last one is finished. As long as the food is appetizing and attractive, it can be served—for all but the most formal occasions—on a platter or even from its cooking pot.

Build Your Plate

The total effect of a dish depends not on its individual components but, rather, on how they are combined. You decide to cook fish. You make a sauce. You must pull the parts together logically, creating texture and balance. You add crunch. You play hot off cold, sweet off sour; you mix plain with rich.

Most important, you must be organized and plan ahead. When I put a dish together, I think of myself as an architect building a high rise with the plate as my blueprint. Start with what you are going to cook. Go back to that fish. It's salmon? You have just made your first choice. Now, start asking yourself questions. Do you want the skin crunchy? To get it that way, will you caramelize it with sugar or dip it in flour? Will you flavor the flour with curry? If so, you may want to add mushrooms to enhance the curry's nuttiness. If you increase the curry and add cayenne, you will have an Indian-inspired dish. Or, you may want to cook the fish in apple juice and coconut milk.

Your family doesn't like skin? You'll need something else for crunch. Couscous? Rice? Bread crumbs? How are you going to cook this fish? What about smoking it? Do you want to marinate it first? Are you going to steam, grill, fry, or sauté it afterward?

What about a sauce? Salmon is rich. It needs acid. Tomato? Do you want an herb to pull the flavors together? Basil? It needs garlic as a companion. Will you blanch it? Or use it raw? If you add saffron to the garlic, it will taste like bouillabaisse. In this case, you may prefer anise to basil.

You have your crunchy fish, your sauce and your acidity. You have your green herb to link them together and add freshness. If it's winter, you'll want something smooth, creamy and heavy such as mashed potatoes. Maybe you'll mix a bit of basil puree into them. If it's summer, you may want green beans or another crisp vegetable. Maybe you'll want both.

If your guests don't like fish undercooked, don't serve it that way, but do add more sauce. You must please your customers. Now you need something fancy or charming for sparkle. Fried herbs? A confetti of beet and carrot chips? Do you have enough color? A fine dice of preserved lemon or melon marinated in lime?

You've completed the blueprint. Heat the plate, but not too much or the fish will overcook. Then build your dish on it.

Entertaining at Home

Chefs have the same problems as you do when they entertain at home. Sometimes you're into it and you are happier cooking the dinner than your guests are eating it. At other times you're not in the mood and nothing works. One day I invited six people for dinner and no one showed up. I waited and waited. They forgot. On another occasion, I was catering a wedding and everything was going wrong. It was hot and I was late. I jammed the cake into the refrigerator and broke all the decorations. At first I panicked. Then I quietly opened the refrigerator door. When my client's dogs came by, I pushed their faces into the cake. "Madam, madam," I began to scream. "Your dogs destroyed my beautiful wedding cake." You've got to be flexible and adjust to the moment.

I used to turn my home into a restaurant when I invited people to dinner and the evening became very tense. Now I cook leg of lamb or something simple and it is relaxing. Recently I served Paul Bocuse a steak, salad and crème brûlée. When you have me for dinner, please make roast chicken, potatoes and chocolate mousse. I will be very happy.

When you entertain, don't let the food be in control. Your friends aren't coming to see a chicken. They're coming to see you. Don't worry about impressing. Prepare something that will bring success to you and comfort to the diners. You must respect your guests and plan a menu that will please them. If you use an exotic unusual item, tell people what they are eating. Once when I served a salad with *foie gras* and black truffles, all the truffles were left on the plates. When I asked why, my friends told me that they didn't want to eat the "burned stuff."

If you are having a formal party, it will be much less stressful if you begin to organize it several days in advance. Since you want your guests to stay for several hours, select three or four small dishes rather than one large quickly gulped one. Serve one dish in the living room or kitchen while people are standing up and milling around. Americans—unlike the French—don't seem to like sitting at the table for a long time.

Write down a countdown schedule and last-minute tasks. If the party is on Saturday, set the table and do some of the marketing and do-ahead preparations on Thursday. Arrange flowers and tackle more *mise en place* on Friday. Reserve Saturday for purchase of perishables and last-minute preparations. Sunday is for sleeping in.

Do not worry whether your guests will like the food. If you taste it and like it, they will, too. It's exciting to give people pleasure. They will know it came from your heart and they will be very appreciative. That is, if you invite the right friends.

Now that I've given you all this advice, I must confess I firmly believe what I've just said, but I think it may be normal to worry a little bit about whether people will like your food. When I bring in plates, I can't help but listen for that moment of silence and awe that interrupts the contented buzz of conversation.

My Rules for the Host

• Be organized.

• Allow enough time; don't start boeuf bourguignon an hour before you want to serve it.

• Concentrate on the food while you're cooking.

• Relax and shower before guests arrive.

• Spend time at the table with your guests, not at the stove.

• Serve whatever bottle of wine guests bring to your home.

• Don't be upset—too upset—if someone doesn't like your cooking. You don't have to speak to that person again.

My Rules for the Guest

• When accepting an invitation, tell the host if there are certain foods you don't eat.

• When invited to a serious cook's home, don't bring a date who doesn't care about food.

• Don't be late.

• Don't be on a diet.

• Don't have a late lunch or eat too much during the day.

• Don't salt your food before tasting it.

• Your primary responsibility as a guest is to enjoy yourself. There is nothing worse than to refuse the host's gift of hospitality.

My Palate and Prejudices

Geographic Influences

This book contains my culinary preferences and prejudices. I will tell you what I like and what I detest; what I have fallen in love with in America and what I miss about my native France. It mirrors many influences. At its core lies the hearty, long-simmered peasant fare from the North of France where I was raised. These simple, gentle pleasures have molded my palate, and I still seek their quiet flavors. As much as I've grown to like spice and heat,

I do temper their intensity. You will see, for example, that I blanch garlic almost every time I use it. The sunny seasonings of Provence and the Riviera also pervade my food, albeit tamed. It's funny, but I never even visited these places until after I moved to the United States.

After French cuisine, I prefer those of the Middle East and North Africa. These lands taught me about using spice, an unknown subject in France. I must acknowledge a debt to Asia as well for its example of yin and yang, of harmony and balance.

Above all, I salute America for teaching me *how* to cook. Today I am a French regional chef and my region is California. It was here that I discovered foods of the world not available in France. I learned about barley, wonton and kataifi—even pasta. After Italian friends got through with me, I was no longer overcooking and oversaucing as the French tend to do. Both the geographic and multicultural climates of California have further expanded my arenas. I have access not only to vegetable gardens all year long but also to a harvest of ethnic international ingredients.

Professional Training

My classical professional training has not, unexpectedly, had an influence on my approach. When I trained in 1961, you had to destroy something and reshape it in order to be considered a great chef. You couldn't just make a potato; you had to turn it into a mushroom first. We learned how to bone poultry and make stocks, the bases on which we built everything else. The downside was that menus were long and turnover small so food could not be fresh. This changed with nouvelle cuisine. As strange as it was, it did help improve French food by encouraging chefs to experiment and create a personal style. Many of the dishes were a joke, particularly in the hands of bad chefs. Do oysters and raspberries go together? It depends upon the chef. The first time I heard about a savory chocolate sauce called mole, it sounded weird, too.

Artistic Fancies

To create texture and solve technical problems, I turn not to my experiences as a chef, but as a pastry chef. Don't be surprised when you come upon a savory crème brûlée, potato chips formed like *tuiles*, and Tomato Rosettes arranged like apples in a tart. These are the signs of a pastry chef at work. I view food as colorful tubes of paint. Spinach and peas tint sauces emerald green while tomatoes with beet juice dye them deep red.

Freshness

The garden freshness of an ingredient is paramount. If I can't get something fresh, I don't use it. I don't even like capers, cornichons or anything blunted by vinegar. I think my partiality to freshness and acidity also explains my love of cold foods. It is these qualities that I emphasize regardless of whether I am preparing food to serve hot or cold.

Crunch

In addition to freshness, the other force driving my food is crunch. With poultry and seafood, even meat, this is expressed most frequently with a crust. In addition to the common bread crumb coating, I often use couscous, onions or kataifi. Why am I so crazy about these crusts? For starters, they give texture and a crackling feeling in the mouth. They hold in juices while providing a crisp contrast, exchanging flavors with the other ingredients they cover. They look great and are extremely easy to do. They do everything a Wellington crust is *supposed* to do, but they don't get soggy. Are those enough reasons?

My other primary way of getting crunch—and drama—is to alternate layers of crisp and moist as in a B.L.T. sandwich or napoleon (the pastry chef comes to the rescue again). Another technique I should probably alert you to is my method of wrapping meat in plastic. It is an easy economical approach that allows food to be completely prepared in advance. Furthermore, when an ingredient is cooked in this package, its flavors are more concentrated.

Ingredients

As far as individual ingredients are concerned, I have my likes and dislikes. Actually it's more like phases. I've been through my cabbage period, bean period and cumin period. When I get sick of one, I just move on to another. Potatoes and apples are always there. After all, I'm French. Garlic, mushrooms and puff pastry appear again and again, for I never tire of them, either. Ginger blows in frequently to give a bite and breath of fresh air similar to that of mint. Salt is another means of crunch. A sprinkle of sea salt or coarse kosher salt on meat, poultry and seafood after cooking tickles the taste buds. With pepper, I look for taste as well as heat, and my choice is black pepper. Tabasco, not white pepper, stands in when I don't want to see black bits in a sauce. To capitalize on pepper's flavor, it must be ground as it is used. Ditto nutmeg and Parmesan cheese. Herbs are always fresh. If one is not available, I substitute something else or use a dried version, figuring about one-third the fresh amount. Often I call upon soy sauce to provide the meatiness traditionally supplied by stocks.

Health

This is the only country where people discuss the fat content of a beautiful dessert while they are eating it. This is pleasure? Even nutritionists agree that small, occasional amounts of butter and cream have their place.

When you want to make a special dish quickly without the benefit of stock, there is no better ingredient to add volume, body, and that velvety mouth feel than cream. A quiche without cream is like a man without a brain.

With so many foods contaminated today, cooks must also be aware of food safety. I do call for eggs in several mayonnaiselike sauces in hopes that producers are going to solve this problem soon. If concern exists about your local supply, I would suggest either eliminating the egg for a thinner, vinaigrette-style sauce or substituting several tablespoons of store-bought mayonnaise or sour cream for the egg to add thickness. Echoing this concern, I have called for store-bought mayonnaise in many a dish in this book. My wish though is that you make your own, for it is ever so much better in flavor.

General Principles

As a chef of habit, I use the following techniques over and over when cooking:

Sniffing and Tasting   I taste and smell all ingredients before using them, particularly butter, oil and nuts, which can turn rancid, to be sure they are in optimum condition.

Long Slow Simmers   I prefer long, slow simmers to rapid reductions, for they allow each part of a dish to cook through while developing complex flavors. I lower the heat on a burner as much as time allows.

Marinades   To bring up flavors, I marinate seafood, poultry and meat, often pushing herb sprigs through the center for intensity.

Preheating Pans   To prevent food from sticking, I heat a skillet, add oil or butter and heat again before adding the food to be cooked.

Oven Cookery   After browning both sides of an ingredient lightly on top of the stove, I finish cooking it in the oven so it doesn't get too hard on the outside before it cooks through.

Degreasing   If round "eyes" remain on a sauce after it has been through a grease separator, I return the sauce to the pan, tilt the pan, and dab the surface with paper towels to remove the droplets.

Keeping Food Warm   To keep food warm while finishing a sauce, I place it between two plates.

Serving Temperatures   Though some food should be served on the hotter side of the continuum and some on the colder, I serve nothing steaming hot or icy cold, temperatures that prohibit flavors from coming through. Food should never be served directly from the refrigerator or freezer or that is all it will taste of.

Equipment

There is nothing like a clean kitchen and a beautiful shiny casserole to put me in a good mood. I have respect and I feel as if I will do a great job. I find it impossible to cook with a bad pot. Sauces burn and ingredients pick up a bad taste. My recommendation is to buy the best quality cookware you can afford. If you buy only one pan a year, within five years you will have an entire set. You will have spent much less money, too, for a good pot lasts a lifetime while cheap ones warp quickly.

My first choice—if I am not using any liquid—is a well-seasoned cast-iron skillet. I like both enameled cast iron and stainless steel-lined copper, although I realize many cooks find these pots too heavy. Less weighty than cast iron, black carbon steel is also a good heat conductor. The quality of a pot is not as important when you are steaming vegetables or boiling liquids as it is when sautéing potatoes that can stick, or stirring a sensitive custard or hollandaise sauce that can curdle. If you do not have a good heavy pot for these jobs to prevent sticking, use one with a nonstick lining. In the past, food didn't brown well in these lined skillets—a real problem when cooking meat. The situation has improved somewhat with the second generation of these pans now on the market. Regardless of the type of pan, choose one that is large enough to hold food without crowding. When cooking, place it on a burner with a comparable diameter so its contents don't scorch. Equally important are knives that can be continually sharpened. The only time you cut yourself is fighting a dull knife. I like a large chef's knife for chopping and slicing, a smaller paring knife and a thin flexible-blade knife for boning. If you serve a lot of smoked salmon, the long scalloped salmon knife makes the job easy. I don't understand how the Chinese do everything with just one knife, their cleaver. I do understand why they like a wok. I'm pulling mine out more and more when I want to cook something quickly.

In addition to my blender, mixer and food processor, there are a few basic tools I call upon constantly. For straining, I turn to a large mallet with a heavy, fine-meshed imported Italian sieve, a conical sieve the French call a *chinois*, or a drum sieve *(tamis)* with a fine-holed screen. This—or a food mill—I also use for mashing potatoes. As strange as this may sound, my Melior coffeepot with its plunger basket mechanism does a great job straining sauces such as raspberry and tomato, leaving me with only one thing to wash.

I have many tongs for turning and transferring food as I cook. Lots of spatulas: wood, metal and plastic; long and short, firm and flexible, narrow, wide and broad (again for transferring). I also depend on my mortar and pestle, brushes for coating, oven and instant-read thermometers, tweezers or small pliers for pulling out fish bones and scissors for snipping chives and prickly tips of artichoke leaves. Sometimes I use things in different ways than they were intended. I find a melon baller handy for hollowing out baked potatoes. A lettuce spinner, which is too rough for tender lettuces, is terrific for eliminating much of the water from potatoes after soaking.

I cannot imagine a kitchen without a good, heavy pepper grinder with an adjustable grind, grease separators in different sizes and an Oven Baking Stone for breads. And, of course, a corkscrew. The thing I reach for most, perhaps, is parchment paper. There is nothing like it for lining molds or cookie sheets, and it sure makes cleanup a snap. Rather than buying the expensive two-sheet rolls in upscale supermarkets, I purchase it in bulk from a baking supplies company listed in the Yellow Pages.

For desserts, I have tart pans with removable bottoms in every size. I have closets full of molds, but I can never find them when I need them. The truth of the matter is that a cook doesn't need all this stuff. You need a good knife and a good pot. That's it. The most important thing in a kitchen is organization.

What you have is what you need. If you don't have a cake pan, use an oven-proof skillet. If you don't own one that is large enough, make a smaller amount of the recipe. If you don't have rings for forming a molded salad, substitute a clean, empty tuna can with its ends cut off. Don't fill your cupboards with expensive molds you'll use once. Improvise.

Conversely, if you like a piece of cookware that I don't suggest, use it. Although I've never owned a microwave oven, many cooks do. If you want to prepare one of my dishes in it, or use it for melting butter or chocolate, do so. Why not?

Wine

Being a chef does not automatically make me a wine expert. Basically, I know what goes with what. When I use wine in a dish, it is the same good quality wine I like to drink. Wine tastes do, however, change. When I was thirty-five, I liked red Burgundies better than red Bordeaux. A man told me I needed to be older to understand the complexity of Bordeaux. I was so insulted. He was right. I'm older now and I prefer Bordeaux.

In this book, I've recommended a wine from either California or France to go with each main dish. These are the styles I know best, and my suggestions should be taken only as a departure point. I love the weight of heavy white Burgundies and California Chardonnays, the spice of Côtes du Rhône and the complexity of Bordeaux and Cabernet Sauvignons. Herbaceous California Sauvignon Blancs or French Pouilly Fumés and spicy Alsatian Gewurztraminers and Rieslings are especially suited to today's fresh acidic food. I reserve Sauternes and liqueurs for after dessert when sugar won't fight these sweet drinks. The blush rosé wines from Provence are fun for an informal outdoor meal. They're best, though, on the Riviera. The view helps.

Choosing a wine should be like cooking. If you don't know something, ask. Don't be intimidated. An expensive wine isn't necessarily the best. Don't be afraid to say you don't like it or that a simpler wine pleases you. Wine likes and dislikes are personal. Buy and try lots of different varieties. You'll soon find out what you like. When you open a nice bottle of wine, it is a precious moment. Make sure you have the right person to share it with.

After each main recipe, you will find a wine suggestion. If I have recommended the French version and you prefer to try the California interpretation, or vice versa, do so by all means. If you like wines from Italy or the Northwestern states, serve those instead. Or make any other substitutions you wish. You will find the following designations for the grapes and wine styles listed below throughout the book:

White Wines

Chardonnay	White Burgundy (French) or Chardonnay (California) Chablis (French) used on occasion
Sauvignon Blanc	Pouilly Fumé or Sancerre (French) or Sauvignon Blanc or Fumé Blanc (California)
Muscadet	Muscadet (French)
Riesling	Alsatian (dry) Riesling (French) or California or German slightly sweet Riesling
Gewurztraminer	Alsatian (dry) Gewurztraminer (French)

Rosé Wines

Rosé	Rosé Côtes de Provence (French)

Red Wines

Beaujolais	Beaujolais (French)
Pinot Noir	Red Burgundy (French) or Pinot Noir (California)
Cabernet Sauvignon	Bordeaux (French) or Cabernet Sauvignon (California)
Syrah	Red Côtes du Rhône (French) or Petite-Sirah (California)
Merlot	Merlot (California)
Zinfandel	Zinfandel (California)

Using This Book

Love in a family is walking into your home and smelling the perfumed aromas of food, a testimony that someone cares enough to cook for you. This act of love nurtured me throughout my youth, and it is this sense of well-being that I hope to foster here.

When I was growing up in rural France, suppers simmered all day long while farmers worked in the fields. Today people eat their food raw or heat it quickly in the microwave. They demand instant, convenient, healthy food that is readily available at the supermarket. They do not sustain themselves from a home garden.

I've taken into account these modern issues, avoiding lengthy preparations, such as peeling artichoke bottoms or piping intricate designs with a pastry bag. With some recipes, however, there are no shortcuts. They will take a little more time and might be better reserved for weekends or special occasions. To ensure success, technique tips are included with each recipe.

Planning Ahead

Fast cooking has to do with organization as much as it has to do with a particular recipe. It requires planning to incorporate shopping into a busy schedule. An ongoing list will enable you to pick up what you need when you are near a store rather than having to make a special trip.

Before cooking, read the recipes through 1-2-3 times and cook them step by step in your head. You may find that you want to modify them for increased efficiency, or just to cut down on dirty dishes. If you are using the food processor, process dry ingredients first, so you won't have to wash between steps. If you don't have a clear understanding of the cooking process in your mind, you won't enjoy it.

Think about which refinements you can let go of when time is very short: Do you have to peel the tomatoes? Strain a sauce? Set the table in the dining room? Can you substitute a simple-to-slice ingredient such as cabbage for spinach, which needs to be stemmed and painstakingly cleaned? Can you premeasure ingredients and wait until friends arrive to cook? Can you make the cooking part of the entertainment and allow guests to help?

Cooking Ahead

Breaking down the preparation into small do-ahead steps often makes cooking seem less daunting and easier to fit into a busy schedule. Sometimes, though, it's easier to make a dish straight through from beginning to end. By the time you cool something, wrap it for the refrigerator or freezer, and then reheat it to continue the recipe, it's often not worth the extra effort.

Flavor needs to be considered as well when deciding whether to prepare a complete dish or some of its stages in advance. Other than soups or stews, few cooked meat, poultry or seafood dishes taste very good when they are refrigerated and then reheated. When chilling isn't a detriment to taste, I recommend refrigerating a dish that has been made ahead. When it will affect it adversely, I say "cover and leave at room temperature," but common sense will need to kick in here.

If your kitchen registers the degrees of a ceramic works, you won't be able to leave a dish at room temperature for as lengthy a period. Ingredients—particularly eggs, fish, poultry, meat and dairy products—will have to be kept in the refrigerator so they don't spoil. If you're cooking in an igloo, ingredients can stay on the counter much longer than the recommended time. "Bring to room temperature" instructions will have to be similarly adjusted according to the thermometer in your kitchen. Since conditions vary, specific times can't be provided. Just don't take risks. If the day is warm and you're not sure how long a dish can stand out, start it later. Be safe, not sorry.

In the recipes that follow, guidelines for planning ahead are geared to the busy person who wants to start even the simplest of meals the day before, or break up the process throughout the day the dish is to be served. Instructions are based on maintaining optimum flavor. As you make these dishes your own, you will find places where you want to shorten or further extend these time frames.

Measurements

Measurements, especially for seasonings, are included as guidelines. Depending on its ripeness, a particular food will vary so much in its intensity that it is impossible to predict how much seasoning it will need. Taste, adjust the seasoning if necessary a bit at a time, and taste again. Repeat this process until the dish is well balanced. To ensure that a preparation doesn't become too salty, use an unsalted or low-sodium chicken stock. These are increasingly available in the supermarket. Better yet, make it yourself. I like a high proportion of vinegar in my dressings. You may not. I like my sauces thin. You may prefer them thicker. My recipes are merely ideas for you to build upon.

I've written exact sizes and shapes so you will know what I have intended. When you see ⅜ inch, though, it does not mean you should take a ruler and measure each cut. I am telling you that I think ¼ inch is too small and ½ inch too big. Again, I am trying to give you a starting line. The important point is to make each piece pretty much the same size so it cooks evenly.

The same principle lies behind my cooking and doneness times: No oven is the same, no burner intensity the same, no pot the same, no ingredient the same, no palate the same. No one can write a recipe that will work for everything and everyone. To know when something is done, check my descriptions of doneness against your eyes, your fingers and, when necessary, your tongue. *The degree of doneness is what's important, not the given time.* Once made, dishes may keep longer than I have stated. Again, I'm starting with a personal view that should be adjusted according to your preferences and schedule.

I don't believe in recipes, other than as guidelines. I believe in good sense and a respect for tradition. Above all, I believe in love and friendship and in having fun.

Thousand-Layer Smoked Salmon Terrine
(page 60)

Marinated Salmon Trout with Warm Potato Salad
(page 102)

Shrimp Porcupines
(page 130)

Mahi Mahi Rice Box
(page 144)

Salmon with Couscous Crust and Tomato Leek Sauce
(page 150)

Tunaburger
(page 156)

Chicken in Red Pepper Sacks
(page 181)

Duck Legs with Beets
(page 201)

Super *Pistou* with Beef
(page 210)

Blackberry Fig Tartlets with Orange Caramel Sauce
(page 332)

Soups

Soup and supper have probably been synonymous in France since fire was discovered. In ancient times, prehistoric peoples prepared their *potages* in a clay-lined pit they dug in the ground and filled with water. Next to this trench, they built a roaring fire to heat large rocks. These they dropped into the water along with some vegetables. Not too long afterward, a dinner bell tolled for hot soup.

When I was growing up in France, a much-used copper caldron had replaced the pit; a big black wood-burning stove the campfire. It was certainly easier for my mother to make soup than it was for her ancestors, but perhaps that was the only difference between the approach of the Gauls and the Richards.

Our soups, like those of the past, were modest dishes. Made from the chicken and lamb we raised, the fish we caught or the vegetables we harvested, bound with a bit of bacon and maybe some cream, they warmed not only our bodies but also our souls. And they were the basis for some of my happiest memories.

In this chapter I've ventured beyond my small backyard plot in France and re-created the soups from around the world that have impressed me most. There is Russian Beet and Cabbage Borscht (page 31) with its great red color and Mexican Avocado Soup with Snapper Seviche (page 22). I've also mixed and matched ingredients: North African couscous substitutes for rice in a Greek lemon broth (page 23), and an American clam chowder intermarries with a French leek and potato soup (page 26).

Although the ingredients I use for soup have changed considerably since I lived in France, my principles for making it have not. First and foremost, soup has to be simple. The more that can be done ahead, the more I like it. Besides, soup is easier to degrease after it is chilled and the fat has risen to the surface to be spooned off. One warning: If making soup in the evening, cool the pot down quickly in a sink filled with ice cubes and cold water. That way you'll be able to chill it before going to bed. Soup must be cooled down before it can be covered and refrigerated. If, however, it is left too long in a warm room, it may ferment.

I do believe that soups like people get better as they get older. Nevertheless, I am very careful not to cook soup too long and destroy its savor. This is soup, after all, not stock. For this reason, I add ingredients at different stages, cooking vegetables al dente and fish or poultry just until opaque. Often I preblanch vegetables and stir them in at the end with minced herbs for a crisp, fresh finish.

My favorite soups are those that develop over time and take on a life of their own. When I go on a ski trip, I put a chicken in a pot with some carrots, onions and water as soon as I arrive at my condo. Before long, I have chicken soup for all that ails me. As the week goes by, I replenish the disappearing broth with different ingredients, depending on my mood. If I've had a good day zipping down the slopes, I find myself choosing sunny green beans and fennel for crunch. If I spend most of the day on my bottom, turnips, rutabagas, potatoes and sausages are added as comfort foods. Sometimes I throw in leftovers from another meal, but as seemingly casual as I am about soup, I never offer one that *looks*, *feels* or *tastes* like a leftover. As an example, see my Smoked Salmon Soup (page 28).

Soups must be deliberately conceived and structured around a specific idea. I may substitute one ingredient for another, but it is always according to a formula. I don't drown two vegetables in ten gallons of water. Proportion, balance and harmony are of utmost importance. And, as I indicated above, a soup must suit a particular mood, appetite and season. For this reason, the soups in this collection range from the sprightly chilled Vine-Ripened Tomato Soup (page 18), to the heartier, more-stew-than-soup Short Rib Stick-to-the-Rib Soup with Corn and Parsley Puree (page 36). I am of the cold or tepid soup school, but if you belong to the hot soup lovers' group, you may want to preheat your soup bowls in the oven.

No matter what ingredients a soup contains, it can be made appropriate for any occasion just by changing its presentation. If either the dinner or your guests are particularly elegant, you may want to puree everything in the blender. A food processor can also be used, but it does not process the mixture as finely. For a sophisticated touch, freeze an ice cube with a twist of lemon inside and add it to a chilled Asparagus Vichyssoise (page 19). Any soup will seem special when a tablespoon of butter is whisked in at the end to provide a silky sheen.

For garnish, spoon caviar, croutons, lemon slices, tomato dice, herb sprigs, grated cheese or a dollop of whipped cream on top. When the rendition is rustic, season with sea salt, mustard and horseradish, pour a slick of olive oil on the surface or balance a hunk of grilled country bread in the bottom of the bowl. My grandfather used to pour a few drops of red wine called *chabrot* into his soups for acidity. It is not my favorite garnish, but it is lusty and wonderful with the Chicken, Mushroom and Barley Soup (page 35) here.

Speaking of wine, I have suggested a wine for each recipe, but I do not recommend serving it with soup unless the broth contains a lot of chunky ingredients or is accompanied by other foods, such as bread, pâté or salad. Otherwise you will be basically having liquid with liquid. A soup is not a bath.

Vine-Ripened Tomato Soup

4 to 6 Servings

Planning Ahead

The soup can be prepared 2 to 3 days in advance. Allow at least 6 to 8 hours for it to chill.

Variation

The character of this soup can be changed merely by varying its garnish. Crab, shrimp or other seafood and/or cooked minced vegetables work particularly well. Think about using up leftovers here, too.

Wine Selection

Chardonnay

I make this soup only during the summer when I have fabulous tomatoes that are even too ripe to slice well. When a beefsteak tomato gets to this point, it is a wonderful thing to behold. Soft, heavy and bursting with juice, it feels as if it will come apart in your hand.

I've kept this soup very simple because I don't want anything to detract from my primary ingredient. Usually I serve it chilled, but I like it warm as well. Whenever I get a windfall of tomatoes, I use the inside pulp for soup or sauce while reserving the outside flesh for salad or terrines.

3 pounds red or yellow tomatoes, chopped

2 medium onions, peeled and chopped

¼ cup tomato paste

Pinch of brown sugar

4 cups unsalted chicken stock

2 to 4 tablespoons balsamic vinegar

¼ teaspoon Tabasco or to taste

Salt and freshly ground black pepper to taste

3 tablespoons olive oil

1½ cups (about ½ pound) ¼-inch mozzarella cubes

¼ cup fresh basil, chive or green onion julienne

Combine the tomatoes, onions, tomato paste, sugar, and chicken stock in a large pot. Bring to a boil, then lower heat and simmer until the mixture is reduced and thickened and the tomatoes can be mashed into a puree, about 30 minutes, stirring occasionally. Puree the soup in a blender (in batches, if necessary) or food processor and strain through a fine sieve into a large bowl, pressing on the ingredients. Add the vinegar and Tabasco to taste. Season with salt and pepper. Cover and refrigerate 6 to 8 hours or until well chilled. (This can be prepared several days ahead.)

To serve, remove the soup from the refrigerator. Whisk olive oil into soup. Ladle into 4 to 6 soup bowls. Garnish with mozzarella cubes and basil. Serve immediately.

Asparagus Vichyssoise

S ince leeks have the same shape as asparagus and were known in France as the "asparagus of the poor," it didn't take a genius to substitute asparagus for leeks in this vichyssoise. Considerably less cream is used, because the potato adds most of the rounded fullness that heavy cream traditionally provided in an asparagus soup. This tuber also cools the chili's heat, so anyone who tastes this soup will know it was created by a French guy who lives near—not in—Mexico.

2 cups unsalted chicken stock

1 pound boiling potatoes, peeled and cut into 1-inch cubes

2 pounds asparagus, tips removed and reserved; white ends discarded

1 cup heavy cream

2 jalapeño peppers or to taste, cored, seeded and minced

Salt and freshly ground black pepper to taste

2 tablespoons Champagne or white wine vinegar

About 1 cup unsalted chicken stock

Salt and freshly ground black pepper to taste

Place 2 cups chicken stock in a large pot. Add the potatoes, bring to a simmer, cover, and cook until almost falling apart, for about 20 minutes. Cut the asparagus stalks in roughly 1½-inch lengths. Stir the stalks into the pot, re-cover and cook just until tender, for about 7 to 8 minutes, stirring occasionally. Puree the potato mixture in a blender (in batches, if necessary) until very smooth, pulsing on/off and stopping to scrape down the sides of the container. Clean the saucepan and strain the soup back into the saucepan through a fine sieve. Add the cream and jalapeños and season with salt and pepper. Bring to a boil over high heat. Stir in the vinegar. Cool, then cover and refrigerate until well chilled, for about 6 to 8 hours. (Can be prepared 1 day ahead.)

Line a rack with paper towels. Cook the asparagus tips in a large pot of boiling water until crisp-tender, for about 5 minutes. Drain and set aside on the rack at room temperature.

To serve, remove the soup from the refrigerator 15 to 30 minutes before presenting. Thin the soup if necessary with additional chicken stock. Ladle into 4 to 6 soup bowls. Season the asparagus tips with salt and pepper and place in the center of each soup bowl. Serve immediately.

Planning Ahead

The soup base can be prepared 1 day in advance. Allow at least 6 to 8 hours for it to chill completely. Cook the asparagus tips at any time during the day the soup is to be served.

Technique Tips

Asparagus should be cooked just until tender. When overcooked, it develops a metallic, off-flavor.

Mixtures containing potatoes should be pureed in the blender rather than in the food processor, because the food processor makes them gummy and glutinous.

Wine Selection

Sauvignon Blanc

Sweet and Sour Corn Soup
with Glazed Red Pepper

4 Servings

Planning Ahead

The soup can be made 1 day in advance. The garnish can be prepared at any time during the day the soup is to be served. Reheat the soup just before presenting.

Technique Tip

Since the exact reduction of the soup will vary according to the type of pot and the amount of heat, it is easiest to adjust the texture of the soup just before serving. If the soup is too thick, thin it with additional stock before reheating. Conversely, if it is too thin, boil the soup down.

Variations

Make as much of the Red Pepper Garnish as you like and reserve any extra in the refrigerator to serve as a relish with grilled chicken or steak.

Use leftover oil and vinegar from the peppers to dress salads.

Wine Selection

Sauvignon Blanc

T his soup with its soupçon of sweet and sour is one of our most popular dishes at Citrus. Even corn purists approve, although they are often suspicious of the Red Pepper Garnish. "What's that strange thing on top?" they ask. Once people taste the piquant peppers, though, they appreciate their haunting aftertaste, similar to that found in a fine wine.

6 large ears of corn, husked and kernels removed

3 cups unsalted chicken stock

1 ounce (¼ stick) unsalted butter

1 large onion, peeled and diced

1 tablespoon brown sugar

1 cup heavy cream or unsalted chicken stock

Additional unsalted chicken stock as necessary

Salt and freshly ground black pepper to taste

RED PEPPER GARNISH

2 small red bell peppers, cut into ⅜-inch dice

3 tablespoons olive oil

1½ tablespoons balsamic vinegar

1 large clove garlic, peeled and minced

1½ tablespoons fresh minced chives or green onions

For the soup, place the kernels in a large pot with the chicken stock. Bring to a boil over medium-high heat, then lower heat and simmer for 15 minutes. Remove 1 cup of corn kernels to a bowl using a slotted spoon; reserve.

Melt the butter in a heavy small skillet over medium-low heat, add the onion, cover, and cook until translucent, for about 10 minutes, stirring occasionally. Add the brown sugar, increase heat to medium, and cook uncovered until the onion has browned, for about 7 minutes, stirring occasionally. Add the onion to the pot with the corn mixture and simmer for 5 minutes.

Transfer the corn mixture to a blender or food processor. Process until it is a smooth puree, about 5 to 6 minutes, pulsing on/off and stopping to scrape down the sides of the container. Clean the saucepan and strain the soup back into the saucepan through a fine sieve. Add the reserved corn kernels. Stir in the cream and/or stock. If the soup is too thick, thin it with additional stock as necessary. Season with salt and pepper. (This can be prepared ahead, cooled, covered and set aside at cool room temperature for several hours or refrigerated for 1 day.)

For the garnish, place the red pepper dice in a small skillet, cover with water and simmer over medium heat until the peppers are very tender, for about 30 minutes; drain. Add the oil, vinegar and garlic to the skillet and cook over low heat until the garlic is translucent, for about 5 minutes, stirring occasionally. (This can be prepared ahead, covered and set aside at room temperature.)

To serve, stir the soup over medium heat to rewarm. Ladle into 4 soup bowls. Remove the red peppers from the skillet with a slotted spoon and place in the center of the soup. Sprinkle the chives over the red peppers. Serve immediately.

Avocado Soup
with Snapper Seviche

**4 First-course or
2 to 3 Main-course
Servings**

Planning Ahead

The Avocado Soup can be prepared at any time during the day it is to be served. Allow at least 1 to 2 hours for it to chill. The seviche base can be prepared several hours in advance, but the fish should marinate only a half-hour to an hour before serving.

Technique Tips

If you like your soup spicier, use more chili peppers.

If the fish is marinated beyond the recommended time, it will become tough and hard, losing its appealing brininess.

Wine Selection

Sauvignon Blanc

Both gazpacho and marinated fish tartar, or seviche, stand as benchmarks of freshness for me. To capture their refreshing quality, I blended these two dishes into a soup with more garnish than broth. Mixing the old world with the new, I removed the avocado from the Latin American seviche and pureed it as the base of the soup while dicing the tomato from the gazpacho in the French manner, *concassée*. I dipped South of the Border again to pick up a nice bite of chili, while keeping the Gallic garnish of chives.

AVOCADO SOUP

  1 large ripe avocado, chopped

  2 cups unsalted chicken stock

  2 tablespoons freshly squeezed lemon juice or more to taste

  Salt to taste

  Tabasco to taste

SEVICHE

  2 tablespoons freshly squeezed lime juice

  1 serrano or other chili pepper or to taste, cored, seeded and
       minced

  1 tablespoon fresh minced cilantro or mint

  1 small tomato, peeled, seeded and cut into tiny dice

  1 tablespoon fresh minced chives or green onions

  1 tablespoon olive oil

  Salt to taste

  Tabasco to taste

  ¾ pound fresh white fish fillets, such as red snapper, halibut or
       sea bass, sliced diagonally into 3/16-inch-wide bite-size strips

  Fresh cilantro or mint sprigs for garnish (optional)

For the Avocado Soup, place the avocado in a blender with the stock and lemon juice. Process several minutes until the mixture is a smooth puree, pulsing on/off and stopping to scrape down the sides of the container. Season with salt and Tabasco. Refrigerate at least 1 hour in the blender or in a covered container.

For the Seviche, mix the lime juice, chili, cilantro, tomato and chives in a small bowl. Whisk in the oil in a slow, thin stream. Season with salt and Tabasco. (This can be prepared several hours ahead, covered, and set aside at room temperature.)

Stir the fish strips into the Seviche base. Cover and refrigerate 30 minutes to 1 hour.

To serve, remove the soup base from the refrigerator 15 to 30 minutes before presenting. Mix well, then ladle into soup plates. Remove the fish mixture from the marinade using a slotted spoon, and arrange in the center of each soup plate. Garnish with cilantro sprigs. Serve immediately.

Lemon Soup with
Mint and Couscous

T his soup was influenced by the Greek avgolemono soup I learned to make during the six months I worked as a pastry chef at the Club Med in Corfu. I was twenty-four years old at that time and did everything with abandon. I bound the soup with egg yolks as my hosts did by mixing two yolks with the lemon juice and then whisking this mixture into a gently-simmering-but-never-boiling-or-it-will-curdle soup just before serving. Today, operating with some maturity and restraint, I have omitted the yolks in deference to the lighter, more modern palate; but for a sublime velvety texture, don't hesitate to add them.

I've replaced the rice used by the Greeks with Moroccan couscous and added the Chinese seasoning paste, hoisin. Why not? It brings an intriguing, unexpected flavor. Since this soup takes less than 10 minutes to both prep and cook, and it's made with nonperishable goods, it pays to keep all the ingredients on hand so you are prepared when unexpected guests drop in.

6 cups unsalted chicken stock

2 tablespoons hoisin sauce

3 tablespoons freshly squeezed lemon juice

6 tablespoons fresh coarsely chopped mint, dill, tarragon, or other fresh herb

¾ cup couscous

2 tablespoons Dijon mustard

Salt and freshly ground black pepper to taste

Bring the chicken stock to a boil in a heavy large saucepan over medium-high heat. Whisk in the hoisin, lemon juice and mint. Stir in the couscous. Cover and set aside off the heat to steep for 5 minutes. Whisk in the mustard. Season with salt and pepper. Ladle into 4 soup bowls. Serve immediately.

4 Servings

Planning Ahead

The ingredients can be prepared at any time during the day the soup is to be served. Cook the soup just before serving.

Technique Tip

If the soup is cooked ahead, the couscous will absorb too much broth. If you prefer to do it this way, just add additional stock before serving and reheat.

Wine Selection
Alsatian Gewurztraminer

Ratatouille Bisque

Planning Ahead

This soup can be completely prepared several days in advance before serving hot or cold. If presenting it cold, allow at least 2 hours for it to chill.

Wine Selection

Rosé Côtes de Provence

I n Citrus's early years, I made a Provençal consommé, a clear broth that was first simmered with leftover vegetables and then strained and clarified. It was a lot of work. French people who came to the restaurant loved its elegance and refinement. Not Americans. So I pureed everything together instead; now all nationalities love this gloriously colored, intensely flavored taste of Provence.

Traditionally you would find a considerable amount of olive oil in a ratatouille, but I have eliminated it here as a token acknowledgment of my continual diet. Although "bisque" usually means a soup made from pureed shellfish, the hue and texture of this mixture is so similar, it seems like the only name to give it. Regardless of what you call this soup, you can serve it hot or cold or even use it as a sauce.

¾ pound (1 small) eggplant, peeled and cut into 1-inch chunks

¾ pound (2 medium) zucchini, trimmed and cut into 1-inch chunks

2 large (about ¾ pound) red peppers, diced

1 pound (about 4 medium) tomatoes, chopped

1 large onion (about ½ pound), peeled and diced

4 large cloves garlic, peeled and quartered

3 cups unsalted chicken stock

4 drops Tabasco or to taste

Salt to taste

1 tablespoon Pernod or anise-flavored liquor (optional)

¼ cup fresh basil or other fresh herb julienne

Place the eggplant, zucchini, peppers, tomatoes, onion, garlic and chicken stock in a heavy large pot. Bring to a boil. Reduce heat to medium and simmer until vegetables are very soft, about 30 minutes, stirring occasionally.

Puree the vegetable mixture in a food processor or blender, pulsing on/off and stopping to scrape down the sides of the container, until it is a smooth puree. Strain into a large bowl (or clean pot) through a fine sieve. Season with Tabasco and salt. Stir in optional Pernod. (This can be prepared ahead, cooled, covered and set aside at cool room temperature for up to several hours or refrigerated for several days.)

To serve, remove from the refrigerator about 30 minutes before serving if presenting chilled. Bring to a boil over medium-high heat if presenting hot. Ladle into 4 soup bowls. Garnish with the basil julienne. Serve immediately.

Emerald Fennel Soup

T he essence of freshness, this emerald soup is a garden in a bowl. Made primarily from fennel and herbs, this broth was formerly known as *Herbes à la Tortue* because turtles eat the greens used in its preparation. Not so long ago, restaurants would make this soup in advance and keep it warm in a *bain marie* (water bath) where it would lose its flavor and color. By the time it was served, it tasted like soap and looked like an army uniform. Remember, this is a young soup. When you're young, you're green. Serve as soon as possible after adding the herbs.

1 medium (about ¾ pound) fennel bulb

½ star anise (optional)

About 4 cups unsalted chicken stock

1 cup chopped green onions (white and light green parts only)

¼ cup packed fresh basil leaves

⅛ cup packed fresh tarragon leaves

¼ cup packed flat-leaf parsley

1 large clove garlic, peeled

2 tablespoons olive oil

Salt and freshly ground black pepper to taste

3 to 4 Servings

Planning Ahead

The soup base can be pre-pared and the herbs blanched at any time during the day the soup is to be served. For the freshest flavor, add the herbs and puree as close to serving as possible. Reheat gently just before presenting.

Variation

Any other fresh herb can be substituted for the basil or tarragon, except cilantro.

Wine Selection

Chardonnay

For the fennel base, remove the fennel fronds from the stalks. Mince the fronds and reserve them. Cut off the stalks. Peel the stalks and the fibrous exterior of the bulb using a vegetable peeler. Cut the stalks into 1-inch pieces and place them in a large pot. Halve, core and chop the bulb coarsely, then add it to the pot with the star anise and chicken stock. Bring to a boil, reduce heat and simmer until the fennel is tender, for about 20 minutes. Discard the star anise.

Meanwhile, line a rack with paper towels. Blanch the green onions, basil, tarragon, parsley and reserved fennel fronds in a large pot of boiling water for 3 minutes. Drain and rinse under cold water. Place on the rack. (This can be prepared ahead and set aside at room temperature.)

To serve, transfer the soup to a blender, along with the blanched greens, garlic and oil. Process, pulsing on/off and stopping to scrape down the sides of the container until the mixture is a smooth puree, for about 5 minutes. Season with salt and pepper. Clean the pot and return the soup to the pot. Bring the soup just to a boil over medium-high heat, stirring occasionally. Immediately ladle it into 3 to 4 soup bowls and serve.

Leek and Potato Soup
with Clams

4 Servings

Planning Ahead
The soup can be completely prepared several hours before it is consumed. Return the clams to the broth and reheat just before serving.

Technique Tips
To rid clams of sand, soak in a bowl of lightly salted water for 30 minutes before cooking. If the water is very sandy at this point, drain and repeat.

When removing clams from liquid with tongs after opening, turn them upside down and shake to add any clam juice to the broth.

Wine Selection
Sauvignon Blanc

When I first arrived in New York City eighteen years ago, a friend pushed me into his old beat-up car and said, "I'm taking you to Boston for some great seafood." I was so excited. At the restaurant, the waiter asked if we wanted some oysters. "Most definitely," I replied. "How about some clams?" "Oh yes." "Some mussels?" "Yes, yes." "Lobster?" "Of course!" I was salivating. "Some scrod, too?" *"Bien sûr.* Certainly," I responded. And so it went. My friend never had a chance to say a word. Me? I was envisioning the greatest seafood feast of my life. The reality was a little less than that. Truthfully, it was a disaster. Everything—oysters, clams, mussels, lobster and scrod—were deep fried in the same batter and served with tartar sauce. If you closed your eyes, you couldn't tell which were the oysters and which was the scrod. The only intriguing dish was the clam chowder. It looked remarkably like glue, but I still found it enchanting, for I had never seen clams in soup before.

Since that notorious night, I've had many different types of clam chowder under my ever-expanding belt, but the following is my favorite. To make it, I've intermingled clam chowder, the American classic, with leek and potato soup, the French standard-bearer, forming a Franco-American international friendship treaty.

CLAMS

28 (about 3 pounds) littleneck clams, scrubbed

2¾ cups water

1¼ cups dry white wine

SOUP

3 medium-large leeks (white and light green parts only), halved
　　lengthwise and thinly sliced crosswise

3 medium (about ¾ pound) russet potatoes, peeled and cut into
　　½-inch cubes

½ cup heavy cream

Salt and freshly ground black pepper to taste

Additional water or cream as necessary

1½ tablespoons fresh minced chives or green onions

To cook the clams, place them in a heavy large skillet. Cover with the water and wine. Bring to a boil, cover the skillet, then reduce heat and simmer for 3 minutes, shaking the skillet occasionally. With tongs, remove the clams that have opened and place them on a tray. Recover and cook for up to 3 to 4 more minutes. Discard any clams that have not opened. Line a fine sieve with a dampened paper towel. Strain the cooking liquid through the sieve into a heavy large saucepan.

For the soup, add the leeks and potatoes to the saucepan with cooking liquid. Bring to a boil, then lower heat and simmer until the potatoes are tender, for about 15 minutes. Add the cream. Coarsely mash the potatoes in the broth to thicken, using a mallet or potato masher. Season with salt and pepper. (This can be prepared ahead and cooled. Cover the clams and soup and set aside at cool room temperature for up to several hours.)

To serve, remove the clams from their shells and mince. Pour any liquid from the shells back into the soup through the sieve and discard the shells. Thin the soup with additional liquid if necessary. Bring to a boil, stirring over medium-high heat. Add minced clams. Ladle into 4 soup bowls. Sprinkle with chives. Serve immediately.

Smoked Salmon Soup

6 Servings

Planning Ahead

The soup can be prepared 4 to 6 hours in advance. Heat just before serving.

Technique Tips

It is unnecessary to use perfect slices of smoked salmon for this soup. Less costly trimmings work fine.

If curds form at anytime while the soup is heating, remove from heat immediately.

Wine Selection

Sauvignon Blanc

If this soup is any indication, dishes made from leftovers can be every bit as good as those that are loved and labored over in classic cuisine. Like my Smoked Fish and Mushroom Salad (page 105), this *dividend* dish came into being when I was hunting for a way to use up bits and pieces of smoked salmon that had accumulated at the restaurant. What do you do most often when you have leftovers? You make soup. In this case, I was also prompted by delicious memories of a Scandinavian smoked herring broth.

Of all the plastic bags with ends of this and that in your refrigerator, smoked salmon is probably the hardest to use because it becomes grainy and lumpy when overheated. This should not be a problem here as long as you watch carefully while warming the puree. Along with a bagel or roll or two, this soup earns a main course status with raves at brunch.

1 pound smoked salmon pieces

4 cups half-and-half

2 teaspoons freshly squeezed lemon juice or to taste

6 ounces salmon roe (caviar) or 1 small cucumber, seeded and finely diced

⅓ cup fresh minced chives, dill or green onions

Toasted mini bagels or rye bread (optional)

Chop the salmon finely in a food processor, pulsing on/off. With the machine running, gradually pour in the half-and-half and lemon juice through the feed tube, stopping occasionally to scrape down the sides and mix in the salmon from the bottom of the container. Transfer the soup to a heavy medium saucepan. (This can be prepared up to 6 hours ahead, covered and set aside at cool room temperature.)

To serve, stir the soup with a wooden spatula over medium-low heat until just warm. Remove from the heat immediately and mix in ¾ of the salmon roe and chives. Ladle into 6 soup bowls. Garnish with the remaining salmon roe and chives. Serve immediately. Pass mini bagels or rye bread, if desired.

Scallop and Celery Root Soup

When a search of my refrigerator revealed some beautiful fat scallops and mushrooms one night, it seemed obvious that the thing to make was a *Sauce Normande*. At the very last minute, I threw in some celery root I'd also uncovered, for what turned out to be one of the best tasting sauces I've ever concocted. Since then, I have become probably—certifiably—celery root's biggest fan. This rich soup is just one of many ways I've brought scallops and celery root together again.

1 small (about ¾ pound) celery root, peeled and shredded

2 cups milk

2 cups clam juice or unsalted chicken stock

Salt and freshly ground black pepper to taste

Additional clam juice or unsalted chicken stock

28 (about 4 ounces) bay scallops

2 tablespoons fresh minced chives or scallions

Bring the celery root, milk and clam juice to a boil in a heavy large saucepan over medium-high heat. Reduce heat and simmer until the root is very tender, for 15 to 20 minutes, stirring occasionally. The mixture may appear curdled. Transfer the mixture to a blender or food processor and process until it is a smooth puree, pulsing on/off and stopping to scrape down the sides of the container. Season with salt and pepper. Clean the saucepan, if necessary. Return the pureed soup to the pan, straining it through a fine sieve if a smoother texture is desired. (This can be prepared ahead, cooled, covered and set aside at cool room temperature for several hours or refrigerated for 1 day.)

To serve, bring the soup to a boil, adding additional clam juice or chicken stock to thin, if necessary. Add the scallops and simmer until just opaque, for about 1 minute. Ladle into 4 soup bowls. Garnish with chives. Serve immediately.

4 Servings

Planning Ahead
The soup base can be prepared up to 1 day in advance. Add the scallops and cook just before serving.

Technique Tip
Shredding celery root or cutting it into julienne, once a hateful task with a knife, has been happily simplified by the food processor. If this machine is not available, cut the celery root into big pieces before cooking. In this case, cooking will probably take longer and more stock may be needed.

Wine Selection
Chablis or White Burgundy

Cabbage and Cumin Soup
for Jean-Louis

4 to 6 Servings

Planning Ahead

Both the soup and the Cabbage Butter can be prepared several days in advance. Reheat the soup just before serving.

Technique Tip

Adding the cold Cabbage Butter just before serving gives the soup a velvety shine and smoothness.

Wine Selection

Chardonnay

I've had some great times skiing with Jean-Louis Palladin, my good friend who is the chef at the Watergate Hotel in Washington, D.C. Since Jean-Louis loves soup as much as I love cabbage, this dish became a reward for both of us after a hard day of slaloming. By throwing leftovers and a carrot or potato into it each day, this nurturing broth lasted the good part of a week. Although cumin is not used in either of the regions in France where Jean-Louis or I come from, we have both taken a fancy to it. I went through a period where I used it in everything. Now I use it more judiciously; but if I make cabbage or carrots without cumin, it tastes as if something is missing.

The Cabbage Butter can be omitted to simplify preparation, but this crisp vegetable finish is what provides a modern freshness to an old-fashioned dish. It also adds a bright green color.

CABBAGE BUTTER

> 1½ pounds green cabbage, quartered and cored
>
> 1 ounce (¼ stick) unsalted butter, at room temperature

SOUP

> 3 slices bacon, cut crosswise into ¼-inch-wide pieces
>
> 1 onion, peeled and chopped
>
> 3½ cups unsalted chicken stock
>
> ¼ teaspoon ground cumin or to taste
>
> Salt and freshly ground black pepper to taste

For the Cabbage Butter, bring a large pot of salted water to a boil. Remove 2 large dark green cabbage leaves, add them to the boiling water and cook 3 minutes. Drain, rinse under cold water and squeeze dry. Process the cabbage and butter in a food processor until smooth, pulsing on/off and stopping to scrape down the sides of the container. Wrap the Cabbage Butter in plastic wrap, forming a log. Freeze briefly or refrigerate several hours until firm. (This can be prepared several days ahead.)

For the soup, cook the bacon in a heavy large pot over medium heat until browned, stirring occasionally. Add the onion, reduce heat to medium-low, cover and cook until translucent, for about 10 minutes, stirring occasionally. Pour the stock into the pot and bring to a boil, stirring to release the browned bits from the bottom of the pot. Slice the remaining cabbage and add it to the pot. Simmer until the cabbage is tender, for about 20 minutes, stirring occasionally.

Process the soup in a food processor or blender to a coarse puree, pulsing on/off. Return it to the pot. Season with cumin, salt and pepper. (This can be prepared ahead, cooled, covered and set aside at cool room temperature for several hours or refrigerated for several days.)

To serve, bring the soup to a boil over medium-high heat, stirring occasionally. Chop the chilled Cabbage Butter and whisk it into the soup. Ladle into 4 to 6 bowls. Serve immediately.

Beet and Cabbage Borscht

I had never even heard of borscht before I moved to this country. Soon after my arrival someone asked me to make it, and I felt like an idiot because I didn't even know what it was. Afterward, I studied borscht by ordering it in Russian restaurants and by making many variations of it. I found I liked it cold or very warm but not boiling hot, and I preferred few beets proportionately. With white wine and chicken stock, this borscht is lighter than the heartier, beefier Russian mixture; but that doesn't mean you can't enjoy a glass of vodka with it.

4 cups unsalted chicken stock

I cup dry white wine

I pound (about 6 cups) savoy or green cabbage, cored and shredded

I large (about 8 ounces) beet, peeled and cut into fine julienne

I small red onion, peeled and thinly sliced

I tablespoon balsamic vinegar

Generous pinch of ground cumin

Salt and freshly ground black pepper to taste

Unflavored yogurt or sour cream (about ½ cup)

Place the chicken stock, wine, cabbage and beet in a large pot. Bring to a boil, reduce heat and simmer until vegetables are tender, for about 30 minutes, stirring occasionally. Add the vinegar, cumin, salt and pepper. (This can be prepared ahead, cooled, covered and set aside at cool room temperature for several hours or refrigerated for several days.)

To serve, remove from the refrigerator for about 30 minutes before serving if presenting chilled. Simmer over medium-high heat to reheat if presenting warm. Ladle into 4 soup bowls. Spoon on a generous dollop of yogurt. Serve immediately.

4 Servings

Planning Ahead
This borscht can be completely prepared several days before serving warm or cold, and it is even better when made in advance. If presenting cold, allow at least 6 to 8 hours for it to chill.

Wine Selection
Alsatian Riesling

St. Tropez–Santa Fe
Black Bean Soup with Basil

4 Servings

Planning Ahead

The black beans should be soaked overnight before cooking and are even better when completely cooked several days in advance. The vegetables can be blanched and the basil pureed at any time during the day the soup is to be served. Reheat the soup just before presenting.

Technique Tips

If time does not allow for soaking the beans overnight, cover the beans with 2 inches of water, bring to a boil and let boil for 2 minutes. Let rest for 1 hour, then continue with recipe.

For maximum flavor, cook the dried beans until they are completely tender and almost falling apart. Too often they are served undercooked, resembling peanuts in their shells. Dried beans may be the sole ingredient I do not look to for crunch.

Wine Selection

Red Côtes du Rhône

This soup is based on the French *soupe au pistou*. When I was first introduced to this Provençal classic during my restaurant apprenticeship, the ingredients were so foreign to me they might just as well have come from China. Parsley was the only herb used in the Ardennes where I was raised, so I had never eaten sweet basil before. In this northern region, it was considered an insult to serve olive oil instead of butter, and we ate garlic in public only with snails.

When I opened Citrus with *Soupe au Pistou* on the menu, southern French people who came to the restaurant complained that the soup wasn't right; it wasn't the way their mothers made it. They were as fussy as Americans are about their clam chowder. After enough of these comments, I decided to make my own version. I substituted the black beans I grew to love while living in Santa Fe for the traditional French *haricots blancs* and added freshly cooked al dente veggies for garnish. Adding a crunchy bite to soup shows more respect than to boil, boil, boil it.

BLACK BEANS

>   1½ cups dried black beans, picked over and rinsed

>   Water

>   12 cups water

>   1 large onion, peeled and diced

>   6 cloves garlic, peeled and minced

>   Salt and freshly ground black pepper to taste

VEGETABLE GARNISH

>   6 ounces green beans, ends snapped and strung, and sliced diagonally into 1-inch pieces (about 1½ cups)

>   2 small (about 8 ounces) zucchini, trimmed and cut into ½-inch dice

BASIL PUREE

>   ⅓ cup olive oil

>   4 large cloves garlic, peeled

>   1½ cups (about 1½ ounces) fresh basil leaves

>   Salt and freshly ground black pepper to taste

>   8 large fresh basil leaves, sliced into julienne

For the black beans, place the beans in a large pot and cover with enough water to come 2 inches above them. Cover the pot and set aside at room temperature to soak overnight.

Drain the beans and return them to the pot. Cover with 12 cups of water. Add the onion and garlic and bring to a boil, skimming off any foam. Reduce heat and simmer until the beans are very tender to taste, for about 2½ hours, stirring occasionally. Add water, if needed, or boil the soup down until it is thickened to the consistency of minestrone. Season with salt and pepper. (This can be prepared ahead, cooled, covered, and set aside at cool room temperature for 6 to 8 hours or refrigerated for several days.)

For the Vegetable Garnish, line a rack with paper towels. Cook the green beans for 3 minutes in a large pot of boiling water. Add the zucchini and cook until the beans are tender, for about 2 more minutes. Drain and rinse the vegetables under cold water and place them on the rack. (This can be prepared ahead and set aside at cool room temperature.)

For the Basil Puree, place the oil, garlic and basil in the blender. Process until the mixture is a smooth puree, pulsing on/off and stopping to scrape down the sides of the container. Season with salt and pepper. (This can be prepared ahead, covered and set aside at cool room temperature.)

To serve, bring the soup to a boil. Season vegetables with salt and pepper. Stir ¾ of the vegetables and puree into the soup. Ladle into 4 soup plates. Divide the remaining vegetables over the top of each soup. Garnish with basil julienne. Serve immediately.

Muguette's Lentil Soup

4 Servings

Planning Ahead

This soup is even better when prepared several days in advance. Reheat before serving.

Wine Selection

Red Côtes du Rhône

My mother's name, Muguette, which means "lily of the forest," is fairly common in France, where women are often given the names of flowers. My mother's life has, unfortunately, been anything but perfumed and delicate. After my father left us, she worked all week long at a factory to support herself and her five children. On Sundays she prepared this soup for us to eat throughout the week. Sometimes she put bacon in it, sometimes sausage. Regardless, we always ate it the same way, picking out the meat first, then the potatoes and, finally, the lentils. I was eight or nine at the time—the grand chef—and it was my job each night to heat the soup and replace the potatoes and carrots. Once the meat was gone, that was it until the following Sunday.

3 slices bacon, sliced crosswise into ¼-inch-wide pieces

1 large onion, peeled and diced

1 large potato, peeled and diced

1 large carrot, peeled and diced

1½ cups lentils, picked over and rinsed

6 cups unsalted chicken stock

Salt and freshly ground black pepper to taste

Cook the bacon in a heavy large pot over medium heat until brown and crisp, stirring occasionally. Add the onion, potato and carrot to the pot, increase heat to medium-high and stir until the vegetables are golden. Add the lentils and chicken stock and bring to a boil. Reduce heat and simmer until the lentils are tender, for about 45 minutes, stirring occasionally. Season with salt and pepper. (This can be prepared ahead, cooled, covered and set aside at cool room temperature for several hours or refrigerated for several days.)

To serve, reheat soup by stirring over medium-high heat. Ladle into 4 bowls. Serve immediately.

Chicken, Mushroom and
Barley Soup

In this recipe I've combined chicken with the Mushroom Barley Soup we prepared at the Broadway Deli for a satisfying meal-in-a-bowl. In order not to overcook the chicken into strings like dental floss, I add it to the soup just before bringing it to the table.

1 tablespoon olive oil

1 small onion, peeled and diced

½ pound mushrooms, ends trimmed and thinly sliced

4 cups unsalted chicken stock

2 tablespoons soy sauce

3 tablespoons pearl barley

2 cloves garlic, peeled and minced

Salt and freshly ground black pepper to taste

2 large chicken breasts or thighs, boned, skinned and sliced into bite-size pieces, at room temperature

About ¾ cup (about 3 ounces) freshly grated Parmesan cheese (optional)

Heat the oil in a heavy medium saucepan over medium-low heat. Add the onion, cover and cook until translucent, for about 10 minutes, stirring occasionally. Add the mushrooms, increase heat to medium-high and cook uncovered until lightly browned, for about 5 minutes, stirring occasionally. Add the chicken stock, soy sauce, barley and garlic. Simmer gently for 45 minutes to cook barley and then blend flavors. Season with salt and pepper. (This can be prepared ahead, cooled, covered and set aside at cool room temperature for up to 4 hours or refrigerated for several days.)

To serve, bring the soup to a boil, add the chicken, reduce heat and simmer just until the chicken becomes opaque, for about 2 to 3 minutes. Ladle into 4 soup plates. Serve immediately. Pass Parmesan, if desired.

4 Servings

Planning Ahead

The soup can be completely prepared—up to the point of adding the chicken—2 days in advance. Reheat the soup with the chicken just before serving.

Variation

Leftover boned, skinned chicken pieces at room temperature can be substituted for uncooked breasts in this recipe. Before serving, bring the soup to a boil and add the chicken off the heat. There is no need to cook it any further.

Wine Selection

Chardonnay

Short Rib Stick-to-the-Rib Soup
with Corn and Parsley Puree

4 to 6 Servings

Planning Ahead

Both the soup and the puree can be completely prepared 2 days in advance. Reheat the soup just before presenting.

Technique Tips

Flanken short ribs are cut from the chuck and contain a large piece of meat over a base of rib bones.

Short ribs will become stringy if overcooked.

Wine Selection

Red Burgundy

T his is another hearty, stewlike soup meal-in-a-bowl. Meaty short ribs, an excellent cut of beef for braising, deepen and enrich the broth. Corn adds color and sweetness. The Parsley Puree, blended like pesto, contributes a contemporary tone to this rustic mélange. Its refreshing, just-mowed herbal character dissipates with simmering, so add it just before serving the soup.

SOUP

1 tablespoon olive oil

1 medium onion, peeled and thinly sliced

1¼ pounds (3 to 4 ribs) beef short ribs, preferably flanken style, trimmed of fat and patted dry

1 tablespoon flour

1 tablespoon red wine vinegar

6 cups unsalted beef stock

2 medium (½ pound) white boiling potatoes, peeled and cut into ½-inch cubes

1 large carrot, peeled and thinly sliced

1 large celery stalk, thinly sliced

1 large ear of corn, husked and kernels removed and set aside

½ pound small mushrooms, ends trimmed and thinly sliced

Salt and freshly ground black pepper to taste

PARSLEY PUREE

1 cup packed flat-leaf parsley

3 small cloves garlic, peeled

¼ cup olive oil

Additional beef stock or water as necessary

For the soup, heat the oil in a heavy large pot over medium heat. Add the onion and cook until golden, for about 5 minutes, stirring occasionally. Add the short ribs to the pot, increase heat to medium-high and brown on all sides, stirring occasionally. Add the flour, reduce heat to low, and stir for 3 minutes to cook flour. Pour in the vinegar and stock and bring to a boil, stirring to release any browned bits on the bottom of the pot. Reduce heat, cover partially, and simmer for 1 hour.

Add the potatoes, carrot, celery, corn and mushrooms to the soup. Cook until short ribs are tender and falling off bones, for about 1 hour. Season with salt and pepper. Remove the short ribs and bones. Trim off any gristle, fat and connective tissue and discard these along with the bones. Cut the meat into ½-inch cubes and return it to the pot. (This can be prepared ahead, cooled, covered and set aside at cool room temperature for several hours or refrigerated for several days.)

For the Parsley Puree, puree the parsley, garlic and olive oil in a blender pulsing on/off and stopping to scrape down the sides of the container. (This can be prepared ahead, covered and set aside at cool room temperature for several hours or refrigerated for several days.)

To serve, bring the soup to a boil, adding more stock or water if it is too thick. Whisk in the Parsley Puree. Ladle into 4 to 6 soup bowls. Serve immediately.

Starters

The nibbles served in France for hors d'oeuvres have been called *amuse-gueule*, although *gueule*, which means "dog face" has pretty much fallen from favor (I bet you can guess why), and the term used now is *amuse-bouche* or "tease the mouth." Foods in this category include olives, cheese, nuts, fresh vegetables or crudités and pâté or *saucisson sec*. These are every-evening items in French homes, not specials for company-is-coming nights.

I wanted this chapter to be more inclusive and broad-based than the term *amuse-bouche* implies, but I was not sure whether to call it Starters, First Courses, Appetizers or Hors d'Oeuvres. I settled on *Starters* when I realized that it is really a catch-all for dishes that don't fit neatly elsewhere in the book.

These recipes center around the finger foods or small appetizers that are passed on platters at a cocktail party or served on plates for a first course at a formal dinner, where they whet the appetite for the entree that follows. When several of these tidbits appear as part of a buffet, they weave a vibrant tapestry of contrast: fresh, acidic, smooth, creamy, piquant, sharp, briny, spicy, fleshy, herbaceous, crisp and crunchy. Make them larger and they are no longer starters but the main course of a meal.

Today, distinctions are blurring between what constitutes a first and main course. At my restaurants, diners often order one or two first courses and call it dinner. A first course at dinner is often a main course at lunch or brunch. To me, it makes more sense to organize these dishes as *Premier Plat* (first plate) and *Deuxième Plat* (second plate) than First Course and Entree, especially since entree means "to enter" and sounds as if it should be the first course, not the main course. If you are confused, please know that I am, too.

Since living in Los Angeles, I serve more starters in my living room when I entertain than anywhere else I have lived, because guests rarely arrive at the same time. They get stuck on the freeway and arrive 45 minutes late. To get around that somewhat, I give an earlier time to people who have a tendency to be late. I still try to keep the cocktail hour short because I hate watching guests getting drunk and bored as they blunt their hunger for dinner.

Probably the best reason for serving a starter or first course is that often these dishes are served cold and can be completely prepared, assembled and arranged on plates before the doorbell rings. Even if they need to be heated, it is still easier for a host to both have a good time and get a meal on the table when it is broken into several small components that can be tackled one by one.

This chapter can be divided into several different categories. It opens with some vegetable dishes that work as a first course salad, a side dish and garnish or as part of a mixed hors d'oeuvres platter's team. There are seafarers that come in and out of their shells to rock some boats and a goat cheese cheesecake (page 56) that becomes the soul of a salad later in the book.

There are also two blockbuster terrines, Eggplant-Tomato (page 46) and Thousand-Layer Smoked Salmon (page 60), that are signature dishes at Citrus. Designed for a large group, they are the oohs and aahs of any party. When I lived in the cold North of France, I stoked up on substantial hearty pâtés that were half goose, duck or pork and half fat for fuel. These seem too heavy for today's diet, so I've switched to lighter vegetable and seafood molds. My cured air-dried duck breast (page 74) is also modern, a lean trade-off for ham.

There is a panoply of tarts: big and small; open-faced and closed; round, rectangular and triangular; composed of purchased puff pastry, egg roll wrappers and an unusual basil crust. The fillings do more things with an onion than your eyes have tears for.

There are even egg concoctions for a first course, the place you're most likely to encounter this ingredient in a French meal. Bowing to British influence, I've combined toast with my Eggs in a Hole (page 70). The chapter finishes with breads, rolls and pastries, such as my Cream Puff Kisses (page 77) and Lacy Cheese Chips (page 76) that can be served by themselves or as accompaniments to the dishes in this and other chapters. Certainly these items can be purchased, but if you do so, buy a nice fresh baguette, not one of those industrial crackers that shouldn't be allowed on the shelves. This is the time to encourage and support the young bakers who are finally giving this country some good bread.

Mushrooms Greek Style

This is the classic marinated mushrooms *à la Grecque* that is always welcome as a first course, a picnic nibble, or as part of a salad or mixed appetizer plate.

When I was a youth in Paris I lived in an attic above a store on a bustling street in the Tenth Arrondissement. To fortify myself for the forced march up to my garret each day, I would stop and buy a small container of these marinated mushrooms. This recipe is less acidic than the standard version with lemon or vinegar, allowing the bite of whole coriander to come through. These seeds are little and crunchy in France, whereas here they're like rocks, so I've crushed them coarsely before adding.

3 tablespoons olive oil

I large onion, peeled and diced

2 cups dry white wine

½ cup unsalted chicken stock

½ cup tomato juice

2 bay leaves

2 teaspoons whole coriander seeds, coarsely crushed

I teaspoon ground coriander

I pound button mushrooms, ends trimmed

Salt and freshly ground black pepper to taste

Heat the oil in a heavy large skillet over medium-low heat. Add the onion, cover and cook until translucent, for about 10 minutes, stirring occasionally. Add the wine, chicken stock, tomato juice, bay leaves, coriander seeds and ground coriander. Bring to a boil and simmer until mixture is reduced to ¾ cup. Add the mushrooms and boil for 2 minutes, stirring continually. Cool completely, stirring occasionally. Season with salt and pepper. Cover and refrigerate for I day. (This can be prepared several days ahead. Remove from refrigerator for about 30 minutes before serving.)

To serve, drain the mushrooms or remove them with a slotted spoon. Arrange them on a platter or in a bowl, or add to a salad. Serve immediately.

4 to 6 Servings

Planning Ahead

The mushrooms should marinate overnight. They can be completely prepared several days in advance.

Variation

Reserve marinating liquid for dressing salads or vegetables.

Wine Selection

Pinot Noir

Chayote with Mustard Mayonnaise

For many years, I ignored chayote at the market because it reminded me of quince, which I had overdosed on in jelly form when I was a small boy. One day I saw the word *chayote* written above this vegetable pear, mirliton or christophine, as it is also commonly known, and I thought that anything with so many interesting names was probably worth trying. It was. A cross between jicama, celery root and watermelon in texture, this fruit of the vine is crisp and refreshing uncooked. I have prepared it here with the mustardy mayonnaise that is commonly combined with celery root in France. Unlike this tough-to-peel, even-tougher-to-slice root vegetable, the chayote can be cut up zip-zip.

MUSTARD MAYONNAISE

¼ cup mayonnaise

1 tablespoon freshly squeezed lemon juice

1½ tablespoons Dijon mustard

1 medium shallot, peeled and minced

½ cup fresh minced chives or green onion

Salt and freshly ground black pepper to taste

2 (about 1 pound total) chayote, peeled

4 radicchio or lettuce cups

For the Mustard Mayonnaise, mix the mayonnaise, lemon juice, mustard, shallot and chives in a small bowl until blended. Season with salt and pepper. (This can be prepared ahead and refrigerated until ready to serve.)

To serve, halve the chayotes from top to bottom. Remove the pit, halve each half lengthwise, and cut crosswise into ⅛-inch slices. Toss with the mayonnaise mixture. Serve immediately in lettuce cups.

Artichokes Citronette

I lived in Brittany until I was three years old. This was certainly not long enough to form an attachment to this beautiful land, but I attribute my great fondness for artichokes, a specialty of this region, to my origins. Eating an artichoke is as much fun for me today as it was when I was a kid and we stripped off the leaves as quickly as possible to get to the heart—our favorite part. As an adult, I consume both the leaves and the heart very slowly and deliberately.

When time allows, I pare down the leaves so the entire thistle is edible. In addition, I often cook an extra whole artichoke and use its leaves for decoration. Regardless of the scenario, I serve this vegetable with Citronette dressing, which is essentially a vinaigrette made with lemon juice instead of vinegar. We rarely use lemon juice in France for dressings, but for me nothing so enhances the flavor of an artichoke.

CITRONETTE

½ cup freshly squeezed lemon juice

1 cup olive oil

Salt and freshly ground black pepper to taste

4 large artichokes

½ cup fresh basil julienne

For the Citronette, place lemon juice in a small bowl. Whisk in the olive oil in a slow, thin stream. Season with salt and pepper. (This can be prepared ahead, covered, and set aside at room temperature.)

For the artichokes, cut any sharp spines off the leaves bluntly with scissors. Break off the stem flush with the bottom of the artichoke. Place the artichokes in a steamer, cover and cook over medium-high heat until the leaves pull out easily and the bottom is tender and easily pierced with a knife, for about 40 to 50 minutes. (This can be prepared ahead and set aside at cool room temperature.)

To serve, place artichokes on 4 plates. Stir the basil into the Citronette and divide it among the plates or present it in 4 small bowls. Serve immediately with a large bowl or plate for the discarded artichoke leaves.

4 Servings

Planning Ahead

The Citronette can be prepared anytime during the day the artichokes are to be served. Steam the artichokes just before presenting hot or several hours in advance to serve warm or at room temperature.

Technique Tips

To determine the freshness of an artichoke, break off its stem. The fresher the artichoke, the sharper the break and the more fibers will protrude.

I prefer steaming artichokes to simmering them in water. Their taste is so much more intense this way, and they do not become waterlogged.

Variation

Any fresh herb or green onion can be substituted for the basil.

Wine Selection

Sauvignon Blanc. Although many people don't like wine with artichokes, I find that the herbal grassy quality of Sauvignon Blanc balances nicely with it.

Warm Asparagus with Tomato and Tarragon Sauce

4 Servings

Planning Ahead

The sauce and croutons can be prepared and the tomatoes prepped at any time during the day the dish is to be served. The asparagus can be cooked in advance, too, and either reheated or presented at room temperature.

Technique Tips

When selecting asparagus, choose smooth, shiny, thick stalks because they have more flavor than thinner spears. Look for firm spears, too, which break with a clean crackle and snap when they are fresh. If spears aren't al dente to start with, they're sure not going to get that way by cooking.

Although many people don't bother to peel asparagus, it is so much more refined in flavor when treated this way. Peeling with a vegetable peeler is very little extra work and it can be done ahead.

To ensure that asparagus is evenly cooked, I sort the spears according to thickness. Beginning with the wider spears, I add them to the cooking water in batches. Knowing that medium-thick spears take about 5 to 6 minutes to

N ot so long ago, asparagus was a seasonal vegetable available only from early March until mid-June. This harbinger of spring was a pleasure we celebrated simply as a first course with a drizzle of mayonnaise, hollandaise or mousseline (a hollandaise with beaten egg whites or cream folded into it). Asparagus for me in those days was the white asparagus that grew in the North of France and was harvested as soon as it poked its tips aboveground. (I never even saw a green stalk until I came here.) We tied the spears in bundles so their softened tips wouldn't fall off, a technique not necessary today with our shorter cooking times, and ate this vegetable with our fingers just like French fries. A chef works so hard to cook food to a proper crunch, it seems a shame to spoil it with a knife and fork that don't have any feelings. I love to see people eating with their fingers in my restaurant. It shows they are enjoying their food.

TARRAGON SAUCE

1 egg yolk (optional), at room temperature

1 tablespoon Dijon mustard

2 tablespoons Champagne vinegar or white wine vinegar

¾ cup olive oil

1 tablespoon fresh minced tarragon

Salt and freshly ground black pepper to taste

3 slices French bread, crusts removed and cut into ⅜-inch cubes

2 pounds asparagus, white ends discarded and stalks peeled

Salt and freshly ground black pepper to taste

1 large (about 4 ounces) tomato, peeled, seeded and minced

For the Tarragon Sauce, blend the egg yolk, if using, and mustard in a blender. With the machine running, add the vinegar, then pour in the oil in a slow, thin stream. Mix in the tarragon and season with salt and pepper. (This can be prepared ahead, covered, and set aside at cool room temperature for 2 hours or refrigerated until 1 hour before serving.)

For the croutons, preheat the oven to 400°F. Place the bread cubes on a baking sheet and toast until brown, for about 5 minutes, turning halfway. (This can be prepared ahead and set aside at room temperature.)

For the asparagus, bring a large pot of water to a boil. Line a rack with paper towels. Divide the asparagus spears according to thickness. Cook, adding thicker spears to the water first, until tender when pierced with a knife, for about 5 to 6 minutes for larger spears. Drain and place on the rack. (This can be prepared ahead and set aside at cool room temperature.)

To serve, reheat the asparagus if desired by shaking in a heavy large dry nonstick skillet over medium-high heat. Season with salt and pepper. Arrange the asparagus on 4 large plates in a fan shape with the ends meeting at the bottom of the plate. Spoon the sauce generously over the asparagus tips. Scatter the minced tomato and the croutons over the stalks. Serve immediately.

cook, I guesstimate when thinner spears should go in. Years of practice make me always right. You'll soon get the hang of it, too.

Variation

To give the sauce a beautiful bright green color, I often add 2 tablespoons of uncooked defrosted frozen baby peas to the blender when I'm making it. Then I sprinkle another several tablespoons of cooked peas over the sauce as a garnish before serving.

Wine Selection

Sauvignon Blanc or Beaujolais

Eggplant-Tomato Terrine
with Parsley-Cilantro Sauce

9 to 18 Servings

Planning Ahead

The eggplant and tomato preparations for the terrine can be done at any time during the day the terrine is to be assembled. Allow about 6 hours for the terrine to gel. Both the terrine and the sauce can be prepared 1 day in advance. If kept much longer, the eggplant will darken and become increasingly bitter.

Technique Tips

If it is difficult to visualize cutting the tomato strips, keep in mind that you are removing the pulp from the interior while opening and flattening the exterior to be used as strips.

Adding beet juice to the tomato mixture intensifies its red color.

I don't salt eggplant as is so often recommended to remove its bitterness because it turns the eggplant dark and, from my perspective, I don't find it bitter.

Although it is not necessary to peel an eggplant, I do it so all the pieces look the same.

With the possible exception of an al dente dried bean, there is nothing worse than an al dente eggplant. Cook it until very tender.

Starters

46

Almost everything I know I learned from history. I am a sponge for tradition and the classic formula; this is a cherished inheritance I protect. Every now and then, though, I find a new way of doing something, an original style that incorporates the past while introducing a freshness and new modern sensibility. This terrine is an example.

Usually when eggplant and tomato appear together in a mold, the tomato is cooked, but in this terrine I left the tomato *au naturel*. While the terrine takes some time to put together, it is easy enough to do. When it is unmolded, you will feel very proud for having made something so beautiful. You will also have enough food to feed the French Legion. The Parsley-Cilantro Sauce is an exercise in balance; the boldness of the cilantro checks the sweetness of the parsley.

TOMATOES

2½ pounds tomatoes (about 10 large), peeled

½ cup (1 tiny) chopped onion

2 cloves garlic, peeled

⅓ cup beet juice (optional)

About 1½ cups tomato juice

Salt and freshly ground black pepper to taste

EGGPLANT

Olive oil (about 1 cup)

2 large (about 3 pounds total) eggplant, peeled and cut lengthwise into ¼-inch-thick slices

1½ envelopes (⅜ ounce total) unflavored gelatin

1 cup fresh coarsely chopped basil

Salt and freshly ground black pepper to taste

Parsley-Cilantro Sauce (page 48)

For the tomatoes, line a tray with parchment or waxed paper. Make a slit down the side of each tomato from stem end to tip. Cut around the interior of the tomato to remove the pulp, gently opening and flattening it into a long strip as you cut. Reserve the strips on the prepared tray. Place the pulp in a heavy small saucepan. Cut any remaining interior ribs off the tomato strips and add them to the saucepan. Add the onion, garlic and beet juice. Bring the mixture to a boil, lower heat and simmer 20 minutes or until reduced and thickened to a saucelike consistency, stirring occasionally.

Puree the mixture in a blender, pulsing on/off and stopping to scrape down the sides of the container. Strain the puree through a fine sieve into a 4-cup measuring cup, pressing on ingredients. Add enough tomato juice to measure 3 cups. Clean the saucepan and return the tomato puree to the pan. Season the puree with salt and pepper. (This can be prepared ahead, covered and set aside at cool room temperature.)

For the eggplant, line 2 large trays with several layers of paper towel. Heat ½ inch of olive oil in a heavy large nonstick skillet until bubbling gently. Cook the eggplant, several slices at a time, until completely cooked, but not colored, turning halfway, for about 4 minutes total. Transfer to the prepared trays using a large slotted spatula. Add additional oil as necessary. (This can be prepared ahead and set aside at cool room temperature.)

To assemble the terrine, sprinkle the gelatin over the tomato puree and stir gently over medium heat until dissolved. Stir the basil into the mixture. Cut a 15-inch-wide piece of parchment paper 9 inches long to fit a 9- × 5-inch loaf pan (or the length of whatever mold is used). Fold the parchment in half, short sides together. Place the parchment on a work surface with the fold running vertically. Blot any excess oil from the eggplant and season with salt and pepper. Arrange 4 large eggplant slices horizontally on each side of the fold with small ends overlapping slightly in the middle at the fold. Add more eggplant slices as necessary, until the paper is completely covered. Holding the short ends, gently insert the paper into the mold, eggplant side up, with the vertical fold down the center of the mold and the ends of the eggplant and paper overhanging the mold.

Spoon a ¼-inch layer of tomato puree into the bottom of the mold. Season the fresh tomato strips with salt and pepper, trim and arrange them in a single layer, covering the puree. Press the strips down firmly into the mold and brush generously with puree. Alternate layers of eggplant, tomato puree, tomato strips and tomato puree, ending with eggplant layer, until the mold is almost filled. Press down firmly after each layer. Fold the overhanging eggplant slices over the mold. Fold paper over all. Place loaf pan on tray. Top with a slightly smaller loaf pan and fill with weights. Refrigerate until the tomato puree is set, for about 6 hours or overnight.

To serve, remove from the refrigerator and unmold 1 hour before serving, pouring off any accumulated liquid. Blot the terrine with paper towels. Cut the terrine into ½-inch-wide slices, sawing with a serrated knife. Place on a larger platter or transfer 1 or 2 slices to 9 to 18 plates, using a wide spatula. Spoon several tablespoons of Parsley-Cilantro Sauce alongside individual servings or pass separately in a sauceboat.

Wine Selection
Chardonnay

Parsley-Cilantro Sauce

Makes About 1½ Cups

Variation

If the egg yolk is omitted, this sauce will be more like a vinaigrette than a mayonnaiselike dressing. Add some commercial mayonnaise if desired.

1 egg yolk (optional), at room temperature

2 tablespoons Dijon mustard

6 tablespoons Champagne or white wine vinegar

¾ cup olive oil

3 tablespoons chopped flat-leaf parsley

3 tablespoons fresh chopped cilantro

Salt and freshly ground black pepper to taste

Blend the yolk, if using, and mustard in a blender. With the machine running, add the vinegar, then pour in the oil in a slow, thin stream. Add the parsley and cilantro to the blender and process until completely pureed. Season with salt and pepper. (This can be prepared ahead and set aside at cool room temperature for 2 hours or refrigerated overnight.)

Eggplant and Arugula Salad

4 Servings

Planning Ahead

Both the eggplant and the Shallot Vinaigrette can be completely prepared and the arugula prepped at any time during the day the salad is to be served. Toss the salad and arrange it just before presenting.

Arugula is not a green I use frequently because it borders on the bitter for me. Bitterness may, in fact, be the main difference between the French and Italian palate, for French people don't generally like the sharp greens Italians favor. Bitterness is not, however, the only quality these greens possess. They have a spicy pepperiness I find very appealing. To satisfy both my French palate and my desire for an intriguing taste, I soften the bitterness with other more neutral ingredients, such as eggplant. In this salad, the small cubes also work like croutons to provide a contrast in texture.

EGGPLANT

¼ cup olive oil

1½ pounds (1 large) eggplant, peeled and cut into ½-inch cubes

2 large cloves garlic, peeled and minced

1 tablespoon fresh coarsely chopped basil or other fresh herb or green onion

Generous pinch of ground cumin

Salt and freshly ground black pepper to taste

SHALLOT VINAIGRETTE

> 2 tablespoons red wine vinegar
>
> 1 tablespoon balsamic vinegar
>
> ¼ cup olive oil
>
> 1 medium shallot, peeled and minced
>
> Salt and freshly ground black pepper to taste
>
> 1⅓ ounces (about 40 sprigs) arugula, thick part of stem discarded
>
> 2 tablespoons fresh basil julienne or other fresh herb or green onion

For the eggplant, place a heavy large nonstick skillet over medium heat and film it with oil. Add the eggplant and cook for 5 minutes, stirring frequently. Add the garlic, basil and cumin; cover, reduce heat to medium-low, and cook until eggplant is very tender, for about 15 minutes, stirring occasionally. Season with salt and pepper. (This can be prepared ahead and set aside at cool room temperature.)

For the Shallot Vinaigrette, mix the red wine and balsamic vinegars in a small bowl. Whisk in the olive oil in a slow thin stream. Stir in the shallot and season with salt and pepper. (This can be prepared ahead, covered and set aside at cool room temperature.)

To serve, toss the arugula with about ¼ of the dressing until it is lightly coated and arrange in a spoke pattern on 4 salad plates using tongs. Mix the eggplant with the remaining dressing and mound in the center of each plate. Sprinkle each portion with basil julienne and serve immediately.

Technique Tip

When choosing an eggplant, look for the male whose bottom indentation is rounder and deeper than a female's shallow oval opening, promising fewer seeds.

Variations

Add chicken or sausage to make this salad a substantial main-course dish.

As an alternative to eggplant, I often mix apples and prosciutto with the arugula for a first-course salad. When arugula is not available, I use watercress.

Wine Selection
Chablis

Mushroom Tarts
with Garlic Cream

6 Servings

Planning Ahead

The Garlic Cream and mushrooms can be cooked and the puff pastry prepared at any time during the day the tarts are to be served. Bake the pastry and fill the tarts just before presenting.

Technique Tips

I slice the mushrooms after they are cooked rather than before to preserve a contrast of color and texture.

I prefer to bake puff pastry at a lower temperature for a longer period of time than most recipes indicate, so I know it will be cooked through and each layer will be crunchy.

Wine Selection

Merlot

When Americans think of French food and garlic, the first thing that usually comes to mind is snails. I tried to serve snails at my restaurant without garlic, but no one would eat them. Actually, not too many people eat them *with* garlic, so I've substituted mushrooms in this tart, and it seems to be a much more popular pairing.

For the mushrooms, I have chosen fresh shiitakes because their pronounced flavor stands up well to garlic. Containing relatively little water, this variety remains firm during cooking and doesn't shrink. If not available, buy whatever type you like. The crisp puff pastry sandwiching this savory filling can also be cut into tiny hors d'oeuvre squares or a grand main-course sheet.

GARLIC CREAM

30 large or generous 1 cup (about 2 heads) cloves garlic, peeled

2 cups heavy cream

Salt and freshly ground black pepper to taste

1 8-ounce frozen puff pastry sheet, defrosted 20 minutes at room temperature

MUSHROOMS

About 2 tablespoons olive oil

1½ to 2 pounds fresh medium shiitake or other type mushroom, ends trimmed

Salt and freshly ground black pepper to taste

6 fresh herb sprigs, such as chervil and parsley (optional)

For the Garlic Cream, place the garlic in a heavy medium saucepan. Cover with 3 inches of cold water. Bring to a boil. Drain and rinse with cold water. Repeat this process 2 more times. Thinly slice garlic. Return it to the same saucepan with the cream. Bring to a boil, then reduce heat and simmer gently until reduced by half or to a thick saucelike consistency, stirring occasionally. Season with salt and pepper. (This can be prepared ahead, covered and set aside at cool room temperature for several hours or refrigerated.)

For the pastry, line a large baking sheet with parchment paper. Roll the pastry into a 10- × 9-inch rectangle on a lightly floured surface. Cut into six 3- × 5-inch squares using a fluted pastry cutter. Transfer to the prepared baking sheet. Cover with plastic wrap and refrigerate at least 1 hour until baking.

For the Mushrooms, place a heavy large skillet over medium-high heat and film with oil. Add the mushrooms and cook until lightly browned and tender, for about 5 minutes, stirring frequently. Halve the mushrooms or slice them into thirds horizontally. Season with salt and pepper. (This can be prepared ahead and set aside at cool room temperature.)

To serve, preheat the oven to 350°F. Discard the plastic wrap. Prick the pastry with a fork. Bake until puffed, golden brown and baked through, for about 30 minutes. Gently slice in half horizontally using a serrated knife. Arrange on 6 plates. Meanwhile, rewarm both the cream and the mushrooms, stirring each over medium-high heat. Spoon ⅙ of the cream onto the bottom of each portion of pastry. Overlap mushrooms on top of the cream, alternating light and dark pieces. Set each pastry cover at an angle on top of the mushrooms so the filling is visible. Garnish each with an herb sprig, if desired. Serve immediately.

Egg Roll Cups with
Cheese Chive Filling

**Makes 20 Cups
to Serve 4 to 6**

Planning Ahead

The Cheese Chive Filling can be made several days in advance. The Egg Roll Cups can be formed at any time during the day they are to be baked, and baked up to several hours before serving. Fill just before presenting.

Technique Tips

These cups can be made in any size, shape or number desired.

Wrap the remaining egg roll wrappers well and refrigerate or freeze them to use at another time or for a different dish.

Variation

Roasted peppers and/or sun-dried tomatoes can be added to the cheese mixture.

Wine Selection

White or Red Burgundy

When I first started making tiny tartlets, my pastry was so thick there was no room for the filling. On top of that, my dough would collapse and shrink into a tough, thick mass. I finally got the technique down, but I'm not sure I would have bothered to do so had I known what delicate shells I could make effortlessly with egg roll skins.

The only drawback is that these shells are so thin they leak when filled and baked. This doesn't stop me, though, from using them to hold cold mixtures, such as a salad, marinated vegetable, cheese dip, smoked fish mousse or seafood cocktail or tartar. Often I make one large cup from an entire egg roll skin to hold a first course or luncheon salad. In this case, I fry the cup in a mold until it holds its shape, but it can be baked in a bowl as well. For a dessert cup, I sprinkle the shells with sugar before baking and mounding with custard, mousse or ice cream and fresh fruit.

CHEESE CHIVE FILLING

8 ounces goat cheese, Montrachet-style, at room temperature

3 ounces cream cheese, at room temperature

1 tablespoon fresh minced chives or green onions

EGG ROLL CUPS

1 ounce (¼ stick) unsalted butter, melted

5   7- × 7-inch egg roll wrappers

About 2 tablespoons minced flat-leaf parsley

For the Cheese Chive Filling, mix the goat cheese, cream cheese and chives in a small bowl with a fork. (This can be prepared ahead and set aside at cool room temperature for several hours or refrigerated for several days. Bring to room temperature before using.)

For the Egg Roll Cups, wipe or brush the excess starch off of both sides of the egg roll wrappers. Brush both sides of the wrappers with melted butter on a clean work surface or tray. Cut each wrapper into quarters. Fit each quarter into a mini muffin tin or other mold, pressing down gently to form a cup. (This can be prepared ahead and set aside at room temperature until baking.)

To bake the cups, preheat the oven to 350°F. Bake until golden brown and crisp, for about 9 to 10 minutes. Transfer to a rack using tongs or fingers.

To serve, divide the filling among the shells using a small spoon. Sprinkle the centers with parsley. Place on a large serving platter. Serve immediately.

Onion and Olive Tartlets

T he onion tart, like bread, has universal appeal and numerous regional interpretations. Bacon is added in Alsace, cream in Normandy, and anchovies in the South of France. In Gascony, the beloved onion is caramelized in goose fat, while in Lyon, red wine is the cooking medium. This Provençal version, made with olives, is designed to be a first course, but you can increase the proportions for a main course—even making one large tart—or add whatever creative touches you wish.

ONIONS

    3 tablespoons olive oil

    2 medium (1 to 1¼ pounds) red onions, peeled, halved and thinly
        sliced

    1 large clove garlic, peeled and minced

    Salt and freshly ground black pepper to taste

    1 8-ounce frozen puff pastry sheet, defrosted 20 minutes at room
        temperature

    8 Niçoise or other black olives, pitted and coarsely chopped

For the onions, heat the olive oil in a heavy large nonstick skillet over medium-low heat. Add the onions, cover and cook until very tender, for about 20 minutes, stirring occasionally. Add the garlic, cover and cook for 5 minutes. Season with salt and pepper. (This can be prepared ahead, cooled, covered and set aside at cool room temperature.)

For the pastry, line a large baking sheet with parchment paper. Roll out the puff pastry on a floured surface into a 13- × 13-inch square. Cut out four 6-inch circles using a sharp floured fluted cutter. Transfer to the prepared baking sheet. Cover with plastic wrap and refrigerate at least 1 hour or until baking.

To serve, preheat the oven to 400°F. Discard the plastic wrap. Prick the pastry with a fork. Mound the onions in the center of each circle of pastry to within ½ inch from the edge. Bake until the pastry is well browned for 30 to 40 minutes. Transfer to 4 serving plates. Sprinkle the olives on top of the onions. Serve immediately.

4 Servings

Planning Ahead
The onions can be cooked and the puff pastry rolled and cut at any time during the day they are to be used. Fill and bake the tartlets just before serving.

Wine Selection
Cabernet Sauvignon

Red Onion Upside-Down Tart

4 to 6 Servings

Planning Ahead

The onions can be cooked on top of the stove and the puff pastry rolled out at any time during the day the tart is to be served. If you are preparing the tart without interruption, pre-heat the oven while cook-ing the onions. Bake the tart 30 to 45 minutes before presenting.

Technique Tips

Use onions that are ap-proximately the same size and shape. I usually use wide flat onions about 3 inches in diameter that I cut in thirds horizontally.

To avoid sticking, use a heavy skillet. I use a sea-soned 11-inch cast-iron skil-let, but a nonstick pan will work well. Heat the pan well before adding butter and then heat the butter before adding onions.

Swirl the pan frequently to be sure onions don't stick.

Considerable liquid may bubble up while the onions bake, but this will evapo-rate by the time onions are caramelized.

Serve the tart immedi-ately after it rests or the pastry will become soggy.

Wine Selection
Beaujolais

I went to a barbecue where roasted whole onions came off the grill looking like pastry-wrapped apples. Brown and caramelized, they were very nice. We don't have large sweet onions like these in France, and I had never seen anything like them before. Since they reminded me of the caramelized apples in an upside-down tart Tatin, I followed the same formula. The technique crossed over from apples to onions beautifully.

6 large (about 3⅛ to 3¼ pounds) red, Maui or Vidalia onions, peeled

2 ounces (½ stick) unsalted butter

2 tablespoons sugar

Salt and freshly ground black pepper to taste

3 tablespoons red wine vinegar

1 8-ounce frozen puff pastry sheet, defrosted 20 minutes at room temperature

Slice the onions into thirds horizontally. Heat a heavy large nonstick skillet over medium heat. Add the butter and allow it to melt. Sprinkle the sugar over the butter. Place a layer of the onions over the bottom of the skillet, flat side down. Season with salt and pepper. Sprinkle with 1 tablespoon of vinegar. Make 2 more layers in this manner, pressing down with hands or large spatula to pack the onions. Dice remaining onions and use them to fill the holes. Reduce heat to low and cook for 30 minutes to begin caramelization, pressing the onions down and shaking the pan frequently in a swirling motion to prevent sticking.

Preheat oven to 350°F. Transfer skillet to oven. Bake for 30 minutes.

Meanwhile, for puff pastry, roll out the pastry sheet to form a circle 1 inch larger than the top diameter of the skillet. (This can be prepared ahead, placed on a baking sheet, covered with plastic wrap, and refrigerated. If chilling several hours, remove from the refrigerator for 15 minutes before placing over onions.)

Remove the skillet from the oven and swirl it to be sure the onions aren't sticking. Prick pastry with fork. Roll up the pastry on a rolling pin and unroll it over the onions. Push the edges of the pastry down between the onions and the sides of the pan using a knife. Return the skillet to the oven and bake until the pastry is golden brown, for about 45 minutes. Let the skillet rest for 15 minutes. Run a spatula around the inside edge of the skillet to free the pastry. Place a large serving tray on top of the skillet and reverse carefully, using towels or potholders, to unmold tart onion side up. Let rest for 15 to 30 minutes. Slice in wedges and transfer to 4 to 6 plates. Serve immediately.

Shrimp Pastry Triangles
with Garlic Butter

C hefs and diners alike are partial to cozily wrapped food *en croûte*. They rarely present seafood this way, though, because it overcooks long before the pastry has had a chance to brown. Rising to this culinary challenge, I figured out a way to produce moist, perfectly cooked shrimp in a crisp-crunchy dough. The key is to roll out the pastry as thin as possible and to refrigerate the shrimp for several hours or until well chilled before baking.

GARLIC BUTTER

> 2 ounces (½ stick) unsalted butter
>
> 2 large cloves garlic, peeled and thinly sliced
>
> ¼ teaspoon anise seed, crushed
>
> ¼ cup fresh minced chervil or flat-leaf parsley or 1½ tablespoons fresh minced chives
>
> 12 large shrimp, shelled and deveined
>
> 1 8-ounce frozen puff pastry sheet, defrosted 20 minutes at room temperature
>
> 1 egg, blended with fork
>
> Salt and freshly ground black pepper to taste
>
> Fresh chervil or parsley sprigs for garnish

For the Garlic Butter, melt the butter with the garlic and anise in a small saucepan over low heat. Stir in the chervil and set aside at room temperature until cooled but still liquid.

Meanwhile, to butterfly the shrimp: Starting from the head end, hold each shrimp rounded side up and cut with a small sharp knife lengthwise down through the center almost to the bottom. Gently open the shrimp and press to flatten.

To assemble, line a large baking sheet with parchment paper. Quarter the pastry lengthwise. Roll ¼ out on a lightly floured surface into a 4- × 20-inch rectangle. If the pastry retracts at any point, let it rest several minutes. Brush the pastry with egg and then with the cool Garlic Butter. Arrange 6 shrimp down the center of the pastry, leaving about 2 inches between each shrimp and 1½ inches on each end. Alternate heads and tails so that the tails of the first, third and fifth shrimp point to the right edge of the pastry and the heads of the second, fourth and sixth shrimp point to the right edge of the pastry. Brush shrimp generously with Garlic Butter. Season with salt and pepper.

(continued)

Planning Ahead
The pastry triangles can be assembled at any time during the day they are to be served. Bake just before presenting.

Wine Selection
Chardonnay

Roll out another ¼ of the pastry into a 4- × 20-inch rectangle. Roll it up on a rolling pin and unroll it over the first quarter of pastry. Seal the 2 layers together, pressing firmly around each shrimp. Following the contours of the shrimp, divide the pastry into 6 even triangles using a fluted pastry wheel or knife. Transfer the triangles to the prepared baking sheet using a spatula.

Form 6 more pastry triangles in the same fashion using the remaining ingredients. Cover with plastic wrap and refrigerate until ready to bake.

To serve, preheat the oven to 450°F. Discard the plastic wrap. Brush the top of the shrimp triangles twice with egg, being careful not to drip down the sides or the pastry won't rise. Mark shallow decorative lines diagonally across the top, using the tip of a sharp knife. Bake until puffed and brown, for 20 to 25 minutes. Transfer to a platter or divide among 4 to 6 plates. Garnish with chervil sprigs. Serve immediately.

Goat/Cheese/Cake

10 to 12 Servings

Planning Ahead
The cheesecake can be assembled up to 1 day before it is baked several days in advance. If baking and serving the same day, allow 6 to 8 hours for it to chill.

D eveloping this savory cheesecake recipe, a mixture of cream cheese and goat cheese, solved a rather frustrating problem at the restaurant. Each day we would bring a selection of cheeses to room temperature so they would be soft enough for the cheese course. Since they were rarely ordered, we usually watched them spoil, and then we threw them out—a very discouraging ritual. After one particularly difficult day, I suffered a loss of self-discipline and ate a cheesecake a friend had brought directly out of the refrigerator. Unlike my chilled French cheeses, this was creamy and unctuous, not hard. Even though it was cold, its texture was *à point*. Since that day, I've been baking a savory cheesecake that can be kept in the refrigerator without spoiling until ordered for a starter, a salad (page 92) or a cheese course.

This loaf also comes to the rescue at party time: It's quick and easy to assemble, can be baked a week ahead and will feed a crowd. Just don't serve it with those stupid industrial crackers or those paper-wrapped breadsticks. Do you know how old those things are?

10 ounces goat cheese, at room temperature

10 ounces cream cheese, at room temperature

1 tablespoon sour cream or plain yogurt (optional)

⅓ cup olive oil

2 eggs, at room temperature

1 tablespoon fresh minced basil or other fresh herb

1 tablespoon fresh minced chives

½ teaspoon freshly squeezed lemon juice

Generous ½ teaspoon anise seed, finely crushed

½ teaspoon freshly ground black pepper

6 drops Tabasco

Greens and cherry tomatoes for garnish

Toast points

Technique Tips

Other soft cheeses such as feta or Brie can be substituted for goat cheese.

Use a plastic wrap to line the loaf pan that has been recommended as safe for microwaving, such as Saran Wrap.

The cheesecake can be baked in individual soufflé dishes or ramekins as well. The baking time will be reduced to 30 to 40 minutes, depending on the size of the dish.

Wine Selection
Red Côtes du Rhône

To assemble, line an 8- × 4-inch loaf pan with enough plastic wrap to extend 3 inches over the sides. Place the goat cheese, cream cheese and sour cream in the bowl of an electric mixer. Blend on low speed. Beat in the olive oil in a slow, steady stream. Beat in the eggs, one at a time. Add the basil, chives, lemon juice, anise, pepper, and Tabasco and mix just until blended. Turn the cheese mixture into the prepared loaf pan. Tap the pan sharply on a work surface to remove air pockets and distribute the filling evenly. Smooth the top with a spatula. Fold plastic over the top. Cover the pan with aluminum foil. (This can be prepared several hours ahead and set aside at cool room temperature or refrigerated 1 day.)

To bake, preheat the oven to 250°F. Place the loaf pan in a larger baking pan. Pour enough water into the baking pan to come ¾ of the way up the sides of the loaf pan. Remove the loaf pan and place the baking pan with the water in the oven to preheat for 15 minutes.

Place the loaf pan in the water bath and bake 1 to 1¼ hours or until slightly puffed and bubbles on the surface are just starting to turn golden. An instant-read thermometer inserted into the center will register 145°F, while a knife inserted into the center will still come out moist and the cake will feel soft. If the water starts to bubble at any time during baking, reduce oven heat. Cool the cheesecake to room temperature, then cover and chill.

To serve, remove from the refrigerator about 30 minutes before serving and unmold it immediately. Spread on toast points or slice using a knife that is rinsed in hot water and dried before each cut. Transfer to a platter with a wide spatula. Garnish with greens and cherry tomatoes.

Summer Tomato Tart
with Basil Crust

4 to 6 Servings

Planning Ahead

The dough for the Basil Crust can be prepared 1 day before it is baked. The crust can be rolled out and baked and the Pastry Cream of Wheat prepared at any time during the day the tart is to be served. The tomatoes can be sliced several hours before arranging on the tart. Spread the Pastry Cream of Wheat on the tart and top with the tomatoes just before broiling and presenting.

Technique Tip

If pastry is too firm to roll out, let it sit briefly at room temperature.

Wine Selection

Alsatian Riesling

At the restaurant, we bake our fruit tarts on long rectangular bands of pastry that are easier to slice evenly than a round tart. I've formed this savory tart similarly, only instead of using the usual puff pastry or *pâté brisée* base, I've made a crust that includes tomato paste, basil and baking powder. The baking powder provides a wonderful crumbly, almost sandy texture—what pastry chefs call a short crust—but it has an aftertaste I don't like, so I add it only when there are other flavorings to mask it.

For my topping, I've placed rows of vine-ripened tomatoes over Cream of Wheat mixed with tomato juice and crunchy celery. I found the box of this polenta-like cereal on the counter one morning after my wife made the children's breakfast, and I tried it out of curiosity. Now I use it all the time for a quick, lowfat, modern-day white sauce or pastry cream. Forget breakfast.

BASIL CRUST

1 tablespoon tomato paste

1 cup (about 1 ounce) loosely packed basil

4 ounces (1 stick) unsalted butter, chopped, at room temperature

1 egg

1 teaspoon sugar

2 teaspoons baking powder

½ teaspoon salt

Several grinds of black pepper

1½ cups flour

TOMATO CREAM OF WHEAT

9 tablespoons (3 packages) instant Cream of Wheat cereal

2 cups tomato juice

2 tablespoons freshly grated Parmesan cheese

3 tablespoons olive oil

1½ tablespoons red wine vinegar

3 cloves garlic, peeled and minced

1 stalk celery, trimmed and finely diced

Salt and freshly ground black pepper to taste

4 large tomatoes, halved and sliced ¼ inch thick

Salt and freshly ground black pepper to taste

Olive oil

About ½ cup (2 ounces) freshly grated Parmesan cheese

¼ cup fresh minced basil

Fresh basil sprigs for garnish (optional)

For the Basil Crust, place the tomato paste, basil, butter, egg, sugar, baking powder, salt and pepper in a food processor. Process until smooth, pulsing on/off and stopping to scrape down the sides of the container. Add ⅓ of the flour and process just until incorporated. Add remaining flour and process just until dough is crumbly. Gather the dough together with your hands, divide in half, and shape each half into a 3- to 4-inch-wide rectangle. Wrap in plastic. Refrigerate at least 1 hour. (This can be prepared 1 day ahead.)

Line a large baking sheet with parchment paper. Roll out each rectangle on a lightly floured surface to slightly larger than 12 × 5 inches. Trim to 12 × 5 inches using a fluted cutter. Arrange rectangles side by side on the baking sheet. Cover with plastic wrap and refrigerate at least 1 hour before baking.

For the Pastry Cream of Wheat, place Cream of Wheat in a bowl. Bring the tomato juice to a boil and whisk it into the Cream of Wheat. Stir in the Parmesan. Add the oil, vinegar, garlic and celery and mix well. Season with salt and pepper. (This can be prepared 4 to 6 hours ahead, cooled, covered and set aside at cool room temperature.)

To bake the crust, preheat the oven to 350°F. Discard the plastic wrap. Bake until slightly puffed and browned, for about 30 minutes. (This can be prepared ahead and transferred to a rack at room temperature.)

To serve, preheat the broiler. Arrange crusts on a baking sheet (or sheets) so they fit under the heat source. Spread half of the Cream of Wheat over each crust. Overlap tomatoes in rows over the Cream of Wheat. Season with salt and pepper. Drizzle lightly with oil. Sprinkle with Parmesan. Place the tarts about 4 inches below the heat source and broil until the cheese is browned and the tarts are heated through, for about 5 minutes, watching carefully. (Or bake in a preheated 500°F oven until rewarmed for 7 to 10 minutes.)

Sprinkle the tarts with minced basil. Slice into 4 to 6 portions using a serrated knife. Transfer to a serving platter or individual plates. Garnish with basil sprigs, if desired. Serve immediately.

Thousand-Layer Smoked Salmon Terrine with Caviar Sauce

12 to 24 Servings

Planning Ahead

The terrine can be completely prepared 3 days in advance. The Caviar Sauce can be prepared at any time during the day the terrine is to be served.

Technique Tips

The key to making this terrine is to keep the ingredients well chilled at all times. If the mousse filling is too soft to hold its shape after adding the fish roe, freeze or refrigerate it until it is firm enough to spread. If the terrine becomes too soft to hold its shape at any time while working on it, freeze or refrigerate it until it firms.

When inverting the trays with salmon over onto the work surface, do it quickly—but not too quickly—with confidence, or the salmon will fall off the paper.

Wine Selection
White Burgundy

This is a terrine without a terrine. Though layered in a rectangular shape, it's constructed free-form rather than in the mold called a terrine. One glance should reveal that a pastry chef's hand is behind this creation. I designed it, in fact, after the many-layered Opera cake. Its smoked salmon filling has basil for an unexpected touch of Provence and flying fish roe for texture. This caviar doesn't have much flavor, but it has tremendous crunch. You should be able to find it in Asian markets, but if not, salmon roe or another type of caviar will be fine. Do, however, use a good quality smoked salmon here. Since the recipe requires a substantial amount, you may be able to purchase it less expensively from a wholesaler.

The technique necessary for this terrine may be hard to imagine, but I would like to encourage you to give it a try. The terrine can be completed in advance, so for your first attempt at least, tackle it during a relaxed period. You will be composing this terrine from three large layers of smoked salmon that are cut into five strips, then stacked, halved, and stacked again to form a 30-layer cake sandwiching a smoked salmon mousse filling. A smaller version can be prepared using only one or two trays—one-third or two-thirds of the recipe—but the beauty of this terrine is that it looks imposing on a buffet and slices into handsome rectangular or triangular wedges. Served with a small salad and/or an egg dish and toast or bagels, there is probably no better centerpiece for a special brunch. Think, too, of presenting it alone for an elegant first course.

3 pounds thinly sliced smoked salmon

SALMON MOUSSE

8 to 9 ounces smoked salmon slices or trimmings

¾ cup packed (¾ to 1 ounce) basil leaves

½ pound chilled cream cheese, coarsely chopped

4 ounces (1 stick) chilled unsalted butter, coarsely chopped

2 to 3 drops Tabasco

¼ cup olive oil

Scant ½ cup unsalted chicken stock

¼ cup freshly squeezed lemon juice

½ ounce (2 envelopes) unflavored gelatin

2 tablespoons flying fish roe, salmon roe or other caviar

Caviar Sauce (recipe follows)

Cucumber slices for garnish (optional)

Line 3 identical 12- × 17-inch baking sheets with parchment paper. Cover the parchment paper completely with the pieces of salmon, overlapping, if necessary. Top each tray with a piece of parchment paper, rubbing and pressing to flatten and adhere it to the salmon. Stack the trays and freeze for 30 minutes while preparing the mousse. (If the trays don't fit in your freezer, refrigerate at least 2 hours or until well chilled.)

For the Salmon Mousse, process the smoked salmon trimmings and basil in a food processor until smooth, pulsing on/off. With the machine running, add the cream cheese and then the butter, several pieces at a time. Add Tabasco and process until smooth, pulsing on/off and stopping to scrape down the sides of the container. With the machine running, pour in the olive oil in a slow, thin stream.

Place the stock and lemon juice in a small pot. Sprinkle the gelatin over the mixture. Stir over low heat until the gelatin is dissolved. Cool until it is tepid. With the food processor running, slowly pour the gelatin mixture into the mousse through the feed tube. Transfer to a large bowl. Stir in the fish roe.

To assemble the terrine, remove the trays from the freezer and discard the top pieces of parchment paper. Spread ⅓ of the mousse evenly over 1 tray with a large flat spatula, covering the salmon completely. Take the salmon layer from the second tray and invert it over the salmon on the first tray, paper side up, forming 2 layers. Rub and press all over the paper so that the 2 salmon layers adhere. Remove the paper. Spread ⅓ of the mousse over this second layer. Invert the third tray over the salmon layers, paper side up. Rub and press the paper so the 3 layers adhere. Invert the tray onto a work surface; remove the tray. Rub the top layer of paper, pressing salmon layers together.

Using a sharp knife and a ruler as a guide, divide the layers equally into five 12-inch strips, each just short of 3½ inches wide. Remove the top paper. Invert 1 strip onto a 13-inch-long cutting board or tray, paper side up. Remove the paper and cover completely with a thin layer of the remaining salmon mousse. Repeat, stacking the remaining strips. Spread any remaining salmon mousse evenly over the top and sides of the terrine. Cover with plastic wrap. Freeze until firm, but not frozen, for about 30 minutes. Cut crosswise in half. Stack one half on top of the other. Smooth and square off the edges using a metal spatula dipped in hot water. Freeze for about 1 hour to firm or refrigerate until well chilled, about 4 hours or overnight. (This can be prepared 3 days ahead.)

To serve, cut into ½-inch-thick slices. If desired, cut each slice in half again diagonally, forming 2 triangles. Transfer the slices to 12 plates using a large, wide spatula. Let sit for 30 minutes. Ladle Caviar Sauce alongside. Garnish with cucumber slices, if desired. Serve immediately. The terrine can also be presented whole on a serving platter.

Caviar Sauce

Makes About 3 Cups

Planning Ahead
The Caviar Sauce can be prepared at any time during the day it is to be served.

2½ cups mayonnaise

¼ cup unsalted chicken stock

3 or 4 tablespoons freshly squeezed lemon juice or to taste

10 drops Tabasco

6 ounces flying fish roe, salmon roe or other caviar

¼ cup fresh minced chives or green onions

2 tablespoons tomato paste or beet juice or to taste

Place the mayonnaise in a small bowl. Stir in the chicken stock, lemon juice, Tabasco, fish roe and chives. Mix in enough tomato paste or beet juice to tint the mayonnaise a slightly lighter shade than salmon. (This can be prepared ahead and refrigerated until 30 minutes before serving.)

Spicy Thai Clams

In France, we make cooking very complicated. We simmer a dish for hours and then reduce, reduce, reduce. In contrast, few Asian dishes take more than two minutes to prepare. With so little time over heat, ingredients remain fresh tasting and flavorful. This approach has significantly influenced my cooking. It has been good for me to travel and see different countries and cultures. Having these new experiences has helped me be more creative and taught me respect for other cuisines.

These clams in their zesty Thai broth is one of the two-minute entrees I enjoyed in Bangkok.

1 cup dry white wine or water

1 tablespoon soy sauce

2 tablespoons fresh coarsely chopped cilantro or other
    fresh herb

1 serrano chili, thinly sliced

1 large shallot, peeled and thinly sliced

1 green onion, thinly sliced

1 large clove garlic, peeled and thinly sliced

1 stalk lemongrass, bulb part only, tough outer peel removed and
    cut into 2-inch strips or peel from 1 lemon (yellow part
    only), cut into fine julienne

32 fresh (about 1¼ pounds) littleneck clams, scrubbed

Toasted or grilled French bread

Place the wine and soy sauce in a heavy, deep, large nonaluminum skillet with the cilantro, chili, shallot, onion, garlic and lemongrass. (This can be prepared ahead and set aside at room temperature.)

Add the clams to the skillet and bring to a boil. Cover and simmer for 3 minutes, shaking pan occasionally. Remove any clams that have opened with tongs. Recover and cook up to 3 to 4 more minutes. Discard any clams that have not opened. Return opened clams to the pan. Ladle into 4 large soup plates with broth. Serve immediately with toasted bread.

4 Servings

Planning Ahead

The ingredients for the broth can be combined at any time during the day the dish is to be served. Add the clams and cook them just before presenting.

Technique Tip

To rid clams of sand, soak them in a bowl of lightly salted water for 30 minutes before cooking. If the water is very sandy at this point, drain and repeat.

Wine Selection

Sauvignon Blanc

Mussels with Basolivaise Sauce

4 Servings

Planning Ahead

The Basolivaise Sauce can be prepared and the mussels steamed at any time during the day the dish is to be served. Spread the sauce over the mussels up to 1 hour before broiling. Broil just before presenting.

Technique Tips

Buy black or green-tipped mussels with tightly closed shells or shells that snap shut when the mussel is touched with a knife.

The water used to heat the ingredients for the sauce should be kept at a very gentle simmer. If it becomes too hot, the egg yolks will curdle.

Variation

This sauce, essentially a cross between pesto and hollandaise, is superb with pasta, meat, poultry, vegetables, mashed potatoes—with anything pesto or hollandaise would complement. The sauce can be made up to 2 hours in advance and kept warm in a widemouthed thermos.

Wine Selection

St. Veran or other White Burgundy

When Citrus first opened, we prepped the butter-based hollandaise and béarnaise sauces each day as any classic French restaurant does. As I got to know California during that period, it increasingly reminded me of the South of France. Slowly pesto and olive oil crept into my cooking. One day I had some beautiful mussels I wanted to offer to special customers as an hors d'oeuvre. I mixed a ladle of hollandaise with a ladle of pesto and spooned an emerald dollop atop each mussel. After this, I readied an additional sauce each day, only now I made it without any butter. Not only was this new, velvety olive oil-based sauce lower in cholesterol but it was a great success. I thought I had invented something brilliant until I read that béarnaise was originally prepared from olive oil a hundred years ago in Bearn, the town in the Pyrenees where many people believe this sauce was born.

So much for the sauce. As for the mussels, this is one underappreciated mollusk in America. Its lack of popularity now is strange, considering that American Indians considered it a staple centuries ago.

BASOLIVAISE SAUCE

5 egg yolks, at room temperature

¾ cup fresh minced basil leaves or more to taste (stems reserved)

½ cup olive oil

1 tablespoon freshly squeezed lemon juice

Salt and freshly ground black pepper to taste

MUSSELS

24 mussels, scrubbed and debearded

Reserved basil stems

1 large shallot, peeled and minced

¼ cup dry white wine

¼ teaspoon freshly ground black pepper

Fresh basil sprigs for garnish (optional)

For the Basolivaise Sauce, place 2 inches of water in a large saucepan and heat until the water is barely shaking. Meanwhile, place the egg yolks in a blender, add the basil and process until pureed, pulsing on/off. Transfer to a stainless bowl and whisk over the heated water until the yolks thicken enough to see the bottom of the pan while whisking. Remove the bowl from the water and whisk in the olive oil in a slow, thin stream. Stir in the lemon juice. Season with salt and pepper. (This can be prepared ahead, covered and set aside at cool room temperature for up to 2 hours or stored in a thermos.)

Place the mussels, basil stems, shallot, wine and pepper in a large skillet. Cover and cook over medium-high heat for 3 to 4 minutes. Transfer mussels that have opened to a baking sheet with tongs. Cover and cook any remaining mussels for about 3 minutes. Transfer open mussels to the baking sheet; discard any that are still closed.

Discard the upper half of each mussel shell. Detach the mussel from the bottom of each shell with a small knife; leave it in the shell. (This can be prepared ahead, covered with plastic wrap and refrigerated until 1 hour before serving.)

To serve, preheat the broiler. Spread the Basolivaise Sauce over the mussels, covering them completely. Place about 2 inches below the heat source and broil just until the sauce starts to brown, watching carefully. Transfer to 4 plates or a large platter. Garnish with basil sprigs. Serve immediately, passing small forks and plates or napkins with the platter.

Scallop Seviche with Carrots and Cumin

4 Servings

Planning Ahead

The carrots can be cooked and the Cumin Vinaigrette prepared at any time during the day the seviche is to be served. Marinate the scallops and carrots for only 15 to 30 minutes before presenting.

Technique Tip

If scallops are marinated longer than 30 minutes, they will toughen.

Variation

Use only fresh, firm scallops for this dish. If they are not available, substitute another shellfish. Cooked shrimp can be used as well; instead of marinating, toss them with the vinaigrette just before serving.

Wine Selection

Chablis or other White Burgundy

I had a friend who loved cumin so much you could smell it as soon as the door opened to his home. His wife hated French people, and every time he invited me to dinner, she would throw part of it at someone. Once I brought a cold poached Salmon Bellevue for a buffet that I had spent hours decorating in aspic, and she heaved it out the door tail-first as soon as I put it on the table. I soon stopped going there for dinner. You know when you're not wanted. Nevertheless, I still think of these people whenever I use cumin today.

I've grown particularly fond of cumin with carrots, and it is a combination I've used frequently over the years, especially with fish. One of my favorite dishes is this Scallop Seviche with Carrots and Cumin presented in the shape of a beautiful blossom.

About 3 large carrots (preferably same diameter as scallops), peeled and cut into 48 ¼-inch-thick coins

CUMIN VINAIGRETTE

2 tablespoons red wine vinegar

1 tablespoon balsamic vinegar

¼ cup olive oil

½ teaspoon ground cumin or to taste

Salt and freshly ground black pepper to taste

16 jumbo (about ¾ pound) sea scallops, sliced in thirds horizontally

4 fresh chervil or parsley sprig bouquets for garnish

Cook the carrot coins in a large pot of boiling salted water until crisp-tender for about 2 to 3 minutes; drain and set aside.

For the Cumin Vinaigrette, whisk the red wine and balsamic vinegars together in a medium bowl. Whisk in the oil in a slow, thin stream. Stir in the cumin. Season with salt and pepper. (This can be prepared ahead, covered and set aside at room temperature.)

To assemble and serve, rewhisk the vinaigrette 15 to 30 seconds before serving. Gently stir the scallops and carrots into the vinaigrette. Let sit for 15 to 30 minutes, stirring occasionally. One at a time, remove 12 scallops and 12 carrots from the vinaigrette with tongs, shake off the excess marinade and arrange alternately in a ring on each of 4 small plates. Place a chervil bouquet in the center of each ring. Blot off any excess vinaigrette on the plates with paper towels. Serve immediately.

Oysters with Tuna Blanket

4 Servings

Chauds-froids (hot-cold) is an old-fashioned French technique in which a classic sauce that is usually served hot is bound with gelatin and served cold instead. The *chauds-froids* concept is one that has always intrigued me intellectually. This delicate interpretation, chilled oysters blanketed by a warm tuna crust, was created for David Shaw, a friend who loves fish tartare.

This is a *chauds-froids* to which you raise a glass of Champagne: an elegant hors d'oeuvre that makes a statement. Exceedingly simple, it is yet one more example that cooking does not have to be difficult and time-consuming for food to taste delicious. Seasoning and timing must, however, be close to perfect since there is no way to mask a mistake. Don't overcook the tuna.

16 Belon or other fresh large unshucked oysters, scrubbed

12 ounces fresh tuna fillet

1 tablespoon soy sauce

2 tablespoons freshly squeezed lemon juice

Salt and freshly ground black pepper to taste

Seaweed or shredded greens for garnish

For the oysters, line a fine sieve with dampened paper towels. Fit the sieve over a small bowl. Open the oysters over the sieve, straining the juices. Discard the top shell. Free the oysters from the bottom shell with a small knife. Rinse and dry the bottom shells. Return the oysters to their shells and place on a baking sheet.

For the tuna, trim the dark oily portions from the tuna. Finely chop the tuna until it has the texture of ground meat, using a large sharp knife. Place in a bowl. Add soy sauce and lemon juice. Add 1 tablespoon oyster juice or to taste. Season with salt and pepper. Mix well, mashing with a fork. Spread the tuna mixture over the oysters, covering completely. Cover the oysters with plastic wrap and refrigerate until ready to serve.

To serve, preheat the broiler. Line a platter or 4 plates with a nest of seaweed or greens. Broil the oysters as close as possible to the heat source until the tuna *just* turns white, for 2 to 3 seconds, watching carefully. Arrange oysters on seaweed. Serve immediately.

Planning Ahead

The tuna mixture can be chopped and spread over the oysters at any time during the day the dish is to be served. Allow several hours to chill the oysters. Cook just before presenting.

Technique Tip

To open oysters, place an oyster rounded side down on a tray or work surface with the smaller hinge end facing you. Holding the oyster down with one hand, insert an oyster knife on one side of the hinge and gently jiggle the knife up and down until it goes in. Push the knife toward the back of the shell until it reaches the muscle attached to the top shell. Cut through the muscle and lift off the top shell.

Variation

Salmon can be substituted for tuna.

Wine Selection

Champagne, Muscadet or Chablis

Scrambled Eggs and
Oysters on the Half-shell

4 Servings

Planning Ahead

The oysters can be shucked and cooked, the cooking liquid reduced and the eggs mixed several hours in advance. Cook the eggs just before serving.

Technique Tip

To open oysters, place an oyster rounded side down on a tray or work surface with the smaller hinge end facing you. Holding the oyster down with one hand, insert an oyster knife on one side of the hinge and gently jiggle the knife up and down until it goes in. Push the knife toward the back of the shell until it reaches the muscle attached to the top shell. Cut through the muscle and lift off the top shell.

Variation

Any herb can be substituted for those called for in this recipe.

Wine Selection

Alsatian Riesling

Oysters and eggs share a special compatibility, perhaps because they both live in shells. Regardless of their affinity, whatever happens between them is very nice. The oyster liquor permeates the eggs as they are scrambled very, very slowly French-style over low heat. This technique, a great job for a guest, gives eggs the buoyancy of a whipped cream cloud without cream. For a lovely brunch or midnight supper, garnish with caviar before serving—if you like caviar. Great drama with very little work.

OYSTERS

16 Belon or other fresh large unshucked oysters, scrubbed

1 teaspoon minced shallot

½ teaspoon Champagne vinegar or white wine vinegar

½ cup clam juice or unsalted chicken stock

EGGS

8 large eggs

1 tablespoon fresh minced chives or green onions

1 tablespoon minced flat-leaf parsley

1 tablespoon fresh minced chervil

2 teaspoons fresh minced tarragon

Salt and freshly ground black pepper to taste

2 tablespoons (¼ stick) unsalted butter

4 fresh bouquets of parsley, chervil or tarragon sprigs

For the oysters, line a fine sieve with dampened paper towels. Fit the sieve over a small saucepan. Open the oysters over the sieve, straining the juices. Set the oysters aside. Discard the top shells. Rinse and dry the bottom shells and divide them among 4 large plates.

Add the shallot, vinegar and clam juice to the saucepan with the oyster juices. Heat until the liquid is just shaking. Add the oysters and simmer gently for 1 minute or until the oysters are barely opaque. Immediately remove the oysters to a plate with a slotted spoon. When cooled, halve the oysters and cover them with plastic wrap. Boil the cooking juices down until reduced to 3 to 4 tablespoons.

For the eggs, whisk the eggs to blend in a large bowl with the chives, parsley, chervil and tarragon. Stir in the reduced oyster liquid. Season with salt and pepper. (This can be prepared ahead to this point and set aside at cool room temperature for up to 2 hours.)

To serve, melt 1 tablespoon butter in a heavy small saucepan over very low heat. Add the egg mixture and whisk continually until smooth and creamy, breaking up curds, for about 15 to 20 minutes. Off the heat, whisk in 1 tablespoon butter and the halved oysters. Mound the egg mixture on top of the oyster shells. Place an herb bouquet in the center of each plate. Serve immediately.

Eggs in a Hole

I t's great fun for me to play in the kitchen. One day while I was fooling around, I made a hole in a piece of toast and then cooked an egg in the hole. I thought I had created something fantastic. My friend offered another perspective. "Big deal," he said. "It's an egg in a hole." So much for scientific discovery. Okay, so it's not a brilliant dish, but it is practical and one of the few ways I know to cook eggs easily for a crowd. It is also a chameleon that changes from a dainty hors d'oeuvre with quail eggs and caviar into a hefty sunny-side-up main course for brunch or supper. Its soft, warm, squirty yolk makes this my favorite choice for breakfast, too.

I've been forewarned that quail eggs are hard to locate, so the instructions here are geared for their larger chicken cousins. Since quail eggs are readily available in Asian groceries, poultry shops and supermarkets in Los Angeles, I was surprised to hear that this is not true all over the country. I suspect that one simple way to get quail eggs would be to ask your grocer for them, thereby creating a demand for their supply. These tiny eggs provide delicious flavor with a minimum of cholesterol, yet another reason for adding them to our diet.

Planning Ahead

The technique and countdown for this dish will change depending on the number of egg-toasts to be made. If you are preparing a simple supper dish for two, it's easy to make this dish in a nonstick skillet on top of the stove just before serving.

Technique Tip

The baking sheet must be preheated before the eggs are broken into the toast holes. If not, the eggs will run all over.

Variations

To prepare the toasts ahead for a crowd, brown one side of each slice of toast in a heavy nonstick skillet, flip the toast over, break an egg into the hole and cook just until the bottom of the egg is set, then carefully transfer to a baking sheet. Before serving, preheat the oven to 500°F and bake until the whites are set, for about 5 to 7 minutes. Season and garnish as directed.

To make quail egg canapés, cut 1½-inch rounds out of ⅜-inch-thick slices of brioche or French bread.

Wine Selection

Chablis or slightly chilled Beaujolais

Starters

TOAST

8 4-inch-wide (at least) pieces of brioche or French bread, sliced diagonally ½ inch thick

About 1 tablespoon olive oil

About 1 tablespoon unsalted butter

EGGS

8 small or medium eggs

Salt and freshly ground black pepper to taste (omit salt if using caviar)

About 1 tablespoon fresh minced chives

1 to 2 ounces salmon roe or other caviar (optional)

For the toast, place a large baking sheet in the oven and preheat the oven to 500°F. Cut 2-inch round holes in the center of each slice of bread using a cookie cutter or knife. Place a heavy large nonstick skillet over medium heat and film it with oil and butter. Add 4 slices of bread and brown them on both sides. Repeat with the remaining bread, adding butter and oil as necessary.

For the eggs, remove the baking sheet from the oven. Immediately arrange the toasts on it and break the eggs into the holes in the bread. Return to the oven and bake until the whites are just set, 5 to 7 minutes. Season each egg with salt and pepper, sprinkle with chives and spoon a dab of caviar next to it. Place 2 toasts on 4 plates, using a broad spatula. Serve immediately.

Asparagus Frittata Terrine

L ike most French chefs, I generally serve asparagus with either a vinaigrette or one of the butter sauces. Seeking a change, I first thought of molding this vegetable in aspic; but I rejected this idea when I realized most people like Jell-O or sweet aspics, not savory ones. My next experiment was to immerse the asparagus in eggs, which also set or gel. The resulting terrine worked as I wished. Though it looks very sophisticated, it is quite easy to duplicate. All you have to do is lay spears in a loaf pan or rectangular mold, pour eggs over them and bake. If asparagus is not in season, substitute cooked small leeks or sliced broccoli stalks. Delicious warm or at room temperature, at brunch, lunch or supper, on a buffet table or in a picnic basket, this terrine looks terrific with its green-gold polka-dot slices.

ONIONS

About 1 tablespoon olive oil

1 medium onion, peeled and finely diced

½ teaspoon sugar

3 large cloves garlic, peeled and minced

1 tablespoon Champagne vinegar or white wine vinegar

Salt and freshly ground black pepper to taste

ASPARAGUS

1½ pounds medium or thick asparagus spears, tough white ends
   broken off and peeled

Salt and freshly ground black pepper to taste

TERRINE

6 eggs, at room temperature

1 tablespoon fresh minced tarragon, dill or mint

Salt and freshly ground black pepper to taste

For the onions, place a heavy small skillet over medium-low heat and film it with olive oil. Add the onion, cover and cook until translucent, for about 10 minutes, stirring occasionally. Add the sugar, increase heat to medium-high and stir until lightly browned. Add the garlic and vinegar and boil until the vinegar has evaporated, stirring occasionally. Season with salt and pepper. Cool to room temperature.

For the asparagus, bring a large pot of water to a boil. Line a rack with paper towels. Divide the asparagus spears according to thickness. Cook, adding thicker spears to the water first, until almost tender when pierced with a knife, for about 3 to 4 minutes for larger spears. Drain and place on the rack. Season with salt and pepper. (This can be prepared ahead.)   *(continued)*

6 Servings

Planning Ahead

The asparagus and onions can be cooked at any time during the day the terrine is to be baked. Bake the terrine just before presenting to serve warm, or several hours or 1 day in advance to serve at room temperature.

Wine Selection

Sauvignon Blanc or Pinot Noir

For the terrine, preheat the oven to 325°F. Butter a loaf pan (approximately 8 × 4 × 2½ inches) and line the bottom with buttered parchment or waxed paper. Place the loaf pan in a larger baking pan. Pour enough water into the pan to come ¾ of the way up the sides of the loaf pan. Remove the loaf pan and place the baking pan with water in the oven to preheat for about 15 minutes.

Trim the asparagus if it is longer than the loaf pan; reserve trimmings. Place a single layer of asparagus spears on the bottom of the loaf pan, alternating tips and ends. Fill in any spaces with trimmings. Spoon over ⅓ of the cooked onions. Continue layering until the asparagus and onion mixtures are used. Break the eggs into a bowl and whisk with the tarragon, salt and pepper until well blended. Pour the egg mixture into the loaf pan. Move a knife between the asparagus spears, jiggling the tip to make sure the egg is evenly distributed. Lightly tap the loaf pan on a work surface. Cover with aluminum foil and place in the water bath. Bake until the eggs are set and a knife inserted into the center comes out clean, for about 50 minutes to 1 hour (time will vary depending on shape of mold). Remove from the water bath.

To serve warm, let the terrine settle for 15 minutes, then run a knife around the rim and unmold. Slice ½ inch thick. Transfer several slices to 6 plates with a large spatula. Serve immediately.

To serve at room temperature, let the terrine cool to room temperature before unmolding and slicing. (This can be prepared ahead, cooled and refrigerated overnight. Bring to room temperature before serving.)

Cream Cheese Gnocchi
with Corn Spinach

**4 Main-course or
6 First-course
Servings**

Planning Ahead

The Corn Spinach can be completely prepared at any time during the day it is to be consumed and reheated just before presenting. The Cream Cheese Gnocchi batter can be prepared at any time during the day it is to be cooked. Poach as close to serving as possible.

T his is my Southwest spinach. To sweeten it, I've used corn in much the same way as the onion in the Mellow Spinach (page 281). Except for the corn, this preparation is similar to the classic French spinach with *Sauce Mornay* or cheesey white sauce. In the same way, the Cream Cheese Gnocchi is a modern version of a traditional French quenelle or mousseline. In using the name "gnocchi," I'm flirting with the Italian style of cooking. If I called this dish "quenelle," I wouldn't sell one today, but as "gnocchi" it walks out the door. Cheese Gnocchi? Cheese Quenelle? Cheese Dumpling? It doesn't matter what you call it. Good cooking is good cooking.

CORN SPINACH

1 ounce (¼ stick) unsalted butter

1 small onion, peeled and diced

2 pounds (2 large bunches) fresh spinach, stemmed, washed, dried and coarsely chopped

Starters

2 large ears of corn, husked and kernels removed

1½ cups heavy cream

Salt and freshly ground black pepper to taste

CREAM CHEESE GNOCCHI

8 ounces cream cheese, at room temperature

2 ounces (½ stick) unsalted butter, at room temperature

½ teaspoon anise seed, finely crushed

½ cup flour

2 eggs, at room temperature

Salt and freshly ground black pepper to taste

For the Corn Spinach, melt the butter in a heavy large deep skillet over medium-low heat. Add the onion, cover and cook until translucent, for about 10 minutes, stirring occasionally. Increase heat to medium-high, stir the spinach into the onion, cover and cook until wilted, for about 5 minutes, stirring occasionally.

Meanwhile, place the corn in a large pot with the cream and bring to a boil over medium-high heat. Reduce heat and simmer for 5 minutes. Puree the corn mixture in a blender until smooth, for about 5 minutes, pulsing on/off and stopping to scrape down the sides of the container. Strain the corn mixture through a fine sieve into the wilted spinach. Simmer the spinach mixture over medium heat until thickened, for about 5 minutes, stirring occasionally. Season with salt and pepper. (This can be prepared ahead and set aside at cool room temperature for 2 hours or re-frigerated.)

For the Cream Cheese Gnocchi, mash the cream cheese, butter and anise in a medium bowl until smooth using a large fork. Add the flour, eggs, salt and pepper and mix just until incorporated. (This can be prepared ahead and set aside at cool room temperature for 2 hours or refrigerated.)

To cook, bring at least 6 inches of water to a gentle simmer in a deep, wide pan. Line a large baking sheet with parchment paper. Using a teaspoon and small spatula to form smooth round gnocchi, shape the gnocchi and drop into gently bubbling water. Make and cook about 10 gnocchi at a time, simmering until gnocchi rise to the surface and feel firm to the touch, for about 5 minutes. Gently transfer to the prepared baking sheet with a slotted spoon. Repeat with the remaining cream cheese batter.

To serve, reheat the Corn Spinach by stirring over medium-high heat. Divide the Corn Spinach among 4 or 6 large soup plates. Arrange the gnocchi on top of the spinach mixture. Serve immediately.

Variations

Arrange cooked Corn Spinach in 1 large or 4 to 6 individual gratin dishes. Top with gnocchi. Sprinkle generously with Parmesan cheese. (This can be prepared ahead and set aside at cool room temperature for 2 hours or refrigerated. Bring to room temperature before gratinéing.)

To serve, preheat the broiler and cook about 4 inches below the heat source until the cheese is melted and golden brown.

The Corn Spinach can also be served as a topping for pasta or as a sauce or side dish with chicken, lamb, beef or seafood.

Wine Selection
Chardonnay

Duck *Ham*

Planning Ahead

Allow 12 to 15 days for the duck to cure. Once cured, the duck will keep for several weeks. As it ages, it becomes increasingly dry.

Technique Tip

To suspend the duck while it cures, hang a hook discretely in the kitchen ceiling over or near the sink. This hook also comes in handy for hanging a jelly bag when clarifying aspic.

Although it is not an American custom to hang cheesecloth-wrapped packages of cured duck breasts from your ceiling to air-dry, the resulting lean *ham* is so delicious and easy to do, you might want to give it a try. Sliced thin, this homemade cold cut can be served plain, with bread, or with ripe melon, figs, pears or other fruit and cheese for an hors d'oeuvre or salad platter. Jicama or blanched turnip or celery root dressed lightly with a vinaigrette are nice partners, too. Or chop and sprinkle Duck *Ham* on pasta as prosciutto often is.

2½ tablespoons coarse kosher salt

1 teaspoon coarsely ground black pepper

1 tablespoon fresh minced thyme or other fresh herb, or
   1 teaspoon dried, crumbled

1 large clove garlic, peeled and minced

2 large duck breasts, boned and trimmed so skin is even with
   meat

Combine the salt, pepper, thyme and garlic in a 9-inch porcelain pie plate or other nonmetallic dish large enough to hold the duck in a single layer. Turn the duck in the salt mixture several times, patting it so the mixture adheres. Cover with paper towels and let it rest at room temperature for 12 hours.

Rinse the duck breasts and pat them dry. Wrap each breast in several layers of cheesecloth. Tie the ends with string and hang the breasts without touching in a cool, dry, airy place until they dry-cure and feel firm to the touch for about 12 to 15 days. Place the cheesecloth-wrapped duck in the refrigerator until serving.

To serve, unwrap the duck and slice paper-thin across the grain on the diagonal; discard the fat. Twist each slice or roll into a curl for an attractive presentation. Serve at room temperature.

Duck *Ham* with
Muscat and Farm Apples

Here, on one small plate, is a souvenir of the countryside with all its magic and simplicity. There is ham from the farm, the fresh bite of apple and the fabulous flavor of the meaty muscat grape—tastes of France that keep families around the big wooden table for hours.

2 Duck *Hams* (page 74)

2 Pippin or other tart apples, peeled and cored

**3 tablespoons Muscat de Beaumes-de-Venise or other muscat or
    sweet Riesling wine**

Slice Duck *Hams* paper-thin across the grain, roll into curls and divide among 4 small plates. Let sit at least for 30 minutes to come to room temperature. Dice the apples as small as possible and place in a small bowl. Toss with the wine and let sit several minutes or until the apples have almost absorbed the wine, stirring occasionally. Divide the diced apples among the plates with the duck curls using a slotted spoon. Serve immediately.

4 Servings

Planning Ahead

The Duck *Ham* must be made 12 to 15 days in advance. Begin the dish at least 30 minutes before serving. Prepare the apples at the last minute so they don't discolor or take on a winey flavor.

Wine Selection

Same wine used to marinate the apples.

Lacy Cheese Chips

Makes About 16

Planning Ahead

The chips can be cooked several hours before serving.

Technique Tips

Use freshly grated imported Parmesan for this dish.

Grate the cheese finely so the chips hold together well. The food processor is a good tool for this job.

Handle the chips carefully as they are somewhat fragile and crumbly.

Wine Selection

Pinot Noir

We have to thank Italy and my friend Piero Selvaggio for these Parmesan chips, which are a cross between a savory lace cookie and a roof tile-shaped *tuile*. Piero considers these very simple to form. And they are . . . once you know the method. It may take one or two trials to get the amount of cheese and cooking time down, but after you do, you'll be surprised how something so delicate and complicated-looking can be so easy to make. You can pass these chips on trays to serve with drinks, soups, or salads or mound them over pasta, mashed potatoes, hamburger patties, vegetable purees or salads. There's nothing like a Caesar with a Parmesan crown. You never know, these cheesy crackers may become as trendy as kiwi once was.

¾ cup (about ¾ ounce) freshly grated Parmesan cheese

4½ teaspoons flour

Mix Parmesan and flour in a small bowl. Arrange 2 rolling pins or bottles on a cloth or baking sheet to secure. Place a heavy small nonstick skillet over medium heat. Sprinkle about ¾ tablespoon of the cheese mixture into a 3- × 1-inch strip, filling in any holes. Cook until the bottom is brown and the cheese melts into the strip, for about 40 seconds, lifting the edge with tongs to check. Turn the strip over onto a rolling pin, brown side up, to firm into a curved chip. Repeat with the remaining cheese mixture. When firm, set aside on a rack. (This can be prepared several hours ahead.)

To serve, carefully transfer to a serving platter or mound over another dish for garnish.

Cream Puff Kisses

W hen I worked for Gaston Lenôtre, the French *pâtissier*, I learned to make cream puffs as smooth, as soft and as small as a baby's bottom. As cute as a Hershey's kiss, these miniature puffs can be floated in soup like fish crackers and sprinkled on salad—after toasting or drying—like croutons. They can be presented by themselves as nibbles or with dishes as mini—almost microscopic—rolls. For flavorings, add any herb or seed you want, some grated cheese, chopped nuts or several drops of a nut oil. Although I have placed this many-faced puff in a savory chapter, it can also be sweetened for dessert. To take this dough as far as it will go, deep fry it for a fritter.

1 ½ tablespoons sesame seeds

¼ cup milk

¼ cup water

2 ounces (½ stick) unsalted butter, chopped

½ teaspoon salt

6 tablespoons flour

2 tablespoons cornstarch, mixed with fork to break up lumps

2 eggs, at room temperature

¼ cup (about ¼ ounce) freshly grated Parmesan cheese

2 teaspoons fresh minced chives or finely minced green onions

Preheat the oven to 350°F. Line 2 baking sheets with parchment paper. Stir the sesame seeds over medium heat in a small dry skillet until brown; set aside. Bring milk, water, butter and salt to a rolling boil in a heavy small saucepan over medium-high heat. Immediately remove the pan from the heat and stir in the flour and cornstarch using a wooden spatula. Let the mixture sit for about 5 minutes.

Make a well in the center of the mixture. Break the eggs into the well and stir until completely incorporated. Stir cheese and chives into the dough.

Place the dough in a pastry bag fitted with ¼-inch plain tip or use 2 spoons to form. Pipe (or spoon) out puffs ½ inch wide and tall on the prepared sheets. Gently push down the tips with a finger. Sprinkle with sesame seeds. Bake until puffed, brown and dry, for about 20 minutes. Serve immediately or cool to room temperature on a rack. Pass in a cloth-lined bowl or basket.

**Makes About
60 ¾-inch Puffs
to Serve 6**

Planning Ahead

The cream puffs taste freshest when baked no more than 1 to 2 hours before serving. They rise highest when baked immediately after the dough is mixed. The dough can, however, be made several days in advance and refrigerated. Before baking, reheat the dough by stirring it over low heat until just warm to the touch.

Or, the dough can be formed into puffs and frozen.

Technique Tips

Although many cream puff recipes call for drying the mixture after the flour is added, I've eliminated this step because it can overactivate the gluten which then makes it difficult for the steam to escape and the puffs to rise and become tender. Adding cornstarch to the flour is another way of reducing the gluten.

If the mixture is too hot when the eggs are added, the puffs will not rise. Allow the mixture to cool to tepid before adding.

Wine Selection
Pinot Noir

Parmesan Génoise

Planning Ahead

This Parmesan Génoise is best eaten warm. Mix and bake the cake up to 1 to 2 hours before serving.

Technique Tips

Since beaten eggs provide the only leavening for this cake, be sure to beat until a thick ribbon has formed before adding other ingredients.

To fold properly, cut a plastic spatula down to the very bottom of the bowl and gently bring the batter on the bottom of the bowl up to the top. Turn the bowl ¼ turn and repeat this procedure. Repeat until the dry ingredients are completely incorporated. Fold gently so the batter doesn't deflate.

The cake pan does not have to be lined with parchment paper if the pan has a lever to release the cake. Butter and flour it anyway.

Snipping chives with scissors is easier than mincing with a knife.

Wine Selection
Pinot Noir

énoise is the basic French cake that you find hiding under buttercream and ganache. Though classically prepared with butter, I removed this ingredient long ago because it made the cake heavy for no good reason. With those creamy frostings, I didn't exactly need a cake that was rich. What I wanted instead was one that was light. When made *ma façon*, the génoise started coming out of the oven nice and light and warm. It was much like an American corn bread without the corn. I thought it might make a good savory cake/bread as well as a dessert. It does.

4 whole eggs, at room temperature

¾ cup flour

I teaspoon sugar

⅛ teaspoon salt

5 turns of whole black peppercorns from a pepper mill

⅓ cup (about ⅜ ounce) freshly grated Parmesan cheese

½ cup fresh minced chives or finely minced green onions

½ cup olive oil

Preheat the oven to 350°F. Line a 9-inch-round cake pan with parchment or waxed paper. Butter and flour the pan and paper, shaking out excess flour. Beat the eggs using an electric mixer on high speed until tripled in volume, pale lemon in color and a thick, slowly dissolving ribbon forms when beaters are lifted, for about 7 minutes. Meanwhile, sift the flour, sugar, and salt together into a medium bowl. Grind the pepper over the bowl. Stir in the Parmesan and chives with a fork. Pour the olive oil and dry ingredients into the beaten eggs, then gently fold these ingredients together until well mixed. Pour into the prepared baking pan. Bake until the cake is puffed, lightly browned and has started to pull away from the sides of the pan, for about 25 minutes. Let sit for 15 minutes. Unmold onto a rack.

To serve, place on a cake platter. Cut into wedges.

Los Angeles Country Bread

Makes I Loaf

When I worked in Gaston Lenôtre's pastry shop, I learned how to produce a delicious, hearty country loaf that could be quickly thrown together without all the fuss of making a starter, proofing yeast, kneading and rising twice that a classic recipe requires. Since I am now in Los Angeles instead of the outskirts of Paris, this has become my Los Angeles Country Bread. Never mind that the freeway is the closest I come to the countryside here.

The batter for this bread is very moist, so it is easier to make it in either the food processor or a heavy-duty mixer than by hand. The recipe can be doubled and made in two batches in a small food processor or in one batch in a larger machine. When shaping the bread, make one loaf or divide the dough in half for two smaller ones. In other words, adapt this bread-making process to suit your lifestyle and equipment. Delicious by itself, this is also an ideal bread to accompany any meal. It is great as well—toasted or untoasted—for sandwiching Rex and Lily Solewiches (page 136).

2 cups bread or all-purpose white flour

½ cup rye flour

1½ teaspoons salt

1½ teaspoons (½ package) dry yeast

1¼ cups warm (100°F) water

For the dough, place the white and rye flours, salt and yeast in a food processor. Process until well blended. With the machine running, gradually pour the water through the feed tube and continue mixing several minutes until it is very elastic. (The dough will be very wet and sticky.) Turn out onto a floured work surface with a stiff spatula and cover with a clean dish towel. Let rest for 40 minutes.

To rise, flour your hands and form a round loaf by rolling the dough into a ball on a work surface and pulling the edges into the center, pinching to seal. Line a 2-quart rounded bowl or basket with the dish towel. Place the dough in the bowl, pinched seam side up. Cover with another dish towel and let rise at room temperature until almost double in size, about 1½ to 2 hours.

To bake, meanwhile, preheat the oven to 400°F. Remove the top towel. Place a baking sheet over the bowl and invert the bread onto the sheet, seam side down; remove the bottom towel. Cut as large a square as possible for decoration on the top surface of the bread, using a single-edged razor or sharp knife tip. Bake the bread for 1 hour or until it sounds hollow when tapped. Cool completely on a rack. Slice with a bread knife just before serving.

Planning Ahead

The bread can be made from start to finish in 3 to 4 hours total, or the dough can be refrigerated overnight after it is formed into a ball and placed in a bowl. If made in advance, allow the dough to sit at room temperature at least 3 hours before baking.

Technique Tips

This bread can also be mixed in a heavy-duty electric mixer fitted with a paddle attachment, then kneaded with a dough hook for 10 minutes or until the dough begins to form a ball around the hook. Or it can be mixed and kneaded by hand, using a dough scraper as an aid.

If an Oven Baking Stone or baking tiles are available, preheat them in the oven. Turn the bread out onto a floured peel and then transfer it to the stone in the oven.

Variation

For Raisin Walnut Bread, mix 1 cup raisins, 1 cup chopped toasted walnuts and 1 teaspoon walnut oil (optional) into the dough just before turning it out onto the floured work surface.

Brioche Dough

Makes 2 Topknot
Brioche Loaves

Planning Ahead

Brioche dough can be prepared at least 1 day and up to 3 days in advance of baking if refrigerated, 1 month if frozen. Defrost frozen dough in the refrigerator overnight before forming. After dough has risen in the refrigerator overnight, allow 5 to 8 hours (depending on size) to form, rise, bake and cool brioche loaves before presenting. This bread is best served within several hours after it is baked.

Technique Tips

The dough is very soft, so it is most easily made using a heavy-duty electric mixer. If one is not available, mix the dough by hand and knead it on a lightly floured surface, using a dough scraper as an aid.

Brioche dough can also be formed into 1 large or 3 small rounds or into smaller rolls.

Variation

For Confetti Brioche, sauté 10 whole, peeled garlic cloves in 1 tablespoon butter until beginning to color. Sprinkle with 2 tablespoons sugar and bake in a preheated 350°F oven

When I was an apprentice, my last task at the end of each evening was to make dough for brioche that would be baked fresh the following morning. The classic recipe demanded that the dough sit out for several hours and rise at room temperature. I was young and didn't want to wait around, so I'd go out. By the time I returned, the dough had over-risen. I knew I had to do something if I wanted to keep my job, so one night I just stuck the dough in the refrigerator as soon as it was mixed—yeast and all. In the morning, the bread was perfect and my boss never knew the difference. I've been making my brioche unclassically ever since.

In the brioche recipes that follow, I have given directions for making the traditional brioche shape with its round top knot as well as two different styles of hors d'oeuvres. This dough is so flexible you can do almost anything with it. Since it keeps for several days in the refrigerator and for at least one month in the freezer, I prepare a complete batch when I make it at home, and then I divide it into breads, rolls and appetizers. Sometimes I freeze half of the dough, sometimes I don't. Sometimes I form it into one large bread, sometimes into 80 rolls. When I have a big party, I use all of it for hors d'oeuvres. It is one of the best recipes I know for feeding a crowd—and everything can be done ahead, including filling and freezing the appetizers and baking them right from the freezer. I don't allow dough trimmings to go to waste, either. If I don't reroll them for appetizers or bite-size buns, I just gather up all the scraps and roll them into a pizza dough.

4 cups (about 1 pound) all-purpose or bread flour

2 tablespoons sugar

2 teaspoons salt

1 package dry yeast

2 tablespoons warm (100°F) water

7 eggs, at room temperature

¾ pound (3 sticks) unsalted butter, chopped, at room temperature

1 egg plus 1 tablespoon water, blended with fork

For the Brioche Dough, place the flour, sugar, salt and yeast in the bowl of a heavy-duty mixer fitted with a paddle attachment. Mix to blend. Add the water and eggs, blend on low speed, then increase the speed to medium and beat at least for 5 minutes or until the dough becomes elastic. With the machine running, gradually add the butter in pieces, then beat for 5 minutes to develop gluten. Place the dough in a large plastic bag, tie loosely and refrigerate overnight. (This can be prepared to this point 3 days ahead and refrigerated or 1 month ahead and frozen. Remove from the refrigerator just before forming.)

To form loaves, divide the brioche dough in half. Butter 2 fluted 6-cup brioche molds or charlotte pans. Working with half of the dough at a time, roll ¾ of it into a ball on a lightly floured surface, pinching the edges to seal. Place the ball pinched side down in the bottom of the mold. Gently make a 2½-inch-wide hole in the center of the dough with your fingertips, opening it about 3 inches deep. Roll the remaining ¼ of dough into a teardrop shape. Drop the teardrop into the hole. Repeat with the second half of dough. Set the loaves aside at room temperature to rise until doubled, for about 3 hours.

To bake, preheat the oven to 350°F. Gently cut around the topknot seam with scissors to free the topknot to rise. Brush the topknot and remaining dough with blended egg, being careful not to drip egg on the seam. Bake until the bread is golden brown and starts to pull away from the edge of the mold, for about 50 to 60 minutes. Turn out onto a rack. Cool for about 2 hours before serving.

until golden brown. Drain off any liquid and chop coarsely. Meanwhile, sauté 3 red and/or yellow finely diced peppers in 2 tablespoons olive oil until tender. Mix in garlic and ½ cup coarsely chopped basil. Cool completely. Stir into brioche dough after butter is added.

Brioche Pillows with
Basil Goat Cheese Filling

**Makes About 80
2-inch Pillows to
Serve 16 to 20**

Planning Ahead

The Brioche Dough can be prepared up to 2 days in advance of baking if refrigerated, 1 month if frozen. Defrost frozen dough in the refrigerator overnight. The Brioche Pillows can be filled and formed on the second day and refrigerated overnight. Remove from the refrigerator about 2½ hours before serving. Bake up to 1 hour in advance or just before presenting.

Technique Tip

Brioche Pillows can also be baked the same day they are formed. After forming, divide among 4 trays instead of 2 and set aside at room temperature for about 1 hour to let rise before baking.

Variations

Brioche Pillows can be cut into any size or shape. Adjust filling amounts accordingly.

Brioche Pizza: Roll dough out into a pizza round, about ⅛ to ¼ inch thick. Bake 10 minutes at 425°F, top with leftover cheese or ratatouille or another topping, and bake for

Starters

82

Brioche Pillows are formed by sandwiching a filling between two layers of dough and cutting the dough into 2-inch rounds. Ideal finger food to pass for appetizers or as accompaniments for soups, salads and egg dishes, the pillows can be filled with either the Basil Goat Cheese Filling, with the Ratatouille Filling for the Brioche Rolls (page 84) or with a ravioli filling or any other mixture of your choice. Hint: These pillows are a great vehicle for using up finely chopped leftovers. For variety, fill half of them with one filling and half with another.

Brioche Dough (page 80)

BASIL GOAT CHEESE FILLING

¼ cup olive oil

1 large clove garlic, peeled

½ cup (about ½ ounce) packed fresh basil leaves

1 egg plus 1 tablespoon water, blended with fork

About 8 to 10 ounces Montrachet or other creamy goat cheese, at room temperature

For the Brioche Dough, prepare according to instructions at least 1 day ahead.

For the filling, place the oil, garlic and basil in a small food processor or blender attachment jar and process until smooth, pulsing on/off and stopping to scrape down the sides of the container. (This can be prepared ahead to this point at any time during the day pillows are filled.)

To form and fill the Brioche Pillows, line 2 large baking sheets with parchment paper. Divide the dough in half and return half to the refrigerator. Divide the other dough half in half again. Roll out 1 piece on a lightly floured surface into a 12- × 14-inch rectangle (about ⅛ inch thick). If the dough retracts while rolling, let it rest several minutes. Press slight indentations into the dough with a 2-inch fluted cutter to indicate where the filling goes. Brush the interior of each circle with blended egg, then with the blended ingredients for the Basil Goat Cheese Filling. Mash the goat cheese into the remaining filling with a fork until well mixed. Place ½ teaspoon of this mixture in the center of each circle.

Roll out the second piece of dough on a lightly floured surface into a 12- × 14-inch rectangle (about ⅛ inch thick). Place over the first sheet of dough. Seal the 2 pieces of dough, pressing down firmly around filling. Flour a 2-inch cutter and cut out the pillows, centering over the mounds. Transfer the pillows to the prepared baking sheets using a spatula. Repeat with the refrigerated half of dough. Cover baking sheets with plastic wrap and refrigerate. (This can be prepared to this point 1 day in advance.)

To bake, remove from refrigerator and take off plastic about 2½ hours before baking. Immediately line 2 more baking sheets with parchment paper. Divide the pillows evenly among the 4 sheets. Let the pillows rest at room temperature until doubled for about 2 hours. Preheat 2 ovens to 425°F (or bake in 2 batches). Arrange 1 oven rack in the top of the oven, 1 in bottom. Brush tops of pillows with blended egg, being careful not to drip down the sides. Bake until puffed and well browned for about 8 to 10 minutes, switching positions of baking sheets halfway through. Arrange the pillows on a platter. Cool for 5 to 10 minutes and serve.

5 minutes more or until pizza bottom is well browned. Cut into pie-shaped wedges and serve immediately.

Wine Selection
Red Côtes du Rhône

Brioche Rolls with Ratatouille

**Makes About 80
2-inch Rolls to
Serve 16 to 20**

T he Brioche Rolls can be served plain with any meal or sliced and filled with the Ratatouille recipe that follows or with any filling of your choice. Although this Ratatouille recipe yields considerably more than you will need for the rolls, it doesn't seem worth the effort to prepare a smaller quantity when the leftovers are so good tossed with pasta, rolled into an omelet or served as a side dish. This Provençal vegetable mélange is also the perfect topping for a pizza made from brioche trimmings (page 80).

Brioche Dough (page 80)

RATATOUILLE

Planning Ahead

The peppers for the Ratatouille can be roasted and peeled the day before the Ratatouille is prepared. The Ratatouille can be completely cooked 2 to 3 days before using. The Brioche Dough can be prepared up to 2 days in advance of baking if refrigerated, 1 month if frozen. Defrost frozen dough in the refrigerator overnight. Brioche Rolls can be formed on the second day and refrigerated overnight. Remove from the refrigerator about 2½ hours before baking. Bake the Brioche Rolls up to 2 hours in advance or just before presenting. Reheat the Ratatouille and fill the rolls just before serving.

Technique Tip

Brioche Rolls can also be baked the same day they are formed. After forming, divide among 4 trays instead of 2 and set aside at room temperature about 1 hour to let rise before baking.

Variation

Brioche Rolls can be cut into any size or shape. Adjust filling amounts accordingly.

2 large red bell peppers

2 large yellow bell peppers or 2 additional large red bell peppers

2 medium green bell peppers

¼ cup olive oil

1 medium onion, peeled and cut into ¼-inch dice

½- to ¾-pound (1 medium) eggplant, peeled and cut into ¼-inch dice

½ pound (about 2 small) zucchini, ends trimmed and cut into ¼-inch dice

1 tablespoon tomato paste

Salt and freshly ground black pepper to taste

4 drops Tabasco

1 egg plus 1 tablespoon water, blended with fork

For the Brioche Dough, prepare according to instructions at least 1 day ahead.

For the Ratatouille, to roast peppers: Preheat the broiler. Arrange the red, yellow and green peppers on a tray below the heat source. Broil the peppers, turning until blackened on all sides. Place in a plastic bag for at least 10 minutes to soften the skin. Peel the peppers using your fingers or a small knife. Remove the core, seeds and ribs, using a paper towel as an aid. Slice lengthwise into ¼-inch-wide strips, then cut crosswise into ¼-inch dice. (This can be prepared ahead, covered and set aside at room temperature for 4 to 6 hours or refrigerated overnight.)

Heat the oil in a heavy large nonstick skillet. Add the onion, cover and cook over medium-low heat for 5 minutes, stirring occasionally. Add the eggplant, cover and cook until the eggplant is very tender, for about 15 minutes, stirring occasionally.

Starters

Add the zucchini, roasted peppers and tomato paste and cook uncovered until zucchini is crisp-tender, for about 5 minutes, stirring occasionally. Season with salt, pepper and Tabasco. (This can be prepared ahead, covered and set aside at room temperature for 4 to 6 hours or refrigerated for several days.)

To form the Brioche Rolls, line 2 large baking sheets with parchment paper. Divide the dough in half and return half to the refrigerator. Roll out other half on a lightly floured surface into a 12- × 14-inch rectangle, about ¼ inch thick. If the dough retracts while rolling, let it rest several minutes. Cut out circles with a lightly floured 2-inch fluted cutter. Transfer to the prepared baking sheets using a spatula. Repeat with the refrigerated half of dough. Cover the baking sheets with plastic wrap and refrigerate. (This can be prepared to this point 1 day in advance.)

To bake, remove from refrigerator and take off plastic about 2½ hours before baking. Immediately line 2 more baking sheets with parchment paper. Divide the rolls evenly among the 4 sheets. Let the rolls rest at room temperature until doubled, for about 2 hours. Preheat 2 ovens to 425°F (or bake in 2 batches). Arrange 1 oven rack in the top of the oven, 1 in bottom. Brush the tops of the rolls with blended egg, being careful not to drip down the sides. Bake until puffed and well browned, for about 7 minutes, switching positions of baking sheets halfway through.

To serve, slice the rolls almost in half horizontally. Reheat Ratatouille by stirring over medium-high heat. Spoon Ratatouille into rolls. Arrange on platter. Serve immediately.

Wine Selection
Rosé Côtes de Provence

Salads

A salad is like chicken soup. When you eat it, you think you are doing something nice for yourself. Serving a salad as a main course or as an accompaniment to fish, poultry and meat is very American. I suspect this practice originated in California where diet-conscious natives eat salad at lunch and dinner and, when given the choice, at breakfast as well.

The French, on the other hand, have not been crazy about salads historically. If you requested one in a restaurant, it was squeezed between the meat and cheese course and was always the same yawn: greens tossed with oil and vinegar and, perhaps, a bit of mustard. Considered a bad match with wine, salads were shunted aside. The *salade composée* became important only when chefs adopted the nouvelle cuisine anything-goes-with-everything attitude. Another factor might have been that we finally learned to cook vegetables al dente.

This chapter is reserved for substantial salads. Lighter mixes are tossed throughout the book. You will find a preponderance of seafood and poultry because that is what people seem to prefer today. Many entries, such as Crab Coleslaw (page 98), Citrus Non-Caesar Salad with Oysters (page 100) and Field Greens with Shrimp, Corn and Ginger (page 96) swing nicely between main course and first course. Going beyond, Limestone Lettuce with Goat/Cheese/Cake, Croutons and Tomatoes (page 92) and Baked Brie Filo Bars with Mesclun and Hazelnuts (page 94) also make a snappy cheese course.

My wish is that these recipes will stand as mere outlines. I believe a salad is a way of emptying the refrigerator and would urge you to subscribe to this theory. Substitute whatever you have, guarding proportion and balance. As with soup, a salad is not a dumping ground for baggies of forgotten peas. Nor is it something to throw carelessly together that looks left over. Rather, it is a way to use fresh, healthful ingredients wisely; a manner of eating a garden on a plate.

A Successful Salad

No matter what constitutes a salad, there are three main rules for its formation. As simple as they are, they are frequently—surprisingly—broken in both homes and restaurants.

1. Greens and other ingredients must be well dried or the leaves will be limp and soggy, their dressing watery and diluted.

2. Components for both salad and its dressing can most often be measured, cut, cooked and otherwise prepped in advance, but each element should be stored separately. If mixed more than a moment before serving, the salad will again be limp and soggy.

3. Dress a salad lightly. Drowning it in dressing will make it—guess what?—limp and soggy.

Greens

There is only one kind of salad green and that is the freshest and crispest your garden or market offers. I have recommended some specific types of greens in the following salads, but they are just suggestions. Since I have access to a beautiful mix of baby greens, I tend to use this mélange for most everything. Called mesclun, it is generally composed of oak leaf lettuce for color, romaine for texture, *frisée* for a bite that doesn't scratch your throat and mâche that, above all, provides taste.

Other greens that wend their way into my salads are watercress, endive, limestone, red leaf and cabbage. Dandelion and radicchio appear, too, if they are small, young and not too bitter. As I mention in the introduction to my Eggplant and Arugula Salad (page 48), I'm not real big on foods that are bitter. If you like this bracing spiciness, you also may want to use arugula, escarole, spinach, flowering kale and other tangier greens.

When washing salad greens, treat them as you would treat your babies: Gently and with respect. Trim off any hard, tough, blemished or discolored edges. Swish carefully in cold water. Shake gingerly, pat dry on a dense bath towel, layer between a flutter of paper towels, pop in a plastic bag and place in the refrigerator for at least several hours to crisp. Whew! There are, unfortunately, no shortcuts to drying greens well. I don't even recommend a salad spinner, for it is too rough on fragile baby lettuces and the tender talking heads in the butter/bibb/Boston/limestone family.

Nongreens

In my book, a salad doesn't have to have greens, as the All-American Deli Salad with its meat, cheese, fruit and vegetables will attest. Nonetheless, the same guidelines should be used in choosing nongreen produce items as green ones. They should be fresh, traveling from garden to table at the peak of flavor. Hopefully, it's your garden they are traveling from. If space allows only a few herbs to be planted, they alone will do a great deal to perk up a salad. In a small plot, I would grow chives and chervil, or chives, chervil and tarragon—what the French call *fines herbes*. And then there is basil which—even the French admit—has become as *de rigeur* as parsley.

When purchasing seasonings, look to ginger, lemongrass and other exotics for spice and to potatoes, vegetables (deep-fried chips, yum) and croutons for texture. By croutons, I mean bread squares that you sauté from leftover brioche or other bread, not those stale, chemical jawbreakers that come in most packages. Peeled, seeded, diced tomatoes add an acidity that complements vinegar and lemon. To peel a tomato, dip it into a pot of boiling water for about 30 seconds and then remove the skin with a small sharp knife. Although I have been known to lay a few caviar or quail eggs here and there, I don't like fancy garnishes for salad and, certainly, ones you can't eat.

I guess I better mention oranges as well since they appear in both my duck and pork salads. Wearing my crazy perfectionist's toque, I peel off the orange skin along with its underlying bitter white pith in one long spiral with a small knife. Then I painstakingly remove the segment between each membrane. This may prove a bit persnickety for cooking at home, where it may be easier to just peel the orange and slice it into rounds. Please at least take out the tacky orange—and lemon—seeds before presenting.

Temperature

Most salad ingredients should be served at room temperature where textures and flavors are most pronounced and perfumes blend more readily. I even remove greens from the refrigerator 15 to 30 minutes before dressing so they taste of themselves. Meat, poultry and seafood are moister and more succulent if they are freshly cooked and left unrefrigerated in a cool kitchen. The only thing I like a bit chilled is tomatoes, which, ironically, must be first ripened and then stored at room temperature. As far as that frozen salad plate and fork that must be held with a glove, I can only say, ridiculous. Pompous buffoonery.

Salad Dressings

I was shocked to see French dressings in America that were thick and sweet and appeared Italian with their inclusion of tomato, and Italian dressings that were simple oil and vinegar mixtures that resembled my dependable French vinaigrette. Generally based on a proportion of two tablespoons oil to one tablespoon vinegar, my blend varies according to the type of green I'm dressing. The thicker the leaf, the more vinegar I include. When baby leaves are young and small, I dress them only with oil and a small amount of vinegar or they soon look like dead cooked spinach. I may add mustard, herbs, shallots or even meat or other cooking juices I save specifically; but, basically, a good salad dressing (vinaigrette) depends solely on two ingredients: a good oil and a good vinegar. In order that the dressing emulsifies or thickens, the oil should be whisked into the mixture in a slow, thin stream, essentially a drop at a time.

Oils

You don't have to view my recipes as a gastronomic adventure in the supermarket. Be practical when purchasing oil. Although roasted hazelnut and walnut oils make warm, wonderful nutty additions to a salad, these oils are expensive and may not be worth the price, especially if you are just using a few drops. Ditto the toasted Oriental sesame oil. You can share these oils with a friend or substitute a good neutral peanut oil (which is also excellent for frying) or an all-purpose olive oil.

In recommending olive oil, I'm taking a giant step from my roots, for my French neighbors in the north hated olive oil so much they refused to vacation in the south where it is used. Here I am, not only suggesting olive oil, but preferring pungent Italian oil to fruitier French bottlings. Regardless of what type you choose, taste the oil first because some are just too green and intense to be used with a delicate lettuce leaf.

To prevent oils from going rancid, store them in a dark airtight bottle in a cool, closed cupboard. Keep walnut, hazelnut and sesame oils in the refrigerator.

Vinegars

I turn to vinegar for acidity much more frequently than I do to lemon, which can be mean and tart. Here again, you don't have to buy fancy vinegars—or many different kinds—to make a good salad dressing. I call for Champagne vinegar because that is the vinegar used in my region, but almost any white wine vinegar will do—other than those that are very strong and cheap. Fruit vinegars taste artificial to me. If I want the taste of raspberries, I mash some fresh fruit into my dressing. That's it. I reserve red wine and sherry vinegars for tomatoes or grilled foods where their dark color doesn't show. The same goes for balsamic vinegar, which is even harder to use correctly because it is sweet. You'll find it mainly in marinades where I want its dark tint and touch of sweetness. As for that vial of concentrated balsamic nectar that has been aged in wooden casks like fine wine and sells for equivalent prices, forget salad dressings. Drink it.

Tossing a Salad

There is no way to toss a salad evenly on a plate, so I serve a dressing on the side only under protest. Diners who request it this way at my restaurants, ironically, end up eating more dressing. The thimbleful I use looks too skimpy when served separately, so I must offer a large ramekin. This is usually consumed in its entirety. If a salad is well dried, it requires very little dressing to taste good. Salad greens are not rafts to float in a lake of vinaigrette.

To prevent a salad from becoming soggy, I spoon on several tablespoons of dressing and then toss ingredients. If more dressing is necessary, I add a little at a time, tossing gently and lightly with my fingertips or two forks until the leaves are just moistened and glistening. No crusher, pincer, wilting action here.

Salt is either added to the dressing or sprinkled on at the last minute so as not to draw water from the leaves. The final step is a grind of black pepper for punch and bite. Not dusty, musty old powdery pepper from a box, but freshly ground in a grinder. (And no, the grinder doesn't have to be six feet tall.) The salad is served immediately. If a diner leaves the table after a salad is presented at one of my restaurants, the waiter exchanges it for a fresh one when he or she returns. A salad is a fragile flower.

Limestone Lettuce with Goat/Cheese/Cake, Croutons and Tomatoes

8 First-course
or 4 Main-course
Servings

Designed specifically to showcase my Goat/Cheese/Cake, this salad makes a menu special regardless of whether it is presented as a first course, a main course or a cheese course. Although there are no Asian ingredients in this mélange, the deliberate balance of flavors and textures—the creaminess of the cheesecake offset by crisp croutons and fresh vegetables—reflects an Oriental influence and sensibility.

Planning Ahead

The cheesecake can be assembled up to 1 day before and baked several days in advance. If baking and serving the same day, allow 6 to 8 hours for it to chill. The lettuce, tomatoes, croutons and vinaigrette can be prepped at any time during the day the salad is to be served. Assemble just before presenting.

Technique Tip

For croutons, I prefer brioche or another type of egg bread which does not harden when the bread cubes cool and crisp.

Wine Selection
Beaujolais

Goat/Cheese/Cake (page 56)

VINAIGRETTE

    2 tablespoons red wine vinegar

    6 tablespoons olive oil

    Salt and freshly ground black pepper to taste

TOMATOES

    1 teaspoon red wine vinegar

    1 tablespoon olive oil

    Salt and freshly ground black pepper to taste

    2 medium tomatoes, peeled, seeded and cut into 1/4-inch dice

CROUTONS

    1 ounce (1/4 stick) unsalted butter

    2 cups 1/4-inch crustless bread cubes, made from brioche or French bread

SALAD

    8 to 9 cups (about 8 to 9 ounces) packed bite-size limestone lettuce or other greens

    About 1/4 cup olive oil

    Freshly ground black pepper to taste

    Fresh whole chives or slivered green onions for garnish

Prepare the Goat/Cheese/Cake. Cool, then cover and chill at least 6 hours or overnight.

For the vinaigrette, place the vinegar in a small bowl. Whisk in the oil in a slow, thin stream. Season with salt and pepper. (This can be prepared ahead, covered and set aside at room temperature.)

For the tomatoes, place the vinegar in a small bowl. Whisk in the oil in a slow, thin stream. Season with salt and pepper. Stir in the tomatoes. (This can be prepared ahead, covered and set aside at room temperature or refrigerated for up to 2 hours to chill slightly.)

For the croutons, melt the butter in a heavy medium skillet over medium heat. Add the bread cubes and stir until medium brown, about 3 minutes. (This can be prepared ahead, transferred to a tray and set aside at room temperature.)

To serve, remove Goat/Cheese/Cake from the refrigerator 30 minutes before serving. Immediately unmold and cut it into ¼-inch-thick slices, using a knife that has been rinsed in hot water and dried before each slice. Gently toss the greens with enough vinaigrette to coat lightly. Divide among 8 or 4 large plates. Transfer 1 (first course) or 2 slices of the cheesecake to the center of each salad using a wide spatula. Drizzle oil over the cheesecake and season with pepper. Scatter the tomatoes and croutons over each salad. Slant several whole chives vertically across the top of each salad. Serve immediately.

Baked Brie Filo Bars
with Mesclun and Hazelnuts

6 Servings

Planning Ahead

The hazelnuts can be toasted several days in advance. The Brie Filo Bars can be formed one day before baking. The Hazelnut Curry Dressing and greens can be readied at any time during the day the salad is to be served. Bake the Brie and toss the salad just before presenting.

Technique Tip

Buy a good quality imported French Brie cheese with a white rind that is lightly flecked with red. The cheese should be completely ripe and creamy throughout with no hard chalky center.

Variation

The Brie can be cut into any desired size or shape and the filo packages fashioned accordingly. Make very small Brie bars or triangles to pass for an hors d'oeuvre.

Wine Selection

Merlot

Brie en Croûte, cheese wrapped in brioche dough or puff pastry, was in vogue for a long time, and yet I never liked it very much. For my taste, there was just too much croûte in proportion to the Brie. By substituting paper-thin filo for the wrapper, the molten cheese can be the focus, as it spurts out like a poached egg yolk as soon as the package is cut. Since a poached egg with dandelions is the most popular bistro salad in France, a green setting seemed ideal for the baked Brie as well. The cheese's earthy flavor, derived from the straw on which it ages, reminds me of hazelnuts, so I've strewn them about here, too. These bars, minus hazelnuts and mesclun, make a terrific hors d'oeuvre nibble.

HAZELNUT CURRY DRESSING

⅓ cup hazelnuts

½ tablespoon confectioners' sugar

½ teaspoon curry powder

1 tablespoon red wine vinegar

2 tablespoons hazelnut oil plus 1 tablespoon olive oil or
    3 tablespoons olive oil

1 large clove garlic, peeled and minced

1 tablespoon minced shallots

Salt and freshly ground black pepper to taste

BRIE FILO BARS

6 sheets filo dough, defrosted overnight in refrigerator if frozen

¾- to 1-pound Brie, cut into 6 rectangular wedges

2 teaspoons whole cumin seed, coarsely crushed

1 egg, blended with fork

6 cups (about 6 ounces) packed bite-size mesclun or other mixed greens

3 tablespoons fresh minced chives or green onions

For the Hazelnut Curry Dressing, preheat the oven to 350°F. Place the hazelnuts in a small baking pan and sprinkle with confectioners' sugar. Bake until well browned, about 20 to 25 minutes, stirring occasionally; cool. Place the hazelnuts in a towel or strainer. Rub them to remove their husks. (They can be prepared ahead and stored several days in a covered container at room temperature.)

Mix the curry powder and vinegar in a small bowl. Whisk in the hazelnut and olive oils in a slow, thin stream. Stir in the garlic and shallots. Season with salt and pepper. (This can be prepared ahead, covered and set aside at room temperature.)

For the Brie Filo Bars, butter a baking sheet. Remove the filo from package and unroll. Remove 1 leaf and cover the remaining filo with plastic wrap and a damp towel. Fold the filo sheet in half crosswise. Turn the sheet so the fold is on the left. Place a wedge of Brie in the middle of the top of the sheet. Sprinkle both sides of the Brie with ⅙ of the cumin seed. Enclose the Brie in the filo by folding over the top of the filo and rolling the Brie twice toward you. Fold the sides of the filo toward the middle as if wrapping a package. Continue rolling the Brie down to the bottom of the filo. Brush the inside edge of the filo with egg and press into the bar to seal. Place the bar on a prepared baking sheet, seam side down. Repeat with the remaining filo, Brie and cumin seed. Brush the bars well with egg. Rewrap remaining filo and refrigerate or freeze for another use. (This can be prepared ahead, covered with plastic wrap and set aside at room temperature for 6 to 8 hours or refrigerated overnight.)

To serve, preheat the oven to 350°F. Remove the plastic wrap and bake the Brie bars until well browned, for about 7 minutes. Meanwhile, gently toss the mesclun with enough dressing to coat lightly and divide among 6 large plates, placing it at the top. Chop the hazelnuts and sprinkle them over the salad, along with the chives. Place a Brie bar at the bottom of each plate. Serve immediately.

Field Greens with Shrimp, Corn and Ginger

4 to 6 Servings

Planning Ahead

The greens can be prepped, the corn cooked and the Ginger Dressing prepared at any time during the day the salad is to be served. The shrimp can be cooked several hours in advance. Toss just before presenting.

Technique Tip

By squeezing the gingerroot and using only its juice, diners don't need to contend with ginger fibers.

Wine Selection

Alsatian Gewurztraminer

For many years, I believed America had the worst shrimp of any country. It was a mystery how people could actually eat those pink, precooked frozen bullets that are best suited for a Saturday Night Special—and I'm not talking about a menu item. That was until I discovered the catch from Santa Barbara. This Pacific shellfish, which is sweet and succulent with a refined elegance, must be cooked the day it is caught, though, or it turns mushy. If this variety is not available, there are, happily, other fresh shrimp beginning to be available. Be sure to use those that are good quality, for I've kept this salad very simple in order that the shrimp can be the star.

GINGER DRESSING

3 tablespoons mayonnaise

3 tablespoons Champagne vinegar or white wine vinegar

1 tablespoon water or orange juice

3 tablespoons olive oil

1 2-inch piece fresh gingerroot, peeled and thinly sliced crosswise

Salt and freshly ground black pepper to taste

1 large ear white (or yellow) corn, husked and kernels removed

About 1 tablespoon olive oil

24 large uncooked shrimp, shelled and deveined

7 cups (about 7 ounces) packed bite-size mixed salad greens

2 tablespoons fresh minced green onions or chives

For the Ginger Dressing, mix the mayonnaise in a small bowl with the vinegar and water or orange juice. Whisk in the oil in a slow, thin stream. Press each ginger slice in a garlic press over a small glass, yielding about 2 teaspoons of juice. Add the ginger juice to the dressing to taste. Season with salt and pepper. (This can be prepared ahead, covered and set aside at room temperature for about 2 hours or refrigerated until 1 hour before serving.)

Cook corn kernels in a pot of simmering water for 5 minutes; drain. (This can be prepared ahead and set aside at room temperature.)

Place a heavy small nonstick skillet over medium heat and film it with oil. Add the shrimp and cook until just pink, for about 2 minutes total, turning with tongs halfway. (This can be prepared ahead and set aside at cool room temperature for several hours.)

To serve, mix the corn and salad greens in a large bowl. Gently toss with enough dressing to coat lightly. Mound the salad in the center of 4 or 6 large plates. Mix the shrimp with several tablespoons of the remaining dressing to coat lightly. Arrange the shrimp around the salad. Sprinkle the salad with green onions. Serve immediately.

Crab Coleslaw

4 First-course
or 2 Main-course
Servings

Planning Ahead

The crab can be cooked, the Russian French Dressing mixed, the peppers roasted and the cabbage and tomatoes prepped at any time during the day the coleslaw is to be served. Assemble the salad just before presenting.

Technique Tips

Don't worry about exact amounts of ingredients. You can never have too much crab. If you don't have enough, just add more cabbage.

The crab can also be steamed in a wok or large pot, turning halfway, for the same amount of time it is boiled.

The fresh tarragon gives an added zip. If it is not available, replace it with another fresh herb such as basil.

Wine Selection
Chardonnay

I grew up eating cabbage that had been boiled for three hours in lard, so the idea of trying this vegetable raw did not appeal to me when I first came to America. Yet, when I finally tried coleslaw with a hamburger, I thought it was delicious. I particularly liked its sweet sauce and wanted to try it in new ways. Since everyone here seems to like crab, I tossed the two together with my French interpretation of Russian Dressing.

Similar in spirit to Crab Louis, this salad can be served in small portions for a first course or as a luncheon or dinner main course. We tried taking it off the menu at Citrus to make room for something new, but we had too many requests for it. You can certainly purchase precooked crabmeat for this slaw, but nothing is as moist and succulent as a crab freshly cooked at home under a watchful eye.

CRAB

> 1½- to 2-pound live Dungeness crab or 6 to 8 ounces
> (1½ to 2 cups) or more cooked crabmeat

RUSSIAN FRENCH DRESSING

> ⅓ cup mayonnaise
>
> 2 teaspoons ketchup
>
> 1 teaspoon freshly squeezed lemon juice
>
> 1 tablespoon fresh minced tarragon or other fresh herb
>
> 1 teaspoon Cognac or bourbon
>
> 1 large clove garlic, pressed
>
> ½ teaspoon curry powder
>
> 2 drops Tabasco
>
> Salt and freshly ground black pepper to taste

PEPPERS

> 1 small red bell pepper
>
> 1 small yellow bell pepper
>
> 1 small green bell pepper
>
> 1 small (about 1¼ pounds) savoy cabbage
>
> 1 small tomato, peeled, seeded and diced

To cook the crab, bring a large pot of water to a boil. Plunge the crab into the boiling water using tongs. Simmer until the crab turns bright red and rises to the surface of the pot, for about 12 to 18 minutes. Drain and cool on a tray.

To crack the crab, pry off the upper top shell. Turn it over and pull up on the triangular apron on the bottom of the shell. Discard the spongy gills, membrane and shell, reserving the golden crab butter and cream lining the shell. Twist off the legs and extract the meat from the legs, claws and body, using a nutcracker, mallet and pick. Shred the crabmeat and place it in 1 bowl and the crab butter/cream in another. (This can be prepared ahead, covered and refrigerated until 30 minutes before serving.)

For the Russian French Dressing, whisk the mayonnaise, ketchup, lemon juice, tarragon, Cognac, garlic, curry powder and Tabasco together in a medium bowl until well blended. Season with salt and pepper. (This can be prepared ahead and set aside at cool room temperature for several hours or refrigerated until 30 minutes before serving.)

For the peppers, preheat the broiler. Arrange the red, yellow and green peppers on a tray below the heat source. Broil the peppers, turning them until blackened on all sides. Place them in a plastic bag for at least 10 minutes to soften their skin. Peel the peppers using your fingers or a small knife. Remove the core, seeds and veins using a paper towel as an aid. Slice the peppers lengthwise into ¼-inch-wide strips, then cut crosswise into ¼-inch dice. Place in a small bowl. (This can be prepared ahead, covered and set aside at room temperature.)

For the cabbage, reserve 4 outer large dark green cabbage leaves. Core and finely shred enough of the remaining cabbage to equal 3 cups. (This can be prepared ahead, wrapped and refrigerated until 30 minutes before serving.)

To serve, stir the crab butter/cream mixture into the dressing to taste. Mix the crabmeat with the cabbage, ½ of the peppers and ½ of the tomato in a large bowl. Stir in enough dressing to coat lightly. Place the reserved cabbage leaves on 4 or 2 large plates. Divide the salad among the cabbage leaves. Sprinkle with reserved tomato and peppers. Serve immediately.

Citrus Non-Caesar Salad
with Oysters

4 Servings

Planning Ahead

The Oyster-Chive Vinaigrette can be prepared and the egg and greens prepped at any time during the day the salad is to be served. The oysters can be shucked and breaded in advance as well, but for the freshest flavor, open them no more than an hour or so before chilling. Freeze the oysters for 20 minutes before cooking. Sauté the oysters and toss the salad just before presenting.

Technique Tips

To open oysters, place an oyster rounded side down on a tray or work surface with the smaller hinge end facing you. Insert an oyster knife on one side of the hinge, hold the oyster down with the other hand and gently jiggle the knife up and down until it goes in. Push the knife toward the back of the shell until it reaches the muscle attached to the top shell. Cut through the muscle and lift off the top shell.

Deep-chilling oysters in the freezer for 20 minutes before cooking prevents them from overcooking and drying out as they crisp and brown on the outside.

W hen I first moved to the States, the most popular salad was a Caesar. I thought it consisted of oysters, greens and hard-cooked eggs, so that's what my customers got when they ordered Citrus Caesar Salad. Now that I've become acclimated, I realize what I was calling a Caesar Salad was really a spinach salad, so feel free to add some spinach and bacon, if you wish.

Taking a cue from fast food, I've breaded and fried the oysters for this salad so they are crisp on the outside and juicy within. Looking very much like a crouton, these marine bread cubes are the perfect anchor for romaine lettuce. The bivalve's briny juices take the vinaigrette seaside.

OYSTER-CHIVE VINAIGRETTE

2 tablespoons red wine vinegar

¼ cup olive oil

1 tablespoon minced shallot

1 large clove garlic, peeled and minced

3 tablespoons fresh minced chives or green onions

Salt and freshly ground black pepper to taste

OYSTERS

24 fresh large unshucked oysters, scrubbed

2 eggs

Salt and freshly ground black pepper to taste

1 cup flour

1 cup bread crumbs

Peanut oil for frying

6 to 8 cups (about 6 to 8 ounces) packed bite-size romaine
    lettuce (preferably tender interior leaves)

1 hard-cooked egg, sieved or finely chopped

For the Oyster-Chive Vinaigrette, place the vinegar in a small bowl. Whisk in the olive oil in a slow, thin stream. Stir in the shallots, garlic and chives. Season with salt and pepper. (This can be prepared ahead, covered and set aside at room temperature.)

For the oysters, line a fine sieve with dampened paper towels and fit the sieve over a small bowl. Open the oysters over the sieve, straining the juices. Remove the oysters from their shells; discard shells.

To bread the oysters, whisk the eggs with salt and pepper in a soup plate until blended. Place the flour in 1 soup plate and the bread crumbs in another. Line a medium baking sheet that will fit into your freezer with parchment or waxed paper. One by one, dredge each oyster in flour, shaking off excess. Dip in egg and then in bread crumbs, coating completely and patting so the crumbs adhere. Arrange the oysters on the prepared baking sheet. (This can be prepared ahead, covered with plastic wrap and refrigerated for several hours.)

To serve, freeze the oysters for 20 minutes. Stir 1 tablespoon sieved oyster juice (or to taste) into the vinaigrette. Line a second medium baking sheet with paper towels. Heat ½ inch of peanut oil in a large skillet over medium-high heat to 375°F. Fry the oysters in batches without crowding until golden brown on both sides, but still moist within about 1 minute. Transfer to the prepared baking sheet to drain using slotted spoon.

Meanwhile, gently toss the greens with enough vinaigrette to coat lightly. Mound on 4 large plates. Arrange oysters around the rim of the salad. Sprinkle with sieved egg. Serve immediately.

Breading can be a messy job with the cook coming out with more breading than the oysters. To do the job neatly without sticking to yourself, use only one hand to hold the oyster and dip it into the flour, egg and bread crumbs.

Wine Selection
Alsatian Riesling

Marinated Salmon Trout with Warm Potato Salad

Planning Ahead

The fish should be marinated at least 2 days and up to 1 week before serving. The vinaigrette can be mixed at any time during the day the salad is to be tossed. Cook and dress the potatoes just before presenting to serve warm or several hours in advance to offer at room temperature.

Technique Tips

To remove the skin from fish, place the fish skin side down on a cutting board and insert a large sharp knife between the skin and meat at the tail end. Cut in a sawing motion, holding on to the edge of the skin and keeping the knife blade slanted down toward the skin.

When marinating the salmon trout, keep it submerged in oil at all times to preserve it. Add more oil as necessary if fillets remain after removing liquid for potato salad dressing.

W hen I fantasize about bistro food, I yearn for plump cured herrings with *Pommes de Terre à l'Huile* (warm potato salad). Herring is generally dry and oversalted here, so to satisfy these cravings, I substitute salmon (sea) trout and make my own cure with onions, carrots, mustard seeds and olive oil. Since the salt and sugar will preserve the fish for a week or two, I make a large batch each time.

Thirty years ago, every French housewife kept a huge jar of this cured fish on hand for unexpected guests or an instant meal. As family members staggered in one at a time after a long hard day, they ate their dinner directly out of the jar. This marinated fish tastes just as good when eaten on a plate. In this case, though, there are dishes to wash.

The potato salad is French-style, so it is mixed with a vinaigrette rather than the expected mayonnaise. Our customers at Broadway Deli are frequently so convinced we forgot the mayo, they send the salad back without trying it first. Once they try it dressed this way, they like it very much. The potatoes are supposed to be served warm to contrast with the cold fish, but they are also delicious at room temperature. To make this a complete healthy meal, add beans, asparagus, zucchini or other crisp green things to the potato salad.

If you serve the fish for several different meals, you may want to make a smaller batch of potato salad and vary the accompaniments.

SALMON TROUT

16 salmon (sea) trout fillets, skinned

½ cup salt

½ cup sugar

Freshly ground black pepper

1 teaspoon mustard seeds, coarsely crushed

2 large carrots, peeled and thinly sliced

1 large red or white onion, peeled and thinly sliced

2 bay leaves, crushed and broken

Corn or vegetable oil

POTATO SALAD

¼ cup red wine vinegar

¼ cup balsamic vinegar

1 cup liquid used in the marinade

Carrots and onions from the marinade

4 large celery stalks, trimmed and thinly sliced

Salt and freshly ground black pepper to taste

6 to 8 pounds red or white boiling potatoes, peeled and cut into
½-inch cubes

For the salmon trout, place the fish fillets in a large glass baking dish. Mix the salt and sugar together and sprinkle over both sides of the fillets. Cover with plastic wrap and refrigerate for 3 hours. Rinse thoroughly to remove the salt and sugar and pat dry with paper towels.

Clean the glass dish. Layer the fillets in the dish, sprinkling each layer with pepper, mustard seeds, carrots, onion and bay leaves. Pour enough oil over the fillets to cover completely. Cover with plastic wrap and refrigerate at least 2 days. (This can be prepared 1 week ahead. Remove from the refrigerator 30 minutes before serving.)

For the potato salad, mix the red wine and balsamic vinegars in a large bowl. Remove 1 cup of liquid from the marinating fish and whisk into the mixed vinegars in a slow, thin stream. Remove carrots and onion from remaining salmon marinade with a slotted spoon. Add to vinegar mixture with celery. Season with salt and pepper if necessary. (This can be prepared ahead, covered and set aside at cool room temperature.)

For the potatoes, steam until tender and easily pierced with a knife, for about 10 to 15 minutes. Immediately place them in bowl with the vinaigrette. Toss well and set aside at room temperature for at least 15 minutes to cool slightly and absorb the dressing, stirring occasionally, or cool to room temperature.

To serve, lightly pat the salmon-trout fillets with paper towels to remove excess marinade. Place 1 fillet in the center of each plate. Spoon some potato salad on each side of it. Serve immediately.

The potatoes must be marinated while still warm to absorb flavorings. When allowed to cool before the dressing is added, they become hard.

Variation
Thin wedges of apple sprinkled with vinegar, oil, salt and pepper is a nice alternative to the potato salad as an accompaniment for the fish.

Wine Selection
Sauvignon Blanc

Tuna Tartare Salad

**4 First-course
or 2 Main-course
Servings**

Planning Ahead

The dressing can be prepared and the greens prepped early in the day the salad is to be served. The tuna can be chopped several hours in advance. Toss the tuna with the greens just before serving.

Technique Tip

For the finest texture, use well-chilled tuna or freeze for 30 minutes before chopping. To keep the fish light and airy, chop by hand with a large sharp knife rather than with a food processor or meat grinder that will mash and compact it.

Wine Selection

Sauvignon Blanc

I've always garnished fish tartare with a small salad of crisp garden-fresh greens, so it was a natural step to mix these items together on the plate as well as in the mouth. The lightness of the greens plays off the dense tuna tones for great texture and flavor contrast. As a first course, the acidity of this salad primes the palate for the plates that follow. Nevertheless, it is also satisfying as a main course at lunch or supper.

1 tablespoon red wine vinegar

1½ teaspoons balsamic vinegar

1 tablespoon soy sauce

2 teaspoons freshly squeezed lemon juice

¼ cup olive oil

1 tablespoon minced shallot

2 teaspoons fresh peeled minced gingerroot

Salt to taste

4 drops Tabasco

1 pound fresh well-chilled tuna fillet

5 cups (about 5 ounces) packed bite-size mixed greens, such as chicory, radicchio, escarole or endive

Mix red wine and balsamic vinegars, soy sauce and lemon juice in a large bowl. Whisk in the olive oil in a slow, thin stream. Mix in the shallot and ginger. Season with salt and Tabasco. (This can be prepared ahead, covered and set aside at room temperature.)

Trim the dark oily portions from the tuna. Slice the tuna thinly, then chop coarsely. (This can be prepared several hours ahead and refrigerated.)

To serve, mix the tuna with the dressing until well coated. Add the greens and toss well. Mound in the center of 2 or 4 large plates. Serve immediately.

Smoked Fish and Mushroom Salad

We created this salad at the Broadway Deli to use up *dividends* from our smoked fish platters. We call them dividends, not leftovers, because they make this salad quite special as either a first course or main course at brunch or lunch. Since these ends or trimmings are a lot less costly than perfect slices, this recipe also offers the means of enjoying luxurious smoked fish without spending an inheritance on it. We have many ethnic delis and fish markets in Los Angeles, so cooks in this city have no trouble finding the varieties of fish listed here. If they are not available in your area, use only smoked salmon or smoked trout for an equally fine result.

HAZELNUT-SOY VINAIGRETTE

2 teaspoons soy sauce

2 tablespoons red wine vinegar

1 tablespoon balsamic vinegar

¼ cup olive oil plus 2 teaspoons hazelnut oil or ¼ cup plus
2 teaspoons olive oil

1 large shallot, peeled and minced

2 tablespoons fresh minced chervil or 1 tablespoon fresh minced
mint or dill

Salt and freshly ground black pepper to taste

24 (about 4½ ounces) button mushrooms, ends trimmed and
thinly sliced

¼ cup freshly squeezed lemon juice

½ pound mixed smoked seafood, such as salmon, trout, halibut,
eel or mussels, sliced into ½-inch pieces

2 medium tomatoes, peeled, seeded and diced

6 cups (about 6 ounces) packed bite-size mixed greens

For the Hazelnut-Soy Vinaigrette, place the soy sauce, red wine and balsamic vinegars in a small bowl. Whisk in the olive oil, then the hazelnut oil in a slow, thin stream. Stir in the shallot and chervil. Season with salt and pepper. (This can be prepared ahead, covered and set aside at room temperature.)

For the salad, marinate the mushrooms with the lemon juice in a large bowl for 15 to 30 minutes, stirring occasionally. Stir in the smoked fish, tomatoes and greens. Gently toss with enough vinaigrette to coat lightly. Mound on 4 to 6 large plates. Serve immediately.

**4 Main-course
or 6 First-course
Servings**

Planning Ahead

The dressing can be prepared and the greens and other ingredients prepped at any time during the day the salad is to be served. Marinate the mushrooms for 15 to 30 minutes before dressing the salad. Dress and toss just before presenting.

Wine Selection
Alsatian Riesling

All-American Deli Salad

2 Main-course
or 4 First-course
Servings

Planning Ahead

The Anchovy Deli Dressing can be mixed at any time during the day it is to be used. The salad ingredients (other than the apple) can be prepared several hours before they are combined. Cut up the apple and toss the salad just before serving.

Wine Selection

Red Côtes du Rhône

This salad without salad greens—actually an all-American combination of a Waldorf, Caesar and Chef's salad—is one I made at my Michel Richard pastry shop for over ten years. In France, the addition of fruit to a salad is very bourgeois, not something you find in an average home. I never even tasted this combination until I was a young man in Paris. I was quite poor in those years, but one day I had a few extra coins in my pocket, and I treated myself to a lobster salad in a restaurant. It arrived garnished with apples and walnuts. I was so shocked and disappointed. This was what I had spent so much money for? I would have sent this travesty-of-a-salad back, but if you do this in France, the chef comes out and cuts your head off with a cleaver. As dismayed as I was, you can bet I ate every last drop of it. I was the one paying. What a surprise. It was very, very nice. With that experience in mind as a souvenir, I often add fruit and nuts to a salad, as I do here.

Please don't be put off by the anchovies in the dressing. I am the first person to pick off these bony skinny fish on top of a Niçoise salad, but when they are minced as they are here, they provide a behind-the-scenes flavor boost like salt and pepper.

ANCHOVY DELI DRESSING

¼ cup mayonnaise

¼ cup red wine vinegar

2 tablespoons freshly squeezed lemon juice

2 tablespoons olive oil

2-ounce can oil-packed anchovies, drained and minced

Salt and freshly ground black pepper to taste

SALAD

¼ pound Gruyère or Emmenthal cheese in 1 piece

½ pound ham in 1 piece

4 celery stalks, trimmed and thinly sliced crosswise on diagonal

14 cornichons or other small tart pickles, thinly sliced on diagonal

1 large Pippin or other tart green apple, cored

¼ cup coarsely chopped toasted walnuts

1 medium-large tomato, peeled, seeded and diced

For the Anchovy Deli Dressing, place the mayonnaise in a small bowl. Gradually whisk in the vinegar and lemon juice. Whisk in the oil in a slow, thin stream. Stir in the anchovies. Season with salt and pepper. (This can be prepared ahead, covered and refrigerated until 1 hour before serving.)

For the salad, cut the cheese and ham into 1- × ¼-inch matchsticks. Place in a small bowl. Add the celery and cornichons. (This can be prepared ahead, covered and set aside at cool room temperature for several hours.)

To serve, dice the apple and add it to the salad ingredients, along with the walnuts and tomato. Gently toss with enough Anchovy Deli Dressing to coat lightly. Mound on 2 or 4 large plates. Serve immediately.

Chicken Medallions with Toasted Sesame Slaw

4 Servings

Planning Ahead

Both the chicken and sauce can be completed 1 day in advance. If preparing the rolls the day they are to be served, allow at least 6 hours for them to chill. Dress the cabbage and slice the rolls just before presenting.

Technique Tips

When encasing the chicken, use only plastic wrap that has been recommended as safe for microwaving, such as Saran Wrap.

To remove the tendon from a chicken breast fillet, hold on to it with the fingers of one hand while scraping it out with a small sharp knife held in the other hand.

To butterfly a chicken breast, place smooth, rounded side up on the work surface. Starting on the right, slice through the center horizontally to ¼ inch of the left side as if cutting open a book. Open the chicken, pressing to flatten the seam.

I am always looking for ways to cut down on labor costs. Since I love to play with gadgets, my solutions almost always involve a new tool. After I saw a demonstration of the Cryovac machine that seals food in plastic, I started encasing everything in sight with the single-mindedness of Christo, the artist who wrapped the Pont Neuf in Paris. Using this method, I can quickly seal marinated or stuffed foods in plastic so they are ready to poach, roast or, even, fry.

In this recipe, I've used the technique to create a sausage—actually a ballottine or rolled chicken breast stuffed with crisp vegetables. By using the plastic, I can form this sausage bundle without having to grind the meat or deal with casings and their strange textures. Cooking chicken in this closed environment concentrates its flavors and keeps it very moist. A first course or main course at lunch or dinner, these rolls can also be passed as an hors d'oeuvre by cutting them into ½-inch-thick rounds and pressing a toothpick into each slice.

CHICKEN ROLLS

1 tablespoon unsalted butter

1 medium leek (white and light green parts only), cut into fine 2-inch julienne

½ large carrot, peeled and cut into fine 2-inch julienne

2 ounces green beans, ends snapped and strung

Salt and freshly ground black pepper to taste

4 large chicken breasts, boned, skinned, trimmed, tendon removed and butterflied

Salt and freshly ground black pepper to taste

SESAME MAYONNAISE

1 cup mayonnaise

1 teaspoon Oriental (toasted) sesame oil

1 teaspoon Champagne vinegar or white wine vinegar

½ teaspoon ground cumin

2 drops Tabasco

1 tablespoon sesame seeds

2 cups thinly sliced savoy or other cabbage

For the Chicken Rolls, melt the butter in a heavy small skillet over medium-low heat. Add the leek and carrot and cook until tender, for about 5 minutes, stirring occasionally. Cook the beans in a large pot of boiling water until just tender, for about 6 to 7 minutes. Drain, halve diagonally and pat dry with paper towels. Cool the vegetables to room temperature. Season with salt and pepper. (This can be prepared ahead and set aside at room temperature until preparing the chicken.)

Overlap 2 butterflied chicken breasts slightly on a large piece of plastic wrap. Cover with a second sheet of plastic wrap and pound lightly with a mallet to form a rectangle of equal thickness. Discard the top layer of plastic and season with salt and pepper. Repeat with the remaining 2 breasts on a separate plastic sheet. Spread the leek, carrot and green beans evenly over the 2 chicken rectangles, leaving about a ¾-inch border. Roll each chicken rectangle up tightly, starting with the narrow end. Wrap in another sheet of plastic and roll up tightly. Twist ends and tie with string.

Bring to a simmer enough water to cover the chicken generously in a wide, deep pot. Submerge the chicken rolls, cover and cook for 15 minutes, turning halfway and adjusting the heat so the liquid is just shaking. Drain, cool to room temperature, then refrigerate until well chilled, for about 6 hours or overnight.

For the Sesame Mayonnaise, mix the mayonnaise, sesame oil, vinegar, cumin and Tabasco in a small bowl. (This can be prepared ahead and set aside at cool room temperature for up to 1 hour or refrigerated overnight.)

Stir the sesame seeds in a heavy small dry skillet over medium-high heat until brown. Mix the cabbage with several tablespoons of Sesame Mayonnaise or enough to coat lightly. Divide the cabbage among 4 large plates. Sprinkle with toasted sesame seeds. Slice the Chicken Rolls ⅜ inch thick and overlap the slices on the plates. Divide the remaining Sesame Mayonnaise among 4 small ramekins. Place on plates and serve immediately.

Variation
If a wide enough pot is available for poaching, make 1 large chicken roll instead of 2 smaller ones.

Wine Selection
Red Côtes du Rhône

Chicken and Green Bean Salad

4 Servings

Planning Ahead

The chicken should be marinated for at least 4 hours or, preferably, overnight. The Tarragon Chive Vinaigrette can be mixed, the beans cooked and the greens prepped at any time during the day the dish is to be served. Cook the chicken and toss the salad just before presenting.

Technique Tips

Cooking the chicken under a weight over medium-high heat results in a flattened bird that is crusty on the outside and moist within, like a steak.

The exact cooking time will depend on the thickness of the breasts and the type of skillet used. Watch carefully because chicken cooks very quickly.

This technique can also be applied to chicken cooked on the grill by weighting the bird or its components with a heavy skillet or brick wrapped in aluminum foil.

To minimize sticking, heat the skillet before adding butter and oil.

T his is my version of the nouvelle cuisine *Salade Gourmande* with its *foie gras* and *haricots verts* (baby green beans) that was served during the seventies. I've found chicken to be a delectable stand-in for the costly *foie gras* and regular green beans a good substitute for the French *haricots verts*. After the original version of this salad was introduced, chefs began adopting the tenets of nouvelle cuisine, cooking green beans only until they were al dente. Neither raw nor overcooked, these toothsome vegetables are pleasing with their waxy taste and crisp bite, but sometimes I really do miss the pasty quality of my mother's limp, cooked-to-death *mange-tout* (eat all), our gigantic variety of bean that is, unfortunately, no longer on the market. Today snow peas are called *mange-tout* in France, but who had even heard of these pods when I was growing up?

CHICKEN

4 large chicken breasts, boned, skinned, trimmed, tendon removed and patted dry

3 tablespoons olive oil

1 tablespoon fresh minced rosemary or 1 teaspoon dried, crumbled

2 tablespoons fresh minced thyme or 2 teaspoons dried, crumbled

2 large cloves garlic, peeled and minced

Salt and freshly ground black pepper to taste

TARRAGON CHIVE VINAIGRETTE

3 tablespoons balsamic vinegar

2 teaspoons Dijon mustard

6 tablespoons olive oil

2 tablespoons minced shallots

2 tablespoons fresh minced chives or green onions

1 tablespoon fresh minced tarragon or other fresh herb

Salt and freshly ground black pepper to taste

1 pound green beans, yellow and green beans or *haricots verts*, ends snapped and strung

5 to 6 cups (about 5 to 6 ounces) packed mixed bite-size greens, including curly endive and baby lettuce

Salt and freshly ground black pepper to taste

3 tablespoons olive oil

Additional olive oil

2 tablespoons fresh minced chives or green onions

12 fresh tarragon sprigs for garnish (optional)

For the chicken marinade, lightly pound the breasts between 2 pieces of plastic wrap with a mallet until they are an equal thickness. Place each breast on a large piece of plastic wrap. Rub both sides with olive oil and sprinkle with rosemary, thyme, garlic, salt and pepper. Wrap in plastic. Refrigerate at least 4 hours or overnight. Bring to room temperature before cooking.

For the Tarragon Chive Vinaigrette, mix the vinegar and mustard in a small bowl. Whisk in the oil in a slow, thin stream. Stir in the shallots, chives and tarragon. Season with salt and pepper. (This can be prepared ahead, covered and set aside at room temperature.)

For the beans, cover a rack with several layers of paper towels. Cook the beans in a large pot of boiling water until just tender, for about 6 minutes. Drain and set aside on the prepared rack.

To serve, trim the ends of the beans and halve them diagonally. Combine ¾ of the beans and mixed greens in a large bowl. Season with salt and pepper. Gently toss with about ¾ of the dressing or enough to coat lightly. Divide among 4 large plates.

Meanwhile, heat a heavy large nonstick skillet over medium-high heat. Add 3 tablespoons of olive oil and heat. Add the chicken breasts. Oil the bottom of a heavy, slightly smaller skillet and place on top of the chicken, pressing to flatten. Cook for 3 minutes. Carefully turn breasts using a spatula (the breasts may stick), reweight and cook until the flesh is just firm when pressed and the breasts are cooked through, for about 3 minutes. Brush both sides of the chicken with the remaining dressing. Slice the breasts diagonally into 4 or 5 pieces. Lay the pieces over the salad. Strew the remaining green beans and chives on top. Garnish with tarragon sprigs, if desired. Serve immediately.

Variation
Chicken breasts for this recipe can also be grilled, poached or baked according to the directions given in the Poultry chapter.

Wine Selection
Chardonnay

Chicken and Guacamole Rings

4 Servings

Planning Ahead

The Cilantro Sauce and vinaigrette can be prepared while the chicken is cooking or at any time during the day the salad is to be served. The chicken can be cooked and the other ingredients prepped several hours in advance. Assemble the salad just before presenting.

Technique Tips

I use a 4-inch pastry ring to form the salad neatly. If this is not available, a clean 12-ounce tuna can with both ends removed will work beautifully as will a spoon and small knife or spatula.

Instead of discarding the chicken bones, return them to the broth with the vegetables and simmer for another 2 hours to make stock, adding water as necessary. Drain the stock, degrease and boil down until rich and concentrated. Cool, then cover and refrigerate for several days or freeze for several months.

T o form this salad, I layer the chicken and guacamole in a round mold, adapting yet another dessert technique for a main course. Popular several years ago, this nouvelle presentation may be considered passé now, but I still find it a neat, elegant way to present a salad that might otherwise look like a mess on the plate. At one time, I combined the chicken with ratatouille and cucumber. Now I'm using guacamole, because its soft creaminess is almost like a fruit mayonnaise. I'm sure another grouping lurks just around the corner. In the meantime, this is your salad to mix and match as you wish.

CILANTRO SAUCE

1½ tablespoons mayonnaise

3 tablespoons heavy cream

3 tablespoons freshly squeezed lime or lemon juice

1½ tablespoons olive oil

4½ tablespoons (about 3 medium) sliced green onions

3 tablespoons fresh coarsely chopped cilantro, basil or mint

Salt and freshly ground black pepper to taste

VINAIGRETTE

1½ tablespoons red wine vinegar

3 tablespoons olive oil

Salt and freshly ground black pepper to taste

CHICKEN

2 carrots, sliced

2 celery stalks, sliced

2 medium onions, peeled and coarsely chopped

6 sprigs parsley

1 bay leaf

6 fresh thyme sprigs or 1 tablespoon dried, crumbled

6 fresh savory or other herb sprigs or 1 tablespoon dried, crumbled

6 black peppercorns, slightly crushed

3- to 3½-pound frying chicken, at room temperature

1 large avocado, peeled, pitted and cut into ⅜-inch dice

I large tomato, peeled, seeded and cut into ⅜-inch dice

I tablespoon freshly squeezed lemon juice

I tablespoon olive oil

Salt and freshly ground black pepper to taste

4 cups (about 4 ounces) packed bite-size lettuce leaves

For the Cilantro Sauce, blend the mayonnaise, cream and lime juice in a small bowl. Whisk in the olive oil in a slow, thin stream. Stir in the green onions and cilantro. Season with salt and pepper. (This can be prepared ahead, covered and refrigerated until 15 to 30 minutes before serving.)

For the vinaigrette, place the red wine vinegar in a small bowl. Whisk in the olive oil in a slow, thin stream. Season with salt and pepper. (This can be prepared ahead, covered and set aside at room temperature.)

For the chicken, place the carrots, celery, onions, parsley, bay leaf, thyme, savory and peppercorns in a large stock pot or casserole. Place the chicken in the pot and cover generously with water. Remove chicken from the pot. Cover the pot and bring to a large rolling boil over medium heat. Add the chicken to the pot, reduce heat so the water is barely shaking, and simmer until the chicken is tender and its juices run yellow when pricked with a fork, for about 30 minutes. Remove the chicken from the broth. Cool. (This can be prepared several hours ahead, covered and set aside at cool room temperature. Cut the chicken into ½-inch cubes, discarding bones and skin, before continuing with recipe.)

To serve, combine the chicken with enough Cilantro Sauce to coat in a small bowl. Mix the avocado, tomato, lemon juice and olive oil in another small bowl. Season with salt and pepper. Place the lettuce in a third bowl and gently toss with enough vinaigrette to coat lightly.

Place a 4-inch pastry ring in the center of 1 large plate. Spoon ¼ of the chicken mixture inside the ring, spreading evenly and packing down tightly. Place ¼ of the avocado mixture on top of the chicken, pressing down. Remove the ring and repeat with remaining chicken and avocado mixtures on 3 more plates. Arrange the dressed greens around the chicken salad using tongs. Serve immediately.

Variation

The chicken can be roasted, grilled or sautéed instead of poached. Leftover chicken can be used as well, but the flavor will be best if the poultry has not been refrigerated.

Wine Selection

Chardonnay

Salads

Stir-fried Chicken and Vegetable Salad

4 Servings

Planning Ahead

The Anchovy Dressing can be prepared and the artichokes cooked and prepped at any time during the day the salad is to be served. The salad mixture can be stir-fried several hours in advance. Allow at least 1½ hours for the salad to cool and marinate before presenting. Assemble the salad just before bringing it to the table.

Technique Tips

If baby carrots are not available, substitute 12 small carrots, leaving 1½ inches of green tops. Cut the bottoms off the carrots so the carrots measure 3 inches in length. Shape the carrots, tapering ends to resemble baby carrots, using a vegetable peeler.

If the carrots are thicker than the asparagus, cook 2 to 3 minutes by themselves before adding the asparagus.

To trim peppers neatly, make a vertical slit down the side of each pepper, open the pepper, flattening it lightly, and scrape out the seeds, core, ribs and white fibers from the interior, slanting a knife almost parallel to the pepper.

an Weimer gave me this salad recipe for the book because it can be adapted to busy schedules. When time is plentiful, nature's garden-fresh artichokes, asparagus, fennel, yellow peppers and carrots can all be utilized. When little opportunity exists for cooking, a bountiful salad can still be put together by stir-frying only two or three of the components and omitting the fennel and artichoke. The chicken itself can be omitted, steering the dish on a straight-and-narrow vegetarian path.

ANCHOVY DRESSING

3 large garlic cloves, peeled

2 2-ounce cans anchovies, drained

½ cup freshly squeezed lemon juice

1¼ cups olive oil

Salt and freshly ground black pepper to taste

4 medium artichokes

3 tablespoons olive oil

1½ to 2 pounds medium asparagus, white ends discarded, stalks peeled and sliced diagonally into 2-inch pieces

40 baby carrots with 1½ inches of green tops, peeled

4 large (1½ to 2 pounds) yellow (or red) peppers, sliced into strips

3 tablespoons olive oil

4 large chicken breasts, boned, skinned, trimmed, tendon removed, patted dry and sliced into 2- × ½-inch strips

1 large (1½ to 2 pounds) fennel bulb

⅓ cup capers, rinsed

Salt and freshly ground black pepper to taste

1 small yellow (or red) pepper, minced

For the Anchovy Dressing, place the garlic and anchovies in a blender. Process until finely chopped. Add the lemon juice and process until pureed, pulsing on/off. With the machine running, pour in the oil in a slow, thin stream. Season with salt and pepper. (This can be prepared ahead and set aside at room temperature.)

For the artichokes, cut any sharp spines off the leaves bluntly with scissors. Break off the stem flush with the bottom of the artichoke. Place the artichokes in a steamer, cover and cook over medium-high heat until the leaves pull out easily and the bottom is tender and easily pierced with a knife, for about 40 to 50 minutes. Pull out the artichoke leaves. Scrape the hairy choke out of the heart using a spoon; discard the choke. (This can be prepared ahead and set aside at room temperature.)

Heat 3 tablespoons of olive oil in a wok or heavy large nonstick skillet over medium-high heat. Add the asparagus, carrots and yellow pepper and toss with a spatula until the asparagus is crisp-tender when pierced with a knife, for about 5 minutes. Transfer to a large bowl.

Heat 3 tablespoons of olive oil in the same wok over medium-high heat. Add the chicken and toss continually until just opaque and cooked through, for about 2 to 3 minutes. Add the chicken to the bowl with the vegetables.

Trim off the fennel fronds and reserve. Cut off the stalks. Peel the stalks and fibrous exterior of the bulb using a vegetable peeler. Halve lengthwise, core and slice the bulb and stalks crosswise into ¼-inch strips. Add the fennel to chicken mixture.

Cool the chicken mixture at room temperature for at least 1 hour. Stir in the capers and ⅓ cup of the Anchovy Dressing or enough to coat the salad lightly. Season with salt and pepper and marinate for 30 minutes, stirring occasionally.

To serve, arrange approximately 15 artichoke leaves around the rim of 4 large plates without overlapping, tips pointed outward. Spoon several drops of Anchovy Dressing on the bottom of each leaf. Toss the salad, adding additional dressing, if necessary. Mound the salad in the center of the plates. Pull out 1 asparagus tip in between each artichoke leaf around the rim of the plate using tongs. Place an artichoke heart in the center of each salad. Spoon several drops of dressing into each heart. Sprinkle minced yellow peppers in the artichoke heart and leaves. Place a sprig of reserved fennel in each heart. Mince the remaining fronds and sprinkle over the salad. Serve immediately. Pass a platter of remaining artichoke leaves and dressing separately, if desired.

Duck Salad with Citrus and Spice

4 Servings

Planning Ahead

The duck can be roasted, the Citrus Dressing prepared and the greens and oranges prepped at any time during the day the salad is to be served. To keep the duck moist, remove the meat from the carcass as close to presenting as possible. Combine the ingredients and toss the salad just before bringing it to the table.

Technique Tips

Utilize only the zest (the orange part of the peel); the underlying white pithy layer can be bitter.

Although a trace of membrane will remain, the oranges can be prepared more quickly by slicing in rounds instead of segmenting.

Refrigerate or freeze the duck fat removed from the pan in a covered container to cook potatoes, rice or vegetables, such as cabbage.

Instead of discarding the duck bones, save them for making stock.

Wine Selection

Alsatian Gewurztraminer

When the sauce for Duck à l'Orange is balanced with a *gastric*, a reduction of vinegar and caramelized sugar, it has a refreshing tartness. Inspired by its pleasing acidity, I've made a tangy orange dressing for this duck salad. Poultry salads of late seem to include everything in the grocery store except the laundry soap. In contrast, I've tried to keep this one pure and simple.

3 oranges

CITRUS DRESSING

3 tablespoons mayonnaise

3 tablespoons freshly squeezed lime juice

3 drops Tabasco

¼ teaspoon sugar

1 tablespoon fresh peeled minced gingerroot

6 tablespoons peanut oil

Salt and freshly ground black pepper to taste

1 tablespoon ground cinnamon

5- to 6-pound duck

Salt and freshly ground black pepper to taste

6 cups (about 6 ounces) packed bite-size curly endive or mixed greens

For the oranges, remove the orange part of the peel from 1 orange using a vegetable peeler. Place the peel in a small pan. Cover generously with cold water. Bring to a boil. Boil 1 minute; drain.

Holding the orange over a bowl, cut the white pith from the first orange and both the peel and white pith from the remaining oranges in 1 large corkscrew strip by starting at the top of the orange and cutting down and around using a small sharp knife. Cut between the coarse whitish membranes to remove each segment, letting the segments fall into the bowl. Squeeze the juice from the membranes into the bowl; discard the membranes. (This can be prepared ahead, covered and set aside at room temperature.)

For the Citrus Dressing, place the mayonnaise in a small bowl. Whisk in the lime juice, 1½ tablespoons orange juice from the squeezed membranes, Tabasco, sugar and ginger until well blended. Whisk in the oil in a slow, thin stream. Coarsely chop the blanched orange peel and add 1½ tablespoons of it to the dressing; discard the remainder. Remove about ⅓ of the orange segments using a slotted spoon. Cut each into 3 sections. Stir into the dressing. Season with salt and pepper. (This can be prepared ahead, covered and set aside at room temperature.)

For the duck, preheat the oven to 325°F. Rub the cinnamon over the duck skin. Season with salt and pepper. Prick the duck all over with a fork. Place the duck on a rack in a roasting pan. Roast 1½ hours, turning halfway. Remove excess rendered fat with a bulb baster as necessary and reserve for another dish. This can be prepared ahead, cooled, covered and set aside at cool room temperature for several hours.

Remove the meat from the duck breasts in one piece by cutting around the breasts and keeping the knife slanted down toward the bone. Discard the skin, slice the fillet diagonally and reserve for garnish. Remove the meat from the rest of the duck, discarding the skin and bones. Cut the duck into bite-size pieces.

To serve, gently toss the greens and duck pieces with about ¾ of the dressing or enough to coat lightly. Divide the salad among 4 large plates. Toss the fillets with enough of the remaining dressing to coat lightly. Arrange slices over salad with 1 end pointing toward the center. Remove the remaining orange segments from the bowl using a slotted spoon. Alternate between duck slices. Serve immediately.

Pea Pod and Calf's Liver Salad

Planning Ahead

The vegetables can be cooked and the Shallot Vinaigrette prepared at any time during the day the salad is to be served. The liver can be sautéed ½ hour in advance. Toss the salad just before presenting.

Technique Tips

This recipe is written for ¼-inch-thick slices of liver because it is most frequently sold precut to this thickness. I find it more succulent, though, when it is ½ to ¾ inch thick. To obtain this thickness, I find out when my market is receiving its liver fresh and have the butcher cut it to order. If the liver is thicker, brown each side briefly and then transfer the skillet to a preheated 325°F oven for 7 to 10 minutes to cook through. In this case, it will probably all fit into 1 large skillet.

Many recipes for liver suggest searing it initially over medium-high heat until it is brown and crusty, but I find it more tender when cooked gently and slowly without browning.

Adding a few drops of red wine vinegar to the skillet at the end of cooking gives the liver a wonderful flavor.

L iver, which has been married to onions for as long as anyone can remember, has largely disappeared from dinner menus unless it's being served as an alternative to pork chops for Sunday supper. Upstaged by salads, it's not much of a lunch item anymore, either. Believing that if you can't beat them, join them, I've joined the liver with snow peas, green beans, broccoli and cherry tomatoes. Now that I have a liver salad, the onions will just have to find another mate.

VEGETABLES

½ pound snow peas, ends snapped and strung

½ pound green beans, ends snapped and strung

Florets from 1 pound (about 4 stalks) broccoli

SHALLOT VINAIGRETTE

3 tablespoons red wine vinegar

1½ tablespoons balsamic vinegar

5 tablespoons olive oil

3 tablespoons minced shallots

Salt and freshly ground black pepper to taste

LIVER

About 2 tablespoons olive oil

1 pound calf's liver, ¼ inch thick, patted dry

Salt and freshly ground black pepper to taste

18 red and/or yellow cherry tomatoes, halved lengthwise

20 large radicchio leaves (about 2 small heads)

For the vegetables, bring a large pot of water to a boil and set a colander over a baking tray. Add the snow peas to water and simmer until crisp-tender, for about 2 minutes. Remove them to a colander with a slotted spoon. Repeat with the green beans (about 6 to 7 minutes) and broccoli (about 4 minutes), cooking each until crisp-tender. (This can be prepared ahead and set aside at room temperature.)

For the Shallot Vinaigrette, mix the red wine and balsamic vinegars in a small bowl. Whisk in the olive oil in a slow, thin stream. Add the shallots and season with salt and pepper. (This can be prepared ahead, covered and set aside at room temperature.)

For the liver, place a heavy large nonstick skillet over medium-low heat and film with oil. Season the liver with salt and pepper. Add to the skillet and cook until just firm to the touch and medium-rare, for about 5 to 7 minutes total, turning halfway. Let rest 5 minutes to ½ hour.

To serve, place the cooked vegetables and tomatoes in a large bowl. Slice the liver diagonally and add it to the bowl. Gently toss the salad ingredients with ¾ of the vinaigrette. Mound the salad in the center of 4 large plates using a slotted spoon. Gently toss the radicchio with enough of the remaining dressing to coat lightly. Ring it around the salad on each plate. Serve immediately.

Wine Selection
Pinot Noir

Pepper-Pork Salad with Blood Oranges and Avocado

4 Servings

Planning Ahead

The pork should be marinated for at least 4 hours or, preferably, overnight in the refrigerator. The greens, tomatoes and oranges can be prepped and the vinaigrette prepared at any time during the day the salad is to be served. Roast the pork and toss the salad just before presenting.

Technique Tip

Although a trace of membrane will remain, the oranges can be prepared more quickly by slicing in rounds instead of segmenting.

Wine Selection

Red Burgundy

When my food does not have the soul of the Mediterranean or the familiar flavors of my northern French youth, it is likely to include Asian and Mexican ingredients. As these disparate influences interact, I feel somewhat like an Alsatian caught between the cultures of France and Germany. This two-country salad has the fresh Mexican bite of orange, avocado and cilantro combined with a Chinese emphasis on texture and sweet-sour peppery spice. I roast the meat at high heat to keep it moist.

MARINADE

I pound pork tenderloin, well trimmed of fat and tendon

¼ cup honey

1½ tablespoons fresh peeled minced gingerroot

I teaspoon finely crushed black pepper

½ teaspoon ground cumin

3 large blood oranges or oranges

VINAIGRETTE

¼ cup Champagne or white wine vinegar

½ cup olive oil

I tablespoon Oriental (toasted) sesame oil

12 drops Tabasco

1½ tablespoons ketchup

2 tablespoons fresh chopped cilantro or other fresh herb

2 teaspoons fresh peeled minced gingerroot

Salt and freshly ground black pepper to taste

SALAD

5 to 6 cups (about 5 to 6 ounces) packed bite-size curly endive

2 small tomatoes, peeled, seeded and diced

I large avocado, cubed

For the marinade, place the pork on a large sheet of plastic wrap. Mix the honey with the ginger, pepper and cumin in a small bowl. Brush this mixture thickly over the pork, covering it completely. Roll the pork up in the plastic, twisting the ends tightly. Place on a tray and marinate in the refrigerator for at least 4 hours or, preferably, overnight. Bring to room temperature before baking.

For the oranges, holding over a bowl 1 at a time, cut off the peel and white pith in 1 large corkscrew strip by starting at the top of the orange and cutting down and around using a small sharp knife. Cut between the coarse whitish membranes to remove each segment, letting the segments fall into the bowl. Squeeze the juice from the membranes into the bowl; discard the membranes. (This can be prepared ahead, covered and set aside at room temperature.)

For the vinaigrette, place the vinegar in a small bowl. Whisk in the olive and sesame oils in a slow, thin stream. Stir in the Tabasco, ketchup, cilantro and ginger. Season with salt and pepper. (This can be prepared ahead, covered and set aside at room temperature.)

To cook the pork, preheat the oven to 500°F. Line a roasting pan with aluminum foil. Place the pork on a rack above the foil and roast until browned and caramelized on the outside and just cooked through, for about 15 minutes brushing with pan juices and turning halfway. Let rest for 15 minutes before carving.

For the salad, meanwhile, place endive, tomato and avocado in a large bowl. Remove the orange segments from the bowl with a slotted spoon and add them to the endive mixture. Slice the pork lengthwise and crosswise into ¾-inch cubes. Add it to the endive mixture. Gently toss the salad with enough vinaigrette to coat lightly. Serve immediately, mounding on a large platter or 4 large plates.

Lamb Salad with
Watercress and New Potatoes

Planning Ahead

The lamb should be marinated for at least 4 hours or, preferably, overnight. The potatoes can be cooked and the vinaigrette and salad ingredients can be readied at any time during the day the dish is to be served. Cook the lamb and assemble the salad just before presenting.

Technique Tips

If neither a lamb loin nor a butcher with a boning knife are available, buy a rack of lamb and bone out the rib eye in a single piece by using a sharp knife and following contours of the rack. Once boned and trimmed, this is one of the easiest cuts of meat to cook and carve, making it an ideal choice for guests.

For potatoes to absorb the dressing adequately, they must be dressed as soon as they are cooked.

This, more or less, is the salad my mother made every summer to take on our swimming outings. Sometimes she made the salad from freshly cooked lamb and sometimes from leftovers. Sometimes she picked a rack, sometimes a leg. On occasion, she even chose chicken. Regardless, there were always baby new potatoes and watercress—the basil of today and the parsley of yesterday. No matter what meat was used, my mother deglazed the cooking pan with a little water or wine and boiled down the juices into a rich concentrate to stir into the dressing. That was her job. Mine was to keep the wine cool. Since there were no ice chests in those days, I put the bottle in the lake to chill, tying it to my wrist with a long string. In this way, I never had to worry about losing our precious beverage, but I sure spent a lot of time untangling myself.

MARINADE

2 (8 to 10 ounce each) lamb loins or rib eyes from 1½ to 1¾ pounds lamb racks, trimmed of all fat and fell (membrane) and patted dry

About ¼ cup olive oil

2 large cloves garlic, peeled and minced

8 fresh large rosemary sprigs or 2 tablespoons dried rosemary, crumbled

8 fresh large thyme sprigs or 2 tablespoons dried thyme, crumbled

VINAIGRETTE

1½ tablespoons red wine vinegar

6 tablespoons olive oil

2 small cloves garlic, peeled and minced

1½ teaspoons fresh minced rosemary or thyme

Salt and freshly ground black pepper to taste

16 baby (about 1 inch diameter) or 10 small (about 1½ inches diameter) unpeeled red boiling potatoes

Salt and freshly ground black pepper to taste

About 2 tablespoons olive oil

Coarse salt

2 cups (about ½ bunch) lightly packed watercress leaves

2 tablespoons mayonnaise

1 medium tomato, peeled, seeded and diced

4 fresh rosemary sprigs (optional)

For the marinade, place the lamb loins on a large piece of plastic wrap. Rub both sides of the loins with oil. Press the garlic, rosemary and thyme into the loins. Wrap in the plastic, twisting the ends tightly, and refrigerate at least 4 hours or overnight. Bring to room temperature before cooking.

For the vinaigrette, place the vinegar in a small bowl. Whisk in the oil in a slow, thin stream. Stir in the garlic and rosemary. Season with salt and pepper. (This can be prepared ahead, covered and set aside at room temperature.)

For the potatoes, steam them until easily pierced with a knife (start checking after 15 minutes). Immediately halve, place in a glass pie plate and drizzle with half of the vinaigrette. Gently toss and turn the potatoes in the dressing. (This can be prepared ahead, covered and set aside at room temperature.)

To cook the lamb, preheat the oven to 325°F. Remove the herbs and most of the garlic from the lamb and season the meat with salt and pepper. Place a heavy ovenproof nonstick skillet large enough to accommodate both loins without crowding over medium-high heat and film with oil. Add the lamb and brown on all sides. Transfer the skillet to the oven and roast the lamb for 10 minutes for medium-rare. Transfer the lamb to a carving board and let it rest for 10 minutes.

To serve, arrange 8 potato halves in a circle in the centers of 4 soup plates; sprinkle lightly with coarse salt.

Slice each lamb loin diagonally into 16 pieces, adding the carving juices to the remaining vinaigrette. Place 2 pieces of meat between each potato half.

Gently toss the watercress with enough dressing to coat lightly and arrange around the lamb and potatoes.

Whisk the mayonnaise into the remaining vinaigrette and place this dressing in the center of the potato circle.

Scatter the tomato on top of the dressing and over the lamb and watercress. Garnish with rosemary sprigs, if desired. Serve immediately.

Variation

Leftover meats can also be used as the base of this salad.

If you want to add another component to this salad for bulk or complexity, a good choice would be steamed artichokes or asparagus. When adding either of these vegetables, make double the amount of vinaigrette and dress the vegetables with extra as needed.

Wine Selection
Cabernet Sauvignon

Seafood

I cannot believe we chefs used to poach fish for 40 minutes, and then leave it in the hot liquid overnight until it got cold. When we were finally finished, we had little rubber bands. Overcooking was an understatement for what we did to these poor creatures. We killed them three or four times and then served them with a ton of béarnaise on the side. Somehow people just accepted this. Even though I was young, I knew there was something very, very wrong with this cooking method. Thank you, nouvelle cuisine for discovering how to cook fish properly.

Going by the Canadian rule of cooking fish, which allows 10 minutes per inch of thickness, even the broadest whole fish won't take much more than 15 minutes. For my taste, I find that 8 or 9 minutes per inch of thickness is more than ample even when I want to cook a fish until it is completely opaque throughout. Thin fillets, such as sole, should be underdone because they will continue cooking on the plate, while meatier fish, such as tuna, salmon and swordfish, are best cooked rare like a steak. I will repeat this ad nauseam throughout this chapter in hopes that I can at least get you to try the delectable flavors of fish cooked this way.

I have devised two methods of cooking thick, beefy fish fillets through to the inside without drying them on the outside. Both systems prevent shrinkage and preserve moisture and tenderness. One technique is to lightly brown both sides of the fish in a skillet on top of the stove and then transfer it to a 200°F oven to cook, uncovered, for 15 minutes. The other approach is a cross between sautéing and steaming. After browning a fish lightly on both sides, I pour between ⅛ and ¼ inch water into the skillet, cover it and cook about 6 minutes on medium heat, turning halfway.

When I prefer my fish crunchy on the outside, I cook it with the skin on, which bastes the fish and keeps it from drying out; or I add a crust, such as those in this chapter made from rice, couscous and onions. I crisp the skin or crust over medium-high heat and then finish the fish in a low oven, again to keep its flesh moist and tender.

To avoid overcooking, start with steaks or fillets that are all the same size. If the fish has a tapered end, just tuck the thinner piece underneath. To make fillets or steaks the same size, pound them lightly with a mallet between two pieces of plastic wrap or waxed paper. Although fillet is defined as "no bones," I probe the surface of a fillet or steak before cooking for hidden bones. These I remove with the tweezers or small pliers I keep in my kitchen for this task. It's a shame people are afraid of bones, for a fish cooked on the bone is so much tastier and fun to eat than one that has been filleted. It's also much easier to recognize whether a fish is fresh when you can examine the entire creature.

If a fish is fresh, its eyes should be bright and clear, gills deep red and skin and flesh gleaming. When it is not optimally fresh, it will look flaccid and flabby, feel gooey and gluey and smell like . . . fish. Fresh seafood smells only of the sea, not of itself. Mollusks should be tightly closed or snap sharply shut when touched. To confirm, ask your fishmonger to show you the tags that must accompany varieties taken from certified waters.

Freshness is, unfortunately, no longer just an issue of maximizing taste but one of food safety as well. It is so sad to think we might be one of the last generations to enjoy fish. I remember the perfect specimens that used to come from the Great Lakes before they were polluted. When I compare them to the bland farm-raised fare offered today in their stead, I feel like screaming: How could we have destroyed this?

When shopping for fish, frequent busy stores that have a high turnover and carefully separate each species as well as cooked from uncooked fish. No matter how you're preparing the fish, tell the fishmonger you are serving it raw as sashimi, and he's apt to be more careful about the condition of the fish he sells you. Another little trick is to create a good relationship with the fishmonger so he'll always give you the best. If you go to a market intending to buy halibut, but the mahi mahi looks better, buy it. Most seafood works interchangeably in a recipe. Use fish the day it is purchased, keeping it in the refrigerator until as close to cooking as possible.

The dishes in this chapter are simple for it is not necessary to create a masquerade around fish. When it is overworked, it looks like an old lady with too much makeup. Chefs love to prepare seafood because we can create recipes with light stocks, something we can't do with meat. Low in fat, it has much to offer the health conscious, and there is little that is as fast and easy to prepare as seafood. Seafood is the entree of choice in most restaurants, yet it is still too rarely cooked at home. Why?

Are people afraid of contamination? Do they know that fresh fish does not smell and will not smell up the house? Do they trust the short cooking times in recipes or overcook it to sawdust and think it is not worth tackling again? Do they destroy their efforts with a squeeze of lemon that makes the fish taste more like lemon than fish? Are they so afraid of bones that they prefer fake crab served with plastic leaves and plastic carrots that are washed and put back on someone else's plate?

Whatever the reason cooks aren't catching up with seafood at home, I'm hoping the recipes in this chapter will prove to be a real fun school of fish. Just keep lemon away from it!

Laurence's Fish Soup

4 Servings

Planning Ahead

The potatoes can be cooked and the soup base prepared at any time during the day the dish is to be served. The shrimp can be shelled and the fish prepped several hours before cooking. Cook the seafood just before presenting.

Technique Tip

If the potatoes are added to the clam juice mixture before the dish is cooked, they will absorb too much liquid.

Wine Selection

Chardonnay

My wife, Laurence, is a very good cook, yet she does not have a lot of time to spend at the stove. When we invite people for dinner and she is the one preparing the meal, she inevitably makes a fish soup or stew, knowing she can put together a dazzling dish in just a few minutes. For Laurence, fish soup is not a particular recipe, but a concept or category that varies according to what is freshest at the market. Most frequently, her seafood swims in a deep, full, rich broth, but every now and then, it wades in a pool that is more like a sauce. In this shallow soup, my Brittany-born wife has looked to other regions of France for inspiration, combining the saffron and tomato of a Provence bouillabaisse with the touch of cream in the Norman marmite.

¾ **pound small red or other boiling potatoes, peeled and cut into ½-inch cubes**

I cup clam juice

½ **cup heavy cream**

¼ **teaspoon saffron threads, crushed and dissolved in 2 tablespoons boiling water**

Salt and freshly ground black pepper to taste

½ **pound medium shrimp, peeled and deveined**

I pound red snapper, sea bass, mahi mahi, halibut or other whitefish fillets, trimmed and cut into ⅓-inch-wide strips

½ **pound bay scallops**

I small tomato, peeled, seeded and diced

Steam the potatoes until tender and easily pierced with a knife, for about 10 minutes. (This can be prepared ahead, covered and set aside at room temperature.)

Place the clam juice, cream and saffron in a heavy large nonstick skillet. (This can be prepared ahead, covered and set aside at cool room temperature for 2 hours or refrigerated.)

To serve, add the potatoes to the clam juice mixture. Season with salt and pepper. Bring the clam juice mixture to a boil, add the shrimp and fish fillets, reduce heat and simmer gently until the shrimp just starts to turn pink, about 2½ minutes total, turning the seafood halfway with tongs. Add the scallops and cook for 1 minute.

Divide the seafood and potatoes among 4 soup plates using a slotted spatula. Quickly bring the cooking liquid back to a boil and ladle over the seafood. Sprinkle with tomato. Serve immediately.

Shrimp with
Green Onion Basil Sauce

It's funny how you become tired of something and stop eating it. Then, after a long absence, you encounter it again, and it tastes so delicious you can't believe you deprived yourself of it. That happened to me with garlic butter. I got so sick of seeing it that I banished it from my table. One day a friend served it to me unwittingly atop these shrimp, and I realized what I had been missing.

GREEN ONION BASIL SAUCE

4 ounces (1 stick) unsalted butter

4 medium (about ½ cup) green onion (white part only), thinly sliced

2 large cloves garlic, peeled and sliced

1 tablespoon Champagne vinegar or white wine vinegar

¾ cup unsalted chicken stock

2 tablespoons fresh minced basil

Salt and freshly ground black pepper to taste

SHRIMP

1 ounce (¼ stick) unsalted butter

24 to 32 large shrimp, shelled and deveined

Salt and freshly ground black pepper to taste

4 fresh bouquets of basil sprigs (optional)

For the Green Onion Basil Sauce, melt the butter and cool it to tepid. Boil the green onions, garlic, vinegar and chicken stock in a heavy small saucepan until the liquid is reduced to 1 tablespoon. Transfer it to a blender with the minced basil. Process until the basil is almost pureed. With the machine running, pour in the butter in a slow, thin stream, forming a thick, emulsified sauce. Season with salt and pepper.

For the shrimp, melt the butter in a heavy large skillet over medium-high heat. Add the shrimp and cook until just pink and opaque, about 2 to 3 minutes total, turning halfway with tongs. Season with salt and pepper.

To serve, ladle a pool of hot sauce in the center of 4 large plates. Arrange the shrimp in a circle over the sauce with their tails meeting in the center. Place the basil bouquets over tails in center. Serve immediately.

4 Servings

Planning Ahead
The Green Onion Basil Sauce can be prepared several hours in advance. Cook the shrimp just before serving.

Variation
The Green Onion Basil Sauce can also be served with cooked asparagus or artichokes.

Wine Selection
Alsatian Gewurztraminer

Shrimp Porcupines

4 Main-course Servings

Planning Ahead

The Purple Sauce can be prepared and the Shrimp Porcupines formed at any time during the day they are to be served. Fry the shrimp just before presenting or several hours in advance and reheat.

Wine Selection

Chardonnay

These little packets of shrimp wrapped in kataifi, the shredded wheat strands used in Middle Eastern cooking, look like golden-brown porcupines when they are fried. Since the kataifi does not absorb oil, these are crisp rather than soggy. The trick to frying these prickly shrimp is to immerse them only partially in oil at first until the kataifi sets at the bottom of the package. Otherwise, the kataifi hairs pull away from the shrimp. Cooking dinner, you know, requires the skills of a hairdresser as well as a chef.

In addition to serving these as a main course, I often present one giant tiger shrimp or several large shrimp as a first course. I like the Purple Sauce with this shellfish for the same reason I like it with the Chicken Kataifi (page 178): It lends freshness, acidity and color. Other sauces, such as the Basolivaise (page 641) and Parsley-Cilantro Sauce (page 48), in particular, work well, too. Sometimes I spoon the Chayote with Mustard Mayonnaise (page 42) alongside as a garnish.

PURPLE SAUCE (PAGE 178)

> 4 cups 1-inch pieces kataifi
>
> ⅓ cup flour
>
> 1 egg, at room temperature
>
> 1 tablespoon water
>
> Salt and freshly ground black pepper to taste
>
> 16 large shrimp, shelled and deveined
>
> Oil (about 4 cups) for deep frying

Prepare the Purple Sauce. (This can be prepared ahead and set aside at cool room temperature for 1 hour, or refrigerated.)

Line a large baking sheet with parchment paper. Pull the kataifi out of the bag and cut it into 1-inch pieces over a bowl. Separate the threads with your fingers. Refrigerate or refreeze the remaining kataifi for another dish.

Place the kataifi on 1 large plate and the flour on another. Whisk the egg with water in a soup plate until blended. Season the egg with salt and pepper. One at a time, dip the shrimp into the flour until well coated, patting off excess. Hold the shrimp with tongs and dip it into the egg, coating completely, and then into the kataifi. Place the shrimp-dipped kataifi in the palm of your hand and compress it into a large neat package, about 2½ inches in diameter. Place on the prepared baking sheet. Repeat with the remaining shrimp. (This can be prepared ahead and set aside, covered, at cool room temperature for 1 hour or refrigerated until 1 hour before frying.)

Seafood

To cook, line a large baking sheet with paper towels. Heat 1 inch of oil in a wok or a large skillet to 350°F, or until bubbles form around a chopstick or a wooden spoon handle immersed in the oil. Using tongs, gradually dip 1 shrimp into the oil, waiting until the bottom layer of the kataifi sets before immersing the shrimp completely. Add additional shrimp in the same manner in batches without crowding. Cook the shrimp until golden brown on both sides, for about 3 minutes total. Transfer to paper towels with tongs or a slotted spoon. (This can be cooked several hours ahead. Reheat on towel-lined tray in a preheated 450°F oven for 2 to 3 minutes.)

To serve, spoon the Purple Sauce in the center of 4 large plates. Arrange 4 shrimp on top of the sauce on each plate. Serve immediately.

■

Crab Brandade

4 Servings

Planning Ahead

The crab can be cooked 1 day in advance according to the directions for Crab Coleslaw (page 98). The Garlic Cream and potato puree can be prepared at any time during the day the brandade is to be served. Reheat the Garlic Cream and the potatoes and combine the ingredients just before presenting.

Technique Tips

Crab is usually so much better when cooked live at home than it is when purchased precooked. If possible, cook a live crab for the Brandade. Or, when cooking live crab for another dish, buy enough so you'll have leftovers to make Crab Brandade for supper the next night.

Crabmeat should remain in small pieces and retain texture. Once it is added, be careful not to overmix.

Mash the potatoes using a potato masher or mallet and sieve rather than a food processor which can make them gluey.

Brandade of salt cod, the popular rustic Provençal entree, is prepared by whisking olive oil and milk or cream into salt cod until it is the texture of mashed potatoes. I was recently reminded of this mound of comfort as I watched a friend bind a crab cake, which flaked like cod. I then tried substituting crab for cod in a brandade, and it worked magnificently, becoming a bit more sophisticated while maintaining its lusty heartiness. Since we are aiming for the texture of mashed potatoes, I added them, too, to get us there faster.

¾ pound (about 3 cups loosely packed) cooked crabmeat, picked over for shells and shredded (page 98)

GARLIC CREAM

15 large or generous ½ cup (about 1 head) garlic cloves, peeled

1 cup heavy cream

1½ pounds (about 6 medium) russet potatoes, peeled and cut into ½-inch-thick slices

½ cup olive oil

1½ tablespoons fresh minced tarragon, marjoram, chives or other fresh herb

Crab butter/cream (optional)

Salt and freshly ground black pepper to taste

Toasted French bread

Prepare two 1½ to 2 pounds live crab (page 98) or pick over and shred precooked crab. (This can be prepared 1 day ahead and refrigerated until 1 hour before serving.)

For the Garlic Cream, place the garlic in a heavy medium saucepan. Cover with 3 inches of cold water. Bring to a boil. Drain and rinse with cold water. Repeat this process 2 more times. Coarsely chop the garlic. Return it to the same saucepan with the cream. Bring to a boil, then reduce heat and simmer gently until reduced by half or to a thick saucelike consistency, stirring occasionally. (This can be prepared ahead, covered and set aside at cool room temperature for several hours or refrigerated.)

For potatoes, meanwhile cover the potatoes with cold water in a medium pot and bring to a boil. Simmer until very tender, for about 20 minutes. Drain and mash to a fine puree. Return the potatoes to the pot. (This can be prepared ahead, covered and set aside at room temperature.)

Stir potatoes over medium-high heat to rewarm. Remove from heat and stir in the olive oil in a slow, thin stream. Reheat the Garlic Cream and slowly stir it into the potato mixture. Mix in the cooked crab. Mix in the tarragon and crab butter/cream to taste, if available. Season with salt and pepper. Mound onto 4 plates. Serve immediately with toast.

Wine Selection
White Burgundy or Chardonnay

Moussaka with
Scallops and Goat Cheese

Wednesday was moussaka night at the Club Med in Corfu when I worked there, and that was the only time you couldn't get me to leave the kitchen and go dancing. I wasn't so crazy about the ground lamb mixture, but I loved the béchamel (white sauce) layer with cheese on top. The French often serve seafood with *Sauce Mornay* (a béchamel with cheese), so this Moussaka with Scallops might be considered a Greek Coquilles St. Jacques.

**4 First-course
or 2 to 3 Main-course
Servings**

EGGPLANT

    1 large (about 1½ pounds) eggplant, peeled and sliced lengthwise
        into ¼-inch-thick pieces

    About ⅓ cup olive oil

    2 tablespoons balsamic vinegar

    Salt and freshly ground black pepper to taste

SCALLOPS

    2 tablespoons olive oil

    2 large cloves garlic, peeled and minced

    ¾ to 1 pound sea scallops, halved horizontally and patted dry

    Salt and freshly ground black pepper to taste

GOAT CHEESE SAUCE

    2 tablespoons flour

    1 cup heavy cream

    About 2½ ounces goat cheese

    1 tablespoon fresh minced chives or green onions

    Generous pinch of ground cumin

    Salt and freshly ground black pepper to taste

(continued)

Planning Ahead
The moussaka components can all be prepared and the dish assembled at any time during the day it is to be served. Broil it just before presenting.

Technique Tips
To get slices that are similar in size, choose an eggplant that is as evenly shaped as possible.

When choosing an eggplant, look for the male whose bottom indentation is rounder and deeper than a female's shallow oval opening, an indication of fewer seeds.

When baking eggplant, cook it until completely tender, but not falling apart.

When assembling the moussaka, save the largest, nicest eggplant slices for the top layer.

Be careful not to over-brown the moussaka under

Seafood

the broiler unless you want little pieces of scallop rubber.

When sautéing scallops or other seafood, I often keep an absorbent terry cloth or paper towel next to the stove to blot off any excess butter or oil after the fish is removed from the pan.

Variation

The moussaka can also be assembled in 4 individual gratin dishes.

Wine Selection

Alsatian Riesling or Sauvignon Blanc

For the eggplant, preheat the oven to 400°F. Arrange the eggplant slices in a single layer on a large baking sheet. Brush both sides with olive oil and bake until tender and easily pierced with knife, for about 15 to 20 minutes. Brush the top of the eggplant slices with vinegar. Season with salt and pepper. (This can be prepared ahead, cooled, covered and set aside at room temperature.)

For the scallops, line a large baking sheet with paper towels. Heat the oil in a heavy large nonstick skillet over medium-high heat with the garlic. Add the scallops and cook until barely opaque, for about 3 minutes total, turning halfway with tongs. Transfer to the prepared baking sheet and turn the scallops to blot them. Season with salt and pepper.

For the Goat Cheese Sauce, place the flour in a heavy small saucepan. Whisk in 3 to 4 tablespoons of the cream and stir to form a thick, smooth paste, adding additional cream if necessary. Whisk in the remaining cream and stir until smooth. Crumble in the goat cheese. Whisk the sauce over medium-low heat until thick and smooth, for about 4 to 5 minutes. Stir in the chives and cumin. Season with salt and pepper.

To assemble, oil a 9- × 12-inch baking dish. Arrange ½ of the eggplant slices side by side in the bottom of the dish, overlapping and trimming as necessary so the layer is even. Arrange the scallops over the eggplant. Spoon over ½ of the sauce. Cover with the remaining eggplant, trimming as necessary, and the remaining sauce. (This can be prepared ahead, cooled, covered and set aside at room temperature for several hours or refrigerated until 1 hour before serving.)

To serve, preheat the broiler. Uncover the baking dish and place about 3 inches below the heat source. Broil for 3 to 4 minutes or until the moussaka is browned and heated through. Divide into 2 to 4 portions with a serrated spatula. Transfer to plates. Serve immediately.

Scallop Asparagus Lollipops

A kebab is impressive to behold, both while it is cooking on the grill and when it is brought to the table. Cut into equal-size pieces, its components cook evenly as their flavors intermingle. It's a great technique, yet once the skewers are removed, the food doesn't look so appealing on the plate. To solve this dilemma, I've come up with a scallop kebab on an edible asparagus spear that resembles a lollipop. Not only do each of these items look the part they are playing, but they are easy to put together. Cornmeal provides my *de rigueur* crunch, while the briny scallops sweeten the asparagus.

ASPARAGUS DRESSING

I egg yolk (optional), at room temperature

I teaspoon Dijon mustard

¼ cup Champagne vinegar or white wine vinegar

½ cup olive oil

2 tablespoons minced shallot

2 tablespoons fresh minced chervil, tarragon, dill or basil

Salt and freshly ground black pepper to taste

8 to 12 medium asparagus spears (see Technique Tips), ends trimmed so spears measure 7 inches

I pound (about 20) medium asparagus spears, white ends discarded and stalks peeled

16 to 20 jumbo (about ¾ to I pound) sea scallops, patted dry

I egg, blended with fork

Salt and freshly ground black pepper to taste

About ⅔ cup cornmeal

Salt and freshly ground black pepper to taste

I ounce (¼ stick) unsalted butter

4 tablespoons olive oil

For the Asparagus Dressing, blend the egg yolk, if using, and mustard in a blender. With the machine running, pour in the vinegar and then pour in the olive oil in a slow, thin stream. Stir in the shallot and chervil with a spatula. Season with salt and pepper. (This can be prepared ahead and set aside at cool room temperature for several hours or refrigerated until 1 hour before serving.)

(continued)

4 Servings

Planning Ahead

The Asparagus Dressing can be completely prepared, the asparagus cooked and the lollipops readied at any time during the day they are to be served. Cook lollipops just before presenting.

Technique Tips

The scallops need to be handled gently so they don't break apart. It is wise, in fact, to have several extra scallops and 7-inch asparagus spears on hand.

When threading asparagus, place the scallop flat on the work surface, encircle the perimeter of the scallop with your hand to hold it together and push and wiggle the asparagus through the scallop. If you have any trouble threading the asparagus, make a slit in the scallop at the point where you want to begin.

If the scallops are too thin, or it is too difficult to thread the asparagus horizontally through the side of the scallop, thread it vertically through the center. In this case, the asparagus will look more like the Michelin tire man than a lollipop.

Seafood

Thread scallops—or shrimp —on Chinese long beans and tie into a necklace for another edible skewer.

Wine Selection

Pouilly Fumé, Sancerre or Sauvignon Blanc

For the asparagus, bring a large pot of salted water to a boil. Line a rack with several layers of paper towels. Cook at least eight 7-inch spears until barely tender, for about 5 minutes. Remove with tongs, rinse under cold water and drain on the prepared rack. Divide the peeled spears according to thickness. Cook, adding thicker spears to the water first, until tender when pierced with a knife, for about 5 to 6 minutes total, for the larger spears. Drain and place on a rack.

To assemble the lollipops, line a large baking sheet with waxed or parchment paper. Treating the asparagus spear like a lollipop stick and the scallops like a piece of hard candy, carefully thread one 7-inch asparagus spear through the middle of the side of 1 scallop and then through the middle of the side of a second scallop. Arrange the scallops so they are centered between the tip and end of the spear. Arrange on the prepared sheet. Repeat with the remaining scallops and 7-inch spears. Brush the top of the scallops and asparagus with egg. Season with salt and pepper and sprinkle with cornmeal. Turn lollipops over and repeat on the second side. Add more cornmeal as necessary to coat completely and press it to adhere. (This can be prepared ahead, covered and refrigerated until 30 minutes before cooking.)

Cut one ½-inch-long tip off the remaining asparagus spears. Cut stalks into ½-inch dice. Set each aside at room temperature on a separate plate and cover.

To serve, season asparagus tips and dice with salt and pepper. Divide diced asparagus among the centers of 4 plates. Drizzle with dressing. Arrange tips around the outside of the plates. Place 2 heavy large nonstick skillets over medium-high heat and film each with half of the butter and oil. Add lollipops to the skillets and cook until crisp and just opaque throughout, for about 8 to 9 minutes total, gently turning halfway.

Carefully transfer 2 lollipops to the center of each plate using a large spatula. Drizzle dressing over the lollipops. Serve immediately.

Rex and Lily Solewiches

4 Servings

Planning Ahead

The ingredients can be prepped and the Lily Sauce prepared at any time during the day it is to be served. The further in advance this sauce is mixed, the more pungent it will be. If you

L ike other Americans, I am always looking for fast food. One day I brought a beautiful piece of rex sole home for lunch. I was not in the mood to fuss, so I just threw the fish in the toaster oven. In a few minutes, I had the filling for a fantastic sandwich. Although you can rarely buy rex sole already filleted, its flavor justifies the minimum effort it takes to bone it after cooking. If you can't deal with this task, substitute a fillet from another type of sole. (Or from any kind of fish, for that matter.)

The Lily Sauce is also fast food for me, for the members of the lily (onion) family are my basic staples. I count on green onions for bite, red for crunch and sweetness, and chives for delicacy and freshness. To provide layers of onionness, I sometimes add a white or yellow onion that has been cooked until it caramelizes.

Seafood

LILY SAUCE

    2 tablespoons mayonnaise

    ¼ cup heavy cream

    2 tablespoons Champagne or white wine vinegar

    2 tablespoons olive oil

    ⅓ cup minced green onion

    ¼ cup minced red onion

    2 tablespoons fresh minced chives

    Salt and freshly ground black pepper to taste

    1 to 1½ pounds rex sole or other sole or whitefish, about
        ½ inch thick, filleted if desired and patted dry

    2 tablespoons olive oil

    Salt and freshly ground black pepper to taste

    8 slices Los Angeles Country Bread (page 79) or other French or
        Italian bread or rolls, cut the same length as fish fillets

    Lettuce or mixed greens, such as escarole, endive, watercress or
        radicchio for 4 sandwiches

    4 small tomatoes, thinly sliced

For the Lily Sauce, whisk the mayonnaise, cream and vinegar together in a small bowl. Whisk in the oil in a slow, thin stream. Mix in the green and red onions and the chives. Season with salt and pepper. (This can be prepared ahead, covered and refrigerated until ½ hour before using.)

For the fish, preheat the oven to 325°F. Line a large baking sheet with parchment paper. Arrange the fish in a single layer on the prepared sheet. Brush with olive oil and season with salt and pepper. Bake for 4 to 5 minutes or until the fish is just opaque throughout. Bone out the fish fillets by cutting down each side of the center backbone, and then cutting from the backbone to the edges of the fish using a sharp knife. Turn the fish over and repeat on the second side.

To assemble the sandwich, grill or toast the bread. Spread the onion sauce on each slice of bread. Place the fish on 4 pieces of bread. Top with greens, tomato slices and second piece of bread. Halve each sandwich crosswise, if desired. Serve immediately.

prefer a mild onion flavor, stir them in at the last minute. Toast the bread and cook the fish just before presenting.

Technique Tips
A flexible narrow blade boning or fish filleting knife comes in handy when boning fish.

When boning fish, keep the knife edge slanted toward the bone.

Wine Selection
Chardonnay

Steamed Red Snapper
with Tomato Herb Sauce

4 Servings

Planning Ahead

The sauce can be prepared at any time during the day it is to be served. Steam the fish just before eating.

Technique Tips

Steaming is a simple technique provided you use a pie plate 1 inch smaller in diameter than the steamer and large enough to hold the item to be steamed in a single layer. I find a wok with a diameter of 13 inches or greater that is fitted with a domed lid to be the perfect tool for this task.

When steaming fish, adjust the heat so the water is simmering gently. Boiling water produces an aggressive steam that toughens the fish.

Variation

The Tomato Herb Sauce is a nice dressing to have in your repertoire for a cold shrimp salad.

Wine Selection

Chardonnay

Unlike the boring Pacific rockfish often incorrectly labeled red snapper, the real red snapper has very sweet tender white flesh. Whenever I have sampled this fish throughout the Gulf where it is caught, I have had it grilled or roasted on the bone with its skin left intact to seal and concentrate juices. Either way, the flavor has been outstanding. I've wanted to duplicate these preparations at the restaurant, but when I've found snapper, it has already been filleted, which makes it difficult to grill or roast without drying out. I tried steaming the fillets instead and found that this method not only kept the fish moist but gave it the clean savor that is particularly satisfying to dieters. When paired with this refreshing Tomato Herb Sauce, the dish earns raves from everyone trying to eat in a lighter, healthier manner.

TOMATO HERB SAUCE

1 tablespoon Dijon mustard

3 tablespoons red wine vinegar

3 tablespoons tomato juice

3 drops Maggi seasoning (optional)

3 tablespoons olive oil

2 tablespoons minced shallots

2 tablespoons fresh minced chives or green onions

2 tablespoons fresh minced tarragon or other fresh herb

¼ cup minced flat-leaf parsley

Salt and freshly ground black pepper to taste

4 (1¾ to 2 pounds total) red snapper, sea bass, mahi mahi or other whitefish fillets, about ½ inch thick

Salt and freshly ground black pepper to taste

3 tablespoons dry white wine

1 hard-cooked egg, finely chopped

For the Tomato Herb Sauce, whisk the mustard and vinegar to blend in a small bowl. Whisk in the tomato juice and Maggi. Whisk in the oil in a slow, thin stream. Mix in the shallots, chives, tarragon and parsley. Season with salt and pepper. (This can be prepared ahead, covered and set aside at room temperature.)

For the fish, arrange the fillets in a single layer, overlapping as little as possible, in a large pie plate or shallow dish that is at least 1 inch smaller in diameter than your wok or steamer. Sprinkle with salt, pepper and wine. Cover the dish with plastic wrap.

Fit the wok or steamer with a rack or overturned cup to support the pie plate. Fill it with enough water to come just below the level of the plate. Bring to a simmer. Place the covered pie plate on the rack. Cover and steam the fish until just opaque and easily pierced with a knife, for about 4 to 5 minutes, turning halfway.

To serve, pat the fish dry with paper towels. Transfer to 4 large plates with a large slotted spatula. Whisk 2 tablespoons of the fish cooking liquid (or to taste) into the sauce. Ladle the sauce over the fish. Sprinkle with egg. Serve immediately.

Sole with Avocado Salsa

T he first time I bought an avocado, I was 18 years old and just married. The fruit was very expensive in France, so it was a big splurge. My wife and I had no idea that this exotic *pear* became soft when ripe, so our splurge turned out to be a hard, flavorless squander. I remember being so angry that I took a hammer and smashed the pit. Some part of this green thing must taste good, I thought.

Now I live in California, the heart of creamy avocadoland. It was not, however, my new home that inspired this salsa but one of my favorite French sauces—the *Sauce Vierge*—a fresh mélange of tomatoes, olive oil and herbs.

AVOCADO SALSA

3 small (8 to 10 ounces total) Roma tomatoes, peeled, seeded and finely diced

2 tablespoons fresh minced cilantro or other fresh herb

1 tablespoon olive oil

2 tablespoons freshly squeezed lime or lemon juice or to taste

2 tablespoons minced red or green onion

1 ripe avocado, finely diced

Salt to taste

4 drops Tabasco

FISH

8 (1½ to 2 pounds total) Dover or other sole fillets

About 3 tablespoons olive oil

Salt and freshly ground black pepper to taste

Fresh cilantro sprigs for garnish (optional)

For the Avocado Salsa, mix the tomatoes with the cilantro, olive oil and lime juice in a small bowl. (This can be prepared ahead, covered and set aside at room temperature.)

Up to 1 hour before serving, add the onion and avocado to the salsa. Season with salt and Tabasco.

For the fish, preheat the oven to 325°F. Line a large baking sheet with parchment paper. Arrange the fish in a single layer on the prepared sheet, tucking the thinner ends of the fillets underneath. Brush with olive oil and season with salt and pepper. Bake until the fish is just opaque throughout for about 4 to 5 minutes.

Transfer 2 fillets to each of 4 plates. Arrange without overlapping. Spoon the salsa lengthwise down the center of each fillet. Place cilantro sprigs between the two if desired. Serve immediately.

Perch with Pistachios
and Escargot Butter

Perch has a nice texture, but it doesn't start out with a whole lot of taste. Adding the Escargot Butter gives it the missing touch. I used essentially the same flavorings for the Shrimp with Green Onion Basil Sauce (page 129) as I did here with the perch, yet these two dishes do not seem at all similar. By substituting parsley for the basil and adding pistachios and clam juice, I have substantially changed the character of this dish. This is an example of how you can use ingredients you like for totally different effects.

About 2 tablespoons olive oil

4 (1½ to 1¾ pounds total) freshwater perch fillets, patted dry

Salt and freshly ground black pepper to taste

ESCARGOT BUTTER

½ cup clam juice or fish stock

3 large cloves garlic, peeled and coarsely chopped

4 tablespoons (½ stick) chilled unsalted butter

¼ cup coarsely chopped flat-leaf parsley

Salt and freshly ground black pepper to taste

⅓ cup pistachio nuts, coarsely chopped

Place a heavy large nonstick skillet over medium heat and film with oil. Season the perch with salt and pepper. Add the fish skin side down to the skillet and cook until opaque throughout, for about 5 minutes total, turning halfway.

For the Escargot Butter, meanwhile boil the clam juice with the garlic in a heavy tiny saucepan until the liquid is reduced to 2 tablespoons. Whisk in 1 tablespoon butter off the heat. Return to very low heat and whisk in the remaining 3 tablespoons butter, 1 at a time, to form a thick creamy sauce. Stir in the parsley. Season with salt and pepper.

To serve, place the perch on 4 plates. Spoon the sauce over the perch. Sprinkle with pistachios. Serve immediately.

4 Servings

Planning Ahead
Prepare the Escargot Butter and fish just before serving.

Technique Tip
If drops of melted butter appear at any time while making the sauce, remove from heat and whisk in 1 tablespoon cold chopped butter.

Wine Selection
White Burgundy

Sea Bass Pochouse

4 Servings

Planning Ahead

The pochouse mixture can be prepared at any time during the day the fish is to be served. Spoon the mixture over the sea bass and cook just before presenting.

Technique Tips

It is not necessary to parboil the pearl onions before adding them to a sauce—an extra step—if the onions are cooked slowly in the sauce over low heat for about 20 minutes.

If the sauce becomes too thick before the onions are cooked, thin it with water.

When adding flour to a sauce, stir it over medium-low heat for 1 minute to eliminate its raw flavor.

Wine Selection

White Burgundy

Anticipating a trip to the Riviera, I began dreaming about fish soup two weeks before my departure. As soon as the airplane touched down in Nice, I went immediately to a restaurant a friend had recommended. "Bring on your bouillabaisse," I said, pounding the table with excitement. A fish soup soon appeared. It contained a variety of freshwater fish, broth, mushrooms, bacon and pearl onions—even some cream—but it bore no resemblance to the feast I was expecting. Where was the fish soup I knew and loved, the one with saffron, tomato and potato?

Once I tried this hearty fish soup, called a pochouse after the pocket where a fisherman keeps his catch, I loved it. Just think, I might never have made this serendipitous discovery had I not been in the wrong restaurant. Even funnier, I needn't have gone down South to form an acquaintance, for it is a specialty of Verdun, a northern city near my home town.

In my interpretation of pochouse, I've used a single piece of sea bass rather than chunks of different fish. I've also eliminated the butter and substantially reduced the cream, allowing delicate seafood flavors to come through. Though no traditionalist would recognize this as an authentic pochouse, for me it has the same spirit. After all, it still contains a lot of garlic. Once again.

POCHOUSE

¼ pound bacon, cut crosswise into ¼-inch pieces

16 pearl onions, peeled

1 large carrot, peeled and thinly sliced

¼ pound (about 6 medium) mushrooms, ends trimmed and thinly sliced

12 small cloves garlic, peeled

3 fresh thyme sprigs or 1 tablespoon dried thyme, crumbled

2 teaspoons flour

1½ cups dry white wine

½ cup heavy cream

Salt and freshly ground black pepper to taste

4 (1½ to 1¾ pounds) sea bass fillets, ½ inch thick

Salt and freshly ground black pepper to taste

Fresh thyme sprigs for garnish (optional)

Grilled bread or toast

For the pochouse, cook the bacon in a heavy large saucepan over medium heat until almost crisp, stirring occasionally. Add the onions, carrot, mushrooms and garlic; increase heat to medium-high and stir until the mushrooms are lightly browned, for about 5 minutes. Reduce heat to medium-low, add the thyme and flour and stir for 1 minute to cook the flour. Add the wine and cream, bring to a boil, then reduce heat and simmer gently until thickened to a saucelike consistency and the onions are cooked through, for about 20 minutes, stirring occasionally. Season with salt and pepper. (This can be prepared ahead and set aside at cool room temperature for about 2 hours or refrigerated until 1 hour before serving.)

To serve, preheat the oven to 325°F. Butter 1 large baking dish or 4 gratin dishes. Arrange the fish in the dish, season with salt and pepper and spoon over the pochouse mixture. Bake until the fish is just opaque, for about 5 minutes.

Divide among 4 large plates or place the gratin dishes on 4 plates. Garnish with thyme sprigs, if desired. Accompany with grilled bread. Serve immediately.

Mahi Mahi Rice Box

Planning Ahead

The rice must be cooked several hours ahead of the fish to cool complete-ly. The fish can be encased in the rice at any time dur-ing the day it is to be served. Bake just before presenting.

Technique Tips

To bring liquid quickly to a boil with the least ex-penditure of energy, cover the pot.

The rice must be com-pletely cooled or even par-tially chilled to adhere to fish. To hasten cooling, spread it out on a baking sheet in a thin layer and/or refrigerate.

If the fillets are not equally thick throughout, pound gently between 2 sheets of plastic wrap.

Individual rice packets can be made instead with smaller, thinner fillets. Ad-just cooking time accord-ingly so the fish doesn't overcook.

Like the Tangy Chicken with Shiitake Crust (page 172), the fish and rice box can also be assembled on two 20-inch sheets of plas-tic wrap that are placed perpendicular to each other like a Greek cross. The rice adheres more readily when compressed

In France, fish is often buried in a salt crust which hardens during baking to seal in its moisture. In this recipe, I've layered fish fillets with tomatoes and seasonings and encased them in cooked rice which absorbs the fish juices and tastes wonderful. (This is more than I can say for the salt.) The first time I tackled this rice-wrapped package, I used some lovely snapper fillets, but the next time I tried this dish, the size and shape of my fishmonger's mahi mahi were much more suited to its preparation. Salmon and sea bass would work well here, too. The trick is to pick two fillets—or one large one that can be halved—that are about the same length and thickness throughout.

RICE

3 cups chicken or fish stock or clam juice

¼ generous teaspoon saffron threads, crushed

1 tablespoon curry powder or to taste

2 large cloves garlic, peeled and chopped

2 tablespoons fresh minced mint or 2 teaspoons dried, crumbled

2 cups white long grain rice

Salt and freshly ground black pepper to taste

FISH

Olive oil

3 large tomatoes, sliced in ¼-inch-thick rounds

Salt and freshly ground black pepper to taste

3 medium cloves garlic, peeled and minced

3 tablespoons fresh minced mint or 1 tablespoon dried, crumbled

About 3 tablespoons olive oil

2 mahi mahi fillets (about 2 pounds total), ¾ inch thick, skinned and patted dry

Fresh mint sprigs for garnish (optional)

For the rice, preheat the oven to 375°F. Bring the stock to a boil in a heavy large ovenproof saucepan over medium-high heat. In a small bowl, stir 2 tablespoons of the stock into the saffron to dissolve, then return to the pan. Add the curry powder, garlic and dried mint (if using). Stir in the rice, return to a boil, cover and bake until the liquid is absorbed and the rice is tender and completely cooked, for about 18 to 20 minutes. Stir in the fresh mint (if using) and season with salt and pepper. Cool completely.

For the fish, lightly oil a large baking/serving dish. Place ½ of the rice in the dish. Using your hands to compact the rice, form a rectangle that is about 1½ inches larger than the fish fillets on all sides. Arrange ⅓ of the tomatoes down the length of the rectangle. Sprinkle the tomatoes with salt, pepper and ⅓ of the garlic and mint and drizzle with about 1 tablespoon olive oil. Place 1 fish fillet on top of the tomatoes. Place ½ of the remaining tomatoes, garlic, mint and olive oil on top of the fish fillet. Season with salt and pepper. Top with the remaining fillet with its tail in the opposite direction of that of the first fillet. Place the remaining tomatoes and seasonings on top of the fillet. Top all with the remaining rice. Cover the fish completely with rice on all sides, using your hands and a spatula to compact the mixture. Arrange any remaining tomatoes down the center of the rice or around the sides of the pan. Season with salt and pepper and drizzle with olive oil. (This can be prepared ahead and refrigerated until 1 hour before baking.)

To serve, preheat the oven to 400°F. Bake until a knife plunged into the rice mixture easily pierces the bottom of the fish, for about 15 to 20 minutes. Remove from the oven and let rest for 5 minutes. Slice into rectangular wedges using a serrated knife. Carefully transfer to 4 plates using a broad spatula. Garnish with mint sprigs, if desired. Serve immediately.

this way, but, unlike the small chicken breasts, these large fillets can become unwieldy, which is why I suggest forming them directly in the dish. Don't hesitate, though, to try the plastic, especially when you have an extra set of helping hands. To do so, gather up the plastic tightly around the fish as if wrapping a gift basket until the rice adheres to the fish. Then unwrap and carefully invert the package in a large baking dish and carefully remove the plastic.

Wine Selection
Chardonnay

Salmon Steak 'n Eggs

4 Servings

Planning Ahead

The salmon can be boned and prepped at any time during the day the dish is to be served. A sauce can be tackled according to its do-ahead directions. Cook the fish just before presenting.

Technique Tip

This technique for cooking salmon, a mixture of steaming and sautéing, allows the fish to stay moist while cooking evenly throughout. It works well with tuna and swordfish, too.

Wine Selection

White Burgundy or Pinot Noir, if served plain. If accompanied by a sauce, the ingredients in the sauce will determine whether a white or red wine is preferable. At brunch—or at any other time—think seriously about Champagne.

One day I was sort of spacing out in front of a salmon steak when it occurred to me that I should take advantage of its horseshoe shape. "Looks like a hole waiting to be filled," I said. I toothpicked the two legs together, forming an egg-shaped cavity. "There is steak and eggs, why not salmon steak and eggs?" I asked. Thus, the perfect brunch dish was born.

As with the salmon, you want to be careful not to overcook the egg because the yolk is much better when it is moist and runny. This can get a little tricky, but as long as the salmon steaks are about one half inch thick and their legs are each about four inches long, both the fish and the egg should come out evenly.

This dish is very nice served plain, but I prefer to accompany it with a sauce, if only for color. Almost all of the sauces paired with the seafood dishes in this book would go well, but if I had only one vote, I would choose the Basolivaise (page 64). If I had two, the Warm Asparagus with Tomato and Tarragon Sauce (page 44) would place second as a sauce side dish accompaniment.

4 (1½ to 1¾ pounds total) salmon steaks with 4-inch legs, ½ inch thick

2 tablespoons unsalted butter

2 tablespoons olive oil

4 large eggs, at room temperature

4 tablespoons water

Salt and freshly ground black pepper to taste

Carefully cut around and remove the bone at the center of the horseshoe of each salmon steak. Cut away a small portion of fish from the end of one leg, leaving the skin. Place the end of the second leg in that cavity and thread a toothpick through the two legs, forming an oval space to hold an egg. Pat the salmon steaks dry.

To serve, divide the butter and oil between 2 heavy large nonstick skillets over medium heat. Divide the salmon between the skillets, separating the legs with your fingers or tongs to form a smooth oval shape. Carefully break an egg into each oval. Divide the water between the skillets, pouring carefully around the salmon. Cover the skillets, reduce heat to medium-low and cook just until salmon is opaque and the egg white is set, for about 5 minutes (white film may develop over yolk). Carefully transfer the salmon steak with egg to 4 plates using a large spatula. Gently remove the toothpicks. Season with salt and pepper. Serve immediately with optional sauce.

Salmon and Cucumber Blanquette

T he word blanquette is mentioned most frequently in association with a veal stew, yet the word actually refers to the classic cream sauce that naps it. As wonderful a dish as Veal Blanquette is, I rarely think of pairing cream with meat today. When I want this type of rich binder, it is generally with fish as in this salmon and cucumber combo.

Though it is not considered nutritionally correct to use cream, I can't think of a better way to make a quick, easy sauce that tastes like heaven and feels like velvet. Besides, you don't have a sauce like this every day, and one-half an egg yolk and two tablespoons of cream are not a problem as long as you balance these ingredients with healthier ones over the next several days. *Vive la crème!*

CUCUMBERS

> 2 cucumbers, peeled, halved lengthwise, seeded and cut crosswise into ¼-inch-wide slices
>
> ½ cup clam juice or fish stock
>
> ½ cup heavy cream
>
> 2 egg yolks, at room temperature
>
> 1 teaspoon Dijon mustard
>
> 2 tablespoons freshly squeezed lemon juice
>
> 2 tablespoons fresh minced chives or green onions
>
> Salt and freshly ground black pepper to taste

SALMON

> 4 salmon (1½ to 2 pounds total) fillets, skinned, or steaks, ¾ inch thick, patted dry
>
> Salt and freshly ground black pepper to taste
>
> 1 ounce (¼ stick) unsalted butter
>
> 2 tablespoons water

For the cucumbers, cook the slices in a heavy medium skillet with the clam juice and cream over medium-high heat until tender when pierced with a knife, for about 5 minutes, stirring occasionally. (This can be prepared ahead, cooled, covered and set aside at room temperature for up to 2 hours or refrigerated.)

To finish the cucumber sauce, whisk the egg yolks, mustard and lemon juice to blend in a small bowl. Bring the cucumber mixture to a boil. Gradually whisk about ½ cup of the cucumber mixture into the egg yolk mixture, then gradually whisk this

(continued)

Planning Ahead

The cucumbers can be cooked at any time during the day the blanquette is to be served. The cucumber sauce can be finished several hours in advance. Cook the salmon just before presenting.

Technique Tips

If the cucumber mixture is allowed to boil after the egg yolks are added, the sauce will curdle.

To add fish cooking juices to the sauce, pour ¼ cup water into the skillet used for cooking the salmon and boil until reduced and thickened, scraping up any browned bits on the bottom of the pan. Strain into the cucumber sauce through a fine sieve, whisking to incorporate.

Wine Selection
Chardonnay

Seafood

mixture back into the cucumbers. Add chives and stir over low heat without boiling until sauce thickens, for about 7 minutes. Season with salt and pepper. (This can be prepared several hours ahead and kept warm in a widemouthed thermos.)

For the salmon, season the fish with salt and pepper. Melt the butter in a heavy large nonstick skillet over medium heat. Turn salmon in butter, add water, cover and simmer until opaque and just cooked through, for about 6 to 7 minutes total, turning halfway.

To serve, ladle cucumber sauce onto 4 plates. Place the salmon in the center of the sauce. Serve immediately.

■

Salmon with
Red Wine Shiitake Sauce

4 Servings

T he red wine serves as a liaison between the fish, which generally seeks more subdued partners, and the earthy shiitake mushrooms that I've sprinkled with several drops of toasted sesame oil to accentuate their heady, damp-forest scent. The overall effect is rich and satisfying—and heartier than you would expect from salmon. Any type of fresh mushroom can be substituted for the shiitake, but beware of reconstituted dried mushrooms that may overpower the dish.

Planning Ahead

The sauce base can be prepared 1 day ahead. The mushrooms can be sautéed at any time during the day the salmon is to be served. Cook fish just before presenting.

Technique Tips

Baking salmon slowly at a low temperature is another technique I use to cook salmon, tuna and swordfish to ensure they will stay moist and cook evenly throughout.

Unless you are working with cèpes, always sauté fresh mushrooms after slicing to seal in their juices.

RED WINE SHIITAKE SAUCE

> 1 teaspoon red wine vinegar
>
> 2 medium shallots, peeled and minced (about ¼ cup)
>
> 2 cups unsalted chicken or veal stock
>
> 1 cup Pinot Noir, Merlot or other dry, fruity red wine
>
> 2 cloves garlic, peeled and minced
>
> 1 large fresh thyme sprig or 2 tablespoons dried, crumbled
>
> 1 teaspoon peanut oil
>
> 1 teaspoon Oriental (toasted) sesame oil
>
> ¼ pound fresh shiitake or other fresh mushrooms, ends trimmed, thinly sliced and patted dry

Seafood

SALMON

4 (1½ to 2 pounds total) salmon steaks, about ¾ inch thick, patted dry

Salt and freshly ground black pepper to taste

About 2 tablespoons peanut or vegetable oil

2 tablespoons minced flat-leaf parsley

Wine Selection
Bordeaux or a wine you have used for the sauce.

For the Red Wine Shiitake Sauce, bring the vinegar to a boil with the shallots in a heavy medium saucepan over medium-high heat. Add the stock, wine, garlic and thyme. Boil until thickened to a saucelike consistency and reduced to about 1 cup. (This can be prepared 1 day ahead and refrigerated.)

Heat the peanut and sesame oils in a heavy medium skillet over medium-high heat. Add the mushrooms and sauté until golden brown, for about 4 to 5 minutes, stirring occasionally. (This can be prepared ahead, covered and set aside at room temperature.)

For the salmon, preheat the oven to 200°F. Pat salmon dry. Season with salt and pepper. Place a heavy large ovenproof nonstick skillet over medium-high heat and film with oil. Add the salmon and brown both sides lightly for about 1 minute. Transfer the skillet to the oven and bake until the salmon is just opaque throughout for about 15 minutes.

To serve, meanwhile, stir the sauce base over medium-high heat to rewarm. Discard the thyme sprig. Stir in the mushrooms. Place each salmon steak in the center of the plate and ladle the sauce over it until completely covered. Serve immediately.

Salmon with Couscous Crust and Tomato Leek Sauce

4 Servings

Planning Ahead

The tomato sauce can be made to the point indicated in the recipe 1 day in advance. The couscous can be prepared and the salmon coated at any time during the day fish is to be served. Cook the salmon and finish the sauce just before presenting.

Technique Tips

To remove salmon skin, cut a slit between the salmon flesh and skin at the tail end, insert a knife in the slit and, holding on to the skin with one hand, cut off in a sawing motion with the knife blade slanted toward the skin.

For coating foods, I like to use Wondra flour. Its texture is so fine it enables a coating to adhere, yet it does not contribute a floury flavor.

If the crust is cooked over too high a heat, it will burn or become hard and overly crunchy.

Wine Selection

Red Côtes du Rhône or Petite Sirah

When I prepare fish, I crisp the skin to contrast with its moist flesh. After carefully harmonizing these textures, I often find people removing the skin because they are squeamish about eating it. So much for my hard work. To restore this balance, I continually search for other ingredients to give fish a crisp crust that diners will like.

One day I was rubbing some couscous between my fingers, much as a Greek rolls his worry beads, when it dawned upon me that my angst had identified the perfect crust. I colored the couscous golden with saffron in honor of its Moroccan roots and cooked up a tomato sauce that went well with this spice. Salmon proved to be an ideal fish for coating because it is both rich enough to handle the dryness of this imposing crust and firm enough to hold it without cracking.

TOMATO LEEK SAUCE

2 tablespoons olive oil

1 medium leek (white and light green parts only), diced

1 cup dry white wine

2 teaspoons coriander seed, finely crushed

2 teaspoons paprika

2 tablespoons freshly squeezed lemon juice

12 oil-packed sun-dried tomatoes, drained and minced

Salt and freshly ground black pepper to taste

COUSCOUS CRUST

¾ cup water

⅛ teaspoon saffron threads, crushed to powder

1½ cups couscous

Salt and freshly ground black pepper to taste

4 skinned salmon fillets (1¾ to 2 pounds total) cut from center, about 1 inch thick

Salt and freshly ground black pepper to taste

About 1 cup Wondra (see Technique Tips) or all-purpose flour

1 egg

3 tablespoons olive oil

1 large tomato, peeled, seeded and diced

2 tablespoons minced flat-leaf parsley

For the Tomato Leek Sauce, heat the olive oil in a heavy large saucepan. Add the leek, cover and cook until translucent, for about 15 minutes, stirring occasionally. Add the wine and coriander. Increase heat to medium-high and simmer until thickened and reduced by about half. Whisk in paprika until dissolved. Stir in the lemon juice and sun-dried tomatoes. Season with salt and pepper. (This can be prepared ahead to this point, cooled, covered and set aside at room temperature for 6 to 8 hours or refrigerated overnight.)

For the crust, bring the water to a boil. Stir several tablespoons of boiling water into the saffron to dissolve, then pour the mixture back into the water. Remove from heat. Stir in the couscous. Cover and let rest for 5 minutes, stirring occasionally. Turn the couscous out onto a tray. Season with salt and pepper. Rub the grains between your fingers to separate them, then divide among four 6-inch-wide pieces of waxed paper.

Squeeze the couscous grains together on each paper, forming a flat layer, about ½ inch thick, that is slightly larger than the salmon fillets. (This can be prepared ahead and set aside at room temperature.)

To coat the salmon, line a tray with parchment paper. Pound the salmon gently between 2 pieces of waxed paper with a meat pounder to an even thickness; pat dry. Season with salt and pepper. Place flour in 1 soup plate. Break the egg into another and blend with a fork. Holding 1 salmon fillet on long edges flat side up, carefully dip the rounded side into the flour, coating completely. Brush off excess flour and dip the floured side into the egg, coating completely. Dip egg side down into couscous to coat, pressing firmly so couscous adheres. If bare spots remain, brush with egg and dip again. Place on prepared tray couscous side up. Repeat with remaining salmon fillets. (This can be coated ahead and set aside at cool room temperature for several hours or refrigerated until 1 hour before cooking.)

To cook, preheat the oven to 350°F. Heat a heavy large ovenproof nonstick skillet over medium-low heat until hot. Add the oil and heat, then add the salmon, crust side down. Cook for 4 minutes, shaking pan occasionally so the salmon doesn't stick. Turn the salmon over using a large spatula. Transfer the skillet to the oven and bake until the salmon is just opaque throughout for about 4 to 5 minutes.

To serve, place salmon on a plate, crust side up. Transfer the Tomato Leek Sauce to the salmon cooking skillet and rewarm by stirring over medium-high heat and scraping up browned bits in the bottom of the pan. Stir in the fresh tomato and parsley. Divide the sauce among 4 plates and top each with a piece of salmon. Serve immediately.

Salmon with Onion Ringlets

4 Servings

Planning Ahead

The Onion Sauce can be prepared 1 day in advance. The onion rings can be fried and the salmon coated at any time during the day the fish is to be served. Cook the salmon just before presenting.

Technique Tips

Fry the onion rings very slowly so they will stay crunchy when removed from the fryer. The frying is really a drying process. You can also bake the onions at 200°F until they are very dry and crisp, for about 1 hour.

To serve the onion rings hot for a garnish, cook ¼ of them only until golden brown when frying. Refry these onions until brown while the salmon is cooking.

Variation

Reserve any leftover sauce for topping a baked potato.

Wine Selection

Chardonnay

T his dish is actually more about onions than about salmon. Not that this vegetable doesn't taste terrific with the fish or form a direct link with it, thanks to the acid in the vinegar. But, basically, the salmon is along for a wild ride; a car seat for the onions to cling to. Chicken, veal or, even, steak would be other good vehicles for this onion trio.

Usually I start with the salmon or the central character on the plate and decide how I want to support it. In this case, though, my idea is to have something that tastes of pure onion in the manner of food prepared in Lyon: onion at its sweetest and crunchiest. Chopped for the crust, the onion here is reminiscent of bread crumbs. Fried for rings, it is an old junk food friend. Pureed for the sauce, the effect is one of silk and satin. If time is an issue, you can omit the sauce, but I wouldn't. It's too good.

ONION SAUCE

1 ounce (¼ stick) unsalted butter

3 small (about ¾ pound) Maui or other sweet onions, halved and thinly sliced (about 3 cups)

¼ cup Champagne vinegar or white wine vinegar

4 cups unsalted chicken stock

¼ cup heavy cream (optional)

Salt and freshly ground black pepper to taste

ONION CRUST

3 small (about ¾ pound) Maui or other sweet onions, sliced into ⅛-inch rings and separated

1 cup flour

Peanut oil (about 4 cups) for deep frying

SALMON

4 skinned salmon fillets (1½ to 2 pounds total), cut from center, about ¾ inch thick

Oil or butter

Salt and freshly ground black pepper to taste

About 1 cup flour

1 egg, blended with fork

For the Onion Sauce, melt the butter in a heavy large saucepan. Add the onions, cover and cook over medium-low heat until translucent, for about 10 minutes, stirring occasionally. Increase heat to medium-high and stir the onions until golden brown, for about 3 minutes. Pour in the vinegar and boil until reduced to a thick glaze, for about 1 minute. Add the chicken stock and simmer until the mixture is reduced to 1½ cups, for about 40 minutes, stirring occasionally. Puree the onion mixture in a blender until very smooth, pulsing on/off and stopping to scrape down the sides of the container. Clean the saucepan, if necessary, and return the sauce to the pan. Add the cream. Season with salt and pepper. (This can be prepared ahead, covered and set aside at cool room temperature for several hours or refrigerated overnight.)

For the crust, toss the onion rings in the flour. Line a large baking sheet with paper towels. Heat the oil in a deep fryer, wok or large saucepan to 325°F or until bubbles rise around a chopstick immersed in the oil. A handful at a time, shake off excess flour, immerse onions in oil and fry slowly until golden brown and very crunchy, for about 20 minutes, turning halfway. Transfer the onions to the prepared sheet to drain using a slotted spatula or tongs. Coarsely chop ¾ of the onions and place them on a tray. Reserve the remaining fried onion rings separately for garnish. (This can be prepared ahead and set aside at room temperature.)

For the salmon, oil or butter a heavy large baking sheet. Pound the salmon gently between 2 pieces of waxed paper with a meat pounder to an even thickness. Season with salt and pepper. Place the flour in 1 soup plate. Blend the egg in another. Holding 1 salmon fillet on the long edges flat side up, carefully dip the rounded side into the flour, coating completely. Brush off excess flour and dip the floured side into the egg, coating completely. Dip egg side down into the coarsely chopped onion rings, pressing firmly so the onions adhere. If bare spots remain, brush with egg and dip again. Place on the prepared sheet onion side up. Repeat with remaining salmon fillets. (This can be coated ahead and set aside at cool room temperature for several hours or refrigerated until 1 hour before baking.)

To serve, preheat the oven to 200°F. Bake the salmon until just opaque throughout, for about 20 minutes. Stir the sauce over medium-high heat to rewarm.

Ladle the sauce into the center of 4 plates. Arrange each salmon fillet in the center of the sauce. Sprinkle with reserved onion rings. Serve immediately.

Tuna Tomato Tart

2 Main-course
or 4 First-course
Servings

Planning Ahead

The onions can be cooked, the vinaigrette prepared, the puff pastry rolled and the other ingredients prepped at any time during the day the tart is to be served. Bake the pastry, assemble the tart, and cook the tuna just before presenting.

Technique Tips

When baking puff pastry, you need to cook it slowly until it is completely dry and crisp in the interior. So much work has gone into creating the layers, it would be a shame to prevent them from rising by undercooking the pastry.

Although the darker, oilier portions of tuna are perfectly safe to eat, I generally trim them off for aesthetic reasons.

Wine Selection

Chardonnay

A t first glance, a recipe named Tuna Tomato Tart may not seem like another variation on an onion tart, but that is exactly what this is. Actually it's a combination of a pissaladière, the Provençal onion and anchovy puff pastry tart, and the *pan bagnat*, a tuna tomato sandwich—also with anchovies—from the same region. Since people *say* they're not crazy about these little fish—I've seen many anchovy haters happily downing them when they weren't visible—I chose tuna instead to garnish the onions. More substantial than either of its inspirations, this tart makes a very satisfying main course as well as a first course. By the way, I've rolled it without a rim, so it may look more like a pillow than a pie shell.

ONIONS

About 2 tablespoons olive oil

2 large onions, peeled, halved and thinly sliced

2 large cloves garlic, peeled and minced

1 tablespoon fresh minced thyme or 2 pinches of dried thyme, crumbled

½ teaspoon sugar

1½ tablespoons red wine vinegar

1 teaspoon soy sauce

Salt and freshly ground black pepper to taste

VINAIGRETTE

1 tablespoon balsamic vinegar

1 tablespoon red wine vinegar

3 tablespoons olive oil

1 large clove garlic, peeled and minced

Salt and freshly ground black pepper to taste

1 8-ounce frozen puff pastry sheet, defrosted 2 hours in the refrigerator

¾ to 1 pound fresh tuna fillet, about ½ inch thick, patted dry and sliced ¼ inch thick

Salt and freshly ground black pepper to taste

2 medium (8 to 9 ounces total) tomatoes, thinly sliced

2 tablespoons fresh minced basil or other fresh herb

Seafood

For the onions, place a heavy large nonstick skillet over medium-low heat and film with oil. Add the onions, cover and cook until very tender, for about 20 minutes, stirring occasionally. Add the garlic, thyme, sugar, vinegar and soy sauce. Cover and cook for 5 minutes. Season with salt and pepper. (This can be prepared ahead, cooled, covered and set aside at room temperature.)

For the vinaigrette, place the balsamic and red wine vinegars in a small bowl. Whisk in the olive oil in a slow, thin stream. Add the garlic and season with salt and pepper. (This can be prepared ahead, covered and set aside at room temperature.)

For the puff pastry, line a large baking sheet with parchment paper. Roll out the puff pastry on a lightly floured surface into a 12½-inch square. Cut out a 12-inch circle using a sharp pastry wheel or knife and a plate as guide. Roll the pastry up on a rolling pin and transfer to the prepared sheet. Cover with plastic wrap and refrigerate for at least 30 minutes.

To cook the pastry, preheat the oven to 400°F 45 minutes before serving the tart. Remove the plastic, prick the pastry all over with a fork and bake until well puffed and brown, for about 30 to 40 minutes. Remove it from the oven, leaving it on the baking sheet. Preheat the broiler.

To serve, meanwhile, stir the onions over medium-high heat to rewarm. Spread them over the baked pastry, leaving a ½-inch border. Arrange the tuna over the onions. Season with salt and pepper. Arrange the tomatoes over the tuna in concentric circles. Brush the tomatoes lightly with the vinaigrette and sprinkle with ⅓ of the basil. Broil 3 to 4 inches below the heat source until tuna is rare or just barely opaque for about 4 to 5 minutes. Spoon the vinaigrette lightly over the tomatoes and tuna. Sprinkle with the remaining basil. Divide the tart into 4 wedges using a large knife. Transfer the wedges to 2 or 4 plates. Serve immediately.

Tunaburgers

4 Servings

Planning Ahead

The tuna patties, condiments and sauce can be prepared at any time during the day they are to be served. Cook the burgers just before presenting.

Technique Tip

For the finest texture, use well-chilled tuna or freeze it for 30 minutes before chopping. Chop it by hand with a large sharp knife rather than with a food processor or meat grinder which will make the fish too dense and compact.

Wine Selection

Sauvignon Blanc

O ne day the tuna I was chopping for tuna tartare looked very much like ground beef to me. "Michel, why don't you make a tunaburger?" I asked myself. I did just that and when I tasted it, I said: "Wow! This is a great sandwich!"

At the restaurant, we serve the burger on a baked-to-fit brioche bun, but any soft spongy roll will work. (One bite of a hard roll and the fish will go all over.) For condiments, I use a flavored mayonnaise or the olive oil, vinegar and tomato that moisten the *pan bagnat* ("bathed bread") sandwich made in the South of France where the art of using *old bread* is practiced. Between these Tunaburgers and my Tuna Tomato Tart (page 154), this popular Niçoise sandwich has had quite an influence on my cooking.

1¾ to 2 pounds fresh well-chilled tuna fillet

4 cloves garlic, minced

¼ cup olive oil

4 anchovies, minced

¼ cup fresh minced basil

Salt and freshly ground black pepper to taste

Sesame Mayonnaise (page 108), Lily Sauce (page 137) or olive oil and red wine vinegar

4 brioche or other soft hamburger buns, halved

1 large tomato, very thinly sliced

4 leaves lettuce (optional)

3 tablespoons olive oil

To form the Tunaburgers, line a baking sheet with waxed paper. Trim off the dark oily portions from the tuna. Thinly slice the tuna, then chop it using a large sharp knife until the fish is the texture of hamburger and presses into a compact ball. Mix in the garlic, olive oil, anchovies, basil, salt and pepper. Taste and adjust for seasoning.

Divide the mixture into 4 balls and form into 1-inch-thick patties. Place the patties on the baking sheet. (This can be prepared ahead, covered and set aside at cool room temperature for 1 hour or refrigerated until 30 minutes before cooking.)

To cook, prepare the Sesame Mayonnaise or Lily Sauce, if using. Heat the buns, if desired. Spread the buns with the sauce or douse with oil and vinegar. Line half with tomato and lettuce.

Meanwhile, heat 3 tablespoons of oil in a heavy large nonstick skillet over medium-high heat until almost smoking. Add the tuna patties and cook for about 1 minute per side for rare; about 1½ minutes for medium-rare. Place the burgers in the buns, the buns on the plates and serve immediately.

Tuna Schnitzel

4 Servings

Like its Austrian namesake, Wiener schnitzel (breaded veal), this is a quick, easy in/out act, but it is unusual in that it is tuna given the bread crumb treatment here. With its crunchy crust a counterpoint to the juicy fish, this dish is delectable when cooked right. Overdone, it becomes a dried-out disaster unless you like cotton batting.

1 cup bread crumbs

Salt and freshly ground black pepper to taste

4 (1¾ to 2 pounds total) tuna fillets, ¾ inch thick, patted dry

Dijon mustard

¼ cup olive oil

To bread the tuna, line a baking sheet with waxed paper. Place the bread crumbs in a soup or pie plate. Season the bread crumbs with salt and pepper, mixing well. One at a time, brush both sides of the tuna fillets with mustard. Dip the tuna into the bread crumbs, coating completely and patting so the crumbs adhere. Transfer to the prepared tray. (This can be prepared ahead, covered with plastic wrap and set aside at cool room temperature for several hours or refrigerated until 1 hour before cooking.)

To cook, preheat the oven to 200°F. Heat the oil in a heavy large ovenproof nonstick skillet over medium-high heat. Add the tuna fillets and brown both sides, for about 3 minutes. Transfer the fillets to a oven-resistant dish and bake until just opaque, about 8 to 10 minutes.

To serve, divide the tuna fillets among 4 plates. Serve immediately.

Planning Ahead

The tuna can be breaded at any time during the day it is to be served. Cook the fish just before presenting.

Technique Tip

Breading can be a messy job, with the cook coming out with more breading than the fish. To do the job neatly without sticking to yourself, use only one hand to both hold the fish and to dip it into the flour, egg and bread crumbs.

Wine Selection

Alsatian Riesling

Tuna with Broccoli
and Anchovy Butter

4 Servings

Planning Ahead

The anchovy butter can be prepared several days ahead and refrigerated or frozen up to a month in advance. The broccoli can be cooked at any time during the day it is to be served. The dish can be assembled up to 1 hour before cooking. Broil just before presenting.

Technique Tips

The Anchovy Butter can be doubled or tripled and refrigerated or frozen for future use in this or other dishes.

The components can also be assembled in 4 gratin dishes. To serve, place the dishes on 4 plates.

Wine Selection

Merlot

Like George Bush, I've never much cared for broccoli, especially the mushy way my mother prepared it. Tuna was never high on my list, either. Once you have memories of badly treated food, it's hard to forget them. It seems, though, that we have more good products than we have good cooks. Recently I had a sensational broccoli dish with anchovies and Parmesan cheese. This reminded me of the tuna served with anchovy butter in the South of France. I then put tuna together with anchovies, broccoli and Parmesan and found a combination I adore.

ANCHOVY BUTTER

> **3 ounces (¾ stick) unsalted butter, at room temperature**
>
> **6 anchovy fillets, minced**
>
> **3 pounds whole broccoli heads or broccoli florets**
>
> **¼ cup (1 ounce) freshly grated Parmesan cheese**
>
> **Salt and freshly ground black pepper to taste**
>
> **4 (1½ to 1¾ pounds total) tuna fillets, ½ inch thick, patted dry**
>
> **Freshly ground black pepper**

For the Anchovy Butter, mix the butter and anchovies together in a small bowl. (This can be prepared ahead and refrigerated for several days or frozen for about 1 month. Finally chop and bring to room temperature before using.)

For the broccoli, cut broccoli florets from stalks and peel them. Peel the stalks and slice them into ¼-inch-thick coins. Cook all the broccoli in a large pot of boiling water until crisp-tender, for about 5 minutes. Drain, reserving ½ cup cooking liquid. Chop the broccoli coarsely and place it in a 9- × 13-inch baking dish. (This can be prepared ahead, covered with plastic wrap and set aside at room temperature.)

To assemble, add the reserved cooking liquid, ¼ cup Parmesan, ¾ of the Anchovy Butter, salt and pepper to the broccoli and mix well. Arrange the tuna fillets over the broccoli in a single layer. Spread the remaining Anchovy Butter over the fillets. Season with pepper. (This can be prepared ahead, recovered and set aside at cool room temperature for up to 1 hour.)

To serve, preheat the broiler. Broil the tuna 3 to 4 inches below the heat source for 3 minutes. Continue broiling 1 to 2 minutes or until the tuna is just rare. Transfer the fish to 4 plates. Spoon the broccoli around tuna. Serve immediately.

Tunados with White Bean Chili Sauce

4 Servings

I used to make a chili with beans and bite-size pieces of tuna, but my customers would talk so much, the fish would overcook on their plates. Once I found that it was too hard to keep a thin tuna slice rare, I refined the dish and served the sauce with a thicker medallion. Since an equivalent piece of beef is called a *tournedo, voilà* my *tunado.* Tuna is the beef of the ocean for me; a steak to serve rare. Please at least try it this way. If you don't like it, you can always cook it longer.

I serve this chili without beans, but you can add them, if you wish, as part of the sauce or on the side, mixed with a vinaigrette. You can also accompany it with a bean dish, such as the White Bean Belly Dancer Rolls (page 274). In anticipation of making this White Bean Chili Sauce, I freeze all leftover bean cooking liquid. When I want to prepare it, I simply strain the defrosted liquid if necessary, and then boil it down until I have a cup of thickened juices. Now you know why I'm always full of beans.

Planning Ahead
The white bean cooking liquid for the sauce base can be collected several months in advance in the freezer. The sauce can be prepared at any time during the day the fish is to be served. Cook the tuna just before presenting.

WHITE BEAN CHILI SAUCE

1 cup strained thickened white bean cooking liquid

½ cup clam juice, fish stock or unsalted chicken stock

1 teaspoon chili powder

¼ teaspoon red wine vinegar

Generous pinch of cayenne pepper

Salt to taste

TUNADOS

2 tablespoons unsalted butter

4 (1½ to 2 pounds total) tuna fillets, ¾ inch thick

2 tablespoons water

Salt and freshly ground black pepper to taste

1 tablespoon fresh minced chives or green onions

1 medium tomato, peeled, seeded and finely diced

(continued)

Since the bean cooking liquid is the thickener for sauce, it must be thickened before using. If it hasn't already thickened while cooking from the starch of the beans, boil enough liquid down to yield 1 cup of thick sauce before using.

Wine Selection

Sauvignon Blanc

For the White Bean Chili Sauce, bring the thickened bean cooking liquid, clam juice and chili powder to a boil in a heavy small saucepan over medium-high heat. Reduce heat and simmer until thickened to a saucelike consistency, for about 2 minutes. Stir in the vinegar, cayenne and salt. (This can be prepared ahead, covered and set aside at cool room temperature for several hours or refrigerated until serving.)

For the Tunados, trim the dark oily parts off the tuna and pat the fillets dry. Melt the butter in a heavy large nonstick skillet over medium heat. Season the tuna with salt and pepper, turn in the butter, add water, cover and cook until opaque, about 4 minutes.

To serve, reheat the sauce by stirring over medium-high heat. Stir in the chives and tomato. Ladle the sauce into the center of 4 plates. Tilt the plates, covering with sauce. Place the tuna in the center. Serve immediately.

Lacquered Swordfish with Green Onions

4 Servings

Planning Ahead

The green onions can be prepared at any time during the day the swordfish is to be served. Coat the fish with the pepper mixture and cook just before presenting.

Technique Tip

Use a ventilation fan while caramelizing the swordfish so your kitchen doesn't become smoky.

When I had my pastry shop, I used to eat at the Japanese restaurant next door almost every day. One of the dishes I liked best was a broiled eel that had been caramelized, a technique I've used here with swordfish. Though dipped in sugar, the fish is not sweet. It has a nutty flavor and a woody aroma that is strangely reminiscent of burnt toast. Now this may not sound very appealing, but when combined with the other haunting flavors and textures of this dish, the end result is fantastic, and one that is very much out of the ordinary.

GREEN ONIONS

   1 tablespoon sesame seeds

   1 tablespoon peanut oil

   1 teaspoon Oriental (toasted) sesame oil

   1-inch piece fresh gingerroot, peeled and finely slivered

   2 large bunches green onions (white plus 3 inches green part only), cut into 1½- × ¼-inch strips

   1 tablespoon water

   2 teaspoons soy sauce

SWORDFISH

Wine Selection
Zinfandel or German slightly sweet Riesling

¼ cup sugar

½ teaspoon freshly ground black pepper

4 (1½ to 2 pounds total) swordfish fillets, 1 inch thick

2 to 4 tablespoons peanut oil

¼ cup soy sauce

For the green onions, stir the sesame seeds in a heavy small dry skillet over medium heat until brown. Transfer to a small glass. Heat the peanut and sesame oils in the same skillet with the ginger over medium-high heat. Add the green onion strips and stir-fry until almost tender, for about 1 minute. Add the water and soy sauce and stir-fry until tender, but still crunchy, for about 1 minute. (This can be prepared ahead, cooled, covered and set aside at cool room temperature.)

For the swordfish, mix the sugar and pepper in a large soup plate. Dip one side of the swordfish in the mixture. Transfer to a large tray. Immediately, place 1 very large or 2 smaller heavy nonstick skillets over medium-high heat and add the oil. Add the swordfish and cook until the bottom is browned and caramelized, for about 3 minutes. Pour the soy sauce into the skillet. Cover the skillet and continue cooking until the fish is glazed and just opaque throughout, for about 1 to 2 minutes.

To serve, rewarm the green onions by stirring over medium-high heat. Transfer the swordfish to 4 plates. Spoon the onions over the swordfish. Sprinkle each with reserved toasted sesame seeds. Serve immediately.

Grilled Swordfish with
Crispy Tomato Onion Relish

4 Servings

Planning Ahead

The Crispy Tomato Onion Relish can be completed several days in advance while each of its components can be prepared separately over the course of 1 day or 2. If the relish is made all at one time, a practical approach is to prepare the tomato pulp while the onions are cooking and then to start cooking the tomato quarters while the pulp is simmering. Marinate the swordfish for about 4 hours and grill it just before serving.

Technique Tip

Use the largest tomatoes available for this relish.

Variations

Instead of frying the tomato quarters for the relish, grill them until blackened over charcoal or broil them 4 inches below the heat source.

Crispy Tomato Onion Relish also makes a wonderful sauce for 1 pound of pasta, such as fusilli, particularly when topped with a generous sprinkling of grated Pecorino or Parmesan cheese.

Being raised on mackerel and herring, the fish of the poor, I did not experience swordfish until I was quite grown-up. What a treat. Swordfish, like tuna, is a fish that is close to beef in its meaty flavor and texture, and it tastes best when eaten rare.

Overcooking will not be a problem, though, if you buy a swordfish steak that is about 1 inch thick. This is an ideal size for grilling, too, because you won't have to worry about the fish falling through the grate, a difficulty I had while learning how to use an American-style brazier. On one occasion, I lost so many trout fillets, I had to go buy more in order to have enough food for dinner.

The grilled swordfish can be successfully paired with most of the other sauces in this chapter, but I think this crisp relish with its fried tomato is quite special, even if I did get carried away with its technique. I like it so much, in fact, that I double or triple the recipe each time I make it to have on hand for an all-purpose barbecue sauce.

CRISPY TOMATO ONION RELISH

2 tablespoons olive oil

1 small (6 to 8 ounces) red onion, peeled and diced (about 1¼ cups)

2 pounds (about 5 large) tomatoes, cored and quartered

1 large clove garlic, peeled

Olive oil

2 tablespoons sun-dried tomato (dry or oil pack) julienne

Salt and freshly ground black pepper to taste

SWORDFISH

2 teaspoons fresh minced tarragon or other fresh herb

1 tablespoon fresh minced thyme or 1 teaspoon dried, crumbled

1 tablespoon minced flat-leaf parsley

½ cup olive oil

4 (1½ to 2 pounds total) swordfish fillets, ¾ to 1 inch thick, patted dry

Salt and freshly ground black pepper to taste

For the Crispy Tomato Onion Relish, heat the oil in a heavy large saucepan over medium-low heat. Add the onion, cover and cook until translucent, for about 10 minutes, stirring occasionally. Transfer the onion to a large bowl; do not wash the pan.

Meanwhile, line a baking sheet with paper towels. Cut the inside pulp, seeds and ribs out of each tomato quarter over a bowl, leaving the skin and flesh. Place the trimmed tomato quarters on the prepared sheet as finished. Pour the tomato pulp mixture into the saucepan used for the onions and add the garlic. Bring to a boil, lower the heat and simmer until the pulp is very tender and soft enough to puree, for about 15 to 20 minutes, mashing occasionally. Strain the cooked tomato mixture into the bowl with the onions through a fine sieve, pressing on the ingredients. Return the mixture to the saucepan.

Meanwhile, heat ½ inch of oil in a large deep skillet over medium-high heat until water droplets sizzle when sprinkled over the oil. Pat the tomato quarters dry with paper towels, add them to the oil without crowding (about 6 at a time) and brown, for about 10 minutes total, turning halfway. Return to the paper-lined tray with a slotted spoon. Repeat with the remaining tomato quarters.

Add the cooked tomato quarters and sun-dried tomatoes to the saucepan with the tomato puree mixture. Bring to a boil, then lower heat and simmer for 15 minutes, stirring occasionally. Season with salt and pepper. (This can be prepared ahead, cooled, covered and set aside at cool room temperature for 4 to 6 hours, or refrigerated for several days or frozen for several months.) Remove from the refrigerator 30 minutes ahead to serve cold or several hours ahead to serve at room temperature.)

For the swordfish, mix the tarragon, thyme and parsley in a large baking dish with the oil. Add the swordfish. Cover and refrigerate for 3 hours, turning after 2 hours. Remove from the refrigerator and let marinate at room temperature for 1 more hour.

To serve, preheat the broiler or grill. Season the fish with salt and pepper. Place on a tray and broil 4 inches below the heat source or grill until barely opaque through-out, for about 6 to 7 minutes total, turning halfway. Place the swordfish on 4 plates. Reheat the relish, if desired, by stirring over medium-high heat or serve tepid or chilled, spooning a dollop alongside the fish. Serve immediately.

Poultry

Probably no category of food offers as many preparation possibilities as poultry. The only way I don't like to fix it, in fact, is on the barbecue where it becomes tough and dry. Given how popular grilled chicken is today, I suspect I'm alone in this opinion. I prefer to poach poultry in plastic, as I have done with the Turkey Corn Dogs (page 194) and Chicken Medallions with Toasted Sesame Slaw (page 108). I know of no better way to keep this meat as juicy and succulent.

Another technique of mine turns a poultry breast into a steak that is crusty on the outside and moist within. To prepare it this way, I cook the breast under a weight over medium-high heat. This may require a bit of legerdemain, but it sounds a lot weirder than it works. For detailed instructions, see Chicken and Green Bean Salad (page 110).

To hasten the preparation of a whole bird and crackle its skin, I remove the backbone and open the bird up as in the Duck Crapaudine with Dried Cherries (page 198). Poultry also responds well to being cooked with a crust. Both shiitake (page 172) and kataifi (page 178) crusts seal in poultry juices while protecting the meat from desiccation. These toppings add intriguing flavors as well. Poultry's neutrality permit it to taste fabulous with a host of exotic ingredients. Celery root, tea and bok choy are just a few of the unique partners I've found for it.

With myriad possibilities for cooking and seasoning poultry, one of my favorite preparations is still the old-fashioned method of roasting a bird. I just wish we'd have more old-fashioned birds to roast. A muscular old rooster that needed hours to become tender developed some savor and complexity. Today's squishy birds are in and out of the pan faster than we can mince their seasonings. This may bode well for speed, but it doesn't do a whole lot for taste. With more and more birds running freely around, quality does, however, happily seem to be improving.

Poultry preparation could be extremely economical if people would buy the whole bird and cut it up themselves. Boning at home also gives you neater pieces and more control over what you actually get. You may, for example, be able to buy only two drumsticks or two thighs when you really want a drumstick with thigh attached. If you do your own boning, you'll have lots of bones to throw into the stock pot and trimmings to grind for filling ravioli or crêpes. The meat will remain juicier if it is not skinned and boned until it is used. Some of the naked legs and breasts being marketed today lose everything they ever had to brag about before they even leave the store.

While we're on the subject, what is half a breast? I sure have seen some strange labels in my supermarket. For the record, every bird—unless it is a freak or has had cosmetic surgery—has two whole breasts that are joined by a breastbone. (Those "parts missing" poultry are another story.) When you buy a package of boned breasts, you are getting whole breasts. These, in turn, can be cut in half at home, but I've never seen them marketed this way. That ends my anatomy lesson for today.

Nonfried Fried Chicken Breasts
with Mustard and Tarragon

I 've been experimenting with ways to create a crisp fried chicken without triggering high-fat alarms. Replacing the chicken skin with bread crumbs for crunch is one solution. Dijon mustard, long a favorite French-homestyle technique for slathering poultry, builds strength of character here, with the tarragon adding a perky note.

1 cup bread crumbs

2 large cloves garlic, peeled and minced

1 tablespoon minced flat-leaf parsley

1 tablespoon fresh minced tarragon or other fresh herb or
    1 teaspoon dried, crumbled

Salt and freshly ground black pepper to taste

1 large egg

3 tablespoons Dijon mustard

¾ cup all-purpose flour

4 chicken breasts, boned, skinned, trimmed, tendon removed and
    patted dry

¼ cup olive oil

4 fresh tarragon sprigs for garnish (optional)

4 Servings

Planning Ahead
The chicken can be breaded the day before it is cooked. Bake it just before serving.

Technique Tip
Breading can be a messy job with the cook coming out with more breading than the chicken. To do the job neatly without sticking to yourself, use only one hand to both hold the chicken and to dip it into the flour, egg and bread crumbs.

Wine Selection
Sauvignon Blanc

To bread the chicken, line a baking sheet with waxed paper. Mix the bread crumbs with the garlic, parsley, tarragon, salt and pepper in a soup plate. Beat the egg with the mustard, salt and pepper in a second soup plate. Place flour in a third. Pound the chicken lightly with a meat pounder between 2 pieces of plastic wrap to an even thickness. One at a time, dredge the chicken breasts in flour, shaking off excess. Dip in egg and then in herbed bread crumbs, covering completely and patting so the crumbs adhere. Transfer to the prepared tray. (This can be prepared ahead, covered with plastic and set aside at cool room temperature for several hours or refrigerated overnight.)

To serve, preheat the oven to 350°F. Heat the oil in a heavy large nonstick ovenproof skillet over medium-high heat. Add the chicken and brown well on both sides. Transfer to the oven and bake until the chicken is just cooked through and feels barely firm when pressed, for about 6 to 7 minutes, turning halfway. Transfer the chicken to 4 plates. Garnish with tarragon, if desired. Serve immediately.

Chicken and Sweet Pea Ravioli

**Makes 46 Ravioli
to Serve 8 to 10**

Planning Ahead

The filling can be prepared and ravioli assembled 1 day in advance. The sauce can be made at any time during the day it is to be served. Cook the ravioli just before presenting.

Technique Tips

This is one of the few instances when I actually come out evenly with the right amount of filling for the number of available wrappers. The recipe can, however, be halved with the remaining egg roll wrappers frozen for another dish.

To serve the ravioli quickly while hot to this large a group, it's helpful to have an extra set of hands. Commandeer a friend to cook the ravioli while you heat the sauce, ladle it onto plates and arrange the cooked packages.

If the sauce is heated too long, it will lose its sprightly green color.

Wine Selection

Champagne or
Chardonnay

T his recipe dates from my pea period. Why another dish with peas, you might ask? Why not? They have a fresh, sweet taste, a bright, beautiful color and a sound nutritional profile. Their starchiness gives the sauce richness without cream and depth without a binder. As a puree, the peas also baste the white chicken meat, which tends to be dry.

In this dish, I've used the pea sauce on ravioli, a universally beloved pasta that is too time-consuming to be tackled frequently at home. With people's desire for speed and convenience in mind, I used egg roll wrappers for my stuffed squares, which means they can be wrapped and rolled in no time. Best of all, this light delicate pasta is fun to play with.

FILLING

2 chicken breasts (about 1½ pounds total), boned, skinned, trimmed, tendon removed and cut into 1-inch pieces

1 cup frozen baby peas, defrosted

4 medium cloves garlic, peeled

¼ cup olive oil

1 egg

Salt and freshly ground black pepper to taste

2 tablespoons fresh minced chives or green onions

1½-pound package egg roll wrappers (twelve 7- × 7-inch sheets)

1 egg, blended with fork

4 to 5 ounces goat cheese

SWEET PEA SAUCE

1 ounce (¼ stick) unsalted butter

1 large shallot, peeled and chopped

1 clove garlic, peeled and minced

2 tablespoons Champagne vinegar or white wine vinegar

2 cups unsalted chicken stock

1 cup frozen baby peas, defrosted

1 cup unsalted chicken stock

Salt and freshly ground black pepper to taste

About 1¼ cups (about 5 ounces) freshly grated Parmesan or Pecorino cheese

About ½ cup fresh minced chives or green onions

For the filling, place the chicken in the freezer for 30 minutes. Process immediately in a food processor, pulsing on/off until the chicken is finely ground and forms a ball. Add the peas, garlic, oil, egg, salt and pepper to the container. Process until the mixture forms a smooth puree. Add the chives and process just until mixed in. (This can be prepared several hours before assembling ravioli, covered and refrigerated.)

To assemble, line 4 large baking sheets with parchment paper. Brush the starch off 1 egg roll wrapper with a brush, then brush 1 side of the wrapper with the blended egg using a second brush. Place 4 dabs (about 2 teaspoonsful each) of chicken mixture (for 4 ravioli) on the wrapper, spaced equidistantly. Top each with about ½ teaspoon of goat cheese, pressing to flatten the mixture. Brush the starch off the second egg roll wrapper using the first dry brush. Place over the first wrapper, stretching to fit as necessary. Press along the edges and around the filling well to seal. Trim the edges and divide the egg roll sheets into 4 ravioli using a fluted cutter. Transfer the ravioli to a baking sheet in a single layer. Repeat with the remaining filling and egg roll wrappers. (This can be prepared ahead, covered with plastic wrap and set aside at cool room temperature for several hours or refrigerated overnight.)

For the Sweet Pea Sauce, melt the butter in a heavy large saucepan over medium heat. Add the shallot and garlic and stir until translucent, for about 3 minutes. Add the vinegar and boil until it is absorbed. Add 2 cups chicken stock and boil until reduced to ⅔ cup.

Meanwhile, puree the peas and 1 cup chicken stock in a blender until smooth. Add the shallot mixture to the pea puree and process until very smooth, for about 4 minutes, stopping to scrape down the sides of the container. Season with salt and pepper. Strain into a clean saucepan through a fine sieve if a finer texture is desired. (This can be prepared ahead, covered and set aside at cool room temperature for several hours or refrigerated.)

To serve, line large baking sheets with paper towels. Fill a large deep wide pot with water and bring it to a boil. Add the ravioli in batches and cook until they float to the surface, for about 3 to 4 minutes. Transfer to the prepared baking sheets in a single layer using a slotted spatula. Meanwhile, reheat the Sweet Pea Sauce just to warm over medium-high heat and ladle some into the center of 8 to 10 soup or dinner plates. Arrange the ravioli around the edge of the plates. Sprinkle with Parmesan and chives. Serve immediately.

Chicken Mushroom Trilogy

4 Servings

Planning Ahead

The chicken should be marinated for at least 4 hours or, preferably, overnight. The mushroom ragoût can be prepared at any time during the day the chicken is to be served. Reheat the ragoût and cook the chicken just before presenting.

Technique Tips

Cooking the chicken under a weight over medium-high heat results in a flattened bird that is crusty on the outside and moist within like a steak.

The exact cooking time will depend on the thickness of the breasts and the type of skillet. Watch carefully; chicken cooks quickly.

This technique can also be applied to chicken cooked on the grill. Weight the bird or its components with either a heavy skillet or a brick wrapped in aluminum foil.

To minimize sticking, heat the skillet before adding butter and oil.

While the mushrooms are cooking, they first render their juices and then the juices evaporate as the mushrooms brown. This

Most people love both chicken and mushrooms, so you will undoubtedly make your friends very happy if you serve this preparation to them. When we made a dish like this in France that called for wild mushrooms, we would gather everything we found in the forest and then take them to the pharmacist in the village to see if they were safe to eat. Now as I look back on this practice, I wonder if he didn't tell us that some of the mushrooms we had picked were bad so he could keep all the great ones for himself. Luckily, the supermarkets in this country are starting to sell some fabulous mushrooms that you don't have to have approved. You won't have to share them, either.

CHICKEN MARINADE

4 large chicken breasts, boned, skinned, trimmed, tendon removed and patted dry

2 cloves garlic, each peeled and sliced into 12 slivers

3 tablespoons olive oil

Salt and freshly ground black pepper to taste

MUSHROOM RAGOÛT

1 ounce (¼ stick) unsalted butter

2 medium shallots, peeled and minced

¾ pound fresh shiitake or other fresh mushroom, ends trimmed and coarsely chopped

¾ pound button mushrooms, ends trimmed and coarsely chopped

1 tablespoon soy sauce

Salt and freshly ground black pepper to taste

1 ounce (¼ stick) unsalted butter

1 tablespoon olive oil

Salt and freshly ground black pepper to taste

1 package (3½ ounces) enoki mushrooms, sandy root ends cut off and discarded

2 ounces (½ stick) chilled unsalted butter, chopped

¼ cup minced flat-leaf parsley

For the chicken marinade, pound the breasts lightly with a meat pounder between 2 pieces of plastic wrap to an even thickness. Place each breast on a sheet of plastic wrap. Cut 6 small slits in each breast and insert a sliver of garlic in each. Rub with olive oil and season with salt and pepper. Wrap in plastic. Refrigerate at least for 4 hours or overnight.

For the Mushroom Ragoût, melt the butter in a heavy large nonstick skillet over medium heat. Add the shallots and stir until translucent, for about 3 minutes. Add the shiitake and button mushrooms, increase heat and cook until tender and lightly browned, for about 5 minutes, stirring occasionally. Stir in the soy sauce. Season with salt and pepper. (This can be prepared ahead and set aside at cool room temperature.)

To serve, heat a heavy large nonstick skillet over medium-high heat. Add 1 ounce butter with oil and heat. Unwrap the chicken breasts and add them to the skillet. Oil the bottom of a heavy, slightly smaller skillet and place it on top of the chicken, pressing to flatten. Cook for 3 minutes. Carefully turn the breasts using a spatula (the breasts may stick), weight again and cook until the flesh is just firm when pressed and the breasts are cooked through, for about 3 minutes. Season with salt and pepper.

Meanwhile, reheat the Mushroom Ragoût over medium-high heat, stirring occasionally. Separate the enoki mushrooms, add to the ragoût and stir until they begin to wilt. Whisk in the chopped butter until it is just melted. Slice the chicken breasts diagonally and arrange them on 4 plates. Ladle the Mushroom Ragoût over the slices. Sprinkle with parsley. Serve immediately.

process takes about 5 minutes. Mushrooms should not be cooked beyond this point or they lose their firm bite.

Variation
The chicken breasts for this recipe can also be poached or baked according to directions in this chapter.

Wine Selection
Red Burgundy

Tangy Chicken with Shiitake Crust

6 Servings

Planning Ahead

The Tangy Sauce can be prepared a day in advance. The crust can be made and the chicken coated at any time during the day the dish is to be served. Cook the chicken and re-heat the sauce just before presenting.

Technique Tips

After 12 minutes of cooking, the chicken will feel firm, but not done. Ignore any doubts and remove it from the oven anyway. The chicken will continue to cook while it rests. If left in the oven longer, it will overcook and dry out. If using medium or small breasts, cook only for 10 minutes.

When slicing cooked breasts on the diagonal, use an electric knife for cleaner, sharper slices.

Wine Selection

Merlot

I n my quest for a crunchy texture, I love to wrap food. This particular wrap is an extension of the Moroccan Merguez sausage crust I enjoy making for lamb. This, in turn, grew out of my desire to improve Beef Wellington, a dish I have always disliked intensely, despite its once-enormous popularity.

I use my crusts like a firm marinade to baste and commingle with the ingredient they are wrapping, as well as to envelop flavors. If you want to play the great chef, this is your opportunity. The chicken with its pebbly mushroom crust will look spectacular and highly professional, yet it is very easy to achieve and completely do-ahead.

TANGY SAUCE

2 medium oranges

2 large shallots, peeled and coarsely chopped

1 cup dry white wine

1 cup balsamic vinegar

2 cups unsalted chicken stock

2 tablespoons tomato paste

Salt and freshly ground black pepper to taste

MUSHROOMS

About 2 tablespoons olive oil

¾ pound button mushrooms, ends trimmed and sliced

¾ pound fresh shiitake or other fresh mushrooms, ends trimmed and sliced

2 large shallots, peeled and coarsely chopped

2 large cloves garlic, peeled and minced

Salt and freshly ground black pepper to taste

6 large chicken breasts, boned, skinned, trimmed and tendon removed

Salt and freshly ground black pepper to taste

2 tablespoons fresh minced chervil, thyme or chives

1 ounce (¼ stick) chilled unsalted butter, coarsely chopped

For the Tangy Sauce, remove the orange part of the peel, without any of the bitter white pith, using a vegetable peeler. Chop the orange peel coarsely and place it in a heavy medium saucepan with the shallots, white wine and vinegar. Boil over medium-high heat until reduced to ½ cup. Add the chicken stock and tomato paste and boil until reduced to 1 cup. Strain the sauce through a fine sieve, pressing on the ingredients. Season with salt and pepper. (This can be prepared ahead and set aside at cool room temperature for several hours or refrigerated overnight.)

For the mushrooms, place a heavy large skillet over medium-high heat and film with oil. Add the button and shiitake mushrooms, shallots and garlic and cook until the mushrooms are lightly browned, for about 5 minutes, stirring occasionally. Cool completely, refrigerating if necessary. Season generously with salt and pepper.

For the coating, remove the small chicken fillets from the underside of the breasts. Grind the chicken fillets in a food processor until they are a smooth paste, pulsing on/off. Add the mushroom mixture and chop coarsely, pulsing on/off.

Line a large baking sheet with parchment. Pat the chicken breasts dry. Pound them lightly between 2 sheets of waxed paper with a meat pounder to an even thickness. Season with salt and pepper. Divide the mushroom mixture into 6 parts.

Place a 12-inch length of plastic wrap on a work surface. Place 1 part of the mushroom mixture in the center of the plastic. Fold the plastic over the mushroom mixture. Pat or roll it with a rolling pin until evenly thick and slightly larger than the chicken breast. Place the breast, smooth rounded side down, on top of the mushroom mixture. Gather the plastic tightly up and around the chicken breast as if wrapping a gift basket, until the mushroom mixture adheres to the top and sides of the chicken breast. Unwrap and gently invert the chicken, uncoated side down, onto the prepared baking sheet. Gently peel off the plastic. Repeat with the remaining mushroom mixture and chicken breasts. (This can be prepared ahead and set aside at cool room temperature for several hours or refrigerated.)

To serve, preheat the oven to 350°F. Bake the chicken for 10 to 12 minutes. Remove from the oven and let rest at room temperature for 12 minutes. Slice the breasts diagonally. Arrange each breast on a plate, fanning out the slices. Reheat the sauce by stirring it over medium-high heat. Stir in chervil. Whisk in the butter. Ladle some sauce alongside the chicken. Serve immediately.

Chicken Vichyssoise

4 Servings

Planning Ahead

The sauce can be prepared several hours in advance. Cook the chicken just before presenting.

Technique Tip

Use red or white boiling potatoes instead of the starchier russet potatoes, which will make the sauce gluey. Puree in a blender, not in a food processor, for the same reason.

Wine Selection

White Burgundy

When I was growing up in France, we often had *poule-au-pot* or chicken braised with leeks and potatoes for Sunday dinner. Although I loved this dish, I hated the way it was served. The platter was passed around the table with the expectation that each of us would be polite and take the least attractive piece of chicken that remained. That meant those who were served first got stuck with the neck or a dried-out wing. Not me. When it was time to sit down, I took off for the bathroom on the pretext of washing my hands. By the time I returned everyone else had their piece, and I was privy to the choicest morsel.

When I first made this chicken with leeks at the restaurant, nobody wanted it no matter which part they got. When I changed the dish's name to Chicken Vichyssoise, it became very popular. There's no reason why it shouldn't be, since everyone's morsel of chicken is a choice one.

VICHYSSOISE SAUCE

3 cups unsalted chicken stock

3 medium-large (about 2 pounds) leeks, (white and light green parts only), halved lengthwise and sliced crosswise into ½-inch pieces

¾ pound boiling potatoes, peeled and cut into 1-inch dice

1 large clove garlic, peeled

1 tablespoon Champagne vinegar or white wine vinegar

Salt and freshly ground black pepper to taste

CHICKEN

2 tablespoons unsalted butter

4 large chicken breasts, boned, skinned, trimmed, tendon removed and patted dry

Salt and freshly ground black pepper to taste

1 tablespoon unsalted butter

For the Vichyssoise Sauce, bring the stock to a boil in a heavy large saucepan. Add the leeks and simmer until tender for about 5 minutes. Remove 1 cup of the leeks with a slotted spoon and reserve for garnish in a heavy small skillet. Add the potatoes, garlic and vinegar to the saucepan with the remaining leeks and simmer until the potatoes are tender, for about 15 minutes. Puree the contents of the saucepan in a blender until smooth, pulsing on/off and stopping to scrape down the sides of the container. Return to a clean saucepan. Season with salt and pepper.

(This can be prepared ahead to this point, covered and set aside at cool room temperature for several hours.)

For the chicken, preheat the oven to 325°F. Melt the 2 tablespoons of butter in a heavy large skillet over medium heat. Season the chicken with salt and pepper and add it to the skillet, turning to coat with butter. Cover the skillet, transfer to the oven and bake until the chicken is just firm to the touch and opaque throughout, for about 10 to 15 minutes, turning halfway.

To serve, add 1 tablespoon of butter to the leeks in the skillet and warm over medium heat, stirring occasionally. Whisk the chicken cooking juices into the sauce. Reheat the sauce and ladle it onto 4 plates. Arrange a chicken breast in the center of the sauce. Spoon warmed leeks over breasts. Serve immediately.

Chicken with Crispy Celery Root

4 Servings

Planning Ahead

The chicken can be poached, the sauce reduced and the celery root garnish fried several hours in advance of serving. Reheat the celery root garnish or serve it at room temperature. Reheat the sauce and chicken before presenting.

Technique Tips

A food processor greatly simplifies the task of cutting the celery root into shreds or julienne.

A grease separator—in small, medium or large—is an invaluable kitchen tool. If not available, degrease the stock by blotting with paper towels.

Wine Selection

White Burgundy

In both French homes and restaurants, we either cook and puree celery root—mixing it occasionally with mashed potatoes—to serve with game, or grate it and dress it raw with mayonnaise for a salad. Period. That's it: A rather narrow focus for such a delectable vegetable. Guessing that this root had great potential, I looked for ways to increase its versatility while preserving its unique celeriac flavor. At first I tried it with fish, but found it a bit too overpowering. Switching to chicken, it balanced out perfectly.

Knob celery is treated to two separate preparations here, braising strips of it in the sauce and deep frying a curly thatch for garnish. (If time is limited, the garnish can always be eliminated.) Served in soup plates, this dish is more like a soup-stew with its thin delicate broth than it is chicken with a sauce.

CHICKEN

4 large unskinned bone-in chicken breasts

4 cups unsalted chicken stock

2 large stalks celery, quartered

2 tablespoons freshly squeezed lemon juice

CELERY ROOT SAUCE

½ cup heavy cream

I small (9 to 12 ounces) celery root, peeled and cut into julienne

Salt and freshly ground black pepper to taste

Peanut or vegetable oil (about 4 cups) for deep frying

For the chicken, place the chicken skin side up in a heavy skillet large enough to accommodate it in a single layer with the stock, celery and lemon juice. Add enough cold water to cover the chicken. Bring to a boil, then immediately reduce heat to the point where the liquid is barely shaking. Cover and poach for 5 minutes. Remove from heat and let stand, covered, for at least 10 minutes. Remove the breasts from poaching liquid; discard skin and bones. Trim the breasts neatly (chicken may not be completely cooked through). (This can be prepared ahead, cooled, covered and set aside at cool room temperature.)

For the Celery Root Sauce, degrease the poaching liquid in a grease separator. Line a sieve with a dampened paper towel. Pour the liquid back into the skillet through the sieve. Boil the liquid over medium-high heat until reduced to I cup. Stir in the cream and I cup celery root julienne. Season with salt and pepper. (This can be prepared ahead, cooled, covered and set aside at cool room temperature.)

For the celery root garnish, line a large baking sheet with several layers of paper towels. Heat the oil to 350°F in a deep fryer, wok or large pot. Fry the remaining celery root, a handful at a time, until golden brown, for about 10 minutes total, turning halfway with tongs or a slotted spatula. Transfer to the prepared sheet. Cover with paper towels. (This can be prepared ahead and set aside at cool room temperature.)

Meanwhile, reboil the sauce 2 minutes; lower heat until the liquid is barely shaking, add the chicken and turn using tongs until heated (or cooked through, if necessary), for about 5 minutes. Transfer the chicken to 4 soup plates using tongs. Ladle over the sauce. Mound the fried celery root on top of the chicken. Serve immediately.

Chicken Kataifi with Purple Sauce

6 Servings

Planning Ahead

The Purple Sauce can be prepared and the chicken coated in kataifi 1 day in advance. Cook the chicken just before presenting.

Technique Tip

After 12 minutes of cooking, the chicken will feel firm, but not done. Ignore any doubts and remove it from the oven anyway. The chicken will continue to cook while it rests. If left in the oven longer, it will overcook and dry out. If using medium or small breasts, cook for 10 minutes only.

Variation

To convert the Purple Sauce to Purple Relish, process only until coarsely chopped. For Red Cabbage Ginger Cole Slaw, stir enough of the mayonnaise mixture into shredded red cabbage to coat generously and marinate for 15 to 20 minutes before serving.

Wine Selection

Pinot Noir

Shopping for food helps keep me creative, especially when I am in a great place and see wonderful ingredients I can't wait to prepare. Whether I am buying supplies for home or the restaurant, I do two tours of a market. First I walk around to see what is available, and then I go back to compose a menu and pick out what I need. Above all, I love to go to ethnic grocery stores. In Los Angeles, every nationality has its own market, except, ironically, the French.

My friend, Robert Robaire, took me to a Greek shop where I found the kataifi. In the Middle East, this shredded wheat is mainly used for desserts, but I've been having a lot of fun using it as bread crumbs to coat foods. It bakes into a beautiful crunch as it does with this chicken, and it fries crisply as in my Shrimp Porcupines (page 130). I even dip the ends of large strawberries into the kataifi and fry them to garnish desserts. Some of my crusts are primarily taste helpers, while this one belongs more in the texture category. To give the chicken some color and zest, I've paired it with this pungent Purple Sauce.

PURPLE SAUCE

⅓ cup mayonnaise

2 tablespoons freshly squeezed lemon juice

1 tablespoon red wine vinegar

1 teaspoon sugar

1½ teaspoons soy sauce

2 thin coins fresh gingerroot, peeled

2 tablespoons olive oil

3 cups (about ¾ pound or ½ small) shredded red cabbage

Salt and freshly ground black pepper to taste

CHICKEN

About ⅓ of 1-pound box kataifi

6 large chicken breasts, boned, skinned, trimmed and tendon removed

Olive oil

About ⅓ cup all-purpose flour

1 large egg

1 tablespoon water

Salt and freshly ground black pepper to taste

For the Purple Sauce, place the mayonnaise, lemon juice, vinegar, sugar, soy sauce and ginger in a food processor fitted with chopping blade. Process until mixed and smooth, pulsing on/off. With the machine running, pour in oil in a slow, thin stream. Add the cabbage and process, pulsing on/off and occasionally scraping down the sides of the container, until finely ground and almost smooth. Season with salt and pepper. (This can be prepared 1 day ahead, transferred to a bowl, covered and refrigerated until 30 minutes before serving.)

For the chicken, tear off six 8-inch sheets of aluminum foil and arrange on a work surface. Remove the kataifi from the box and form a 6-inch square of kataifi, about ¼ inch thick, on each sheet of aluminum foil, using scissors and fingers to pull the strands in the same direction. Pull the strands apart with your fingers and neaten the squares. Return the remaining kataifi to the refrigerator or refreeze it for another dish.

Coat a large baking sheet lightly with olive oil. Pound the chicken lightly between 2 sheets of plastic wrap with a meat pounder to an even thickness. Place the flour on a plate. Whisk the egg with water, salt and pepper in a soup plate. One at a time, dip both sides of the chicken breasts in the flour, patting off excess. Holding with tongs, dip in the egg and then place in the center of each kataifi square. Wrap with kataifi, enclosing chicken completely and shaping into an oval with your hands. Remove chicken packets from the aluminum foil and place on the prepared sheet. (This can be prepared ahead to this point, covered with plastic wrap and set aside at cool room temperature for several hours or refrigerated overnight.)

To serve, preheat the oven to 350°F. Remove the Purple Sauce from the refrigerator, if necessary. Bake the chicken for 10 to 12 minutes. Remove and let sit for 10 minutes. Place the chicken on 6 plates. Ladle the Purple Sauce alongside. Serve immediately.

Chicken Curry with
Apple and Coconut Milk

4 Servings

Planning Ahead
The Curry Sauce can be completely prepared at any time during the day the rag-oût is to be served. Poach the chicken in the sauce just before presenting.

Technique Tips
This technique of poaching small pieces of chicken breast in a sauce that has been completely prepared in advance is an ideal do-ahead method that works sensationally when enter-taining. Many chicken recipes can be adapted to utilize this approach.

When adding flour to a sauce, cook for at least 3 minutes over medium-low heat to remove its unpleas-ant raw quality.

Variation
Hard cider can be sub-stituted for apple juice.

Wine Selection
California or German slightly sweet Riesling

I go out to eat very seldom, but when I do, I prefer Asian to French food, which is too much like what I have at home. Often I am inspired by these nights on the town and bring back an idea to use at Citrus. This dish came from one such jaunt. Its sauce was a bit heavy for my traditional French palate, so I added some apple juice to make the ragoût fruiter and to lighten the load of coconut milk.

CURRY SAUCE

   1 tablespoon peanut oil

   1 small onion, peeled and diced

   2 tablespoons curry powder

   ¼ teaspoon ground anise seed

   Generous pinch of ground cinnamon

   Generous pinch of ground cayenne pepper

   1 teaspoon all-purpose flour

   ½ cup unsalted chicken stock

   ¾ cup canned coconut milk

   ½ cup unsweetened apple juice

   Salt and freshly ground black pepper to taste

   1 small Pippin apple, peeled, cored and cut into tiny dice

   1 tablespoon freshly squeezed lemon juice

   5 large chicken breasts, boned, skinned, trimmed, tendon
       removed, sliced crosswise into ¼-inch-wide pieces and
       patted dry

For the Curry Sauce, heat the oil in a heavy large nonstick skillet. Add the onion and cook over medium heat until lightly browned, for about 3 minutes, stirring occasionally. Add the curry, anise, cinnamon, cayenne and flour; lower heat to medium-low and stir 3 minutes. Pour in the chicken stock, coconut milk and apple juice. Bring to a boil, then lower heat and simmer until reduced and thickened to a saucelike consistency. Season to taste with salt and pepper. (This can be prepared ahead, covered and set aside at cool room temperature for several hours or re-frigerated.)

To serve, mix the apple and lemon juice in a small bowl. Bring the Curry Sauce to a boil. Add the chicken and lower heat until liquid is just shaking. Poach the chicken until just opaque throughout, for about 3 minutes total, turning halfway with tongs. Ladle the curry into 4 plates or soup plates. Sprinkle with the apples. Serve immediately.

Chicken in Red Pepper Sacks

T his is my variation of a Provençal *Petit Farci*, a vegetable stuffed with ground pork or rice. Although I like this idea, I hate these particular common fillings. I'd rather have honest bread crumbs and olive oil than create volume by using such vulgar food. Other than hamburger, Americans don't like forcemeat anyway, because they are always wondering what is in it. To get around this suspicion—and my distaste for bulky fillers—while utilizing this amusing presentation, I roll up a piece of chicken and stick it in a red pepper sack. This is a lot of fun and quite easy to do. Add a sauce, if you like, maybe some pesto, and some vegetables on the side or coming out of the top to look as if there are groceries spilling out of the bag.

4 large chicken legs with thighs attached, skinned

¼ cup olive oil

2 large cloves garlic, peeled and minced

¼ cup fresh minced basil or other fresh herb

Salt and freshly ground black pepper to taste

4 large red bell peppers (see Technique Tip)

Olive oil

Salt and freshly ground black pepper to taste

4 fresh basil sprigs for garnish (optional)

To bone the chicken legs, place chicken leg skin side down on a washable cutting surface. Using a small sharp knife and starting at the end of the drumstick, cut closely down to and along both sides of the bone. Repeat the procedure with the thigh bone. Holding on to the end of the drumstick bone, remove the drumstick by cutting around the bone and scraping off the meat as it is released. Cut through the thigh joint, being careful not to cut through the meat. Remove the thigh bone in the same manner. Cut out the joint. Holding on to the ends of the tendons, scrape the meat off of the tendons and remove. Trim the boned leg, if necessary, and pound it gently with a meat pounder between 2 pieces of plastic wrap to an even thickness. Repeat with the remaining legs.

(continued)

Planning Ahead
The chicken legs should be boned and marinated for at least 4 hours or, preferably, overnight. The peppers can be prepared at any time during the day the dish is to be served. Place chicken in the peppers and bake just before presenting.

Technique Tip
The red pepper cases should be approximately the same size. Choose even, almost rectangular-shaped, peppers with flat bottoms that will easily hold the boned, rolled chicken legs.

Variation
Two thighs can be substituted for 1 chicken leg with the thigh attached.

Wine Selection
Chardonnay

Place each leg on a large piece of plastic wrap. Rub both sides of the boned leg with olive oil and sprinkle with garlic, basil, salt and pepper. Wrap up and marinate at least 4 hours in refrigerator.

For the peppers, slice off the tops and carefully remove seeds and veins, being careful not to cut through peppers. Rub the inside of the peppers with oil and sprinkle with salt and pepper. Stand the peppers upright in a deep 8-inch square pan or one just wide enough to hold the peppers. If necessary, trim the peppers' bottoms to flatten. (This can be prepared ahead to this point and set aside at room temperature.)

To serve, preheat the oven to 350°F. Roll the marinated chicken up jelly-roll fashion and place inside the red peppers. Bake until the chicken juices run clear when pricked with a fork, for about 30 to 35 minutes. Transfer the peppers to 4 large plates using a spatula. Garnish each with a basil sprig, if desired.

Coq au California

4 Servings

Planning Ahead

The chicken should be marinated overnight. Cook it just before serving or several hours in advance and then reheat gently.

Technique Tips

The chicken has much better flavor and texture if not refrigerated in between cooking and serving.

When adding flour to a sauce, cook for at least 3 minutes over medium-low heat to remove its unpleasant raw quality.

When cooking with wine, choose a good quality bottle that you would be happy to drink.

While growing up in France, my wine experience was generally limited to bottlings produced by friends of friends. I didn't know much about wine, although I remember harboring the suspicion that most of what I was drinking would taste better if I used it as vinegar in a salad dressing. One night after CTA (coming to America), Gaston Lenôtre, the French *pâtissier* who was my teacher and mentor, ordered a bottle of Corton Charlemagne at Ma Maison restaurant in Los Angeles where we were dining together. I didn't even like white wine, and yet all of a sudden here was this nectar creating a miracle in my mouth. It is amazing how a glass of wine can change your life.

After that momentous occasion, I initially looked to the wines of my native country, but, increasingly, I've discovered the great vintages here in California. As I watch the smart winemakers who work so hard and are so dedicated to their profession, I am overwhelmed by the same, almost mystical aura that I experience visiting the great kitchens in France. As a toast to these creators I've created Coq au California, an American equivalent to Coq au Vin, the classic chicken dish that emerged from the winemaking traditions of France. Let's all raise our glasses to good food and wine everywhere.

MARINADE

   4 large chicken legs with thighs attached, skinned

   4 fresh thyme sprigs or 1 tablespoon dried, crumbled

   4 cloves garlic, peeled and crushed

   1½ cups Cabernet Sauvignon or other dry red wine

2 slices bacon, halved lengthwise and cut crosswise into
   ¼-inch-wide pieces

½ ounce unsalted butter

16 pearl onions, peeled

2 medium carrots, peeled and thinly sliced

1 tablespoon all-purpose flour

1 cup unsalted chicken stock

1 tablespoon tomato paste

16 (10 to 12 ounces total) medium-large button mushrooms,
   ends trimmed

Salt and freshly ground black pepper to taste

Wine Selection

Cabernet Sauvignon or the same wine used in marinade.

For the marinade, place the chicken legs in a single layer in a large nonmetallic dish. Add the thyme, garlic and wine. Cover and refrigerate overnight, turning the chicken several times with tongs.

To cook, preheat the oven to 300°F. Melt the butter in a heavy large pot over medium heat and cook the bacon until brown, stirring occasionally. Add the onions and carrots and cook until golden. Add the flour and stir for 3 minutes over medium-low heat. Pour in the chicken stock with the tomato paste and stir, scraping up any browned bits on the bottom of the pan. Add the marinade and bring to a boil. Add the chicken legs, cover and transfer to the oven. Cook for 30 minutes, turning the chicken and stirring halfway. (This can be prepared several hours ahead and set aside at cool room temperature.)

To serve, remove the chicken from the pot using tongs. Add the mushrooms to the cooking liquid and boil until the sauce is thickened and reduced by about half to approximately 1¼ cups, for about 20 minutes. Discard the herb sprigs. Season with salt and pepper. Remove the vegetables with a slotted spoon and arrange on 4 plates. Turn the legs in the sauce, heating gently if cold, and place in the center of plates. Spoon the remaining sauce over the legs. Serve immediately.

Chicken Polenta
Pot Pie with Spinach

4 Servings

Planning Ahead

The Cream of Wheat Crust must be prepared at least several hours in advance of using to set. The spinach filling can be completely made and the chicken prepped the night before serving. Assemble the pie and bake just before presenting.

Technique Tips

To seed tomatoes, halve them horizontally and squeeze the seeds out over the sink. Tomatoes can be peeled if desired.

Chicken thighs (or substitute legs or legs with thighs attached) are preferable to breasts for the pie, because dark meat stays moister and stands up better to braising.

Wine Selection

Cabernet Sauvignon

Made with Cream of Wheat, the polenta here is similar to the one I used for my savory Summer Tomato Tart with Basil Crust (page 58). It is so quick and easy to make, I wouldn't be surprised if it appeared increasingly on my table. In this case, I've used it for my interpretation of a chicken pot pie. The white wheat polenta satisfied my demands for the crust perfectly; the spinach for a creamy filling.

CREAM OF WHEAT CRUST

> 1½ cups tomato juice
>
> 7½ tablespoons instant Cream of Wheat
>
> 3 tablespoons freshly grated Parmesan cheese
>
> Salt and freshly ground black pepper to taste

SPINACH FILLING

> 1 small onion, peeled and diced
>
> ½ cup heavy cream
>
> 1 pound spinach, stemmed, washed, well dried and cut into strips
>
> 1 large clove garlic, peeled and minced
>
> 2 medium tomatoes, seeded and diced
>
> 3 tablespoons freshly grated Parmesan cheese
>
> ½ cup unsalted chicken stock
>
> Salt and freshly ground black pepper to taste
>
> 6 large chicken thighs, boned, skinned, halved and patted dry
>
> Salt and freshly ground black pepper to taste
>
> 2 tablespoons freshly grated Parmesan cheese

For the Cream of Wheat Crust, turn a 9-inch porcelain or glass pie plate over on parchment paper. Trace around the rim of the plate, using a dark heavy pen. Turn the parchment over. If circle is not visible, redraw so it is. Bring the tomato juice to a boil in a heavy medium saucepan. Add the Cream of Wheat and Parmesan cheese and stir over medium heat until very thick, for about 5 minutes. Season with salt and pepper. Turn out onto the prepared parchment. Spread the mixture evenly within the circle using a spatula. Place the parchment on a tray and refrigerate several hours or overnight or freeze about 1 hour until crust is well chilled and firm.

For the spinach filling, mix the onion and cream in a heavy large saucepan. Simmer over medium-low heat until the cream is reduced, thickened and almost completely absorbed by the onions, stirring frequently. Increase heat to medium-high and gradually stir in the spinach. Cover and cook until completely wilted, for about 3 minutes, stirring occasionally. Mix in the garlic, tomatoes, cheese and chicken stock. Season with salt and pepper. Cool completely. (This can be prepared several hours ahead and set aside at cool room temperature or refrigerated overnight.)

To serve, preheat the oven to 350°F. Spoon ½ of the spinach mixture into a 9-inch pie plate. Season the chicken with salt and pepper and place over the spinach mixture. Spread the remaining spinach mixture over the chicken. Invert the parchment with the crust over the pie; peel off the paper and discard it. Press the edges of the crust into the rim of the pie plate to seal. Sprinkle the crust with cheese. Bake for 25 minutes.

Preheat the broiler. Place the pie plate under the heat source to brown the cheese, watching carefully. Cut into 4 wedges and transfer each to a soup plate using a wide spatula. Ladle the cooking juices into the plates. Serve immediately.

Chicken Macaroni and Cheese with Butternut Squash

4 Servings

Planning Ahead

All of the components for this *pot pie* can be cooked several hours before serving. Assemble the pie and heat it under the broiler just before presenting.

Technique Tip

Chicken thighs and legs are preferable to breasts for the pie, because dark meat stays moister and stands up better to braising.

Variation

The *pot pie* can also be cooked in one large 12- to 14-inch gratin pan.

Wine Selection

Chardonnay

I could never eat pumpkin or winter squash. They were both the same to me: tasteless. I was telling a chef friend how boring I thought they were and he said, "Michel, use some Parmesan. It will make a big difference." I did. It did. I had squash and I had cheese. This made me think of macaroni. Then I had macaroni and cheese with a beautiful color. Why not some chicken, too, I thought? And then I had dinner.

1 large tomato

1 medium (about 1½ pounds) butternut squash, peeled, halved lengthwise and cut into large pieces

6 ounces macaroni

1 tablespoon olive oil

2 tablespoons olive oil

3 large (1¾ to 2 pounds total) chicken legs with thighs attached, patted dry

2 large cloves garlic, peeled and minced

1 tablespoon fresh minced sage or 1 teaspoon dried, crumbled

Salt and freshly ground black pepper to taste

2 tablespoons olive oil

¼ cup (about 1 ounce) freshly grated Parmesan cheese

Salt and freshly ground black pepper to taste

¼ cup (about 1 ounce) freshly grated Parmesan cheese

Bring a large pot of water to a boil. Add the tomato for 30 seconds to loosen its peel. Remove the tomato with a slotted spoon. Add the squash. Boil for 15 minutes or until very tender when pierced with a knife. Transfer the squash to a food processor with a slotted spatula. Add the macaroni to the water. Cook until al dente, for about 10 minutes; drain. Toss the macaroni with 1 tablespoon of olive oil in a large bowl. Meanwhile, puree the squash in the food processor until smooth, pulsing on/off and stopping to scrape down the sides of the container. Peel the tomato, seed and cut it into ¼-inch dice. (This can be prepared ahead, components covered and set aside at room temperature until serving.)

Heat 2 tablespoons of olive oil in a heavy large nonstick skillet over medium-high heat. Add the chicken legs and brown them on both sides. Cover, reduce the heat to medium-low and cook 15 minutes, turning halfway. Stir the garlic and diced tomato into the pan. Recover and cook for 5 minutes.

Remove the chicken legs from the skillet with tongs and discard their skin and bones. Cut the meat into bite-size pieces. Place in a large bowl. Mix the cooked garlic, tomato, pan juices and sage into the meat. Season with salt and pepper. (This can be prepared to this point several hours ahead, covered and set aside at cool room temperature.)

To serve, preheat the broiler. Heat 2 tablespoons of oil in the chicken-cooking skillet over medium-high heat. Add the squash puree and stir until heated through. Mix in the cooked macaroni and ¼ cup cheese. Season with salt and pepper.

Divide ½ of the squash mixture among four 6- or 7-inch gratin pans, spreading evenly over the bottom. Divide the chicken mixture over the squash mixture. Top with the remaining squash mixture, spreading evenly. Sprinkle with ¼ cup cheese. Place the gratin pans about 4 inches below the heat source. Broil until the cheese browns. Place the gratin pans on 4 large plates. Serve immediately.

A Chicken in Every
Teapot with Vegetables

Planning Ahead

The vegetable mixture can be prepared several hours in advance. Steam the chicken just before presenting.

Technique Tips

A wok works perfectly for this task, but any type of pot will do as long as the chicken can be suspended on a rack above the vegetables and covered completely with a lid so steam doesn't escape.

When steaming chicken, adjust the heat so the water is simmering gently. Boiling water produces an aggressive steam that can toughen the chicken.

Wine Selection

White Burgundy or Côtes du Rhône

Not so long ago, French peasants were very poor. Their preoccupation was with hunger, not with presentation. In those days, they cured their root vegetables and layered them with salt to last through the winter, removing them as necessary to make a soup called Vegetable Tea. This homey broth was as nurturing and comforting as a *tisane,* an herbal tea drunk before bedtime, or the *poule-au-pot,* or chicken in a pot, served by wealthier farmers for Sunday supper.

I very much wanted to include a recipe in this book from the French tradition of food as love and emotional sustenance. This old-fashioned soupy chicken stew comes as close to those sentiments as possible without putting you through the trouble of curing all the vegetables. I hope it will give you the flavor of a pre-nouvelle cuisine era when people didn't worry whether a dish was good looking; just good tasting.

VEGETABLES

1 medium (5 to 7 ounces) rutabaga, peeled and cut into 1-inch pieces

1 medium (5 to 7 ounces) turnip, peeled and cut into 1-inch pieces

1 large carrot, peeled and cut into 1-inch segments

2 medium (about ½ pound) red boiling potatoes, peeled and cut into 1-inch pieces

1 large leek (white and light green parts only), halved lengthwise and sliced crosswise into ⅛-inch-wide pieces

1 small onion, diced

About 4 cups unsalted chicken stock

Salt and freshly ground black pepper to taste

3¾ to 4 pounds roasting chicken, at room temperature

3 chamomile tea bags

1 tablespoon Dijon mustard

Salt and freshly ground black pepper to taste

2 tablespoons fresh minced chervil or flat-leaf parsley

For the vegetables, place the rutabaga, turnip, carrot, potatoes, leek and onion in a wok or the bottom of a steamer. Pour over the chicken stock. (This can be prepared to this point several hours ahead, covered and set aside at cool room temperature.)

To steam the chicken, bring the vegetable mixture to a boil. Place a steamer rack above the vegetable mixture. Season the chicken with salt and pepper and place it on the rack. Cover completely. Reduce heat and steam the chicken for 20 minutes. Add the tea bags to the steamer and additional stock if reduced below approximately 2 cups liquid. Turn the chicken, re-cover and steam until it is cooked and its juices run yellow when a thigh is pricked with a fork, for about 10 to 15 minutes.

To serve, transfer the chicken to a carving board with tongs; carve the chicken into individual serving pieces. Remove the skin if desired. Degrease the vegetable mixture, if necessary. Bring it back to a gentle simmer. Remove the tea bags. Whisk in the mustard. Season with salt and pepper. Ladle vegetables and broth into 4 soup plates. Place the chicken on top of the vegetables. Sprinkle with chervil. Serve immediately.

Roast Chicken with Garlic, Shallot and Potato

Planning Ahead

The only advance preparation is readying the chicken and prepping the other ingredients. Roast the chicken just before it is served.

Technique Tips

Cooking garlic and shallots unpeeled enhances their flavor and prevents them from burning. To eat, just squeeze them out between your fingertips onto the accompanying toast. Cutting off the tops will make it easier to extract the pulp.

By roasting the chicken on its side, the juices from the leg can continuously baste the drier breast.

When turning the chicken and vegetables halfway through cooking, it may be easiest to temporarily place the rack with the chicken on a tray.

Variation

If fresh thyme is not available, substitute 2 tablespoons dried thyme. Crumble the thyme and sprinkle it all over the chicken rather than using it as described for the fresh sprigs.

Wine Selection

Cabernet Sauvignon

I f you want to be successful with chicken, just cook it classically like your grandmother—or my French grandmother—did with lots of garlic, shallot and potato to sop up the good cooking juices. It's so simple to prepare, everyone can have good results. Sometimes I feel so much pressure to come up with a new way to cook chicken, but there have been so many great dishes created before me, why should I do something different? What is more beautiful than a crispy roasted bird? We used to have chicken only on Sundays, but we are very lucky now; we can have it every day.

3¼ to 3½ pounds roasting chicken, patted dry

3 to 4 tablespoons olive oil

Salt and freshly ground black pepper to taste

8 fresh large thyme sprigs (see Variation)

24 large unpeeled shallots, washed and tops cut off

2 large heads garlic, separated into unpeeled cloves and washed, tops cut off

24 baby (about 1 inch diameter) red unpeeled boiling potatoes, pricked or 12 small (about 1½ inches diameter) red unpeeled boiling potatoes, halved

¼ cup olive oil

¼ cup water

Fresh thyme sprigs for garnish (optional)

Grilled or toasted bread

Preheat the oven to 375°F. Rub the chicken with olive oil. Season with salt and pepper. Place 4 thyme sprigs in the cavity. Scatter the shallots, garlic, potatoes and 4 thyme sprigs on the bottom of a large roasting pan. Drizzle the oil and water over the vegetables. Season with salt and pepper. Place a rack over the vegetables. Place the chicken on its side on the rack. Bake until the juices in the thigh run yellow when pricked with a knife and the drumstick moves easily in socket, about 1 hour, basting occasionally. Turn the vegetables over and the chicken to its second side halfway through with tongs.

To serve, place the chicken on a large carving board. Scatter the vegetables around. Carve and serve immediately at the table. Garnish each serving with thyme sprigs. Accompany with grilled bread.

Roast Chicken with Bok Choy and Juniper Berries

Although this roasted chicken bears no resemblance to *choucroute*, the idea for it actually started with my recollections of this wonderful Alsatian platter of potatoes, sausages, smoked meats, sauerkraut and juniper berries. In Alsace, *choucroute* was everyday fare. In our region, which was only 20 kilometers away—a great distance in France culturally—it was a special event, consumed only once or twice a year. I remember walking in the door on that momentous occasion and being assaulted by its perfume. I miss the aromas of the old days; of going home and smelling your favorite dish on the stove; knowing that someone was trying to please you. People are so busy that you rarely find anyone cooking anymore. We are losing the most fabulous part of going home.

I substituted bok choy for cabbage here because it looked intriguing to me in the market. Since it is milder in flavor than cabbage, I enlivened it with some soy sauce. The Alsatians may not recognize this as their own, but it should taste delicious, and make your house smell good.

4 Servings

Planning Ahead
The bok choy can be cooked at any time during the day the chicken is to be served and sauce completely prepared several hours in advance. Roast the chicken and reheat both sauce and bok choy just before presenting.

Wine Selection
Alsatian Gewurztraminer

BOK CHOY

½ ounce (⅛ stick) unsalted butter

4 large green onions (white and light green part only), thinly sliced

1½ tablespoons soy sauce

8 heads baby bok choy, sliced crosswise into ½-inch-wide strips

Salt and freshly ground black pepper to taste

JUNIPER SAUCE

¼ cup red wine vinegar

30 juniper berries, finely crushed in a mortar

1 cup unsalted chicken stock

1 teaspoon sugar

2 teaspoons soy sauce

½ cup heavy cream

Salt and freshly ground black pepper to taste

3¼ to 3½ pounds roasting chicken, patted dry

Peanut oil

Salt and freshly ground black pepper to taste

(continued)

For the bok choy, melt the butter in a heavy large skillet or wok over medium heat. Add the onion and stir until translucent, for about 3 minutes. Mix in the soy sauce. Add the bok choy, increase heat to medium-high and stir-fry until just tender, for about 3 minutes. Season with salt and pepper. (This can be prepared ahead, cooled, covered and set aside at room temperature until serving.)

For the Juniper Sauce, boil the vinegar in a heavy small saucepan until reduced to a glaze. Stir in the juniper berries and the chicken stock and reduce by half. Add the sugar, soy sauce and cream and boil until thickened and reduced to a saucelike consistency, about ⅔ cup, stirring occasionally. Strain the sauce, if desired, to remove juniper berries. Season with salt and pepper. (This can be prepared ahead, cooled, covered and set aside at cool room temperature for several hours.)

For the chicken, preheat the oven to 375°F. Rub the chicken with peanut oil. Season with salt and pepper. Place the chicken on its side on a rack in the roasting pan. Bake until the juices in the thigh run yellow when pricked with a knife and the drumstick moves easily in socket, for about 1 hour, basting occasionally and turning the chicken to its second side halfway through with tongs.

To serve, carve the chicken into individual serving pieces. Pour the chicken cooking and carving juices into the bok choy and stir over medium-high heat to rewarm. Place the bok choy in the center of 4 plates. Top with a piece of chicken. Stir the sauce over medium-heat to rewarm. Ladle the sauce over the chicken. Serve immediately, passing any additional sauce separately.

Babar's Jumbo
Pasta Shells with Turkey

4 Servings

Planning Ahead

The shells can be stuffed 1 day in advance. They can be baked and their sauce made several hours before serving. Gratinée the shells just before bringing to the table.

Wine Selection

Merlot, or orange juice for Chloe

My motto has always been: Buy it and try it. I was browsing in the supermarket and saw these big shells that resembled escargots waiting to be filled. Then I saw some ground turkey that looked as if it was ready to be a filling. I hadn't realized you could buy turkey ground. It was such a nice change from buying a whole bird, I've purchased it many times since. I was a bit worried about the turkey tasting dry, so I added some ricotta to my shopping cart for moistness. I then started from scratch, working with foods I had never worked with before, and came up with a recipe I liked very much, and one that was healthy and economical, too.

When my little daughter Chloe, who loves Babar the Elephant, saw this dish for the first time, she called it Babar's ears. She loves the flavor of this dish, so you might think about serving it to your little Babar lovers as well.

STUFFED SHELLS

½ pound (about 24) jumbo pasta shells

½ pound ground turkey

½ pound ricotta cheese

¼ cup (1 ounce) freshly grated Parmesan cheese

¼ cup olive oil

¼ cup minced flat-leaf parsley

2 small cloves garlic, peeled and minced

Salt and freshly ground black pepper to taste

About 1½ cups unsalted chicken stock

SAUCE

¼ cup milk or heavy cream

2 tablespoons all-purpose flour

1 teaspoon Dijon mustard

Salt and freshly ground black pepper to taste

¼ cup (1 ounce) freshly grated Parmesan cheese

For the stuffed shells, bring a large pot of water to a boil. Add the pasta shells and cook until al dente, for about 10 to 12 minutes; drain.

Meanwhile, mix the turkey, ricotta, Parmesan, oil, parsley, garlic, salt and pepper in a medium bowl until well blended. Stuff the shells with the mixture, pressing down gently to eliminate any air pockets. Place the filled shells open side up in a 9- × 13-inch baking dish. Set aside covered at cool room temperature for several hours or refrigerate until 1 hour before baking.

To bake, preheat the oven to 400°F. Pour the chicken stock into the baking dish with the shells. Re-cover and bake 30 minutes.

For the sauce, remove the cooking juices with a bulb baster and strain into a measuring cup through a fine sieve. Whisk the milk, flour and mustard together in a heavy small saucepan until smooth. Gradually whisk in 1 cup of the cooking juices, adding additional stock if necessary. Whisk over medium heat until thickened. Season with salt and pepper. Spoon the sauce over each shell. Sprinkle with ¼ cup Parmesan. (This can be prepared ahead, covered and set aside at cool room temperature for several hours.)

To serve, preheat the broiler. Uncover and place the baking dish about 4 inches below the heat source. Broil until the shells are golden brown, for about 4 to 5 minutes, watching carefully. Place 6 shells on each of 4 plates. Serve immediately.

Turkey Corn Dogs

**Makes 8 Sausages
to Serve 4**

Planning Ahead

The sausages can be prepared and wrapped in plastic wrap 1 day before poaching. Once poached, they can be kept several days. Sauté just before serving.

Technique Tips

The technique used here for wrapping and poaching the turkey can be used to make sausages with any ground meat mixture.

To encase the sausage, use only plastic wrap that has been recommended as safe for microwaving, such as Saran Wrap.

When forming the sausages, dip your hands occasionally into a bowl of cold water so your fingers won't stick to the meat.

Twist the ends tightly to compact the meat and avoid air pockets and holes.

The water should be barely simmering so the sausages will remain tender and well shaped.

Wine Selection
Red Burgundy

I first made these sausages when I was challenged on a TV show to serve six people a gourmet dinner for $20. Although I selected turkey because it was the least expensive ground meat in the market, an added bonus is its low fat that makes these hot dogs for dieters. My plastic wrap-poaching technique may sound weird to the uninitiated—or even to the initiated—but it is quick and easy to do.

¾ cup unsalted chicken stock

1 large ear corn, husked, kernels removed and coarsely chopped

1 pound ground turkey

⅓ cup pecans, toasted and coarsely chopped

Salt and freshly ground black pepper to taste

1 ounce (¼ stick) unsalted butter or 2 tablespoons olive oil

4 sausage-length French bread rolls or hot dog buns

Coarse-grained or other Dijon mustard

Place the chicken stock in a small pan, add the corn and simmer briskly until the corn completely absorbs the stock, for about 10 minutes, stirring occasionally. Cool completely, for about 30 minutes.

To assemble the sausages, mix the turkey, pecans, cooled corn, salt and pepper in a medium bowl. Divide the mixture into 4 parts. Tear off four 15-inch-long sheets of plastic wrap. Working with ¼ of the mixture at a time, place the mixture in the center of the plastic wrap. Form into a 1-inch-wide sausage. Fold the plastic wrap over the meat, sliding your hand across to smooth and even it out, then roll up the sausage, jelly-roll fashion, in the plastic, twisting ends tightly. Tie the middle, then the ends with string, dividing into 2 equal-sized sausages. Repeat with the remaining sausage mixture. Place the sausages on a tray. (This can be prepared ahead and set aside at cool room temperature for several hours or refrigerated overnight. Bring to room temperature before cooking.)

To poach, fill a deep large skillet at least 10 inches in diameter with water and bring to a gentle simmer. Add the sausages, cover and poach 8 minutes or until just firm to the touch, adjusting the heat so the water is barely bubbling and turning halfway with tongs. Remove the sausages from the water and let cool for at least 5 minutes. (This can be prepared ahead, cooled completely, covered and set aside at cool room temperature for several hours or refrigerated until 1 hour before sautéing.)

To serve, melt the butter in a heavy large nonstick skillet over medium-high heat, unwrap the sausages, add them to the skillet and brown on all sides, for about 5 minutes. Serve immediately on a platter or 4 plates. Accompany with rolls or buns and mustard.

Turkey à l'Orange

I love the American Thanksgiving holiday because you don't have to worry about religion and getting to services on time. Since the celebration starts late in the afternoon, there are many good hours to spend with family and friends. In France, our main holiday is Christmas, and its festivities don't start until midnight. By that time, all I usually want to do is go to sleep.

This big unstuffed turkey will be terrific either for Thanksgiving or for Christmas, or for any time you are awake, for I've updated the proverbial Orange Sauce usually served with duck to be light and refreshing. This sauce may get the versatility award because it goes beautifully with any type of poultry—either whole or in parts—no matter whether it is roasted, grilled, poached, sautéed or fried.

ORANGE SAUCE

6 oranges

½ cup sugar

Water

6 tablespoons Champagne vinegar or white wine vinegar

4 cups strained orange juice

6 tablespoons Grand Marnier

1 tablespoon plus 1 teaspoon all-purpose flour

4 cups unsalted chicken or other poultry stock

TURKEY

12- to 15-pound fresh turkey, patted dry

Peanut oil or 1 ounce (¼ stick) unsalted butter, melted

Salt and freshly ground black pepper to taste

1 tablespoon fresh peeled minced gingerroot

Salt to taste

Tabasco to taste

(continued)

10 to 12 Servings

Planning Ahead

The Orange Sauce can be almost completely prepared 1 day in advance. Finish the sauce and cook the turkey just before serving.

Technique Tips

Oranges vary in the amount of juice they yield. Generally you'll need 12 to 16 oranges for 4 cups of juice, but to be on the safe side, purchase extra.

To keep the turkey moist and self-basting, insert a flavored butter under its skin: Mix 6 tablespoons room temperature unsalted butter with 2 tablespoons minced fresh thyme, tarragon, savory, marjoram or other favorite herb. Starting at the neck end, gently loosen the skin by gradually inserting your fingers between the skin and meat. Keeping your fingers toward the meat and being careful not to tear the skin, move your hand down over the breast and legs. When the skin is completely loosened, chop the herb butter and distribute small pieces of it under the skin over the breast and legs.

Wine Selection

California or German slightly sweet Riesling or Champagne

For the Orange Sauce, remove the orange part of the peel, without the bitter white pith, using a vegetable peeler. Chop coarsely. Blanch the peel in a small pot of simmering water for 3 minutes; drain. (This can be prepared ahead, wrapped in plastic and set aside at room temperature.)

Place the sugar in a heavy large saucepan. Cover with water. Cook over low heat until the sugar dissolves, swirling the pan occasionally. Increase the heat and boil until the sugar caramelizes and turns a deep mahogany, watching carefully so the mixture doesn't burn. Stand back and pour in the vinegar, off the heat, avoiding splatter. Add the orange juice, Grand Marnier and blanched peel. Return to the heat and simmer until reduced to 3 cups.

Place the flour in a small bowl. Whisk in several tablespoons of the stock or enough to form a smooth paste. Whisk in the remaining stock. Add the stock to the saucepan and simmer until thickened and reduced to 3 cups or to a saucelike consistency, for about 30 minutes. (This can be prepared ahead, cooled, covered and set aside at cool room temperature for several hours or refrigerated.)

For the turkey, preheat the oven to 325°F. Rub the turkey with oil, sprinkle with salt and pepper and place on a rack in a roasting pan, breast side up. Roast, basting with pan juices every 30 minutes. If the turkey becomes too brown, tent with aluminum foil. If the turkey is not coloring evenly, turn halfway through. Roast until the thermometer registers 155°F to 160°F when inserted into the thickest part of the breast, about 2½ to 2¾ hours for a 12-pound turkey. Let the turkey rest for 30 minutes before carving.

Add the ginger, salt and Tabasco to the sauce. Stir over medium-high heat to rewarm. Slice the turkey and arrange on a platter or on 10 to 12 plates. Spoon several tablespoons of the sauce over each serving or pass it separately in a sauceboat. Serve immediately.

Roast Turkey Breast
with Lemon and Thyme

4 to 6 Servings

R egardless of whether turkey is whole or in parts, a strange ritual surrounds its cooking in this country. Before it is roasted, people worry about how long to cook it, what technique to employ and whether it will be juicy. Afterward, they glom on a gravy that looks like wallpaper paste to hide its dryness. Wouldn't it be easier just to cook it right in the first place? Since the fail-safe method below will yield a moist, juicy breast, I've made a fresh light lemony sauce without flour that would also be nice with a big bird. There should be no unhappy groans at the groaning board. With turkey so inexpensive, everyone should be happy, including the hosts.

MARINADE

2½ to 3 pounds fresh bone-in turkey breast, patted dry

2 tablespoons peanut or olive oil

2 large garlic cloves, peeled and minced

1½ tablespoons fresh minced thyme or 2 teaspoons dried thyme, crumbled

Salt and freshly ground black pepper to taste

SAUCE

1½ cups unsalted chicken stock

8 4-inch fresh thyme sprigs or 2 teaspoons dried thyme, crumbled

2½ tablespoons strained freshly squeezed lemon juice or to taste

Salt and freshly ground black pepper to taste

Salt and freshly ground pepper to taste

1 ounce (¼ stick) chilled unsalted butter, chopped

4 to 6 fresh thyme sprigs for garnish (optional)

Planning Ahead

Marinate the turkey at least 4 hours or, preferably, overnight. The sauce base can be prepared at any time during the day it is to be served. Cook the turkey just before presenting, allowing about 30 minutes for it to rest before carving.

Technique Tip

To ensure that the breast remains moist and juicy, I cook the meat only until a meat thermometer registers 150°F. I then let it rest outside of the oven for about 30 minutes while it continues to cook and becomes opaque throughout.

Wine Selection

Chardonnay

For the marinade, place the turkey breast on a large piece of plastic wrap. Rub the oil and press the garlic and thyme onto both sides of the breast. Season with salt and pepper. Wrap and refrigerate at least 4 hours or overnight.

For the sauce base, boil the chicken stock and thyme in a heavy small saucepan until reduced by half. Add the lemon juice and season with salt and pepper. (This can be prepared ahead, cooled, covered and set aside at cool room temperature for several hours or refrigerated.)

To cook the turkey, preheat the oven to 325°F. Arrange the breast on a rack in a heatproof roasting pan. Season with salt and pepper. Roast until the thickest center portion registers 150°F on a meat thermometer, about 1 to 1¼ hours. Let rest 30 minutes before carving.

To serve, pour the sauce base into the turkey roasting pan. Bring to a boil over 2 burners, stirring until all the browned bits are dislodged. Strain back into a saucepan through a fine sieve, pressing on the ingredients. Degrease if necessary. Carve the turkey on a diagonal into thin slices. Overlap the slices on 4 to 6 plates. Bring the sauce to a boil. Quickly whisk in the butter, then immediately remove from the heat. Ladle the sauce over the turkey. Garnish with thyme sprigs, if desired. Serve immediately.

Duck Crapaudine with Dried Cherries

Planning Ahead

The cherries should be soaked at least 4 hours before using in the sauce. The sauce can be prepared at any time during the day the duck is to be served. Roast the duck just before presenting.

Technique Tips

Air drying, part of the process for producing Peking duck, facilitates the crisping of the skin. If you order ahead, many Chinese markets will sell a duck that is already air-dried. If one of these markets is nearby, purchase an air-dried duck for this—and all other—duck recipes, proceeding with the recipe as written.

Refrigerate or freeze the duck fat removed from the roasting pan in a covered container to cook potatoes, rice or vegetables such as cabbage.

If sauce becomes too thick while standing, thin with water as necessary.

Variation

This sauce is also excellent on chicken or game hens.

*C*rapaudine (toad) is a French technique for cooking chicken or duck that crisps the poultry's skin while reducing its cooking time. When utilizing this method, a cut is made down both sides of the backbone, the backbone is removed and then the bird is opened up and flattened until it looks more like a toad than a duck. After roasting, the bird emerges moist and succulent with crunchy mahogany skin to serve plain or with a sauce.

For my sauce, I use the dried cherries that have recently appeared on the market. Not only is it fun to experiment with a new dried fruit, but, unlike the fresh variety, this one can be used all year long.

SOUR CHERRY SAUCE

I cup dried sour cherries

I cup tepid water

I tablespoon red wine vinegar

I tablespoon kirsch (optional)

½ teaspoon Chinese five-spice powder or mixture of ground cloves, cinnamon and anise seed

I teaspoon all-purpose flour

2 tablespoons sugar

Water to cover

5- to 6-pound duck, patted dry

Salt and freshly ground black pepper to taste

For the Sour Cherry Sauce, soak the cherries in water for at least 4 hours or overnight at room temperature, stirring occasionally. Stir the vinegar, kirsch, five-spice powder and flour into the cherry mixture.

Meanwhile, place the sugar with water to cover in a heavy small saucepan. Cook over low heat until the sugar dissolves, swirling the pan occasionally. Increase heat and simmer until the sugar caramelizes, watching carefully. Stand back and pour in the cherry mixture off the heat, avoiding splatter. Return to the heat and simmer gently until the caramel dissolves and the sauce thickens and reduces slightly, for about 5 minutes, stirring occasionally. (This can be prepared ahead, cooled, covered and set aside at cool room temperature.)

For the duck, preheat the oven to 325°F. Remove the backbone by cutting down the length of the duck on both sides of the bone with a knife or poultry shears. Open the duck up and press down on its breast bone to flatten. Place on a large rack in a roasting pan. Season with salt and pepper. Prick the skin all over with a fork. Roast 1½ hours, skin up. Remove fat from the pan to a container as necessary, using a bulb baster.

To serve, carve the wings and legs off the duck; separate the drumsticks from the thighs. Remove the breast meat from the bone in 1 piece; slice thinly on the diagonal. Place ½ of the breast and leg or thigh on each of 4 plates. Reheat the sauce by stirring over medium-high heat. Ladle over duck. Serve immediately.

Wine Selection
Merlot or California or German slightly sweet Riesling

Apple Pie Duck

The sauce can be prepared at any time during the day the dish is to be served. Roast the duck just before presenting.

Technique Tip

The apples should retain their texture in this sauce. If they begin to overcook before the sauce is reduced, remove them temporarily with a slotted spoon.

Wine Selection

Chardonnay

Muscovy ducks, which are much meatier than the meager Peking and Long Island varieties commonly sold, are increasingly available. Before roasting, I rub my duck with cinnamon to reinforce the sweetness of its skin. This spice, like the couplers linking cars of a train, is also the transition to the apples in the sauce.

APPLE CINNAMON SAUCE

3 tablespoons sugar

Water

1 pound (about 3 large) Golden Delicious or Pippin apples, peeled, quartered, cored and thinly sliced

1 cup unsweetened apple juice

½ cup dry white wine

1 teaspoon ground cinnamon

Salt and freshly ground black pepper to taste

DUCK

2 tablespoons ground cinnamon

2 teaspoons sugar

5½- to 6-pound duck, patted dry

Salt and freshly ground black pepper to taste

1 ounce (¼ stick) unsalted butter, chopped

For the Apple Cinnamon Sauce, place the sugar with water to cover in a heavy small saucepan over medium-low heat. Cook until the sugar dissolves, swirling the pan occasionally. Increase heat and boil until the sugar caramelizes, watching carefully. Stand back to avoid splatter, add the apples and cook over medium-high heat until browned, stirring occasionally. Pour in the apple juice and wine, stir in the cinnamon, reduce heat and simmer until reduced and thickened to a saucelike consistency. Season with salt and pepper. (This can be prepared ahead, cooled, covered and set aside at cool room temperature.)

For the duck, preheat the oven to 325°F. Mix the cinnamon and sugar and rub over the duck skin. Season with salt and pepper. Prick the duck all over with a fork. Place the duck on a rack in a roasting pan. Roast 1½ hours, turning halfway with tongs. Remove the fat from the pan to a container as necessary, using a bulb baster. Let rest 10 minutes.

To serve, carve the wings and legs off of the duck; separate the drumstick from the thigh. Remove the breast meat from the bone; slice thinly on the diagonal. Place ½ of the breast and leg or thigh on 3 or 4 plates. Reheat the sauce by stirring over medium-high heat. Whisk in the butter. Ladle over the duck. Serve immediately.

Duck Legs with Beets

O ne day I made borscht and was trying to decide how I wanted to present it. I had some duck legs I didn't know what to do with, so I boned them out and made them into a mousse. I then cut the mousse into wedges and fried it to serve with the soup. I called the dish Duck Fries with Beets. It was pretty weird, but everybody liked it. Since then, I've often cooked duck with beets as I have here. The sweetness of the beets goes well with the gamey duck flavor, and the red color is just great. With the caramelized beet chips, the overall effect is wonderfully rustic and nutty, although if time is a problem, this garnish can be omitted.

Since I prefer to cook duck breasts rare and legs well done, I frequently cook them separately. It is hard to find ducks sold cut up like chickens, so I often buy three or four birds at once and then divide them up and freeze them by parts, reserving the carcass and any remaining scraps to simmer for stock. I've used only the legs for this dish. If you want to use the breasts as well, follow the directions under Technique Tips.

4 Servings

Planning Ahead
The duck legs, sauce and chips can all be prepared several hours in advance and reheated before serving. The beet chips can also be presented at room temperature.

BEET SAUCE

> 2 tablespoons coarsely chopped duck fat with 2 tablespoons water or unsalted butter

> 4 large duck legs with thighs attached, patted dry and pricked with fork

> 2 medium (about 12 ounces total) beets, peeled and diced

> 1 small onion, peeled and diced

> 2 cloves garlic, peeled and halved

> 1½ cups Cabernet Sauvignon or other dry red wine

> Salt and freshly ground black pepper to taste

BEET CHIPS

> Peanut or vegetable oil (about 4 cups) for deep frying

> 3 medium (about 18 to 20 ounces total) beets, peeled and thinly sliced

> Salt to taste

> Fresh thyme sprigs for garnish (optional)

(continued)

When cutting up ducks, reserve loose fat in the refrigerator or freezer to render for cooking.

To slice beets thinly (easily), use the slicing blade of a food processor or a mandoline.

To cook boned breasts, trim off excess fat, prick skin, pat dry and pound gently between 2 sheets of plastic wrap with a meat pounder to an even thickness.

Heat a heavy large nonstick skillet over medium heat. Add the breasts skin side down. Cook until the skin is brown and crisp and the fat is rendered out, for about 30 to 45 minutes, depending on the type of duck. Remove fat occasionally with a bulb baster. Turn and cook the second side 3 to 4 minutes for rare or until just firm to the touch. Let sit for 10 minutes before carving diagonally into ¼-inch-thick slices.

Variation

Beet chips can be baked until crisp instead of fried in a 350°F oven for 20 to 30 minutes.

Wine Selection

Zinfandel

For the sauce, preheat the oven to 300°F. Heat a heavy large nonstick skillet over medium heat. Add the duck fat with water and cook until it is rendered. Add the duck legs skin side down to the skillet. Cook until the fat is rendered out of the duck legs and the skin is crisp and brown. Turn and brown the second side. Remove all fat from the skillet with a bulb baster and reserve for another use. Add the beets, onion and garlic to the skillet. Pour in the wine. Bring to a simmer. Cover the skillet and transfer to the oven. Bake until the legs are tender and their juices run clear when pricked with a fork, about 1¼ to 1½ hours, turning several times. Remove the duck legs to a tray. Remove the beets, onion and garlic to a food processor or blender with a slotted spoon. Place cooking juices in a fat separator or degrease. Wash the skillet.

Process the vegetables until finely chopped, pulsing on/off and stopping to scrape down the sides of the container. Pour the degreased juices through the feed tube and continue processing until mixture is a smooth puree, for at least 5 minutes. Strain the sauce back into the clean skillet through a fine sieve, pressing on the ingredients. Simmer, if necessary, to reduce and thicken to a saucelike consistency. (There should be about 1½ cups sauce.) Season with salt and pepper. Return the duck legs to the sauce. (This can be prepared ahead, covered and set aside at cool room temperature.)

For the chips, line a large baking sheet with several layers of paper towels. Heat oil in a deep fryer, wok or large pot to 325°F. Fry the beets in small batches, adjusting the heat as necessary so the chips cook slowly and turning until brown on both sides, for about 15 to 20 minutes total. Transfer to the prepared baking sheet in a single layer using tongs or a slotted spoon. The beets will be limp when removed from the fryer, but will crisp immediately. (This can be prepared ahead and set aside at cool room temperature.)

To serve, preheat the oven to 450°F, remove the paper towels from the baking sheet and reheat the beet chips for 5 minutes or until warm, or serve at room temperature. Season with salt, if desired. Reheat the legs on both sides, if necessary, by simmering gently in the sauce in the covered skillet. Ladle the sauce into the center of 4 large plates. Place a leg in the center of sauce. Garnish with beet chips and thyme sprigs, if desired. Serve immediately.

Meat

I must confess that from a chef's perspective, it is less fun to cook meat than other foods. No matter what we do with a steak, a chop or a rack, it is basically the same style. It is what it is. The focus becomes the accompaniments, and, occasionally, the sauce. Flavors need to be strong to stand up to meat, whereas my personal preference is for more subtle delicate tones. With one person liking meat rare and another well done, it's harder to cook meat for a group than fish or chicken, which are pretty much done to the same degree for all. Every once in a while, though, I have a yearning for meat; an emotional craving for a big T-bone or prime rib. Then I go to a steak house and I'm disappointed. I'm looking for taste more than size; a refined little portion. As the years pass, I think a steak must taste best when you're 25.

The fact that meat cookery is less than exciting to a chef is exactly what makes it a good choice for home-cooked meals: It can be handled quickly and simply in a straightforward manner. When people want a steak, they are not looking for an elaboration. They want meat and maybe fries or mashed potatoes. It is a fast jump from pan to plate. If you treat each cut properly, you will have the satisfaction of providing a delicious meal with no fuss.

We have the best beef in the world in this country. When you buy beef, buy choice or aged prime, which is definitely worth a detour. If you're going to indulge in meat, let it be the best available. Meat should look fresh and red. If you look at it long enough, you instinctively recognize when it is good. Better yet, if you make friends with your butcher, you will be assured of quality all the time. Trim it very well, removing all visible fat and any tendon or fell (membrane). Give it a head start by marinating overnight. Learn how to prepare it properly and don't start cooking until it reaches room temperature.

I'm not a grilling fan, even for the beef or lamb team. The only food that tastes good to me charred is a hot dog on a stick. Barbecuing toughens, shrinks and dries meat, cooking the interior unevenly while armoring the exterior. For this reason, I prefer to dry my meat, brown it on both sides in a skillet on top of the stove and then finish cooking it in the oven, turning it halfway to head juices in the opposite direction. When I want that barbecued smokiness, I brown meat very lightly in the beginning, undercook it slightly and throw it on the grill for just a few moments at the end.

Don't rush to serve meat when it has finished cooking. It needs about 15 minutes to relax, cook through to the interior and distribute juices evenly. Doneness is not a guessing game or a matter of cut-it-up-and-see-what-it-looks-like-inside. You can recognize when meat is done to your liking by touch. If meat is very rare, it feels somewhat like the muscle between the thumb and index finger when it is relaxed. When you stretch your fingers, the muscle tightens, resembling the texture of meat cooked medium. When meat feels like the muscle in a clenched fist, it's all over, unless you like your meat well done.

When I think about meat, I really do think of it as a hunk, but more and more, I like to cut it up and stir-fry it. Other than the food processor, I can't think of a tool better suited for today's busy health-oriented lifestyle than the wok. It is definitely worth the expense and cupboard space it occupies. There is no better recipe for getting a delicious dinner to the table quickly than: "Cut everything you want to cook the same size, throw it in the wok and toss it around. Eat it."

At the other extreme, the slow simmering Short Rib Terrine with Mustard Dressing (page 206), Braised Beef with Carrots (page 221), Lamb Pilaf with Cardamom (page 237) and Lamb Shanks with *Ras el Hanout* (page 238) are, perhaps, the dishes that come from the depths of my being. People complain they don't have time to stew meat today, but time can't buy what these dishes offer in terms of outright satisfaction.

As I mentioned, a sauce for lamb or beef is more of a decoration than a requirement. For a simple sauce that catches pan drippings, degrease any pan juices, pour a little stock or wine into the skillet and boil it down while you scrape up browned bits on the bottom. Whisk in a little chopped chilled butter to bind the juices, strain if you wish, and *voilà*, you have a sauce.

More than the sauce, it is the seasoning—the salt, pepper, and any spices or flavorings—that heightens the meat. Until you taste the difference, it's hard to imagine how much better it is seasoned with sea salt or kosher salt than with regular salt. I also use *fleur de sel*, the finest white salt skimmed off the top of the beds in Brittany.

Although I've spoken mainly about beef and lamb so far, pork is one of my favorite meats. In France, no part of the pig is wasted, whereas here only a few cuts are generally used. To be good, pork has to be moist. If pork is overcooked, give it to the dog. I love liver, too, and other offal, but here again—as with some of the more exotic poultry and wild game—I can't get people to eat it. Veal, on the other hand, is very popular even though it is rather bland. Yet, it, too, is a cinch to cook. With an interesting sauce or side dish, you have the props in place for a wonderful evening of *bonhomie*.

Short Rib Terrine
with Mustard Dressing

8 to 16
First-course Servings
or 6 to 8 Main-course
Servings

Planning Ahead

It's best to order the meat for this terrine in advance to ensure that such a large amount will be available. The terrine should be made at least 24 hours before serving to allow it to set. Prepare the dressing at any time during the day the terrine is to be presented. To offer the terrine chilled, remove it from the refrigerator 30 minutes early.

One morning I found myself with a huge pile of short ribs left over from a gigantic pot-au-feu I had made for a party. I removed all the bones and stacked the meat in a terrine, pressing the layers together to meld with the meat's natural gelatin. The next day I unmolded this terrine and served it for another celebration to great acclaim. Everyone who tastes this accidental creation loves it, regardless of whether they have it hot or cold; as a first course or main course. It was even voted one of the best dishes of 1990 by the *Los Angeles Times*. Nevertheless, when I put this terrine on the menu, I have a hard time selling it. When you say braised beef, people's eyes glaze over. Today, it's anything that's grilled that goes. Perhaps I'll change its name to Grilled Short Rib Terrine.

SHORT RIBS

12 pounds large short ribs (preferably flanken-style cut from the chuck)

Salt and freshly ground black pepper to taste

3 medium unpeeled onions, washed and quartered

3 large unpeeled carrots, sliced

2 celery stalks, sliced

3 tomatoes, quartered

2 whole unpeeled heads garlic, washed, halved crosswise and cloves separated

10 fresh thyme sprigs or 3 tablespoons dried thyme, crumbled

½ bunch flat-leaf parsley

2 large bay leaves

1 tablespoon black peppercorns, crushed

2 quarts or more unsalted chicken or beef stock

MUSTARD DRESSING

¼ cup Dijon mustard

1 egg yolk (optional), at room temperature

½ cup red wine vinegar

1 cup olive oil

2 medium shallots, peeled and minced

¼ cup fresh minced chives or green onions

Meat

½ cup minced flat-leaf parsley

Salt and freshly ground black pepper to taste

Coarse salt

Small salad of mixed greens or marinated vegetables to garnish
when serving cold

Steamed or stir-fried vegetables to garnish when serving hot

For the short ribs, preheat the oven to 300°F. Season the short ribs with salt and pepper. Place in a large roasting pan. Scatter the onions, carrots, celery, tomatoes, garlic, thyme, parsley, bay leaves and peppercorns over the meat. Pour in enough chicken stock to cover the meat. Bring to a boil over medium-high heat. Cover the pan, transfer to the oven and braise 2½ to 3 hours or until the meat is very tender and falling off the bones.

To assemble the terrine, immediately remove the short ribs from the broth with a slotted spoon. Working with the meat while it is still warm, remove all the fat, gristle and bones from the short ribs, keeping the meat in 1 large strip, if possible. Line a 9- × 5-inch loaf pan with plastic wrap, letting several inches overhang. Pack the trimmed short ribs into the terrine lengthwise in several layers, pressing down and placing the ribs as close together as possible. Fold the plastic over to cover.

Place the terrine on a tray to catch the juices. Place a second 9- × 5-inch loaf pan over the terrine to compress air pockets. Tie the loaf pans together with string at each end. Put a spoon under each knot and turn it to tighten the string. Pour off any juices that accumulate. Refrigerate at least 24 hours.

Strain the short rib cooking broth through a fine sieve, pressing on the ingredients. Cover and refrigerate to serve with warm short ribs.

For the Mustard Dressing, mix the mustard and egg yolk, if using, in a blender. With the machine running, pour in the vinegar and then the oil in a slow, thin stream. Stir in the shallots, chives and parsley with a spoon. Season with salt and pepper. (This can be prepared ahead, covered and set aside at cool room temperature for several hours or refrigerated until 30 minutes before serving.)

To serve, remove the terrine from the refrigerator, cut the strings and remove the top loaf pan. Invert the terrine onto a cutting board. Immediately slice it into ½- to ¾-inch-thick slices, using a sharp knife and broad spatula. Allow 1 to 2 slices for a first course; 2 to 3 slices for a main course.

To serve cold, place slices on a platter or on individual plates. Let sit at room temperature for 30 minutes. Before serving, sprinkle lightly with coarse salt and ladle dressing alongside. Garnish with a small mixed green salad or marinated vegetables.

To serve warm, place cold slices on individual ovenproof plates. Preheat the oven to 350°F. Reheat meat for 5 minutes. Spoon off the firm layer of fat from the short rib cooking broth. Reheat and ladle several tablespoons over each slice of meat. Sprinkle lightly with coarse salt. Ladle dressing alongside. Garnish with steamed or stir-fried vegetables.

Technique Tips

Flanken short ribs are cut from the chuck and contain a large piece of meat over a base of rib bones. In order for the individual short ribs to meld together, the terrine must be assembled while the short ribs are still warm and the terrine must be weighted as described above.

Since the meat is bound together only by its natural gelatin, the union is a delicate one. To keep the slices from breaking, slice the terrine immediately after it is removed from the refrigerator and reheat the slices directly on individual serving plates.

To degrease the braising liquid easily, refrigerate it overnight and spoon off the firm layer of fat that rises to the surface. Freeze any leftover juices to use as a base for soups or meat sauces.

If the egg yolk is omitted, the Mustard Dressing will be more like a vinaigrette than a mayonnaise-like sauce. Store-bought mayonnaise or sour cream can be added instead of the egg yolk.

Variation
Use the dressing also as a sauce for cold vegetables.

Wine Selection
Red Côtes du Rhône

Meat

Michel-Michel Shabu-Shabu

Planning Ahead

The beef can be sliced, the vegetables prepped and the horseradish simmered in the broth several hours in advance. Cook the vegetables just before serving to maintain their freshness.

Technique Tips

Meat is easiest to slice thinly when it is partially frozen.

If a meat pounder is not available, use the bottom of a heavy pot.

When pounding the meat, use a down-and-out motion.

Meat pounded to paper thinness will cook just from the heat of the broth.

Wine Selection

Beaujolais or beer

A shabu-shabu I ordered one night in a Japanese restaurant reminded me of both a fondue Bourguignon and pot-au-feu, the hearty, honest French fare that is part of my soul. It is amazing how similarly dishes are constructed in each culture, with only herbs and seasonings to give them a particular ethnic identity. In this adaptation, I've used the horseradish and mustard that accent Western soup-stews to contrast with the Eastern vegetables. I now frequently incorporate ginger, soy sauce and toasted sesame oil in my cooking, but I rarely produce a dish that feels so explicitly East meets West as this one.

¾ to 1 pound beef tenderloin, preferably a single piece cut from center, trimmed of all fat

4 to 5 cups unsalted beef stock

2-inch piece fresh horseradish root, peeled and grated or 1-inch piece fresh gingerroot, peeled and cut into fine julienne

1 small (about ¼ pound) rutabaga, peeled, halved lengthwise and thinly sliced

1 small (about 4 to 5 ounces) zucchini, ends trimmed and thinly sliced

1 large carrot, peeled and sliced into thin sticks (about 2 × ¼ inch)

8 (about 2 ounces) button mushrooms, ends trimmed

8 large (about ½ pound) whole napa cabbage leaves

¼ pound snow peas, ends snapped and strung

Salt and freshly ground black pepper to taste

4 teaspoons Dijon mustard

1 teaspoon prepared horseradish

Freshly ground black pepper to taste

Freeze the meat for 1 hour, then cut it into 12 to 16 thin slices. Pound each slice between 2 pieces of plastic wrap until paper thin, using a meat pounder. Rewrap and refrigerate until 1 hour before serving.

Bring 4 cups of the stock and the grated horseradish to a boil in a large pot. Lower the heat and simmer gently for 10 minutes. (This can be prepared to this point, covered and set aside at cool room temperature for several hours or refrigerated.)

To serve, strain the stock and return it to the pot, adding additional stock as necessary to measure 4 cups. Bring the stock to a boil. Add the rutabaga, zucchini, carrot and mushrooms, cover and simmer gently for 5 minutes. Stir in the cabbage and snow peas, re-cover and simmer for 5 minutes. Season with salt and pepper.

Meanwhile, arrange the meat slices in the bottom of 4 soup plates. Mix the mustard and prepared horseradish. Spread over the meat. Grind some pepper over the meat. Ladle the broth and vegetables over the meat. Serve immediately.

Super *Pistou* with Beef

4 Servings

Planning Ahead

Pistou is even better when prepared several days in advance. The macaroni and zucchini can be cooked several hours before serving. Add them to the soup and reheat just before presenting.

I n 1965, I was proud to receive the award for the best apprentice of the Champagne region. What this meant in reality, though, was that I was now free to get my first job as a slave. By day, I worked in a *boulangerie*/patisserie in Reims and at night, in the few hours I was allowed off, I slept in the attic above with rats, one of whom had babies in my bed. The owner was a tough, mean Niçoise woman who screamed at the bakers and threw food at us as if we were animals. Her one indirect act of kindness occurred each Thursday when she made a large pot of *pistou*, the Provençal version of minestrone. If her husband was home, we got nothing. But if he was out fooling around, which he usually was, each of us got a small bowl of this wonderful basil-scented broth. I would have liked never to think about this witch-woman again, but I just can't forget her delicious soup. I have added meat, so you will be able to eat lots of it for an ample, hearty meal.

About 2 tablespoons olive oil

2 pounds beef rump, chuck or other stew meat, cut into 1-inch pieces and patted dry

2 medium leeks (white and light green parts only), halved lengthwise and sliced crosswise into ½-inch pieces

4 large cloves garlic, peeled and minced

1 cup unsalted chicken stock

2 cups tomato juice

2 medium carrots, peeled, halved lengthwise and sliced crosswise into ½-inch pieces

1 medium (about 10 to 12 ounces) fennel bulb

1 large potato, peeled and cut into ½-inch dice

Salt and freshly ground black pepper to taste

¼ cup fresh minced basil

¾ cup dry elbow macaroni

2 medium zucchini, ends trimmed and sliced crosswise into ½-inch-thick rounds

2 tablespoons olive oil

Salt and freshly ground black pepper to taste

¼ cup (about 1 ounce) freshly grated Parmesan cheese

¼ cup fresh minced basil

2 tablespoons olive oil

Preheat the oven to 325°F. Place a heavy large nonstick casserole over medium-high heat and film with oil. Brown the beef in batches on all sides, adding additional oil as necessary. Transfer the meat to a plate as it is browned using tongs. Add the leeks to the casserole with the garlic, reduce heat to medium-low, cover the casserole and cook until tender, for about 15 minutes, stirring occasionally. Pour in the chicken stock and tomato juice, increase heat and bring to a boil, stirring to release any browned bits on the bottom of the casserole. Return the meat and any juices to the casserole, stir in the carrots, cover and bake for 1 hour.

Trim off the fennel fronds and reserve for another use. Cut off the stalks. Peel the stalks and fibrous exterior of the bulb using a vegetable peeler. Quarter the bulb, core and dice the bulb and stalks. Add the fennel and potato to the stew and bake until the meat is tender when pierced with a knife, for about 1½ hours, stirring occasionally. Season with salt, pepper and basil. (This can be prepared ahead, cooled, covered and set aside at cool room temperature for several hours or refrigerated for several days.)

Bring a large pot of water to a boil over medium-high heat. Add the macaroni. Cook for 7 minutes. Add the zucchini. Cook for 5 minutes or until the macaroni is al dente; drain. Toss the macaroni and zucchini with oil. Season with salt and pepper. (This can be prepared ahead and set aside at room temperature.)

To serve, add the macaroni mixture to the *pistou* and stir over medium-high heat to reheat. Ladle into 4 soup plates. Sprinkle with Parmesan and basil. Drizzle with olive oil. Serve immediately.

Technique Tips

When browning beef, do not crowd the pan or the beef will steam rather than brown.

If the liquid reduces too much while the stew is cooking, add more chicken stock before reheating.

Wine Selection

Zinfandel, Pinot Noir or Red Côtes du Rhône

Meat

Meat Loaf with Brown Lentils

6 to 8 Servings

Planning Ahead

The lentils can be cooked 1 day before the meat loaf is prepared. If cooking the same day, allow 3 to 4 hours for them to cool to room temperature (or chill more quickly in the refrigerator). The meat loaf can be formed several hours before baking. If serving hot, bake just before presenting. If offering cold, bake a day or two in advance.

Wine Selection
Cabernet Sauvignon

When I opened Broadway Deli, I knew I had to have a meat loaf on the menu. What I didn't know was how much I would like it. After trying many different versions of this comfort food, I ended up with what is essentially a pâté mixed with the lentil stuffing my mother uses to fill tomatoes for baking. The lentils keep the meat loaf moist while reinforcing its country character. The best part of the meat loaf for me, though, is the ketchup on top.

LENTILS

¼ pound (about 4 slices) bacon, finely diced

1 small onion, peeled and finely diced

1 tablespoon tomato paste

1 cup brown lentils, picked over and rinsed

4 cups unsalted chicken stock

2 fresh large sprigs thyme or 1 teaspoon dried, crumbled

MEAT LOAF

1½ pounds regular ground beef

½ pound ground pork

¼ cup chicken stock

2 eggs

3 large cloves garlic, peeled and minced

½ cup minced flat-leaf parsley

1½ teaspoons salt

Freshly ground black pepper to taste

Red Cabbage Ketchup (page 277) or ketchup

For the lentils, cook the bacon and onion in a heavy large nonstick pot over medium heat until the bacon is brown, stirring occasionally. Stir in the tomato paste and lentils. Add the chicken stock and thyme. Bring to a boil. Lower heat and simmer gently until the lentils are very tender, for about 45 minutes, stirring occasionally. Drain the lentils. Cool to room temperature. (This can be prepared ahead, cooled, covered and set aside at cool room temperature for several hours or refrigerated overnight.)

Meat

For the meat loaf, preheat the oven to 350°F. Lightly mix the beef, pork, cooled lentils, chicken stock, eggs, garlic, parsley, salt and pepper in a large bowl with your hands or a large fork. Place a large fine-holed rack in a 9- × 13-inch baking dish. Form the meat mixture into a loaf shape about 2 inches thick and place on the rack. Bake for 40 minutes, basting occasionally. Spread Red Cabbage Ketchup or ketchup on top of the meat loaf, about ¼ inch thick. Bake for 15 minutes.

To serve hot, cut immediately into slices about ¼ inch thick and transfer to 6 to 8 plates using a large spatula.

To serve cold, cool, cover and refrigerate for at least 6 hours or several days. Remove from the refrigerator and slice immediately. Let sit 1 hour before serving.

Steak with Garlic-Ginger *Jus*

T here is a French accent on the sauce for this steak and a Chinese inspiration behind both the seasonings and the stir-fry technique. This high-heat cooking method is particularly good for meat and poultry because it tenderizes while sealing in juices. We frequently use a wok at Citrus because its shape lends itself so readily to moving ingredients around with a spatula. With everything prepped, we are able to instantly respond to orders from hungry guests.

2 tablespoons olive oil

1½ to 2 pounds boneless top sirloin steak, trimmed, cut crosswise into ¼-inch-wide strips and patted dry

½ cup unsalted chicken stock

4 cloves garlic, peeled and thinly sliced

1 tablespoon peeled, slivered fresh gingerroot

1 tablespoon minced flat-leaf parsley

Salt and freshly ground black pepper

2 tablespoons (¼ stick) chilled unsalted butter, chopped

Heat the oil in a wok or heavy large skillet over medium-high heat. Stir-fry the beef until browned on the outside, but very pink within, for about 2 minutes. Transfer the meat to a plate. Add the chicken stock, garlic and ginger to the wok. Boil until reduced to 2 tablespoons. Meanwhile, season the meat with salt and pepper. Mix parsley and butter into the reduced juices off the heat. Stir in the meat. Divide among 4 plates. Serve immediately.

Planning Ahead

The ingredients can be prepped at any time during the day the dish is to be served. If desired, the garlic-ginger mixture can be reduced in advance in a separate pan. Stir-fry the steak and finish the sauce just before presenting.

Wine Selection
Red Burgundy

Stir-fry Sesame Beef with Celery and Belgian Endive

4 Servings

Planning Ahead

The ingredients can be prepped and organized in separate bowls, as they are in Chinese restaurants, several hours in advance of cooking. Stir-fry the dish just before serving.

Wine Selection

Pinot Noir

For many, many months, I presented a roast squab at Citrus on a bed of endive with mushrooms and lots of crisp celery for crunch. These vegetables went so well together that I looked for a way to use them in the book, along with something that would be more accessible for the home cook than squab. Beef proved the perfect answer. While I was trying to be practical, I thought I would adopt the Chinese conveyor-belt system of stir-frying ingredients together in a wok or even a skillet. The Chinese are so smart. They do everything in one pot, whereas the French need six. In keeping with the streamlined Asian approach, there is no need to make a sauce for the beef; just thicken its cooking juices with cornstarch.

8 medium cloves garlic, peeled and minced

8 green onions (white and light green parts only), thinly sliced

1 tablespoon cornstarch

¼ cup unsalted chicken stock

2 tablespoons red wine vinegar

1 tablespoon soy sauce

1 tablespoon peanut oil

1 teaspoon Oriental (toasted) sesame oil

1 pound fresh shiitake or other fresh mushroom, ends trimmed and thinly sliced

1 teaspoon peanut oil

3 stalks celery, trimmed, quartered lengthwise and thinly sliced crosswise

1 tablespoon peanut oil

3 medium (about ¾ pound) Belgian endive, thinly sliced crosswise in rings

Salt and freshly ground black pepper to taste

Meat

1 tablespoon peanut oil

1¼ to 1½ pounds flank steak, sliced cross-grain into ⅛-inch-wide strips and patted dry

Salt and freshly ground black pepper to taste

Celery leaves for garnish

Mix the garlic and onions in a small bowl. Place the cornstarch in a large bowl. Whisk enough chicken stock into the cornstarch to form a smooth paste, then whisk in the remaining chicken stock, vinegar and soy sauce.

Heat 1 tablespoon peanut oil with the sesame oil in a wok or heavy large skillet with about ⅓ of the garlic-onion mixture over medium-high heat. Add the mushrooms and stir-fry just until crisp-tender, for about 2 minutes. Add the cornstarch mixture and stir-fry until thickened. Return the mushroom mixture to the cornstarch bowl.

Heat 1 teaspoon peanut oil in the same wok over medium-high heat. Add the celery and stir-fry until crisp-tender, for about 1 minute. Return to the bowl.

Heat 1 tablespoon peanut oil in the same wok with about ⅓ of the garlic-onion mixture over medium-high heat. Add the endive and stir-fry until crisp-tender, for about 2 minutes. Return to bowl. Season with salt and pepper.

Heat 1 tablespoon peanut oil in the same wok with the remaining garlic-onion mixture over medium-high heat. Add the meat and stir-fry until just browned on the outside, but still very rare within, for about 1 minute. Return the mushroom mixture to the wok and stir-fry until the beef is cooked to rare or the desired degree of doneness, for about 1 minute. Season with salt and pepper.

To serve, scatter the endive over the bottom of 4 plates. Mound the meat mixture over the center of the endive. Sprinkle with celery. Garnish the plates with celery leaves. Serve immediately.

Steak/*Frites* with Shallot Glaze

4 Servings

Planning Ahead

The Shallot Glaze can be completely prepared at any time during the day the steak is to be served. The potatoes can be fried for the first time several hours in advance. Cook the steak just before presenting, while refrying the potatoes.

Technique Tip

To fit the steak into your skillet, it may be necessary to divide it into 2 to 4 pieces, or to cook it in batches or in 2 pans.

Variation

The steak can also be broiled.

Wine Selection

Cabernet Sauvignon

Although I put the *frites* (French fries) recipe with the other potato dishes, they are as inseparable from the steak for me as fish is from chips for the Brits. Of course, they will go well with other dishes, too. Most other dishes. Together with a flank steak—or what we call *bavette*—and Shallot Glaze, you will have the real taste of France.

The only steak I knew growing up was one made from horsemeat, and this is something I still must have today whenever I go back to France. Every Thursday I bought six of these fillets for my family for only ten francs, about $2. I accompanied them with *frites*, followed by a green salad. For dessert, I served strawberries in red wine. I was just a young boy, but I felt like a grand chef.

SHALLOT GLAZE

½ cup (about 4 medium-large) shallots, peeled and thinly sliced crosswise

2 tablespoons red wine vinegar

½ cup dry white wine

⅔ cup unsalted chicken stock

1 large clove garlic, peeled and minced

1 teaspoon soy sauce

Salt and freshly ground black pepper to taste

Frites (page 264)

STEAK

About 2 tablespoons peanut or olive oil

1½ to 1¾ pounds flank or skirt steak, trimmed and patted dry

Salt and freshly ground black pepper to taste

For the Shallot Glaze, boil the shallots with the red wine vinegar in a heavy small saucepan until the vinegar is reduced to a glaze. Add the wine and boil until the sauce is syrupy. Add the chicken stock, garlic and soy sauce and boil until it has reduced and thickened to a saucelike consistency. Season with salt and pepper. (This can be prepared ahead, cooled, covered and set aside at cool room temperature for several hours or refrigerated.)

Prepare the *frites* and fry them once according to instructions.

Season the steak with salt and pepper. Place a heavy large nonstick skillet over medium-high heat and film with oil. Add the steak and brown on both sides, for about 5 minutes total. Slice diagonally crosswise. Overlap the slices on a plate. Reheat the Shallot Glaze and spoon it over the meat. Serve immediately with a fistful of *frites*.

Black Olive Tuxedo Steak

When I am hungry for a steak, it's generally for a huge hunk of meat without embellishment. Recently, though, after my friend Silvio De Mori slathered a magnificent T-bone Florentine-style with olive oil, garlic and sea salt at his restaurant, Tuttobene, I went back to the beloved Provençal ingredients and my technique of using a crust to seal in natural juices. Mixing olives and bread crumbs, I formed a crisp, tapenadelike topping for a fillet. I suspect Silvio would not recognize this steak as the one on his restaurant menu, but it certainly was the inspiration.

GARLIC OIL

> 6 tablespoons olive oil
>
> 3 large cloves garlic, peeled and thinly sliced

OLIVE CRUST

> ⅔ cup minced Niçoise olives or black olive spread, paste or tapenade
>
> ¼ cup bread crumbs
>
> 2 tablespoons olive oil
>
> 4 (1½ to 1¾ pounds total) room temperature fillet or New York steaks, 1 inch thick, patted dry
>
> Salt and freshly ground black pepper to taste
>
> 2 tablespoons olive oil
>
> 1 tablespoon balsamic vinegar

For the Garlic Oil, mix the oil with the garlic in a small glass. Cover with plastic wrap and set aside at room temperature for at least 4 hours.

For the Olive Crust, mix the olives, bread crumbs and oil in a small bowl. (This can be prepared ahead, covered and set aside at room temperature.)

To cook the steaks, preheat the broiler. Season the steaks with salt and pepper. Heat 2 tablespoons of the Garlic Oil in a heavy large nonstick heatproof skillet over medium-high heat. Add the steaks and brown the bottoms, for about 4 minutes. Remove from heat. Spread the Olive Crust over the top of the steaks, covering completely. Broil 3 inches below the heat source for about 4 minutes for rare, or to taste. Let rest for 10 minutes. Place the steaks on 4 plates and drizzle with Garlic Oil and balsamic vinegar. Serve immediately.

4 Servings

Planning Ahead
The Garlic Oil and Olive Crust can be prepared at any time during the day the steak is to be served. Cook the steak just before presenting.

Technique Tips
If the olive mixture is salty, you may not want to season the steaks with additional salt.

To cook a steak to the desired degree of doneness, learn what it feels like when it has reached that point. The longer a steak is cooked, the firmer its surface becomes.

Variation
Diced sautéed onions, chopped tomatoes or mushrooms (cooked until all their liquid has evaporated) can be substituted for olives in the crust.

Wine Selection
Bordeaux

New York Pepper Steak
with Raisins

4 Servings

Planning Ahead

The raisins should be marinated at least several hours in advance or overnight. The sauce can be prepared at any time during the day the steak is to be served. Cook the steak just before presenting.

Wine Selection

Pinot Noir

Sugar-sweetened foods were an important part of the privileged bourgeois French diet historically, so it is not at all unlikely to encounter raisins in a composed salad or in a game sauce, such as Grand Veneur, a rich peppery red wine reduction.

Although the raisins and port used in this sauce suggest game as an accompaniment, not steak, these ingredients work surprisingly well together, combining a hearty robustness with the sweetness Americans seem to love. Actually, I got the idea for this entree one evening when my son started eating raising while we were washing dishes after a steak dinner.

PORT RAISIN SAUCE

½ cup raisins

1 cup port

1 cup unsalted chicken stock

¼ teaspoon ground cinnamon

Salt to taste

STEAK

1 teaspoon black peppercorns, coarsely ground

4 (1½ to 2 pounds total) room temperature New York steaks,
     ¾ to 1 inch thick, patted dry

Salt and freshly ground black pepper to taste

About 2 tablespoons olive oil

¼ cup water

1 ounce (¼ stick) chilled unsalted butter, coarsely chopped

For the Port Raisin Sauce, marinate the raisins with the port in a heavy small saucepan for at least 2 hours or overnight, stirring occasionally. Boil down until the port is reduced by half, stirring occasionally. Add the chicken stock and reduce by half again. Season with cinnamon, salt and pepper. (This can be prepared ahead, cooled, covered and set aside at cool room temperature for several hours or refrigerated.)

For the steak, press the ground peppercorns into the steak and season with salt. Place a heavy large nonstick skillet over medium-high heat and film with oil. Add the steaks to the skillet and cook until brown on both sides and just firm to the touch, for about 7 to 8 minutes total for medium-rare. Transfer to a warm plate. Discard the fat from the skillet. Pour the water into the skillet and stir over medium-high heat, scraping up any browned bits on the bottom of the pan. Pour deglazed juices into the Port Raisin Sauce. Slice the steak diagonally. Arrange on 4 large plates. Pour any carving juices into the Port Raisin Sauce and boil until the sauce is thickened and reheated. Quickly whisk the butter into the sauce. Ladle over the meat. Serve immediately.

Steak Bourguignon

T his is a Beef Bourguignon for the year 2000. It has the red wine sauce and wonderful flavors of its old-fashioned namesake, plus a preparation time of only half an hour compared to the traditional three to four hours. Another bonus for these busy times is that you get two meals from one small effort. The sauce is strained to serve over steak, leaving many good ingredients in the strainer to serve with pasta for a second dinner. There are all kinds of benefits to updating a classic dish to fit today's lifestyle.

4 Servings

Planning Ahead

The sauce can be prepared 2 days in advance. The strained ingredients can be refrigerated or frozen for a future dish. Cook the steak and reheat the sauce with the mushrooms just before serving.

BOURGUIGNON SAUCE

I tablespoon peanut oil

I large onion, peeled and finely chopped

3 slices bacon, diced

½ pound ground beef

½ medium carrot, peeled and finely chopped

I tablespoon all-purpose flour

3 cups Pinot Noir or other dry red wine

2 tablespoons tomato paste

2 cloves garlic, peeled and minced

I fresh large thyme sprig or I½ teaspoons dried thyme,
    crumbled

Salt and freshly ground black pepper to taste

About 2 tablespoons peanut oil

4 (I½ to 2 pounds total) room temperature fillet or other
    steaks, about ¾ to I inch thick, patted dry

Salt and freshly ground black pepper to taste

4 large mushrooms, ends trimmed and finely diced

3 tablespoons flat-leaf parsley, coarsely chopped

(continued)

The sauce should simmer for 3 minutes after the flour is added to eliminate its raw taste.

Variation
Smoked turkey or chicken can be substituted for bacon in this sauce.

Wine Selection
Pinot Noir or whatever wine is used in the sauce

For the Bourguignon Sauce, heat the peanut oil in a heavy medium nonstick saucepan over medium-low heat. Add the onion, cover and cook until translucent, for about 10 minutes, stirring occasionally. Add the bacon, ground beef and carrot, increase heat to medium and cook until the bacon and beef brown, mashing the beef with a fork to break it up. Add the flour, reduce heat to low and stir for 3 minutes. Add the wine, tomato paste, garlic and thyme; increase heat and bring to a boil, stirring to release any browned bits on the bottom of the pan. Lower heat so the sauce is barely simmering. Cook for 30 minutes, stirring occasionally. Strain the sauce into a clean heavy small saucepan through a fine sieve, pressing on the ingredients. (Transfer the strained ingredients to a covered container. Refrigerate or freeze to use as a sauce for pasta.) Degrease the strained sauce and, if necessary, boil until it has reduced and thickened to the desired consistency. Season the sauce with salt and pepper. (This can be prepared ahead and set aside at cool room temperature for several hours or refrigerated.)

For the steaks, season the meat with salt and pepper. Place a heavy large nonstick skillet over medium-high heat and film with oil. Add the steaks to the pan and cook until brown on both sides and just firm to the touch, for about 8 minutes total for medium-rare. Let rest for about 10 minutes.

To serve, add the diced mushrooms to the strained sauce and simmer gently until the mushrooms are cooked, for about 3 minutes, stirring occasionally. Stir in the parsley. Place the steaks on 4 plates. Ladle the sauce over the meat. Serve immediately.

Braised Beef with Carrots

T his long, slow simmering represents the old way of French cooking. Early in November each year, we filled a big black iron pot with the meat and vegetables for this dish and hung it in the fireplace to cook for six hours. When we returned home at the end of that day, we removed the lid ceremoniously, celebrating the wonderful aromas that told us winter had officially started. Before people taste this braised meat, they often say it doesn't sound very exciting. They don't say that afterward, but even if they did, why should I change a recipe my family has enjoyed forever?

About 1 tablespoon olive oil

2 to 3 pounds beef tri-tip, eye of round or brisket, patted dry

Salt and freshly ground black pepper to taste

4 slices bacon, cut crosswise into ¼-inch-wide strips (optional)

6 large carrots, peeled and thinly sliced

1 medium onion, peeled, halved and thinly sliced

2 large cloves garlic, peeled and minced

1 cup unsalted beef stock

2 fresh 5-inch thyme sprigs or 1 tablespoon dried thyme, crumbled

2 tablespoons fresh minced chervil or flat-leaf parsley

Coarse salt

Dijon mustard (optional)

4 Servings

Planning Ahead
The vegetables can be prepped in advance, but basically this is a throw-together-and-cook dish. Braise the beef either the day before or the day of serving.

Variations
If you have mushrooms, celery or other vegetables you want to use up, add them along with the carrots. Simmer boiled potatoes briefly in the sauce after it is reduced.

Wine Selection
Red Burgundy

To braise the beef, preheat the oven to 325°F. Place a heavy large nonstick ovenproof casserole over medium-high heat and film with oil. Add the beef, season with salt and pepper and brown on all sides, for about 5 minutes. Remove the beef. Add the bacon and cook over medium heat. Return the meat to the pan with the carrots, onion, garlic, stock and thyme. Bring to a boil, then cover and bake for 2 hours or until very tender, turning halfway with tongs and lowering heat if necessary so the liquid is barely simmering. (This can be prepared ahead, and set aside at cool room temperature for several hours or cooled and refrigerated overnight. Reheat, covered, in a preheated 300°F oven for about 20 minutes or until warm.)

To serve, remove the meat from the pan, degrease the cooking liquid if necessary, and boil juices down until reduced and thickened to a rich broth. Thinly slice the meat and arrange on a platter or 4 plates. Spoon the cooking juices and vegetables over the meat. Sprinkle with chervil and coarse salt. Serve immediately. Pass the mustard, if desired.

Prime Rib with
Blue Cheese Dressing

3 to 4 Servings

Planning Ahead

The sauce base can be pre-pared at any time during the day it is to be served. Cook the meat and whisk the cheese into the sauce just before presenting.

Technique Tip

When choosing a rib roast, look for one that has been cut from the portion of the rib closest to the loin—the small end—and contains a large rib eye muscle, as opposed to one from the large end cut closer to the less tender chuck.

Wine Selection

Bordeaux

My first impressions of American food came from watching French TV cowboys who chomped on rib steaks and roasts that were bigger than their plates. The frontier sure is shrinking; today my single-rib roast serves three to four modern he-men. Although meat portions seem to have changed, not so the salad with blue cheese dressing that accompanies them. With respect for this tradition, I've incorporated blue cheese into my sauce along with some rosemary to lasso my pioneering spirit.

BLUE CHEESE DRESSING

1 tablespoon unsalted butter

½ small onion, peeled and finely chopped

½ cup dry white wine

½ cup unsalted chicken stock

2 large cloves garlic, peeled and minced

1 fresh 5-inch rosemary sprig or ¾ teaspoon dried rosemary, crumbled

Freshly ground black pepper to taste

RIB ROAST

1¾ to 2 pounds beef single-rib roast (about 2 inches thick), trimmed

Salt and freshly ground black pepper to taste

About 2 tablespoons olive oil

2 ounces room temperature blue cheese, crumbled

1 teaspoon Dijon mustard

Fresh rosemary sprigs for garnish (optional)

For the Blue Cheese Dressing, melt butter in a heavy medium saucepan over low heat. Add the onion, cover and cook until translucent, for about 10 minutes, stirring occasionally. Add the wine, chicken stock, garlic and rosemary and simmer over medium heat until thickened and reduced by about half, for about 10 minutes. Remove the rosemary sprig. Season with pepper. (This can be prepared ahead, cooled, covered and set aside at cool room temperature for several hours or refrigerated.)

For the roast, preheat the oven to 350°F. Pat the meat dry and season with salt and pepper. Heat a heavy large nonstick ovenproof skillet over medium-high heat and film with oil. Brown the meat well on both sides. Transfer to the oven and bake for about 13 minutes, or until a meat thermometer registers 120°F for rare. Let rest for 10 to 15 minutes before carving.

To serve, cut the rib eye off the bone and present the bone to an honored guest. (Me, I hope.) Slice the meat diagonally and overlap on 3 to 4 plates. Bring the sauce to a boil over medium-high heat, add the blue cheese and quickly whisk in just until small pieces remain. Stir in mustard. Taste and adjust seasoning. Spoon the sauce across the middle of the meat. Garnish with rosemary sprigs, if desired, and serve immediately. Pass additional sauce separately.

Roasted Beef Ribs with
Parsley, Sage, Rosemary and Thyme

Planning Ahead

The sauce can be made and frozen several months in advance. Cook the ribs just before serving.

Variations

The ribs can be broiled or grilled as well as baked, in which case reduce the cooking time to 10 to 15 minutes total for rare. Cook 3 to 4 inches from the heat source so the ribs will brown on the outside and still stay rare within. If desired, add soaked mesquite or other wood chips to the fire for flavoring.

Any leftover sauce can be used for pasta or to baste grilled poultry or pork as well as beef.

Wine Selection

Bordeaux

I f you are dubious about the conversion of Michel Richard, the French chef, to an all-American cook, this rib recipe should lay those doubts to rest. I had long been fascinated by the gargantuan racks sold at RJ's The Rib Joint in Beverly Hills. After some prodding from my son, I finally stoked up the grill for ribs one Sunday and started simmering this herb-filled barbecue sauce. I tried offering a salad at Citrus that included rib meat, but there weren't many takers. I guess people thought the salad would come with a huge bone lying across the plate.

TOMATO-SAGE BARBECUE SAUCE

2 tablespoons olive oil

1 small onion, peeled and diced

4 cloves garlic, peeled and sliced

3 fresh thyme sprigs or 1 teaspoon dried thyme, crumbled

1 fresh 3-inch rosemary sprig or 1 teaspoon dried rosemary, crumbled

16-ounce can Italian-style tomatoes

1 tablespoon dark brown sugar

2½ tablespoons red wine vinegar

1 tablespoon coarse-grained mustard

1 teaspoon Worcestershire sauce

Salt and freshly ground black pepper to taste

1 tablespoon fresh minced sage leaves or 1 teaspoon dried sage, crumbled

1 tablespoon minced flat-leaf parsley

4 to 5 pounds beef ribs

For the Tomato-Sage Barbecue Sauce, heat olive oil in a heavy medium nonstick saucepan over medium-low heat. Add the onion, garlic, thyme and rosemary. Cover and cook until the onions are translucent, for about 10 minutes, stirring occasionally. Add the tomatoes, sugar, vinegar, mustard and Worcestershire sauce and bring to a boil. Reduce heat and simmer gently until the sauce is reduced and thickened, for about 30 minutes, stirring occasionally and mashing the tomatoes to break up. Remove the thyme and rosemary sprigs. Puree the sauce in a processor or blender,

Meat

pulsing on/off and stopping to scrape down the sides of the container. Season with salt and pepper. (This can be prepared ahead, cooled, covered and set aside at room temperature for several hours, refrigerated for several days or frozen for several months. Stir in the sage and parsley before continuing with the recipe.)

For the ribs, preheat the oven to 350°F. Brush the ribs generously on both sides with the sauce. Place on a rack in a roasting pan and bake for 1 hour or until brown and crusty, turning halfway and basting occasionally with additional sauce. Slice in between the ribs, place on 4 plates or a platter and serve immediately. Reheat extra sauce and pass separately.

Stuffed Napa Cabbage with Pork and Tomato Sauce

2 to 4 Servings

Planning Ahead

The Tomato Sauce can be prepared several days or months in advance, or even while the cabbage is cooking. The cabbage can be filled the day before it is to be served. Allow about 30 minutes for the stuffing ingredients to cool before using. Bake the cabbage roll just before presenting.

Variations

This recipe can readily be doubled. To do so, prepare 2 separate rolls and bake them side by side.

For a deeper red sauce, cook a small diced beet with the tomatoes.

Wine Selection

Red Burgundy

I n Europe, stuffed cabbage is primarily a way of using up leftover beef or pork. A peasant dish that simmers for several hours, it is generally served with a sauce made from its braising juices. At once rustic and refined, I regard cabbage as too elegant to be relegated solely to leftovers, so I've prepared this dish from scratch. Rather than the ruffled savoy, the cabbage of kings in France, I chose the Oriental napa cabbage, an easy variety to work with. Its leaves are simple to remove, they contain no hard core to cut out and their rectangular shape is more conducive to wrapping than the spherical leaves from a round head. The Tomato Sauce completes my interpretation of stuffed cabbage as a fresh, modern vegetable roll. After you try it, you'll most likely understand why *petit chou* (small cabbage) is a term of endearment in my country.

TOMATO SAUCE

  2 tablespoons unsalted butter

  1 small onion, peeled and diced

  1 small carrot, peeled and sliced

  1 small celery stalk, trimmed and sliced

  1 pound tomatoes, chopped

  Salt and freshly ground black pepper to taste

CABBAGE

  1¾- to 2¼-pound napa cabbage

  2 tablespoons unsalted butter

  1 small onion, peeled and minced

  1 pound ground pork

  1 teaspoon ground cumin

  Salt and freshly ground black pepper to taste

  1 cup unsalted chicken stock

Meat

For the Tomato Sauce, melt the butter in a heavy medium saucepan over medium-low heat. Add the onion, carrot and celery. Cover and cook until translucent, for about 10 minutes, stirring occasionally. Add the tomatoes and bring to a boil. Reduce heat and simmer briskly until the tomatoes are soft, mashing occasionally, for about 15 minutes. Reduce heat to medium-low and continue cooking for 30 minutes, stirring occasionally. Puree in a food processor, pulsing on/off and stopping to scrape down the sides of the container. Strain through a fine sieve, pressing on the ingredients. Season with salt and pepper. (This can be prepared ahead, covered and set aside at room temperature for several hours, refrigerated for several days or frozen for several months.)

For the cabbage, remove 10 of the best outside leaves, trim the ends and blanch in a large pot of boiling water for 1 minute. Drain and pat dry with paper towels. Thinly slice enough of the remaining cabbage to measure 3 to 4 cups.

Melt the butter in a heavy medium saucepan over medium heat. Add the thinly sliced cabbage and onion. Cover and cook until well wilted, for about 10 minutes, stirring occasionally. Cool completely, for about 30 minutes. Mix in the pork and cumin. Season with salt and pepper.

Place a 2-foot-length of plastic wrap on a work surface. Overlap blanched cabbage leaves lengthwise on the plastic, alternating stem end at top and bottom of plastic, to form a 13-inch-wide rectangle. Spread the pork filling over the cabbage to within 1 inch of each edge. Using the plastic wrap as a guide, tightly roll up the cabbage, starting from the long side. Transfer to a 9- × 13-inch baking dish seam side down and carefully remove the plastic. (This can be prepared ahead, covered and set aside at cool room temperature for several hours or refrigerated overnight until 1 hour before baking.)

To serve, preheat the oven to 350°F. Pour the stock into the baking dish. Cover the dish with aluminum foil and bake for 1 hour. Slice the cabbage roll into 12 slices using a serrated knife. Transfer to the top of 2 to 4 plates in a line using a large slotted spatula. Reheat the Tomato Sauce by stirring over medium-high heat. Ladle under the cabbage. Serve immediately.

Pork Kebabs with
Apricot Marmalade

4 to 6 Servings

Planning Ahead

The sauce can be prepared several days in advance. Cook the kebabs just before serving.

I am constantly searching for ways to use dried or underripe fruits, which are like vegetables in their complex flavors and crisp, firm textures. I thought this slightly sweet Apricot Marmalade would work well with Pork Kebabs, regardless of whether they were grilled indoors during the winter or barbecued outdoors in the summer. In these dog days, the kebabs can be eaten right off the grill, the way they are on the streets of Greece and Turkey.

APRICOT MARMALADE

¼ pound (about 1 cup or 22) small dried apricots

Warm water

¾ cup warm water

1 tablespoon sugar

1 tablespoon freshly squeezed lemon juice

½ tablespoon soy sauce

1 small clove garlic, peeled and chopped

½ generous teaspoon fresh minced peeled gingerroot

¼ star anise or ⅛ teaspoon anise seed, crushed

Salt and freshly ground black pepper to taste

KEBABS

2 pounds pork tenderloin, well trimmed of fat and tendon

⅓ cup sugar

Salt and freshly ground black pepper to taste

For the Apricot Marmalade, cover the apricots with warm water in a small bowl and soak until softened for about 15 minutes; drain. Reserve 12 apricots on a plate. Cover the plate and set aside at room temperature.

Place the remaining apricots in a blender with ¾ cup water, sugar, lemon juice, soy sauce, garlic and ginger. Process several minutes until smooth, pulsing on/off and stopping to scrape down the sides of the container. Place in a heavy medium saucepan with the star anise. Bring to a boil. Reduce heat and simmer gently over medium heat until the sauce is thickened and reduced to about ⅔ cup, stirring frequently. Discard the star anise. For a smoother texture, strain the sauce through a fine sieve. Season with salt and pepper. (This can be prepared ahead, cooled, covered and set aside at room temperature for 6 to 8 hours or refrigerated for several days. Bring to room temperature before serving.)

For the kebabs, preheat the broiler. If a second oven is available, preheat it simultaneously to 325°F. Halve the pork lengthwise, then cut it crosswise into 1¼-inch pieces. Thread the pork and the 12 reserved apricots on 4 skewers. Place the sugar on a large plate. Dip each skewer in the sugar, turning to coat all sides of the meat. Season with salt and pepper. Line a broiler pan with foil. Place the skewers in the pan. Broil the pork as close to the heat source as possible, turning to brown all sides, for about 7 minutes. Transfer the meat to the preheated 325°F oven (or reduce the heat to 325°F) and bake until just cooked through, for about 5 to 7 minutes. Arrange the kebabs on a serving plate, removing skewers. Reheat the sauce if desired and spoon alongside. Serve immediately, passing any remaining sauce separately.

Dipping the kebabs in sugar enables them to caramelize. This in turn adds a crunch and complexity as well as a hint of sweetness.

Wine Selection
Chardonnay

Lamb Chops with
Sweet Pea and Spinach

4 Servings

Planning Ahead

The sauce base can be prepared at any time during the day it is to be served. Cook the chops and finish the sauce just before serving.

Wine Selection

Red Burgundy

When I was an apprentice, we paired lamb *au jus* with spinach as automatically as steak with *frites*. One day I realized this marriage would be even stronger if the spinach and *au jus* were combined into a garden-fresh sauce. With the addition of a pea puree and some sprinkles of vinegar, this relationship matured into a union blessed evermore by garlic.

SPINACH PEA SAUCE

I ounce (¼ stick) unsalted butter

I small onion, peeled and chopped

I clove garlic, peeled and minced

2 tablespoons Champagne vinegar or white wine vinegar

½ cup unsalted chicken stock

¾ cup frozen baby peas, defrosted

½ cup unsalted chicken stock

LAMB CHOPS

About 2 tablespoons olive oil

8 rib lamb chops, well trimmed and patted dry

Salt and freshly ground black pepper to taste

½ pound (about ½ bunch) small leaf spinach, stemmed, washed, well dried and coarsely chopped

Salt and freshly ground black pepper to taste

For the Spinach Pea Sauce, melt the butter in a heavy large saucepan over medium-low heat. Add the onion, cover and cook until translucent, for about 10 minutes, stirring occasionally. Add the garlic and vinegar. Boil until reduced to a glaze. Add ½ cup chicken stock and boil until reduced by half.

Meanwhile, puree the peas and ½ cup chicken stock in a blender until smooth, pulsing on/off. Add the onion mixture to the pea puree and process until very smooth, for about 4 minutes, stopping to scrape down the sides of the container. Strain back into a clean saucepan through a fine sieve. (This can be prepared to this point, covered and set aside at room temperature for several hours or refrigerated.)

For the lamb chops, preheat the oven to 425°F. Place a heavy large nonstick ovenproof skillet over medium-high heat and film with oil. Add lamb chops and brown quickly on both sides. Transfer the skillet to the oven and bake until just firm to the touch, for about 5 minutes for medium-rare. Season with salt and pepper.

To serve, meanwhile, stir the sauce over medium-high heat just until rewarmed. Add the spinach and stir just until wilted, for about 3 minutes. Season with salt and pepper. Ladle the sauce into the center of 4 plates. Cross tips of 2 lamb chops in the center of each plate. Serve immediately.

Rack of Lamb with Tomato Crust

I n Provence, a rack of lamb is often capped with garlic, parsley and bread crumbs and then garnished with a broiled tomato filled with . . . garlic, parsley and bread crumbs. Although the tomatoes are very nice with the lamb, the repetition is pretty dull. When the tomatoes are added to the topping instead, they form a self-basting lamb crust, transforming the rack into a handsome centerpiece for a dinner party.

TOMATO CRUST

> ½ pound very ripe tomatoes, peeled and seeded or canned tomatoes, coarsely chopped
>
> 2 teaspoons tomato paste
>
> 1 tablespoon fresh minced rosemary or flat-leaf parsley
>
> 2 ounces (½ stick) unsalted room temperature butter, chopped
>
> ⅓ cup fresh bread crumbs
>
> 1 egg white

LAMB

> 1¾- to 2-pound (8 ribs) rack of lamb, trimmed of all fat and fell (membrane) and patted dry
>
> Salt and freshly ground black pepper to taste

For the Tomato Crust, simmer the tomatoes in a heavy small saucepan over medium heat until reduced and thickened into a dry paste, stirring occasionally, for about 15 minutes. Cool for at least 15 minutes. Mix in the tomato paste, parsley, butter, bread crumbs and egg white. (This can be prepared ahead, covered and set aside at cool room temperature.)

For the lamb, preheat the oven to 425°F. Season the lamb with salt and pepper. Spread the Tomato Crust over the top of the lamb. Place on a rack in a roasting pan bone side down and roast for 25 minutes for rare. Preheat the broiler. Brown the crust under the broiler. Let rest for 15 minutes. Slice in between the ribs. Overlap 2 chops on each plate. Serve immediately.

2 to 4 Servings

Planning Ahead
The Tomato Crust can be prepared at any time during the day the lamb is to be served. Cook the lamb just before presenting.

Wine Selection
Bordeaux

Meat

Rack of Lamb with
White Bean Sauce and Salad

4 Servings

Planning Ahead

The lamb should be marinated at least four hours or, preferably, overnight while the beans should soak overnight before cooking. Both the white bean salad and the sauce can be prepared a day in advance. Cook the lamb just before serving.

Technique Tip

When serving no other courses other than a green salad or vegetable, you may want to increase the amount of lamb to 3 or 4 chops per person. The Bean Salad and sauce are ample for either scenario.

Wine Selection

Red Côtes du Rhône

I f I ever had any doubts that cassoulet was not a dish to make in California, it was proven to me one afternoon when my friend André insisted we have it, despite a thermometer reading of 88 degrees. We turned the air conditioning on high, and we ate cassoulet until our nostalgia for this Toulousien specialty—with its beans, lamb, pork, sausage and preserved goose—had entirely dissipated. Funny, we haven't gotten nostalgic for this dish since.

I don't really understand why cassoulet doesn't work better in California since it is a specialty of the South of France where it is equally warm. When you think about the raw fish served in cold countries, such as Norway, and the heavy beans, rice and tortillas favored in hotter climates, such as Mexico, the world's eating patterns don't make any sense.

I do, however, still yearn for the flavors of lamb and beans playing off each other, so I often serve a lighter, son-of-cassoulet recipe, such as the one here. I like this combination so much, in fact, that I've pureed half the beans for the sauce and dressed the second half for a salad to accompany the meat. This French grandmother's postcard from the past now bears the stamp of a modern California chef.

BEANS

½ pound white beans, picked over and rinsed

LAMB

1¾- to 2-pound (8 ribs) rack of lamb, trimmed of all fat and fell (membrane) and patted dry

¼ cup olive oil

4 cloves garlic, peeled and minced

4 fresh 2-inch rosemary sprigs or 1 tablespoon dried rosemary, crumbled

¼ pound pancetta or bacon, coarsely chopped

1 medium onion, peeled and diced

1 fresh 6-inch rosemary sprig, minced or 2 teaspoons dried rosemary, crumbled

1 bay leaf

2½ quarts (10 cups) unsalted chicken stock

2 large cloves garlic, peeled and minced

BEAN SALAD

 1½ tablespoons olive oil

 ¾ tablespoon red wine vinegar

 Salt and freshly ground black pepper to taste

 Salt and freshly ground black pepper to taste

 4 fresh large rosemary sprigs for garnish (optional)

For the beans, place the beans in a large bowl. Cover with enough water to come 2 inches above the beans. Cover and set aside at room temperature to soak overnight.

For the lamb marinade, place the lamb rack on a large sheet of plastic wrap and rub with the olive oil. Sprinkle with garlic and arrange the rosemary sprigs over lamb. Wrap in plastic and marinate at least for 4 hours or, preferably, overnight in the refrigerator. Bring to room temperature before roasting.

Place the pancetta in a heavy large pot over medium heat. Cook until browned, stirring occasionally. Add the onion, rosemary and bay leaf; reduce heat to medium-low, cover and cook until the onion is translucent, for about 10 minutes, stirring occasionally.

Drain the beans and add to the pot. Add the chicken stock and garlic. Bring to a boil, skimming off any foam. Reduce heat and simmer until the beans are very tender to taste, for about 2½ to 3 hours, stirring occasionally, and adding more liquid, if necessary.

For the Bean Salad, remove 2 cups of the beans with a slotted spoon and place in a bowl. Mix with the oil, vinegar, salt and pepper. (This can be prepared ahead, cooled, covered and set aside at cool room temperature for several hours or refrigerated overnight. Bring to room temperature before serving.)

For the Bean Sauce, continue simmering the remaining beans for 1 hour or until almost falling apart. Transfer to a food processor using a slotted spoon. Add ¾ cup of the cooking liquid, stock or water. Process until finely pureed, pulsing on/off and stopping to scrape down the sides of the container. Strain into a small saucepan through a fine sieve, pressing on the ingredients. Add additional liquid, if necessary, to thin to a saucelike consistency. Season with salt and pepper. (This can be prepared ahead, cooled, covered and set aside at cool room temperature for several hours or refrigerated overnight.)

To serve, preheat the oven to 425°F. Place the lamb on a rack in a roasting pan, bone side down. Season with salt and pepper. Roast 25 minutes for rare. Let rest for 15 minutes. Slice in between ribs.

Arrange the Bean Salad on 4 plates. Reheat the Bean Sauce, thinning if necessary, and ladle a large portion in the bottom. Arrange chops in pairs on each plate so that tips meet in the center of the sauce. Place a rosemary sprig vertically between chops. Serve immediately.

Lamb Loin with Eggplant Puree
and Tomato Rosettes

4 Servings

Planning Ahead

The lamb should be marinated for at least 4 hours or, preferably, overnight. The eggplant can be completely prepared and the tomatoes readied for cooking at any time during the day the dish is to be served. Reheat the eggplant and cook the lamb and tomatoes just before presenting. If only one oven is available, bake the tomatoes first and rewarm them if necessary while the lamb is settling.

Technique Tips

If neither a lamb loin nor a butcher with a boning knife is available, buy a rack of lamb and bone out the rib eye in one piece using a sharp knife and following the contours of the rack.

Once boned and trimmed, this is one of the easiest cuts of meat to cook and carve, making it ideal for guests.

For more attractive rosettes, use tomatoes that are the same size and shape.

Wine Selection
Bordeaux

This roasted lamb is composed of three different dishes that interweave as they play off each other to form a single entree. Garlic, tomatoes and eggplant, the Mediterranean triumvirate, rule together logically here as elsewhere, balancing the lamb, whose texture is always wonderful, but whose flavor can overpower. The garlic stands up to the lamb, while the eggplant provides a creamy contrast, and the tomato freshens the garlic. The tomatoes, arranged in overlapping slices like apples in a tart, are a dead giveaway that a pastry chef has had a hand in this dish.

LAMB MARINADE

2 (8 to 10 ounces each) lamb loins or rib eyes from 2 lamb racks (1½ to 1¾ pounds total), trimmed of all fat and fell (membrane) and patted dry

¼ cup olive oil

2 large cloves garlic, peeled and minced

8 fresh large rosemary sprigs or 2 tablespoons dried rosemary, crumbled

8 fresh large thyme sprigs or 2 tablespoons dried thyme, crumbled

EGGPLANT PUREE

1½ pounds eggplant

About 2 tablespoons olive oil

9 large cloves garlic, peeled

1 tablespoon olive oil

1½ teaspoons ground cumin

Salt and freshly ground black pepper to taste

TOMATO ROSETTES

5 to 7 medium (about 12 ounces) Roma tomatoes, thinly sliced

Salt and freshly ground black pepper to taste

3 tablespoons olive oil

About 2 tablespoons olive oil

Salt and freshly ground black pepper to taste

Meat

For the Lamb Marinade, place the lamb loins on a large piece of plastic wrap. Drizzle completely with olive oil and sprinkle with garlic. Arrange rosemary and thyme sprigs over the lamb. Wrap in plastic and refrigerate for at least 4 hours or overnight. Bring to room temperature before cooking.

For the Eggplant Puree, preheat the oven to 350°F. Line a baking sheet with parchment paper or aluminum foil. Halve the eggplant lengthwise. Brush the cut surface with olive oil. Place cut side down on the prepared sheet. Bake for 50 to 55 minutes or until extremely soft.

Place the garlic in a small pan, cover with cold water, bring to a boil over medium-high heat; drain. Repeat this process 2 times.

Scoop out the interior of the eggplant. Place in a food processor with the garlic. Process until completely smooth, pulsing on/off and stopping to scrape down the sides of the container. Mix in the olive oil, cumin, salt and pepper. Strain the mixture through a fine sieve into a heavy small saucepan. (This can be prepared ahead, covered and set aside at room temperature.)

For the Tomato Rosettes, line a baking sheet with four 6-inch squares of parchment paper. Trace a 4-inch circle on each square in heavy ink. Turn the squares over. If circles are not visible, redraw them so they are. Starting with the edge, overlap the tomato rounds in a spiral to the center of the circle. (This can be prepared ahead, covered and set aside at room temperature.)

To cook the tomatoes, preheat the oven to 400°F. Season the tomatoes with salt and pepper and drizzle with olive oil. Bake until softened, for about 10 minutes.

To cook the lamb, preheat a second oven (or increase oven heat) to 450°F. Remove the herbs and most of the garlic from the lamb. Place a heavy nonstick ovenproof skillet large enough to accommodate both loins without crowding over medium-high heat and film with oil. Add the lamb and brown well on all sides. Transfer the skillet to the oven and roast the lamb for 6 to 8 minutes for medium-rare. Let sit for 15 minutes before carving.

To serve, run a broad spatula under the tomatoes to loosen them. Invert the tomato rosettes onto 4 large plates. Carefully peel off the parchment. Thinly slice the lamb diagonally. Season with salt and pepper. Stir the lamb cooking and carving juices into the eggplant. Reheat the eggplant by stirring over medium-high heat. Spoon below the tomatoes. Flank the lamb slices on either side of the eggplant puree. Serve immediately.

Farmhouse Leg of Lamb

6 Servings

Planning Ahead
The lamb should be marinated for at least 4 hours or, preferably, overnight. Roast it just before serving.

Technique Tip
Cooking garlic and shallots unpeeled enhances their flavor and prevents them from burning. To eat, just squeeze them out between your fingertips onto the meat or the accompanying toast.

Wine Selection
Red Burgundy, Bordeaux

A roast leg of lamb in France is like roast chicken in this country. You have it on Sunday or when friends come over, and it is the ultimate in easy cooking. There is little to do but insert a few slices of garlic, sprinkle on a little spice and pop the meat in the oven. Actually, it may be more like a lazy, casual barbecue, for the dish is fun to make, it serves lots of people and the price is right.

MARINADE

- 5- to 7-pound leg of lamb, fell (membrane) removed, trimmed and patted dry
- 2 tablespoons olive oil
- 4 large cloves garlic, peeled and thinly sliced
- 1 teaspoon ground cumin
- 8 fresh 2-inch rosemary sprigs or 1½ tablespoons dried rosemary, crumbled
- 8 fresh 2-inch thyme sprigs or 2 tablespoons dried thyme, crumbled
- 24 medium unpeeled shallots, tops sliced off
- 40 unpeeled cloves garlic, tops sliced off
- About ½ cup unsalted chicken stock
- Salt and freshly ground black pepper to taste
- Toast or grilled bread

For the marinade, place the lamb on a large sheet of plastic wrap. Rub with olive oil. Cut slits all over the lamb. Place a slice of garlic in each slit. Sprinkle with cumin. Strew rosemary and thyme sprigs over the lamb. Wrap and refrigerate for 4 hours or overnight. Bring to room temperature before roasting.

To cook, preheat the oven to 450°F. Scatter the shallots and garlic in the bottom of a large roasting pan. Moisten with the chicken stock. Place a large rack over the vegetables. Unwrap the lamb, season with salt and pepper and place on the rack with herb sprigs. Roast for 15 minutes, reduce heat to 350°F and continue roasting for an additional 45 minutes for medium-rare or until a thermometer inserted into the center of the meat registers 130°F. Cover with aluminum foil and let the meat rest for 15 minutes before carving. To serve, cut into thin slices. Transfer to a platter or 6 plates. Spoon the shallots and garlic over the slices. Serve immediately with toast.

Lamb Pilaf with Cardamom

T his is an Indian stew made by a California potpourri chef who uses ingredients from all over the world: me. Actually, this dish was based on an impressive crunchy pilaf some Iranian friends made by simmering lamb for seven hours with aromatic basmati rice. I had never tasted this dish before, but as soon as I saw it unmolded, I knew what it was. I had heard about it from Chef Raymond Olivier for so many years, I had already tasted it in my mind. When I started making it one Sunday afternoon, I didn't know why I was putting these ingredients together, but when it was finished, I knew where I got the idea. What I haven't figured out is why such a famous dish would choose such a bad word as pilaf for its name.

About 2 tablespoons olive oil

2 large onions, peeled and diced

1¾ to 2 pounds trimmed lamb stew meat (about 2 × 1 inches) from the leg, patted dry

4 large cloves garlic, peeled and minced

2 teaspoons curry powder

1 teaspoon crushed cardamom seed

Large pinch of cayenne pepper

1½ cups basmati or long grain white rice, washed well

3 cups unsalted chicken stock

Salt and freshly ground black pepper to taste

Preheat the oven to 325°F. Place a heavy large nonstick casserole over medium-low heat and film with oil. Add the onions, cover and cook until translucent, for about 10 minutes, stirring occasionally. Increase heat to medium-high and stir the onions until they are golden brown. Remove the onions to a plate, add the lamb to the casserole in batches and brown on all sides, adding oil as necessary. Return the onions to the casserole, along with the garlic, curry, cardamom and cayenne. Stir in the rice. Pour in the chicken stock. Bring to a boil; stir. Cover and bake until the meat is tender and the liquid is absorbed, for about 45 minutes. Sprinkle with salt and pepper. Stir the rice, fluffing it with a fork. Serve immediately.

4 Servings

Planning Ahead
The onions can be cooked and the ingredients prepared at any time during the day the pilaf is to be served. Cook the stew just before serving.

Technique Tip
In order that the meat and rice finish cooking at the same time, use lamb meat cut from the leg. Meat cut from the shoulder or another less tender part will take several hours to cook.

Variation
For crunchy rice, unmold the stew onto an ovenproof platter, preheat the broiler and place close to the heat source to crisp and brown.

Wine Selection
Zinfandel

Meat

Lamb Shanks with *Ras el Hanout*

4 Servings

Planning Ahead

The ingredients can be prepped at any time during the day the lamb shanks are to be braised. They can be cooked a day in advance and reheated. If the sauce is dry, add more stock before reheating.

Technique Tip

To grate only the nonbitter colored part of oranges or other citrus fruit, use the fine grate of a four-sided grater. After grating, remove the grated peel from the inside of the grater with your hand, then bang the grater hard on a work surface to release any remaining peel.

Wine Selection
Zinfandel

When I was in Morocco, a friend introduced me to *ras el hanout*, a varying blend of aromatic spices made from the dregs of the spice barrels. Imagine my surprise when I found a bottle labeled *ras el hanout* at my local supermarket in Los Angeles. Of course I had to buy it for a Moroccan-style dish. To show it off, I chose lamb shanks. This is yet another delicious, easy-to-prepare underutilized cut of meat. To give the braised juices in this dish a bright note, I add an acidic component toward the end of simmering. In this case, both the apple and tomato bring a contemporary spark of freshness.

4 lamb shanks (about 1 pound each), patted dry

4 teaspoons *ras el hanout* or any mixture of allspice, cumin, cardamom, cinnamon, cloves, coriander, mace and/or nutmeg, ground to a coarse powder, or 4 teaspoons mixed ground spices

About 2 tablespoons olive oil

1 medium onion, peeled and finely diced

1 large carrot, peeled, quartered lengthwise and diced

1 cup unsalted chicken stock

6 medium cloves garlic, peeled and minced

Grated rind (orange part only) and juice of 1 large orange

¾ to 1 pound (about 2 small) fennel bulbs

1 small tomato, peeled, seeded and diced

1 Pippin or other green apple, peeled, cored, diced and tossed with 1 tablespoon lemon juice

Salt and freshly ground black pepper to taste

Preheat the oven to 325°F. Massage the lamb shanks with the *ras el hanout*. Place a heavy deep large nonstick skillet over medium-high heat and film with olive oil. Brown the lamb well on all sides. Set aside on a plate. Add the onion and carrot to the pan, reduce heat to medium-low, cover and cook until the onion is translucent, for about 10 minutes, stirring occasionally. Add the chicken stock with garlic, orange rind and juice. Bring to a boil, stirring to release any browned bits clinging to the bottom of the pan. Return the lamb to the pan, cover and bake for 1½ hours, turning every 30 minutes.

Trim off the fennel fronds, mince and reserve 2 tablespoons. Cut off the stalks. Peel the stalks and fibrous exterior of the bulb using a vegetable peeler. Quarter the bulb, core and dice the bulb and stalks. Mix the fennel into the lamb with the tomato and apple. Season with salt and pepper. Cover and bake until the lamb is very tender and almost falling off of the bone, for about 30 minutes.

To serve, divide the lamb among 4 large plates using tongs. Ladle the vegetables over the lamb using a slotted spatula. Degrease the remaining juices in a fat separator and pour over the lamb. Sprinkle with reserved minced fennel fronds. Serve immediately.

Liver with Onion and
Preserved Lemon Confit

iver is one dish both the French and Americans enjoy in the same manner: smothered with onions. I've broadened its nationality even further by adding the preserved lemons that are the backbone of Moroccan cooking. Utilizing only the skin, these tender, salt-cured citrus fruits have the acidity of the vinegar usually used in this preparation, as well as a unique flavor. I always knew the true flavor of citrus fruit lies in its skin, but other than grating and blanching it on occasion, I never really used it before going to North Africa. Unlike the juice of the lemon, the skin is piquant when it is cured without being overwhelmingly tart. I find the preserved lemon skin a much better flavoring than lemon juice for delicate foods such as fish, for it adds acidity without destroying the ingredient's intrinsic flavor.

ONION AND PRESERVED LEMON CONFIT

> 2 whole Preserved Lemons (page 241), rinsed and quartered completely
>
> 1 ounce (¼ stick) unsalted butter
>
> 2 large onions, peeled, halved and thinly sliced
>
> Large pinch of sugar
>
> ¼ cup red wine vinegar
>
> 1 cup unsalted chicken stock
>
> 2 fresh large thyme sprigs or 1 tablespoon dried thyme, crumbled
>
> Salt and freshly ground black pepper to taste

LIVER

> About 2 tablespoons olive oil per skillet
>
> 4 pieces (1¾ to 2 pounds total) calf or beef liver, sliced ¼ inch thick, patted dry
>
> Salt and freshly ground black pepper to taste
>
> 2 tablespoons fresh chopped thyme or 2 teaspoons dried thyme, crumbled

For the Onion and Preserved Lemon Confit, fill a heavy large saucepan halfway with water. Bring to a boil. Meanwhile, scrape the pulp from the interior of the preserved lemon quarters; discard. Dice the lemons into ⅜-inch pieces. Add the lemon dice to the boiling water and blanch for 5 minutes to remove salt; drain.

Dry the same saucepan, add the butter and melt it over medium-low heat. Add the onions, sprinkle with sugar, cover and cook until translucent, for about 10 minutes, stirring occasionally. Uncover, increase heat to medium-high and stir until the onions are golden brown. Pour in the vinegar and boil until it is absorbed, stirring occasionally. Add the chicken stock, thyme and blanched preserved lemons and bring to a boil. Reduce heat and simmer until the onion mixture is thickened and the liquid is almost absorbed, stirring occasionally, for about 30 minutes. Season with salt and pepper. (This can be prepared ahead, cooled, covered and set aside at cool room temperature for several hours or refrigerated.)

For the liver, place 2 heavy large nonstick skillets over medium-low heat and film with oil. Season the liver with salt, pepper and thyme. Add 2 pieces of liver to each skillet. Cook until medium-rare, for about 5 to 7 minutes total, turning halfway.

To serve, transfer the liver to 4 plates. Reheat the Onion and Preserved Lemon Confit by stirring over medium-high heat. Discard the thyme sprigs. Spoon the onion mixture on top of the liver. Serve immediately.

Wine Selection
Chablis

Preserved Lemons

I keep two jars of these lemons in my refrigerator at all times: one that is ready to use and one that is in the process of curing. Whenever I want to add a special flavor to vegetables, salads, veal, pork, chicken and fish dishes, in particular, I find myself reaching for a preserved lemon. Once it is cured, this fruit has a lovely acidic tang that complements a variety of foods without overwhelming them.

10 tablespoons salt

1 tablespoon sugar

3 large juicy lemons, washed

To cure, mix the salt with the sugar in a small bowl. Place 1 tablespoon of salt mixture in the bottom of a large clean jar. Quarter the lemons to within ½ inch of the stem end. Open gently, remove any surface seeds and sprinkle with about 1 tablespoon of the salt mixture. Place in the jar. Add any remaining salt mixture to the jar. Refrigerate at least 1 month, turning the jar upside down daily to rest on its opposite end. The salt will draw out the lemons' juice to form a liquid brine.

To use, remove as many lemons as desired from the jar and scrape out the pulpy interior with a spoon or a knife; discard. Cut the peel into desired size and blanch for 5 minutes in boiling water to eliminate excess saltiness. Use as desired. Refrigerate the remaining lemons in the brine.

Makes 3 Preserved Lemons

Planning Ahead
Allow at least 1 month for the lemons to cure. Once cured, they can be kept for many moons in the refrigerator.

Technique Tips
To prevent contamination while the lemons are curing, do not touch with your fingers or metal implements.

Lemons can be prepared in any quantity using the proportions of 10 tablespoons salt to 1 tablespoon sugar.

Veal Chops Italian-style with Garlic, Rosemary and Parmesan

4 Servings

Planning Ahead
Marinate the veal at least 4 hours or, preferably, overnight. The sauce can be prepared at any time during the day the dish is to be served. Cook the meat just before presenting.

Technique Tips
Pushing fresh herbs through the center of meat as done here allows the herbal flavor to permeate. This technique can be used with any stiff herb or any type of meat or seafood with at least ½ to ¾ inch thickness.

If fresh rosemary sprigs are not available, sprinkle chops with about 1½ tablespoons dried, crumbled rosemary before marinating and omit insertion of sprigs through center of chops.

Wine Selection
White Burgundy

T he French cook very little veal at home because they consider it to be bland. I like it, nonetheless, as long as it is still moist and not overcooked. Since Italy's veal is rarely bland by the time they've finished garnishing it, I've borrowed the country's popular blend of rosemary, garlic and Parmesan cheese that can be found in almost every region. Although veal is becoming evermore expensive, it is still very elegant, quick-to-prepare party fare. And there are not many main courses more economical in terms of time.

MARINADE

> 4 (2 to 2¼ pounds total) veal rib chops, ¾ to 1 inch thick, trimmed and patted dry

> ¼ cup olive oil

> 2 cloves garlic, peeled and thinly sliced

> 8 fresh 5-inch rosemary sprigs

PARMESAN SAUCE

> ¾ cup unsalted chicken or veal stock

> 1 fresh 5-inch rosemary sprig or 1 teaspoon dried rosemary, crumbled

> 3 large cloves garlic, peeled

> ¾ cup heavy cream

> Salt and freshly ground black pepper to taste

> 3 tablespoons olive oil

> 1 ounce (¼ stick) chilled unsalted butter, finely chopped

> 2 tablespoons freshly grated Parmesan cheese or to taste

> Fresh rosemary sprigs for garnish (optional)

For the marinade, place each chop on a large piece of plastic wrap. Rub with olive oil. Press the garlic onto all sides of each chop and sandwich with rosemary sprigs. Wrap in plastic and refrigerate for at least 4 hours or overnight. Bring to room temperature before cooking.

For the Parmesan Sauce, simmer the chicken stock, rosemary and garlic gently over medium-low heat in a heavy small saucepan until reduced by half, for about 7 minutes. Add the cream, reduce heat and simmer gently until reduced and thickened to a saucelike consistency, stirring occasionally. Strain through a fine sieve, pressing on the ingredients. Clean the pan and return the sauce to the pan. Season with salt and pepper. (This can be prepared ahead, covered and set aside at cool room temperature for several hours or refrigerated.)

For the veal, preheat the oven to 350°F. Brush the garlic off of the veal; reserve the rosemary. Make 2 side-by-side horizontal slits on both long edges of each veal chop. Insert 1 sprig of rosemary into a slit on one side of a veal chop and push through the meat so it comes out a slit on the opposite side. Place a second sprig into the second slit and push it through. Repeat with the remaining 3 chops. Pat chops dry and season with salt and pepper.

Heat the 3 tablespoons of olive oil in a heavy large nonstick ovenproof skillet over medium-high heat. Add the veal chops and brown lightly on both sides, for about 3 minutes total. Transfer to the oven and continue cooking until just opaque throughout and firm to the touch, for about 7 to 10 minutes.

To serve, bring the sauce to a boil. Whisk in the butter off the heat. Stir in the Parmesan. Arrange the veal chops on 4 plates. Remove the rosemary from the slits. Spoon some sauce over the chops. Garnish with fresh rosemary sprigs, if desired. Serve immediately.

Veal Chops with Barley and Leeks

4 Servings

Planning Ahead

Marinate the veal at least 4 hours or, preferably, overnight. The leeks can be cooked at any time during the day the dish is to be served. Prepare the barley just before presenting. Begin cooking the chops for about 15 minutes after the barley is placed in the oven.

Wine Selection

Pinot Noir

O nce again, with veal in front of me, I look first to the Italian larder for inspiration. As a change, I wanted a companion for the chops rather than an integrated sauce or seasoning team. I also desired something rustic with considerable texture. Risotto seemed like a logical choice, but after some reflection, I chose barley instead because it is easier to make and has a fabulous bite. Unlike rice, barley also has a starchiness that reminds me of potatoes. Once a Frenchman starts thinking about potatoes, the idea of leeks can't be far behind. At this point, we cross the Italian border back into France.

MARINADE

4 (2 to 2¼ pounds total) veal rib chops, ¾ to 1 inch thick, trimmed and patted dry

About ¼ cup olive oil

4 large cloves garlic, peeled and minced

2 tablespoons fresh minced thyme or 2 teaspoons dried thyme, crumbled

BARLEY

2 tablespoons olive oil

2 large leeks (white and light green parts only), quartered lengthwise and cut crosswise into ½-inch pieces

1¼ cups pearl barley

2½ cups unsalted chicken stock

Salt and freshly ground black pepper to taste

3 tablespoons olive oil

1 ounce (¼ stick) unsalted room temperature butter, chopped

3 tablespoons freshly grated Parmesan cheese

Salt and freshly ground black pepper to taste

¼ cup water

1½ tablespoons fresh minced thyme or ½ teaspoon dried thyme, crumbled

For the marinade, place each chop on a large piece of plastic wrap. Rub with olive oil. Press the garlic into both sides of the chop and sprinkle with thyme. Wrap in plastic and refrigerate for at least 4 hours or overnight. Bring to room temperature before cooking.

For the barley, preheat the oven to 350°F. Heat the oil in a heavy large nonstick casserole. Add the leeks, cover and cook over medium-low heat until soft, for about 10 minutes, stirring occasionally. Stir in the barley. Add the chicken stock, bring to a boil, cover and bake until the liquid is absorbed and the barley is tender, for about 30 minutes.

Meanwhile, to cook the veal, brush the thyme and garlic off of the veal so seasonings don't burn. Pat the chops dry. Season with salt and pepper. Heat the oil in a heavy large nonstick skillet over medium-high heat. Add the veal chops and brown lightly on each side, for about 3 minutes total. Transfer the skillet to the oven and continue cooking until just opaque throughout and firm to the touch, for about 7 to 10 minutes.

To serve, stir the butter and Parmesan into the barley. Season with salt and pepper. Ladle some barley into the center of 4 plates. Place a chop in the center of the barley. Pour water into the veal skillet. Stir over medium-high heat to release any browned bits on the bottom of the pan. Pour juices over veal. Sprinkle with thyme. Serve immediately.

Veal Chops with Saffron and Caramelized Onions

4 Servings

Planning Ahead
Marinate the veal at least 4 hours or, preferably, overnight. The onions can be prepared up to 1 day in advance. Cook the chops just before serving.

Technique Tip
Before adding saffron to a mixture, crush the threads using a mortar and pestle and stir in several tablespoons of hot liquid. This will dissolve the spice as well as extract its maximum flavor.

Wine Selection
Chardonnay, Côtes du Rhône

Michel Ohayon, the owner of Koutoubia, the best Moroccan restaurant in Los Angeles—and probably in the country—served me a tagine with lamb shanks and saffron/ginger-flavored onions that was so delicious it gave me goose bumps. (Tagine is a Moroccan stew, but also refers to the pyramid-shaped cooking vessel used to cook the stew.) I have made the rich, caramelized onions many times since, sometimes serving them with lamb as Michel does and sometimes with veal. I chose veal for this occasion because it gives this chop a new dimension, and I wanted to introduce you to this combination. Besides, it will be some time before I make this dish again; I don't have any more space for new goose bumps.

MARINADE

> 4 (2 to 2¼ pounds total) rib veal chops, ¾ to 1 inch thick
>
> ¼ cup olive oil
>
> 6 large cloves garlic, peeled and minced
>
> 1 teaspoon ground cumin

ONIONS

> 2 tablespoons olive oil
>
> 2 large onions, peeled, halved and thinly sliced
>
> 1 tablespoon Champagne vinegar or white wine vinegar
>
> 1 teaspoon dark brown sugar
>
> 1 cup unsalted chicken stock
>
> 2 teaspoons fresh minced gingerroot or 1 teaspoon ground ginger
>
> ¼ teaspoon saffron threads, crushed
>
> Salt and freshly ground black pepper to taste
>
> 3 tablespoons olive oil

For the marinade, place each chop on a large piece of plastic wrap. Rub with olive oil. Press the garlic into both sides of the chop and sprinkle with cumin. Wrap in plastic and refrigerate for at least 4 hours or overnight. Bring to room temperature before cooking.

For the onions, heat the oil in a heavy small skillet over medium-low heat. Add the onions, cover and cook until translucent, for about 10 minutes, stirring occasionally. Add the vinegar, increase heat to medium-high and boil until evaporated. Add the brown sugar and stir until the onions are browned. Add the chicken stock and ginger. Bring to a boil. Ladle several tablespoons of this liquid into the crushed saffron and stir to dissolve.

Return saffron mixture to the pan. Lower heat and simmer until the liquid is absorbed, for about 30 minutes, stirring occasionally. (This can be prepared ahead, cooled, covered and set aside at cool room temperature for several hours or refrigerated overnight. Bring to room temperature before using.)

To cook, preheat the oven to 350°F. Brush the garlic off of the meat so it does not burn. Pat the meat dry and season with salt and pepper. Heat the oil in a heavy large nonstick ovenproof skillet over medium-high heat. Add the veal and brown lightly on both sides, for about 3 minutes total. Spoon the cooked onions over veal. Transfer to the oven and continue cooking for 7 to 10 minutes or until the veal is just opaque throughout. Divide the chops among 4 plates. Serve immediately.

Rabbit with Endive and Sage

Both rabbit and endive have rustic country flavors, so I've braised the two together with some orange to give a nice fresh fruity taste. The soft greens balance what is too often dry, overcooked meat. For some unfathomable reason, people don't believe something can be cooked in as short a time as a recipe states, and their lack of trust results in some pretty bad food. I also don't understand why rabbit isn't more popular in this country. This chicken-without-feathers is lean with giant, meaty legs. It is easy to prepare and goes well with many different garnishes.

Rabbits are so easy to raise, they could be an important inexpensive food source in this country. You take a male and a female and boom, a few weeks later, you have lots of baby rabbits. I was nine years old when I killed my first rabbit with a rolling pin. My mother had said she needed a man to do this job, and my brother wouldn't touch it. I felt so strong. After that, I'd continually ask, "Mummy, do you want a rabbit for dinner tomorrow?" I was well on my way to becoming a butcher and a chef.

(continued)

4 Servings

Planning Ahead

The endive can be braised several hours before serving. Brown the rabbit, add to endive and cook just before presenting.

Meat

Choose endive heads that are approximately the same size.

Reserve the rabbit liver and kidneys to garnish a salad. Before serving, cook in a heavy skillet over medium-high heat until crisp and brown on the outside, but rare within.

Wine Selection

Cabernet Sauvignon

ENDIVE

2 tablespoons dark brown sugar

1 ounce (¼ stick) unsalted butter, finely chopped

1 large orange

4 to 5 (about 1 pound) medium endives, ends and outside leaves trimmed and halved lengthwise

⅓ cup unsalted chicken stock

Salt and freshly ground black pepper to taste

RABBIT

About 2 tablespoons olive oil

1 cut-up rabbit, patted dry

2 tablespoons Dijon mustard

2 tablespoons olive oil

2 tablespoons (about 15 large leaves) fresh minced sage or 1 tablespoon dried, crumbled

Salt and freshly ground black pepper to taste

For the endive, preheat the oven to 350°F. Sprinkle sugar on the bottom of an 8- × 10-inch or other medium baking dish or gratin pan. Scatter the butter over the sugar. Remove the orange part of the peel in strips without the bitter white pith using a vegetable peeler; chop finely. Sprinkle the peel over the butter. Arrange the endives in a single layer, cut side down. Squeeze the orange juice over the endive and pour over the chicken stock. Season with salt and pepper. Cover the pan with aluminum foil. Poke steam holes in the foil. Bake for 30 minutes. (This can be prepared ahead to this point and set aside at cool room temperature for several hours. Reheat the oven to 325°F before continuing.)

For the rabbit, place a heavy large skillet over medium-high heat and film it with oil. Add the rabbit to the skillet in batches and brown both sides.

Turn the endives cut side up using tongs. Whisk the mustard, olive oil, sage, salt and pepper to blend in a small bowl. Brush on both sides of the rabbit. Arrange the rabbit on top of the endives. Return to the oven and bake uncovered for 40 to 45 minutes or until the rabbit is tender when pierced with a knife, basting occasionally. Transfer to 4 plates. Spoon pan juices over the rabbit and endive. Serve immediately.

Side Dishes

Side, by definition, means "an aspect of" or "subordinate to." This may have been true of side dishes in the past. But as cooking and eating habits become simpler today, the side dish is being integrated with the main course. Throughout the book, you'll find dishes such as the Lamb Chops with Sweet Pea and Spinach (page 230) and the Veal Chops with Barley and Leeks (page 244), where the moist vegetable also substitutes for the sauce. Some side dishes even have their 15 minutes of fame when presented by themselves as a first course. If the number of recipes in this chapter seems sparse, it is because veggies (what I call vegetables) appear so frequently as part of an entree elsewhere.

Furthermore, as health issues force us to evaluate our diets today, we should be increasing proportions of rice, grain and vegetable *sides* while scaling down portions of meat and poultry. Like the Prince and the Pauper, it is time for meat to switch places with the garnish.

During the wintertime in France, veggies once meant only potatoes, leeks and dried beans. Fresh vegetables were the products of spring and summer. When the first *primeurs* (spring vegetables) arrived at the farmers' market, it was a festive, exciting time for a young chef. More people frequented the restaurants, and there was more activity in the streets. The seasons controlled our natural rhythms.

When I first moved to this country, it was difficult to find produce at any time of year. I couldn't even locate a staple as basic as leeks to make soup. I wasn't homesick for my country, but I sure missed its *haricots verts*. Now, almost two decades later, we can find more vegetables and fruits here than we need. Just the number of mushrooms alone is staggering. Often I combine them, choosing button for flavor, shiitake for texture and cèpes for strength. The influx of Asian immigrants has brought lemongrass, snow peas and bok choy to add to a burgeoning ethnic larder.

As this bounty has proliferated, our seasonal markers have sadly disappeared. I cannot encourage you enough to purchase produce only at the peak of its season and ripeness. It not only tastes better at this point, but it is less expensive, too. Buy it also as close to the time of consumption as possible. As produce matures, it loses its vitamins, costing you money in nutritional waste.

There is a little more leeway in items stored out of the refrigerator, such as onions, potatoes, garlic, shallots and tomatoes. Tomatoes, though, are great only in summertime.

When you buy vegetables, choose heavy firm specimens with shiny unblemished skin that smell sweetly of what they are. Be sure you're not the one buying some of the bruised flabby green beans, rotten peppers, moldy corn and open-gilled mushrooms that I see in some of the supposedly superior supermarkets.

Basically, you can serve any kind of vegetable with any kind of dish, but make an effort to balance the textures of other ingredients. If you have a soft fish like sea bass, a crunchy vegetable such as asparagus will heighten its effect more than a smooth eggplant puree. If you make a pea puree, you may want to add some whole peas as well to give the sauce a snap. Adding a particular herb or garlic to a vegetable will help it liaison with other ingredients on the plate. Conversely, if you have basil and garlic, a direct bridge would be to red peppers, zucchini or another Provençal vegetable.

To peel or not to peel? If this is the question, the answer is "yes." Do it while you talk on the telephone, but do it if you can possibly work it into your schedule. Peeling broccoli, asparagus or even cauliflower gives these vegetables a refined edge.

Although it is still fashionable to interpret al dente for vegetable cookery as raw, I do not like my veggies undercooked. What is most important to me above all is taste. Instead of boiling or sautéing my vegetables until they are crisp and light, I often roast them. They may not be as sprightly when prepared this way, but their flavors develop more fully.

The potato is in a class by itself. It can be silky, soft or crunchy; and there are so many ways to prepare it. My favorite way of cooking potato is to sauté it as chips . . . except for *frites* . . . except for mashed. . . . I even use potato in a chocolate cake recipe. With my Japanese Benriner Turning-Slicer, I create long strands of potato to serve as Potato Fettuccine with Tomato and Basil (page 254) or to wrap other foods. If you tie a roast with these potato cords, you can eat them.

If I had to vote, though, I guess my award for "Best in Show" would go to mashed potatoes. When I'm looking for something soothing to make me feel wonderful, this is definitely my first stop. I could give you 200 recipes for potato purees, but you should be the one to be creative and decide whether you want to add two tablespoons of basil or leek.

Mashing a potato correctly is easy to do as long as you have the right tool. A potato masher works for those from the lumpy side of the mashed potato track, but not for those like me who define a perfect mashed potato as one having an ethereal grain. To derive this sensation, I use a food mill or mallet and large-holed French *tamis* (drum sieve). The potatoes must be tamped through the holes in an up-and-down motion, because dragging elasticizes them. People complain that this sounds difficult, but it is actually easier and faster than lumping with a masher. Food processors and blenders, our high-speed friends, make potatoes, unfortunately, gluey and sticky. Use the starchier heavy-bodied russets for purees (and *frites*), while reserving red or white boiling potatoes for steaming.

I am very much against the idea that each main course must come with a starch and a vegetable. Each plate is peerless and requires a different garnish. You can have a vegetable at lunch and a potato at breakfast. As long as you have five servings of vegetables (and/or fruits) every day, you don't need to have everything at once. What does it mean that you have to have something leafy daily? This is not sex.

B.L.T. Potato Salad

4 Servings

Planning Ahead

The Tarragon Dressing can be made at any time during the day the salad is to be served. The bacon can be cooked several hours in advance. Cook and dress the potatoes just before presenting to serve warm or several hours earlier to offer at room temperature.

Technique Tips

When the potatoes are steamed instead of boiled, they do not become waterlogged.

The potatoes should be tossed with the dressing immediately after they are cooked. When allowed to cool before the dressing is added, they become hard.

For maximum flavor, serve the potato salad tepid or at room temperature.

English speakers use so many abbreviations that it has been difficult for me to learn this language. Some of these abbreviations are used so often I feel I should know their definition; yet I don't, and I'm always too embarrassed to ask. B.L.T. was one of these codes that I interpreted incorrectly, so I was happy when I finally had lunch with someone who ordered one. Now that I know what it is, I frequently eat this sandwich when I am on the road, particularly when room service offers it as a triple decker club. I've taken a bit of license with this all-American favorite in converting it to a salad, but I've found potatoes to be as good a partner as bread with the crunchy "B" and fresh "L" and "T."

TARRAGON DRESSING

 1 egg yolk (optional), at room temperature

 1 tablespoon Dijon mustard

 2 tablespoons Champagne vinegar or white wine vinegar

 ¼ cup olive oil

 2 tablespoons flat-leaf parsley

 1 tablespoon fresh minced tarragon or other fresh herb

 Salt and freshly ground black pepper to taste

 1½ to 2 pounds red or white boiling potatoes, peeled and cut into ½-inch cubes

 1 large tomato, peeled, seeded and diced

 Salt and freshly ground black pepper to taste

 4 slices bacon, sliced crosswise into ¼-inch-wide pieces

 Lettuce leaves

 1½ tablespoons fresh minced chives or green onions

For the Tarragon Dressing, blend the yolk, if using, mustard and vinegar in a blender. With the machine running, pour in the oil in a slow, thin stream. Add the parsley and tarragon to the blender and process until completely pureed, pulsing on/off and stopping to scrape down the sides of the container. Season with salt and pepper. (This can be prepared ahead, covered and set aside at cool room temperature for several hours or refrigerated until 1 hour before using.)

For the potatoes, steam until tender and easily pierced with a knife, for about 10 to 15 minutes. Immediately place in a large bowl. Add the tomato. Season with salt and pepper and toss with the Tarragon Dressing. Set aside at room temperature for at least 15 minutes to cool slightly and absorb the dressing, stirring occasionally, or cool to room temperature.

For the bacon, cook the bacon in a heavy large skillet over medium heat until crisp and brown, stirring occasionally. Line a baking sheet with paper towels. Transfer the bacon to the sheet to drain using tongs or a slotted spoon. (This can be prepared several hours ahead.)

To serve, line a large bowl or 4 plates with lettuce leaves. Mix the bacon into the potato salad, then spoon the salad on top of the lettuce. Sprinkle with chives. Serve immediately.

Potato Fettuccine with
Tomato and Basil

4 Servings

Planning Ahead

The olive oil and garlic mixture can be prepared, the potatoes prepped and the dressing ingredients mixed at any time during the day the Potato Fettuccine is to be served. Cook the potatoes just before serving to present warm or several hours in advance to offer at room temperature.

Variation

If you have a mandoline, a food processor with a variety of blades or another type of cutting tool, you might try slicing the potatoes into other pasta shapes, such as fine angel hair or linguini. The cooking times for the potato pasta will vary according to its size.

I was cutting my potatoes with my Japanese Benriner Turning-Slicer, and they came out in long fettuccine-like strips. These look like pasta, why not cook them like pasta, I thought. And so I did. With the garlic, tomatoes, olive oil and Parmesan, I intermarried a potato and pasta salad. If you don't have the magic machine, use a regular vegetable peeler instead.

I must admit that I prefer potatoes to pasta because they present a chef with more opportunities for creativity. Pasta depends upon its sauce to make it different, whereas potatoes give the sauce a special aura. If pasta was based solely on potato starch, it would be fabulous. Keep your eyes open. Soon we're going to see restaurants that serve only potatoes.

¼ cup olive oil

2 cloves garlic, peeled and crushed

3 large (1 to 1¼ pounds) russet potatoes, peeled

1 large tomato, peeled, seeded and diced

1 cup (about 1 ounce) fresh loosely packed basil, chopped, or other fresh herb

1 small clove garlic, peeled and minced

About ¼ cup (about 1 ounce) freshly grated Parmesan cheese

Salt and freshly ground black pepper to taste

Bring the olive oil and garlic to a simmer in a tiny pot over medium heat. Set aside off the heat.

Fill a large bowl with cold water. Working over the bowl, slice down potatoes lengthwise with a vegetable peeler to form fettuccine strands. Change the water repeatedly to remove the potato starch, until the water remains clear. (This can be prepared ahead and set aside at room temperature in the bowl covered with water.)

To cook, bring a large pot of salted water to a boil. Place a large clean bath towel on a work surface. Place the tomato, basil, garlic and Parmesan in a large bowl. Drain the potatoes. Add them to the boiling water. Cook until tender, for about 1½ minutes, watching carefully. Drain the potatoes, turn out onto the towel; pat dry. Add the potatoes to the tomato mixture. Remove the garlic from the oil in the tiny pot using a slotted spoon. Add half of the garlic oil to the potatoes. Toss gently. Add additional oil and Parmesan as desired. Season with salt and pepper. Serve immediately warm or later at room temperature in a vegetable dish or on 4 large plates with an entree.

Parsnip Potato Puree

The parsnip is a vegetable I discovered in the United States. To me, it combines the sweetness of beets with the sharpness of celery root and, to a lesser extent, turnips. These are flavors I like very much, as long as they are not too strong. The potato dilutes the strength of the parsnip, while the two ingredients together add up to a brand new taste that is wonderful with game, lamb and poultry.

Once you get started with mashed parsnips, don't stop. A delicious puree can also be made by combining the potato with rutabaga, carrot, cauliflower, kohlrabi, celery root, turnip and pumpkin or winter squash; with almost any starchy vegetable. (See Red Square Potato Puree, page 257.) To prepare a puree with one of these other vegetables, use the same proportions and techniques described here.

1 pound parsnips, peeled and quartered crosswise

1 large (about 6 ounces) russet potato, peeled and quartered

Salt and freshly ground black pepper to taste

2 ounces (½ stick) unsalted room temperature butter, chopped

1 tablespoon minced flat-leaf parsley

Place the parsnips and potato in a medium pot and cover generously with cold salted water. Bring to a boil over medium-high heat. Reduce heat and simmer until very tender and almost falling apart, for about 20 minutes; drain. Set a large-holed sieve over the same pot. Mash the vegetables through the sieve, using a large mallet and up/down motion. (This can be prepared ahead, covered and set aside at room temperature.)

To serve, stir the puree over medium-high heat using a wooden spatula until warm. Add the butter and stir until smooth. (This can be prepared 1 hour ahead and kept warm in a larger pan of gently simmering water [*bain marie*]. Stir occasionally.) Mix in the parsley. Mound in a vegetable dish or spoon out onto 2 to 4 large plates with an entree. Serve immediately.

2 to 4 Servings

Planning Ahead
The Parsnip Potato Puree can be prepared at any time during the day the puree is to be served. If prepared in advance, re-heat and complete it before serving. Once completed, the dish can be kept warm in a water bath for about 1 hour.

Technique Tips
Potatoes become elastic and unpleasantly gluey when pureed in a food processor or blender or when pushed or dragged by a mallet or potato masher. In France, we use a drum-shaped sieve called a *tamis* to achieve a smooth texture. If one is not available, tamp the potatoes through a large-holed sieve by using a large mallet and a straight up-and-down arm movement. Although this may sound like a lot of work, it is easier than wielding a hand-held potato masher. A food mill is another good device for this task.

Unlike potatoes, parsnips are fine when pureed in the processor. If desired, cook the potato and parsnip separately, and puree the potatoes through a sieve and the parsnips in the processor.

Garlic Mashed Potatoes Ali-Bab

4 Servings

Planning Ahead

The Garlic Cream and Potato Puree can be prepared at any time during the day the dish is to be served. If the puree is made in advance, reheat it and whisk in the remaining ingredients before presenting. Once completed, this dish can be kept warm in a water bath for about 1 hour.

Technique Tips

This recipe will, indeed, serve 4, but a single mashed potato fan, like me, can easily consume all of it.

When boiling potatoes, simmer them very gently. If the water boils rapidly, the potatoes can break apart and become waterlogged.

Potatoes become elastic and unpleasantly gluey when pureed in a food processor or blender or when pushed or dragged by a mallet or potato masher. In France, we use a drum-shaped sieve called a *tamis* to achieve a smooth texture. If one is not available, tamp the potatoes through a large-holed sieve, using a large mallet and a straight up-and-down arm movement. Although this may sound

My customers at Citrus constantly ask me what is different about my mashed potatoes. "Why are they so delicious?", they query. The answer is simple: Ali-Bab. My fifty-fifty formula, one pound butter to one pound potatoes, comes directly from his book, *Gastronomie Pratique*, published in 1907. As I've said many times, today's chefs aren't inventing anything even when we think we are. I've cut the proportion of butter here substantially, but feel free to use any amount you want. If you desire the real mashed potatoes my restaurant patrons get, follow Ali-Bab's formula for an extraordinary experience.

It is funny. I am a pastry chef, yet this is the only dish in the restaurant in which I use so much butter. It makes me sad that people feel so guilty about food. Having potatoes with butter—or butter with potatoes—once every two months isn't going to hurt anyone. Our clients tell us they can't eat anything fattening because they are on a diet, but when we serve them these potatoes, all we see is joy.

GARLIC CREAM

¼ cup (about 8 large) peeled garlic cloves

¼ cup heavy cream

POTATO PUREE

1 pound (about 4 medium) russet potatoes, peeled and quartered

¼ cup heavy cream

3 ounces (¾ stick) unsalted room temperature butter, coarsely chopped

Salt and freshly ground black pepper to taste

For the Garlic Cream, place the garlic in a heavy medium saucepan. Cover with 3 inches of cold water. Bring to a boil. Drain and rinse with cold water. Repeat this process 2 more times. Coarsely chop the garlic and return it to the same saucepan with the cream. Bring to a boil, then reduce heat and simmer gently until reduced by half or to a thick saucelike consistency, stirring occasionally. (This can be prepared ahead, cooled, covered and set aside at cool room temperature for several hours or refrigerated.)

For the Potato Puree, place the potatoes in a heavy medium pot. Cover with cold salted water and bring to a boil. Reduce heat and simmer until tender, for about 20 minutes; drain. Set a large-holed sieve over the same pot. Mash the potatoes through the sieve, using a large mallet and up/down motion. (This can be prepared ahead, covered and set aside at room temperature.)

Up to 1 hour before serving, add ¼ cup heavy cream to the Garlic Cream and reheat until warm, stirring occasionally. Meanwhile, place the potato pot over medium-high heat and stir using a wooden spatula until the potatoes are warm and dried out. Stir in the butter several pieces at a time. Mix in the warm Garlic Cream in a slow stream. Season with salt and pepper. (This can be prepared 1 hour ahead and kept warm in a larger pan of gently simmering water [*bain marie*]. Stir occasionally.) Mound in a vegetable dish or spoon out onto 4 large plates with an entree. Serve immediately.

like a lot of work, it is easier than wielding a hand-held potato masher. A food mill is another good device for this task.

Red Square Potato Puree

A beet by itself is like a vampire's blood: too red and too strong. When pureed with potatoes, its intensity is toned down and it acquires the starchiness it inherently lacks. And the color is fabulous. Like the potatoes, the vinegar plays a moderator's role, balancing the beets and softening their sweetness. I used to serve both baked beets and mashed potatoes as separate garnishes with venison and other game, but I like them even better bound together. They're simpler to prepare this way, too.

4 to 6 Servings

Planning Ahead
The potato beet puree can be prepared at any time during the day it is to be served. If prepared in advance, reheat and complete before serving. Once completed, the dish can be kept warm in a water bath for about 1 hour.

POTATOES

> 5 medium (about 1¼ pounds) russet potatoes, peeled and quartered
>
> 2 teaspoons red wine vinegar
>
> Salt and freshly ground black pepper to taste

BEETS

> 4 medium (about 1 to 1¼ pounds) beets, peeled and quartered
>
> ¼ cup milk
>
> Salt and freshly ground black pepper to taste
>
> 2 ounces (½ stick) unsalted room temperature butter, chopped
>
> 2 tablespoons fresh minced chives or green onions   *(continued)*

Side Dishes

Potatoes become elastic and unpleasantly gluey when pureed in a food processor or blender or when pushed or dragged by a mallet or potato masher. In France, we use a drum-shaped sieve called a *tamis* to achieve a smooth texture. If one is not available, tamp the potatoes through a large-holed sieve by using a large mallet and a straight up-and-down arm movement. Although this may sound like a lot of work, it is easier than wielding a hand-held potato masher. A food mill is another good device for this task.

Variation

Beet greens can be served with the puree, if desired. To prepare the greens, discard the stalks and slice the greens into strips. Heat 2 tablespoons of olive oil in a heavy large skillet over medium-high heat. Add the greens, cover and cook until wilted and tender, for about 5 minutes, stirring frequently. Season with salt and pepper.

For the potatoes, place in a medium pot and cover with cold salted water. Bring to a boil over medium-high heat. Reduce heat and simmer until very tender and almost falling apart, for about 20 minutes; drain. Set a large-holed sieve over the same pot. Mash the potatoes through the sieve, using a large mallet and up/down motion. Stir in the vinegar. Season with salt and pepper. (This can be prepared ahead, covered and set aside at room temperature.)

Meanwhile, cover the beets with cold salted water in a medium pot. Bring to a boil over medium-high heat. Reduce heat and simmer until very tender and easily pierced with a knife, for about 20 minutes; drain. Puree the beets with the milk in a blender until smooth, pulsing on/off and stopping to scrape down the sides of the container. Season with salt and pepper. Strain the beet puree into the potatoes through a fine sieve, pressing on the beets. (This can be prepared ahead, covered and set aside at room temperature.)

To serve, stir the puree over medium-high heat until warm, using a wooden spatula. Add the butter and stir until smooth. (This can be prepared 1 hour ahead to this point and kept warm in a larger pan of gently simmering water [*bain marie*]. Stir occasionally.) Mix in the chives. Mound in a vegetable dish or spoon out onto 4 to 6 large plates with an entree. Serve immediately.

Quiche-in-a-Potato

The French have many tricks for cooking potatoes, but stuffing large russets as the Americans do is not one of them. This manner of presenting the potato offers a little surprise, and is yet another idea I've adopted from my new country. I'm not sure this recipe adds a new dimension to the baked potato or to quiche, but real men should like it, regardless.

6 large (about 12 ounces each) evenly shaped russet potatoes, scrubbed and pricked all over with a fork

Peanut oil

Salt and freshly ground black pepper to taste

½ pound Swiss cheese, grated

1 cup heavy cream

2 eggs

1½ tablespoons minced green onions or fresh chives

Salt and freshly ground black pepper to taste

To bake the potatoes, preheat the oven to 350°F. Rub the potatoes with oil, place on a rimmed baking sheet and bake until very tender and easily pierced with a knife, for about 1½ hours. Hollow out the potato with a knife and small spoon or melon baller, leaving ½-inch-thick boat-shaped shell. Reserve scooped-out potato for salad or another use.

For the filling, return the potato shells to the baking sheet. Season the shells with salt and pepper. Press ¾ of the cheese into the shells. Whisk the cream, eggs and green onion together. Season the cream mixture with salt and pepper. (This can be prepared ahead. Set shells aside at room temperature and refrigerate the cream mixture until 1 hour before rebaking potatoes.)

To serve, preheat the oven to 350°F. Carefully ladle the cream mixture into the potatoes. Sprinkle the remaining cheese on top. Bake immediately until puffed and browned, for 25 to 30 minutes. Let sit for 5 to 10 minutes or until tepid before serving. Transfer to a platter or to 6 small or main-course plates. Serve immediately.

6 Servings

Planning Ahead

The potatoes can be cooked and the quiche filling mixed at any time during the day the dish is to be served. Stuff the potatoes and rebake just before presenting.

Variation

Bake the quiche filling in tiny steamed, hollowed-out red potatoes to pass for hors d'oeuvres.

Potato Risotto with Mushrooms

4 to 6 Servings

Planning Ahead
The potatoes can be diced and the other ingredients prepped at any time during the day the risotto is to be served. The risotto can be partially cooked about 1½ hours before eating. Complete the cooking just before presenting.

Technique Tip
The potatoes need to be cut as close to the size of rice grains as possible. As you chop the potatoes, the temptation is to cut the dice bigger and bigger. Resist.

I like to tease and joke, but with respect, so no one gets hurt. When I am in the kitchen, I play around with new ideas because it's fun to see my customers' reactions. I enjoy being a magician and creating a surprise on the plate. One of the best ways for me to do so is to make one ingredient look like another. In this *trompe l'oeil* dish, I fool the eye by cutting the potatoes into such tiny dice they look like the Arborio rice used for making risotto. Silvio De Mori, a friend who owns many Italian restaurants, is always lecturing me that the French don't know how to cook a proper risotto. At long last, after tasting this rendition, he told me he was very impressed. I was elated.

I may make foods look different than what they are, but I never call them something they are not. It makes me angry to order a dish named "Potatoes with Truffles" and then get one measly slice of chopped truffle that you need a magnifying glass to find.

2 pounds (about 8 medium) russet potatoes, peeled

2 cups heavy cream

¼ to ½ pound shiitake or other fresh mushrooms, ends trimmed and thinly diced

¼ cup (about 1 ounce) freshly grated Parmesan cheese

Salt and freshly ground black pepper to taste

To prepare the potatoes, carefully cut potatoes into thin, even slices using a knife or food processor with a slicing blade. Cut the slices into ⅛-inch-wide strips. Cut the strips crosswise into very fine dice the size of rice grains. As the potatoes are cut, place them in a large bowl of cold water. (This can be prepared ahead to this point and set aside at room temperature in the bowl covered with cold water.)

To cook, bring 1 cup of the cream to a boil in a heavy large nonstick saucepan over medium-high heat. Drain the potatoes and add them to the cream. Simmer gently, adjusting the heat, until the cream is absorbed, stirring occasionally. Pour in ½ of the remaining cream with all of the mushrooms. Simmer gently until the cream is absorbed, stirring occasionally. (This can be prepared to this point about 1½ hours ahead and set aside at cool room temperature.)

To serve, bring to a simmer and pour in the remaining cream. Simmer until thickened and the cream is absorbed (the potatoes will start to meld together), for about 20 minutes. Stir in the Parmesan. Season with salt and pepper. Mound in a vegetable dish or spoon out onto 4 to 6 large plates with an entree. Serve immediately.

Mini Potatoes Alex Humbert

4 Servings

Chef Alex Humbert created these sublime potatoes during his long tenure at the venerable Maxim's restaurant in Paris. One of the best of the many variations on a crisp potato cake, this dish should be called *Pommes Alex Humbert* rather than *Pommes Maxim,* the French name by which it is known. To prepare his signature dish, Chef Humbert would sauté overlapping slices of potato in a large skillet until they formed a crisp cake he served sliced in wedges. Unless you have a well-seasoned cast-iron skillet, the potatoes can stick and become difficult to handle. To simplify the process, I make mini single servings on aluminum foil or parchment paper squares that slip off easily after the potatoes are baked.

3 small (¾ to 1 pound total) russet potatoes, peeled

1 ounce (¼ stick) unsalted butter, melted

Salt and freshly ground black pepper to taste

Cut the potatoes into thin, even slices using a knife, a mandoline or a food processor with a slicing blade. Place in a large bowl of cold water. (This can be prepared to this point and set aside at room temperature in the bowl covered with cold water. Drain before continuing with the recipe.)

To cook, preheat the oven to 450°F. Dry the potatoes well in a bath towel. Cut four 6-inch squares of parchment paper or aluminum foil. Line 1 large or 2 small baking sheets with a single layer of squares. Brush the squares lightly with melted butter. Overlap the slices on the squares in a circular pattern, forming 4 flowers, each about 4 inches in diameter.

Brush each flower with melted butter. Season with salt and pepper. Bake until the potatoes are brown and easily pierced with a knife, for about 25 minutes.

To serve, slide a long narrow spatula under each flower to loosen it from the paper. Switch to a large broad spatula and carefully transfer the flowers to 4 small or main-course plates. Serve immediately.

Planning Ahead

The potatoes can be sliced at any time during the day they are to be served and arranged up to ½ hour or so before they are cooked. Bake just before presenting.

Technique Tips

For the most attractive appearance, use potatoes that are the same size.

When loosening and removing the potatoes from the parchment, keep the spatula flat with the tip tilted toward the parchment, not the potatoes.

Baker's Memory Potatoes

Planning Ahead

The onions can be cooked and the potatoes sliced at any time during the day the dish is to be prepared. But the further ahead the potatoes are sliced and the longer they sit in the water, the crisper they become and the harder it will be to get the layers to adhere. If time allows, slice the potatoes just before arranging. The potatoes and onions can be layered up to a half hour before cooking. Bake just before serving.

Technique Tips

For the most attractive appearance, use potatoes that are the same size.

Potatoes are easiest to work with and will stick together most readily if their starch is not washed out. Nevertheless, I prefer the flavor of rinsed potatoes so, if necessary, I just push them back into their sandwich shape.

When removing potatoes from parchment, keep the spatula flat with the tip tilted toward the parchment, not the potatoes.

I n the old days, one baker would feed an entire French town. Late in the morning, this important man would remove the freshly baked loaves from his large hot communal oven and replace them with casseroles the villagers had mixed at home and dropped off on their way to work. When it was time for the midday meal, people would stop by once again to pick up their hot food along with a fresh baguette for what was an early version of a cooperative take-out.

Probably no dish was carried up and down the streets of France more frequently in those years than *Pommes Boulangères,* the baker's potatoes that were layered with onions. In re-creating a one-stop version of this dish—to be both mixed and baked at home—I have tried to make this rustic favorite a bit grand while retaining its wonderful savor. Recalling the many happy recollections this heirloom dish has given me, I want to offer my clients memorable food to sweeten their reminiscences ten years from now.

ONION FILLING

> 2 tablespoons peanut oil
>
> 2 small (about ⅔ to ¾ pound) onions, peeled and finely diced
>
> 1 tablespoon fresh minced thyme or 1 teaspoon dried thyme, crumbled
>
> 1 tablespoon Champagne vinegar or white wine vinegar
>
> Salt and freshly ground black pepper to taste

POTATOES

> 1¼ pounds (about 5 medium) russet potatoes, peeled
>
> 2 ounces (½ stick) unsalted butter, melted
>
> Salt and freshly ground black pepper to taste

For the Onion Filling, place a heavy medium saucepan on medium-low heat and add the oil. Add the onions and thyme, cover and cook until very tender, for about 20 minutes, stirring occasionally. Add the vinegar, bring to a boil and stir until absorbed. Season with salt and pepper. (This can be prepared ahead, cooled, covered and set aside at room temperature.)

For the potatoes, carefully cut potatoes into thin, even slices using a knife, a mandoline or a food processor with a slicing blade. Place in a large bowl of cold water. (This can be prepared to this point and set aside at room temperature in the bowl covered with cold water. Drain before continuing with the recipe.)

To cook, preheat the oven to 450°F. Dry the drained potatoes well in a lettuce spinner and a clean bath towel. Line a large baking sheet with parchment paper. Trace four 5-inch circles on the parchment with dark ink. Turn the paper over. If the circles are not visible, redraw them so they are. Brush the circles lightly with butter. Overlap the potatoes to cover the bottom of each circle, using the least attractive slices for the center. Brush lightly with butter. Season with salt and pepper. Divide the onions among the centers of the circles. Flatten onions to ⅛-inch-thick circles using a spatula. Overlap 1 layer of potatoes around the rim of each circle, leaving part of the onion center exposed. Brush the top layer of potatoes lightly with butter. Season with salt and pepper. Press down on the top layer, sealing it to the bottom layer. Bake until brown and crisp, for about 30 minutes. Press the layers together and neaten edges several times while baking.

To serve, slide a long narrow spatula under the potatoes to loosen them from the paper. Switch to a broad spatula and carefully transfer the potatoes to 4 small or main-course plates, neatening the edges if necessary. Serve immediately.

Frites (French Fries)

Planning Ahead

The potatoes can be peeled and cut at any time during the day they are to be cooked. They can be fried for the first time several hours in advance and for the second time just before serving.

Technique Tips

For the crispest crust, cut the fries about ¼ inch thick.

With its tapered bottom, a wok enables you to fry with a minimum amount of oil. Regardless of what pan you use, cook the potatoes in small batches without crowding so they will fry, not steam.

To develop a thick crisp crust that will prevent steam from escaping from the interior of the potatoes and making them soggy, fry the potatoes slowly.

In order for both the interior of the potato to cook completely and the exterior to crisp without burning, it is necessary to fry potatoes twice. After the potatoes are cooked once and removed from the oil, the exterior cools immediately while the interior continues to cook through. The exterior browns and crisps on the second frying.

I don't know if the French invented French fries, but it is certainly the most famous French dish in America, even if Americans claim it as their own by drowning it in ketchup. Not so long ago, these golden sticks were street food in France. Folks bought a cornet of fries on the way to the movies and gathered in the square to visit and eat. During the movie, fancies turned to peanuts in the shell, but, once out in the open again, it was another cornet to munch on while walking home.

Not only did we purchase our potatoes on the streets in those days, we also made them at home where our *négresse*, a big black cast-iron pot with a removable basket, awaited our whim on the back burner. It was filled with oil and ready to go whenever we wanted *frites*, which was just about daily. We fried the potatoes twice to be sure they cooked through, taking turns being responsible for each immersion. Volunteers were hard to come by for the first frying. Not so the second, when we could eat the *frites* right out of the fryer.

2 pounds (about 8 medium) russet potatoes, peeled, sliced lengthwise and cut into ¼- to ⅜-inch-wide sticks

Peanut oil (about 4 cups) for deep frying

Salt to taste

Place the potatoes in a large bowl of cold water. Change the water repeatedly to remove the potato starch, until the water remains clear. (This can be prepared ahead to this point and set aside at room temperature in the bowl covered with cold water. Drain before cooking.) Dry the potatoes well in a lettuce spinner and a clean bath towel.

To cook the first time, line 2 large baking sheets with paper towels. Heat the oil to 350°F in a deep fryer, wok or large pot. Fry the potatoes in small batches without crowding until completely cooked, but barely colored, turning occasionally. Transfer to the prepared sheets in a single layer using a slotted spatula. (This can be prepared ahead and set aside at room temperature.)

To serve, line another baking sheet with paper towels. Preheat the oven to 200°F. Reheat the oil to 350°F. Fry the potatoes in small batches until crisp and golden brown, turning occasionally. Transfer the cooked potatoes to the prepared sheet using a slotted spatula and keep them warm in the oven while cooking the remaining potatoes. Sprinkle with salt. Transfer to a large bowl. Serve immediately.

Potato Pancakes A.K.A. Latkes

4 Servings

A friend of mine was complaining that her big Hanukah party was ruined every year because she either spent the night in the kitchen frying the ritual latkes (potato pancakes), or reheating rounds she had made ahead that became soggy. "What do I do?" she asked. To answer her question, I drew upon my experience as a pastry chef, which has taught me many tricks over the years for solving cooking as well as baking problems. The cutting, rolling and baking techniques I adopted for these latkes are the exact ones I employ for making cookies, for it was their crunch I sought here. As my friend requested, these crisp cakes can be prepared ahead, except for the final baking. This is a rare virtue, indeed, for a potato recipe and one that certainly makes it ideal for entertaining. And not just for Hanukah.

Planning Ahead

These pancakes can be completely prepared in advance. If they are not, allow at least 1 hour to weight the potatoes. Bake just before serving.

1 pound (about 4 medium) russet potatoes, peeled

2 tablespoons olive or peanut oil

1 tablespoon unsalted butter

Olive or peanut oil

Salt and freshly ground black pepper to taste

Cut the potatoes into long thin strips (about $\frac{1}{16}$ to $\frac{1}{8}$ inch wide) by hand or in the food processor, using the julienne or shredder blade. Place the potatoes in a large bowl of cold water. (They can be prepared ahead to this point and set aside at room temperature in the bowl covered with cold water. Drain before cooking.) Dry the potatoes well in a lettuce spinner and a clean bath towel.

Place a heavy large nonstick skillet over medium-high heat. Add the oil and butter and heat. Add the potatoes and stir-fry until tender, for about 5 minutes. Turn out onto a baking sheet and push the potatoes together into a rectangular shape, about $\frac{1}{4}$ inch thick. Roll with a rolling pin to flatten further. Cover with a sheet of plastic wrap.

Oil a large baking sheet. Cut out $2\frac{1}{2}$- to 3-inch-round pancakes by pressing a fluted cookie cutter into the potatoes. Transfer the pancakes to the prepared sheet with a spatula. (This can be prepared ahead to this point, covered with plastic wrap and set aside at room temperature until baking.)

To serve, preheat the oven to 325°F. Discard the plastic and season the potatoes with salt and pepper. Bake until crisp and brown on both sides, for about 30 minutes, turning halfway. Transfer the pancakes to a serving platter or to 4 small or main-course plates with a large spatula. Serve immediately.

Sweet Potatoes with Rosemary

4 Servings

Planning Ahead

The potatoes can be cooked at any time during the day they are to be served. Sauté just before presenting.

Americans appear to love sugar, particularly with sweet potatoes. The French adore rosemary, which is a classic counterpoint to something sweet. So what we have here is sweet sweet potatoes balanced with an aromatic herb. I have adopted the American habit of serving sweet potatoes with turkey in my home, yet I find that they go equally well with almost any meat, poultry or seafood dish.

1¼ to 1½ **pounds sweet potatoes, peeled, quartered lengthwise and sliced crosswise into ¾-inch-thick rounds**

1 **ounce (¼ stick) unsalted butter**

1 **tablespoon dark brown sugar**

1½ **teaspoons fresh minced rosemary or ½ teaspoon dried, crumbled**

Freshly ground black pepper to taste

Fill a heavy large nonstick skillet with water. Bring to a boil, add the sweet potatoes and cook until tender when pierced with a knife, for about 10 minutes; drain. (This can be prepared ahead, placed on a tray, cooled, covered and set aside at room temperature. Reserve skillet for reheating potatoes.)

To serve, melt the butter in the same skillet over low heat. Add the brown sugar and stir until melted. Add the sweet potatoes, sprinkle with rosemary and pepper, increase the heat to medium-high and stir until the potatoes are brown on all sides, for about 3 minutes. Mound in a vegetable bowl or spoon out onto 4 plates with an entree. Serve immediately.

Sweet Potato Puree with Prunes

When we serve game in France, we partner it as automatically with prunes as you do with sweet potatoes. For me, the next logical step was to partner the two partners. I think you call this a square dance. Although the resulting puree has the same strange colors as your Halloween festival, I find I very much like the flavors together as well as the bite of dried fruit in the mix. Cinnamon, reserved for apples in France, adds a charming nuance to the potatoes.

2 ounces (about 6 large) pitted prunes

1¼ to 1½ pounds sweet potatoes, peeled and cut crosswise into ¾-inch-thick rounds

Salt and freshly ground black pepper to taste

Generous pinch of ground cinnamon

2 ounces (½ stick) unsalted room temperature butter, chopped

Soak the prunes in warm water to cover for 20 minutes. Drain and quarter, using scissors.

Cook the sweet potatoes in a medium pot of boiling water until tender when pierced with a knife, for about 10 minutes; drain. Puree the potatoes in a food mill or food processor, pulsing on/off and stopping to scrape down the sides of the container. Return them to the pot. Season with salt and pepper. Mix in the cinnamon. (This can be prepared ahead, covered and set aside at room temperature.)

To serve, stir the potatoes over medium-high heat until hot. Add butter and stir until melted. Stir in the quartered prunes until just mixed through. Mound in a vegetable dish or spoon out onto 4 plates with an entree. Serve immediately.

4 Servings

Planning Ahead

The puree can be prepared at any time during the day it is to be served. Reheat and stir in the butter and prunes just before presenting.

Technique Tips

It is easier to cut sticky prunes with scissors than with a knife.

When mixing prunes into the puree, stir in just to distribute. Overmixing will cause the mixture to turn black. At this point, the taste will still be delicious, but the appearance may be a bit disconcerting.

Giant Potato Chips

Makes About 16
6-inch Chips to Serve 6
to 8

Planning Ahead

The potato puree can be made and the chips immediately formed at any time during the day they are to be served. Bake the chips just before presenting.

Technique Tips

The chips must be formed immediately after the ingredients are mixed and while the puree is warm or the mixture becomes difficult to spread and the chips will be too thick.

At the restaurant, I use a stencil I made to form these potatoes. To do so, I cut an 8-inch circle with a handle on it from the cover of a large plastic container and then cut a 6-inch circle out of its interior. A stencil could also be made from heavy cardboard. If a stencil is available, there is no need to draw the circles first on parchment. To form the chips, I place the stencil on the parchment, scoop the potatoes into the center of the stencil and then spread the mixture with a spatula. When I am finished, I lift off the stencil.

I wanted to make the perfect *tuile:* a thin crunchy cookie with the texture of a potato chip. After I tried several methods, I realized I wasn't going to get what I wanted by making a cookie with flour. Since my ideal *tuile* resembled a potato chip, I thought, Why not just make a potato chip? So that is exactly what I did, using egg white to bind the potato. Now I have something new and spectacular looking on the plate. It's amazing what you can accomplish when you do what you say you are going to do.

1 pound (about 4 small) russet potatoes, peeled and quartered

4 ounces (1 stick) unsalted room temperature butter, chopped

½ teaspoon sugar

Salt and freshly ground black pepper to taste

4 (½ cup) egg whites, at room temperature

1½ tablespoons sesame seeds (optional)

Draw four 6-inch circles on each of four 15- × 15-inch pieces of parchment paper in heavy ink. Turn each paper over and place on a separate baking sheet. If circles are not visible, redraw them so they are. Cover the potatoes with cold salted water in a medium saucepan. Bring to a boil over medium-high heat. Reduce heat and simmer until very tender and easily pierced with a knife, for about 15 to 20 minutes; drain. Immediately set a large-holed sieve over a large bowl. Mash the potatoes through the sieve, using a large mallet and up/down motion. Stir in the butter, sugar, salt and pepper. Stir in the egg whites in a very fine stream so they do not curdle.

Working quickly while the potato mixture is warm, spread about 2 tablespoons of the mixture evenly over each circle with a flexible spatula, covering completely. Smooth and form the edges of each chip using your fingers and the spatula. Stir the sesame seeds in a heavy small dry skillet over medium-high heat until brown. Sprinkle them over the potatoes, pressing into the puree. (This can be prepared ahead to this point, covered with plastic wrap and set aside at room temperature.)

Preheat the oven (or ovens) to 350°F. Remove the plastic and bake the chips (in batches, if necessary) until brown on both sides, for about 25 to 30 minutes, turning halfway, if necessary. Slide a long narrow spatula under the potatoes to loosen from the parchment. Switch to a large broad spatula and stack on a large platter or on 6 to 8 small or main-course plates. Serve immediately.

Potato Gold Bricks

The Japanese Benriner Turning-Slicer has been one of my most trusted pieces of equipment ever since an ex-girlfriend showed me how to use it for shredding a daikon radish into long, slender, spaghettilike strands. Though my ardor for this woman cooled, not so my infatuation with her machine. Slicing the potatoes for this gold brick and for the Potato Fettuccine with Tomato and Basil (page 254) are only two of the many tasks I depend on this miracle tool to perform. You can find it at stores selling Japanese cookware.

Never mind, though, if you don't have either the cutter or the large electric deep-fryer basket I use at the restaurant. Dramatic Potato Gold Bricks can easily be made with the *batterie de cuisine* you already have at home. No fast-food French fries these, but slow finger food to linger over. Four pounds of potatoes may sound excessive for four people, but you'll know the proportions are right when you see the expression on people's faces.

4 pounds (about 16 medium) russet potatoes, peeled

Peanut or other oil for deep frying

Salt to taste

To prepare the potatoes, grate or cut them into long thin strips (about ¹⁄₁₆ to ⅛ inch wide) by hand, with a mandoline or in a food processor using the julienne or shredder blade. Place the julienne in a very large bowl of cold water. Change the water repeatedly to remove the potato starch, until the water remains clear. (This can be prepared ahead to this point and set aside at room temperature in the bowl covered with cold water. Drain before cooking.) Dry the potatoes well in a lettuce spinner and a clean bath towel.

To cook the potatoes, line a large baking sheet with several layers of paper towels. Divide the potatoes into 4 batches. Rinse a deep fryer basket in cold water; shake dry. Place ¼ of the potatoes in the wet basket. Place the basket in a deep fryer. Pour in enough oil to come at least 3 inches above the top of the potatoes. Remove the basket. Heat the oil to 350°F. Immerse the deep fryer basket in the oil and fry until the potatoes are well browned, for about 10 minutes. Tamp down the potatoes occasionally while cooking using a spoon or spatula. Lift the basket out of the oil, shake off the oil over the deep fryer and run a spatula around the edge to free the potatoes. Turn out onto the prepared baking sheet. Repeat with the remaining 3 batches. Season with salt. Serve immediately on 4 large plates or set aside to reheat or serve at room temperature.

To reheat, preheat the oven to 400°F. Remove the paper towels from the baking sheet and reheat the potatoes for 5 minutes or until warmed through.

4 Servings

Planning Ahead

The potatoes can be grated at any time during the day they are to be fried. Fry just before presenting or several hours in advance to reheat or serve at room temperature.

Technique Tips

To grate the potatoes, use a hand grater, a mandoline, a Japanese slicer or a food processor fitted with a julienne or shredder blade.

To cook the potatoes, use a round or rectangular deep fryer basket or metal mesh sieve.

Wetting the fryer basket prevents the potatoes from sticking.

Consider purchasing a good, instant-read thermometer to measure the temperature accurately for deep frying. If a thermometer is not available, check the oil temperature by immersing a chopstick or wooden spoon handle in the oil. The oil is ready when it starts to bubble up enthusiastically around the handle.

Singapore Breakfast Rice

Planning Ahead

The onion and shallot can be cooked at any time during the day the rice is to be served. Cook the rice just before presenting.

We do not add a lot of ingredients to rice in France. But after eating this grain with soy sauce for breakfast in Singapore, I wanted to extend its frontiers and cook it like the Asians do. The ginger and soy sauce give this a decided Oriental accent, which complements most dishes very nicely. And not just at breakfast.

1 ounce (¼ stick) unsalted butter

1 small onion, peeled and coarsely chopped

1 large shallot, peeled and minced

1 cup long grain white rice

2 cups unsalted chicken stock

1 tablespoon soy sauce

1 tablespoon fresh peeled minced gingerroot

Salt and freshly ground black pepper to taste

Melt the butter in a heavy medium saucepan over low heat. Add the onion and shallot, cover and cook until translucent, for about 10 minutes, stirring occasionally. Increase heat to medium-high, add the rice and stir until golden. Add the chicken stock with the soy sauce and ginger and bring to a boil. Reduce heat to low, cover and simmer gently until the rice is tender and the liquid is absorbed, for about 20 minutes. Let rest off the heat 10 minutes, covered. Fluff with a fork. Mound in a vegetable dish or spoon out onto 4 plates with an entree. Serve immediately.

Saffron Barley

I n France, people tend to use indigenous ingredients, whereas in America, they pull from international larders. Even knowing this, I was surprised to find so many foodstuffs here that I had never sampled before. Barley was one of them. The first time I tried it, I asked for the name of this new rice with such a great chewy texture. Since discovering its identity, I've kept this cereal as a staple in my cupboard. It's so easy to use and brings excellent flavor and texture. I've added saffron to this particular recipe to give the barley an unusual Mediterranean flair. Saffron is so good with fish, it has made this flavored barley a new unexpected side dish for seafood. From the combinations I have tried, though, I would say that the Saffron Barley goes quite well with everything. Well, maybe not with chocolate.

  I tablespoon peanut oil

  I small onion, peeled and diced

  1½ cups pearl barley

  3 cups unsalted chicken stock

  ⅛ teaspoon saffron threads, crushed

  Salt and freshly ground black pepper to taste

Heat the oil in a heavy medium saucepan. Add the onion, cover and cook over medium-low heat until translucent, for about 10 minutes, stirring occasionally. Stir in the barley. Add the chicken stock and bring to a boil. Stir 2 tablespoons of the hot stock into the saffron to dissolve and return the mixture to the saucepan. Cover, reduce heat to medium-low and simmer until the liquid is absorbed, for about 30 minutes. Season with salt and pepper. Fluff the grains with a fork. Mound in a vegetable dish or spoon out onto 4 plates with an entree. Serve immediately.

4 Servings

Planning Ahead
The onion can be cooked several hours in advance. Cook the barley just before serving.

Technique Tip
Dissolving crushed saffron in a hot liquid before adding to a mixture brings out its flavor.

Garlic Rigatoni Gratin

4 Servings

Planning Ahead

The components can be completely prepared and the dish assembled at any time during the day it is to be served. Brown the gratin just before presenting.

Technique Tip

When cooking garlic in cream, use a large deep pan so the cream doesn't boil over.

Variation

Mixture can also be divided among 4 individual gratin dishes.

From the name of this dish, you might think I've been affected yet again by Italian cooking. It's not me, however, but Lyon which is under the influence. The Romans founded this city of onion cookery, and this is one of its typical dishes—even if it has no onions in it. In this gastronomic capital, the gratin is made with either long macaroni tubes or perciatelli, but I've substituted rigatoni since I've had difficulty finding anything here but elbow-shaped pasta. If you can get the hollow cylinders about 8 or 9 inches long, use them by all means. Traditionally, this gratin is made by arranging macaroni side by side in an oval baking dish and layering it with a béchamel sauce. I've used my favorite Garlic Cream instead and tossed it all together.

GARLIC CREAM

30 large or generous 1 cup (about 2 heads) cloves garlic, peeled

2 cups heavy cream

½ pound rigatoni

Salt and freshly ground black pepper to taste

¼ cup (about 1 ounce) freshly grated Parmesan cheese

For the Garlic Cream, place the garlic in a heavy large saucepan. Cover with 3 inches of cold water. Bring to a boil. Drain and rinse with cold water. Repeat this process 2 more times. Coarsely chop the garlic. Return to the same saucepan with the cream. Bring to a boil, then reduce heat and simmer gently until reduced by half or to a thick saucelike consistency, stirring occasionally. (This can be prepared ahead, cooled, covered and set aside at cool room temperature for several hours or refrigerated. Reheat gently before mixing with pasta.)

Cook the rigatoni in a large pot of boiling water until al dente, for about 12 minutes; drain. Stir the pasta into the Garlic Cream. Season with salt and pepper. Butter an 11- or 12-inch gratin pan. Spread the pasta evenly in the pan. Sprinkle with the cheese. (This can be prepared ahead, covered and set aside at cool room temperature for several hours or refrigerated. Bring to room temperature before continuing with the recipe.)

To serve, preheat the broiler. Uncover the gratin and broil 6 inches below the heat source until golden brown, for about 3 to 4 minutes, watching carefully. Pass at the table or spoon out onto 4 small or main-course plates. Serve immediately.

Corn Pancakes

B efore coming to America, I thought corn was food for pigs. Not only have I learned to use this vegetable for people, but I have also grown quite fond of it. In this instance, I've called on both the corn kernels and the dried meal to texture pancakes. I offer these either as a side dish for poultry or I make them a star, gilding them with crème fraîche, chives, dill, capers—or caviar—and smoked salmon for a first course or light main course at brunch or supper.

3 tablespoons all-purpose flour

⅓ cup cornmeal

3 tablespoons milk

2 ounces (½ stick) unsalted butter, at room temperature

½ teaspoon salt

2 drops Tabasco

3 eggs, separated, at room temperature

1 large ear corn, husked and kernels removed

½ teaspoon baking powder

1½ tablespoons fresh minced chives or green onions

Pinch of cream of tartar

About 1 ounce (¼ stick) unsalted butter

For the batter, blend flour, cornmeal, milk, butter, salt, Tabasco and egg yolks in a food processor or blender, pulsing on/off and stopping to scrape down the sides of the container. (This can be prepared ahead to this point, covered and set aside at cool room temperature for several hours or refrigerated until 2 hours before completing.)

To serve, preheat the oven to 150°F. Add the corn kernels and baking powder to the batter and process, pulsing on/off until the corn is coarsely chopped. Transfer to a bowl. Stir in the chives. Meanwhile, beat the egg whites with the cream of tartar using an electric mixer until stiff peaks form but are not dry. Gently fold ¼ of the whites into the corn mixture, then fold in the remaining whites.

Preheat a griddle or heavy large nonstick skillet over medium heat. Melt the butter on the griddle. Drop a rounded tablespoon of batter onto the griddle and cook until bubbles appear and begin to pop. Turn and brown the second side lightly. Place the cooked cakes in a single layer on a baking sheet in the preheated oven to keep warm. Repeat with the remaining batter, adding more butter as necessary. Arrange on a platter or on 6 plates with any desired accompaniments. Serve immediately.

Makes About 12 (3-inch) Pancakes or 18 (2-inch) Pancakes to Serve 6

Planning Ahead

The batter can be partially prepared in advance at any time during the day the pancakes are to be served. Cook the pancakes just before presenting.

Technique Tip

If it is difficult to cook the pancakes before serving when guests are present, place the griddle near the table and cook as you eat.

Side Dishes

273

White Bean Belly Dancer Rolls

4 to 6 Servings

Planning Ahead

The beans can be cooked several days before filling the rolls. The rolls can be filled and frozen several months in advance. Fry or bake just before serving.

I enjoy taking the French recipes from my youth and my apprenticeship and giving them a modern international twist. White beans appeared in many guises while I was growing up, yet I never encountered them in either a Mexican refried state or a crunchy Middle Eastern filo dough wrapper.

No longer just a side dish, these rolls reflect their multiple origins as an appetizer, first course or even main course for a light lunch or supper. Serve them plain, with sour cream and chives or with salsa, guacamole, Avocado Salsa (page 140) or Crispy Tomato Onion Relish (page 162). As filo dough assumes new roles, this pastry becomes a citizen of the world.

½ pound Great Northern or other white beans, picked over and rinsed

2 slices bacon, diced

4 fresh 4-inch thyme sprigs or 1 tablespoon dried thyme, crumbled

2 tablespoons olive oil

1 large tomato, peeled, seeded and chopped

Salt and freshly ground black pepper to taste

6 sheets filo dough, defrosted overnight in refrigerator if frozen

1 egg, blended with fork

Peanut oil

For the beans, place them in a large pot. Cover with enough water to come 2 inches above the beans. Cover the pot and set aside at room temperature to soak overnight.

Drain the beans. Cook the bacon in the same pot over medium heat until brown and crisp, stirring occasionally. Return the beans to the pot along with the thyme. Add enough water to come 4 inches above the beans and bring to a boil, skimming off any foam. Reduce heat and simmer until the beans are very tender to taste and almost breaking apart, for about 2½ hours, stirring occasionally and adding additional water as necessary. Drain the beans. Place in a medium bowl and mash coarsely with a mallet or potato masher. Stir in the olive oil and tomato. Season with salt and pepper; cool. (This can be prepared ahead, covered and set aside at room temperature for several hours or refrigerated for several days.)

To assemble the rolls, line a large baking sheet with parchment or waxed paper. Remove the filo from its package and unroll. Remove 1 sheet and cut in half crosswise. Cover one of the ½ sheets and the remaining filo with plastic wrap and a damp towel so they do not dry out. Fold the uncovered ½ sheet in half crosswise, place a generous ¼ cup of beans lengthwise in a 5-inch band 1 inch in from the edge. Brush all 4 sides with egg. Fold the sides over and roll up jelly-roll style. Place seam side down on the prepared baking sheet. Repeat with the remaining filo sheets. Rewrap remaining filo and refrigerate or freeze for another use. (This can be prepared ahead, covered with plastic wrap and set aside at cool room temperature for several hours, refrigerated for several days or frozen on trays for several months. When frozen, wrap in freezer bag or paper. Defrost overnight in refrigerator before cooking.)

To serve, line a baking sheet with paper towels. Heat ¾ inch of oil in a large skillet until it reaches 375°F on a thermometer or until the oil starts to bubble up enthusiastically around a chopstick or wooden spoon handle immersed in the oil. Fry the rolls in batches until golden brown on both sides, for about 7 minutes total. Drain on the prepared baking sheet. Arrange on a serving platter or divide among 4 to 6 plates. Serve immediately plain or with sour cream or a dipping sauce.

Variation

To bake the rolls instead of frying, preheat the oven to 450°F. Melt 1 ounce (¼ stick) unsalted butter. Brush the rolls with the butter and bake until brown, for about 15 to 20 minutes.

To serve bean rolls as an appetizer, make them half the size described here or smaller and pass with a dipping sauce such as Avocado Salsa (page 140) or Crispy Tomato Onion Relish (page 162).

Fresh Corn Polenta

4 Servings

Planning Ahead

The polenta can be completely prepared in advance. Cook just before serving.

Technique Tips

Scrape the corn into a large baking dish or tray so the mixture doesn't spatter.

Experiment with different spoons and knives to determine which tool performs this task the quickest.

When a recipe with so few ingredients can be so easy to make and so delicious to eat, you know you have one of the world's great dishes. To make a corn puree, I used to cut the kernels off the cob, blend them in the food processor and then strain them through a fine sieve. Not only did this take three steps and many more dishes, but I also lost a lot of the good corn pulp in the strainer along with the skin. One day I stumbled on an American Indian woman at a street fair in Santa Fe who was removing the corn pulp as I describe below, and I've been copying her method ever since. It does take some time to scrape out all the corn, and, admittedly, it can be a fairly messy job, but it's all do-ahead, and the resulting thick, coarse puree is the sweetest corn I've ever had. The texture of this corn essence resembles that of polenta, but its taste is pure, intense and fresh.

6 large ears of corn, husked

⅓ cup (about 1¼ ounces) freshly grated Parmesan cheese or to taste

Salt and freshly ground black pepper to taste

1 to 3 ounces (¼ to ¾ stick) chilled unsalted butter, chopped

Brush the silk off of the corn. Using a very sharp knife, and slicing from top to bottom of cob, cut a slit through the center of each corn kernel. Holding the corn over a large deep baking dish or tray, scrape the pulp out of the corn kernels with a large soup spoon or the back of a heavy large knife, leaving the corn skin. (This can be prepared ahead, covered with plastic wrap and set aside at room temperature.)

To serve, heat a heavy large saucepan over medium heat. Add the corn puree and stir until the corn liquid is absorbed and the mixture thickens, for about 3 to 4 minutes. Stir in the cheese. Season with salt and pepper. Stir in the butter. Mound in a vegetable dish or spoon out into 4 plates with an entree. Serve immediately.

Red Cabbage Ketchup

Makes About 1 Cup

I had been making coleslaw from green cabbage on a regular basis. "Why not use red cabbage?" I asked myself one day. "It would be prettier." Soon I started using red cabbage for the coarse puree that accompanies my Shrimp Porcupines (page 130) and Chicken Kataifi (page 178). This purple sauce has a sweet/sour tang that is reminiscent of ketchup. Not surprisingly, it wasn't too long before I was making my own condiment, too. Unlike the fresh Purple Sauce, a blend of raw ingredients, this ketchup is cooked. It also has a beet to dye it deep red. Beautiful and quite delicious, when placed upon a ground beef patty, you have a hamburger, ketchup and coleslaw in one bite.

Planning Ahead

The ketchup can be completely prepared several days in advance. Reheat if serving warm.

2 tablespoons butter

1 tablespoon oil

1 large red onion, peeled and thinly sliced

½ small red cabbage, cored and shredded

1 medium red beet, peeled and thinly sliced

1 tablespoon honey

3 tablespoons red wine vinegar

1 cup water

½ teaspoon ground ginger

2 drops Tabasco or to taste

Salt and freshly ground black pepper to taste

Melt the butter with the oil in a heavy large skillet over medium-low heat. Add the onion and cabbage, cover and cook until the onion is translucent, about 10 minutes, stirring occasionally. Mix in the beet, honey, vinegar, water and ginger. Cover and cook over medium-low heat until the cabbage and beet are very soft, for about 1 hour, stirring occasionally. Transfer the vegetables to a blender or food processor using a slotted spoon. Puree the mixture until it becomes a thick, smooth sauce, adding cooking liquid as necessary. Season with Tabasco, salt and pepper. (This can be prepared ahead, cooled, covered and set aside at room temperature for several hours or refrigerated for several days.)

To serve, remove from refrigerator and reheat, if desired, to serve warm by stirring over medium-high heat. Spoon ketchup out onto plates or on top of its accompaniment.

Oven-dried Herb Tomatoes

Planning Ahead

The tomatoes can be baked at any time during the day they are to be served.

Variation

Combine with leftover Eggplant Puree (page 234) and Parmesan or Pecorino cheese and chives to serve as a sauce for pasta.

When Judy Zeidler first served me these oven-dried fruits, I wasn't very excited. They looked just like the sun-dried tomatoes I knew and didn't love, the ones that taste like an old piece of leather and smell like an attic that hasn't been opened for years. When I tasted hers, though, I found they were absolutely delicious, with a deep, concentrated flavor; a reminder of the tomato's true potential. These tomatoes make a nice side dish, particularly with steaks and lamb chops, or a more integrated garnish when heaped, for example, atop whitefish. I often sprinkle them as well over a sauce or pasta.

1 pound (about 10 to 12) Roma tomatoes, halved lengthwise

1 teaspoon sugar

Salt and freshly ground black pepper to taste

About 2 tablespoons olive oil

4 large cloves garlic, peeled and minced

24 fresh large sage or basil leaves, finely shredded

Preheat the oven to 250°F. Brush a large baking sheet with olive oil or line with parchment paper. Gently scoop out the seeds, pulp and interior of the tomatoes using a melon baller or small spoon. Place the tomatoes cut side up on the baking sheet. Sprinkle with sugar, salt and pepper. Drizzle with olive oil. Scatter the garlic and sage over the tomatoes. Bake for 2 hours or until the tomatoes are wrinkled and dried. To serve warm or at room temperature, mound in a vegetable dish or spoon out onto 4 plates with an entree.

Celery Crunch with Anise

4 Servings

We rarely cook celery today in France, other than in a *mirepoix*, that dependable mixture of carrot, onion and celery employed as a flavoring base. In the past, we braised the stalks, but that is considered old-fashioned today. To update this vegetable, I've created a very simple dish; my favorite kind of recipe. Many people automatically dismiss celery as boring, but by using it in both its raw and cooked state, I can offer multiple tastes and textures with only one main ingredient. Oh yes, there is also a little pinch of anise for a teasing taste of Provence.

Planning Ahead

The dish can be partially cooked several hours before serving. Reheat and stir in the raw celery just before presenting.

- **1 bunch celery with 8 to 10 stalks**
- **About 1 tablespoon olive oil**
- **1 medium onion, peeled and minced**
- **1 teaspoon anise seed, finely crushed or 1 teaspoon ground anise seed**
- **¾ cup unsalted chicken stock**
- **Salt and freshly ground black pepper to taste**

Remove the leaves from the celery stalks and mince. Trim the celery stalks and peel off any fibrous strings on the exterior using a knife. Quarter the stalks lengthwise and cut crosswise into ¼-inch pieces.

Place a heavy medium nonstick saucepan over medium-low heat and film with oil. Add the onion and minced celery leaves, cover and cook until the onions are translucent, for about 10 minutes, stirring occasionally. Add ¾ of the diced celery, the anise seed and the chicken stock to the pan. Bring to a boil, reduce heat, cover and simmer until the celery is tender, for about 20 minutes, stirring occasionally. Boil down, if necessary, until the liquid is reduced and thickened to a saucelike consistency. Season with salt and pepper. (This can be prepared ahead, cooled, re-covered and set aside at cool room temperature for several hours.)

To serve, reheat the celery by stirring over medium-high heat. Stir in the remaining ¼ uncooked celery off the heat. Mound in a vegetable dish or spoon out onto 4 plates with an entree. Serve immediately.

Side Dishes

Forest Mushrooms with Hazelnuts and Parsley

4 Servings

Planning Ahead

The hazelnuts can be toasted and husked several days in advance. The mushrooms can be sautéed several hours before serving, but they will be more attractive if cooked at the last minute. Add the hazelnuts and parsley just before presenting.

Technique Tips

To prevent the mushrooms from absorbing too much water and steaming rather than browning, clean them by wiping with a damp paper towel rather than by immersing in water; dry well.

In order that mushrooms remain firm, add remaining ingredients and remove from heat as soon as the fungi brown well.

Whenever I taste a mushroom, I picture myself gathering this bounty in the forest on a foggy day, and it is this damp, earthy sensuality that I try to re-create whenever I cook any type of fungi. Hazelnut oil adds a woodsiness, while nuts crunch like twigs underfoot and parsley clings like a soft, fuzzy moss. Garlic, tamed by blanching in most of my other recipes, rages here to give the preparation a rustic force. I used to do very complicated things with mushrooms, but I've gone back to a simple *persillade* to show them off in all their dewy glory.

3 tablespoons peanut oil

1 tablespoon hazelnut oil

18 large (about 1 pound) mushrooms, ends trimmed and quartered

4 medium cloves garlic, peeled and minced

Generous pinch of curry powder

Salt and freshly ground black pepper to taste

12 hazelnuts, toasted, husked and coarsely chopped

½ cup minced flat-leaf parsley

Heat the oil in a heavy large skillet or wok over medium-high heat. Add the mushrooms and stir-fry until lightly browned. Add the garlic and curry powder and stir-fry for 1 minute. Season with salt and pepper. Stir in the hazelnuts and parsley. Mound in a vegetable dish or spoon out onto 4 plates with an entree. Serve immediately.

Mellow Spinach

As much as I like spinach, I find it has an underlying harshness that masks its clean pure savor. To soften its edge, I often mix this vegetable with an apple, pear or banana—yes, banana—puree. These flavors are not strong enough to be recognizable, yet they mellow the spinach while allowing it to maintain a garden freshness. As a change from the fruit, I've turned to the sweetness of onion for this crustless quiche. A wonderful accompaniment to everything in the fish, fowl and meat departments, it also makes quite a showy first course when baked in individual soufflé dishes, especially when several tablespoons of a lemon or tomato sauce are spooned over.

2 cups unsalted chicken stock

2 large onions, peeled and diced

¼ teaspoon freshly grated nutmeg

1½ to 2 pounds (about 2 bunches) fresh spinach, stemmed, washed, dried and coarsely chopped

¼ cup (about 1 ounce) freshly grated Parmesan cheese

Salt and freshly ground black pepper to taste

3 large room temperature eggs, blended with fork

Bring the stock to a boil with the onions in a heavy large deep skillet over medium-high heat. Reduce heat and simmer until reduced to 1½ cups, for about 20 minutes. Puree the mixture in a blender with the nutmeg until it is a smooth puree, pulsing on/off and stopping to scrape down the sides of the container. Return to the skillet over medium-high heat. Gradually stir in the spinach. Cover the pan, reduce heat and cook until the spinach is wilted, for about 3 minutes, stirring occasionally. Mix in the Parmesan. Season with salt and pepper. Whisk the eggs into the spinach mixture in a fine stream. Butter a 10-inch gratin pan or baking dish. Pour the spinach mixture into the pan. (This can be prepared ahead and set aside at cool room temperature for several hours.)

To serve, preheat the oven to 375°F. Bake until browned, set and slightly puffed, for about 25 to 30 minutes. Let rest for 5 minutes. Cut into wedges, transfer to 4 first-course or main-course plates and serve immediately.

Planning Ahead

The spinach mixture can be prepared several hours before serving. Bake just before presenting.

Technique Tips

If time allows, cool the spinach mixture to room temperature before stirring in the eggs. If the mixture is still warm, whisk vigorously while adding the eggs so they don't curdle.

If a nice serving dish is not desired to bring the baked spinach to the table, it can be baked in its original skillet.

Garlic Crème Brûlée

4 to 6 Servings

Planning Ahead

The custard can be prepared several hours before baking. If prepared in advance, wait to preheat the oven with a water bath until just before baking. Bake the custard up to 1¾ hours before serving.

When I saw how successful my dessert crème brûlée was, I began to think about a savory version. Basically, I created a gratin with a crunchy cheesy top I call the *tête de cuvée* after the free-run juice used to make the finest Champagne. To ensure there is lots of topping, I make the creamy custard layer very thin. The result? Each time you dip in your spoon, you pull out a bite of crispy silk. I'd like to try cooking a piece of lamb or fish on top of the Garlic Crème Brûlée so their juices might intermingle. If you have a chance to experiment with this combination before I do, I would appreciate knowing how it works out.

1 cup (about 30 large cloves from 2 large heads) cloves garlic, peeled

2 cups milk, at room temperature

7 large egg yolks

About 1 teaspoon salt

Freshly ground black pepper to taste

⅓ cup (about 1¼ ounces) freshly grated Parmesan cheese

Preheat the oven to 300°F. Place a 10-inch glass or porcelain pie plate in a larger baking pan. Pour enough water into the pan to come ¾ of the way up the sides of the pie plate. Remove the pie plate and place the baking pan with water in the oven to preheat for 15 minutes.

Place the garlic in a small saucepan, cover with water and bring to a boil; drain. Repeat this process 2 more times.

Blend the milk, egg yolks and blanched garlic in a blender or food processor until mixture is a smooth puree, pulsing on/off and stopping to scrape down the sides of the container. Season with salt and pepper. Strain into the pie plate through a fine sieve. (This can be prepared ahead, covered and set aside at cool room temperature for several hours. Remove the cover before baking.)

Place the pie plate in the water bath. Bake until the custard is set and a knife inserted into the center comes out clean, for about 1 hour. (This can be prepared ahead, removed from the oven and kept warm in the water bath for 20 to 30 minutes.)

Preheat the broiler. Remove the pie plate from the water bath. Sprinkle with Parmesan cheese. Place 3 inches below the heat source and broil until golden brown. Let rest for about 10 minutes. Spoon out onto 4 to 6 plates with an entree. Serve immediately.

Cauliflower Cheese Gratin

I like cauliflower either raw or so well cooked it becomes almost creamy like the fondant used to glaze desserts. Green beans can be cooked just until they are al dente with a bit of a bite. So can asparagus and broccoli, but not cauliflower. People never seem excited about cauliflower, but this is probably because they've only sampled the vegetable undercooked. Of all the ways I've ever had cauliflower, I like it best with the same *Sauce Mornay* or cheese sauce I've eaten it with since I was a young boy. I've modernized that old-fashioned sauce here by eliminating the flour, but this is still my beloved cauliflower bride in its pure white dress.

1 large (1½ to 1¾ pounds) cauliflower, outer leaves removed, cored and cut into florets

2 eggs

½ cup heavy cream

5 tablespoons (about 1¼ ounces) freshly grated Parmesan cheese

¼ teaspoon freshly grated nutmeg

Salt and freshly ground black pepper to taste

For the cauliflower, cook in a large pot of boiling water until tender when pierced with a knife, for 10 to 12 minutes. Drain, rinse under cold water and shake to dry.

To assemble the gratin, butter or oil a 1½-quart soufflé dish or casserole. Whisk the eggs with the cream to blend in a large bowl. Stir in 3 tablespoons of the Parmesan cheese and season with nutmeg, salt and pepper. Chop the cauliflower coarsely and stir into the cheese mixture. Turn into the prepared dish. Sprinkle with the remaining 2 tablespoons cheese. (This can be prepared ahead, covered and set aside at cool room temperature for several hours or refrigerated overnight. Bring to room temperature before baking.)

To bake, preheat the oven to 325°F. Place the soufflé dish in a large baking pan. Pour enough water into the pan to come ¾ of the way up the sides of the dish. Remove the dish and place the baking pan with water in the oven to preheat. When preheated, gently put the soufflé dish into the water bath and bake until the custard is softly set when tested with a knife, for about 45 to 50 minutes. Adjust the oven heat as necessary so the water is just gently bubbling. Remove the cauliflower from the water bath and let settle for 10 minutes at room temperature. Spoon out onto 4 plates. Serve immediately.

4 Servings

Planning Ahead

The cauliflower can be cooked at any time during the day the gratin is to be assembled. The gratin can be completely prepared up to 1 day before it is to be baked. It can be baked up to 30 minutes before serving and kept warm in a water bath.

Technique Tips

For more tender cauliflower, peel the floret stems with a small sharp knife before cooking.

If the florets are not approximately the same size, cut the larger ones in half or thirds as necessary.

To prevent the cauliflower custard from curdling, keep water in the water bath at a gentle simmer. If water reaches a boil, the mixture can curdle.

To keep cauliflower warm after it is baked, remove it from the oven and leave it in the water bath where it will stay warm for 30 to 45 minutes.

Bouillabaisse of Fennel

4 to 6 Servings

Planning Ahead

The bouillabaisse can be completely prepared several hours in advance. Reheat just before serving.

This thick stew contains all the members of a bouillabaisse, that heady fish soup served in the South of France—except for the . . . fish. Its components—fennel, tomato, garlic, saffron and olive oil—are the perfumes of Provence, and they percolate into a wonderful aromatic sauce for almost any poultry, meat or seafood. In this case, though, they comprise the dish itself, not the secondary sauce, providing an opportunity to appreciate these Mediterranean sun-worshipers at their most intense and powerful.

2½ to 3 pounds (about 4 medium) fennel bulbs

3 tablespoons olive oil

1 large onion, peeled and thinly sliced

8 large cloves garlic, peeled and coarsely chopped

1 28-ounce can chopped tomatoes

1 cup dry white wine

1 tablespoon fennel seeds, crushed

¼ teaspoon saffron threads, crushed

Salt and freshly ground black pepper to taste

¾ cup coarsely chopped Niçoise or other black olives

2 tablespoons olive oil (optional)

Trim off the fennel fronds, mince them and reserve 3 tablespoons. Cut off the stalks. Peel the stalks and fibrous exterior of the bulb using a vegetable peeler. Halve the bulb lengthwise, core and cut stalks and bulb crosswise into ¼-inch-thick half-rounds.

Heat the oil in a heavy large skillet over medium-low heat. Add the onion, cover and cook until translucent, for about 10 minutes, stirring occasionally. Add the garlic and fennel, cover and sweat 10 minutes, stirring occasionally. Add the tomatoes, wine and fennel seeds and bring to a boil. Stir 2 tablespoons of the boiling liquid into the saffron to dissolve, then return the mixture to the skillet. Reduce heat and simmer for 45 minutes, stirring occasionally. Increase heat and boil until the liquid is reduced and thickened to a saucelike consistency. Season with salt and pepper. (This can be prepared ahead and set aside at cool room temperature.)

To serve, simmer over medium heat to rewarm, stirring occasionally. Stir in the olives, reserved fennel fronds and optional oil. Mound in a vegetable dish or divide among 4 to 6 soup bowls or plates with an entree. Serve immediately.

Baked Zucchini and
Tomato Arènes de Nîmes

T his vegetable casserole is often called a gratin or *tian* after the type of dish in which it is baked, but I named my version Arènes de Nîmes because its concentric circles of vegetables remind me of spectators in the amphitheater of this southern French town. Another example of Provence's bounty, the combination of zucchini, tomato, garlic, olive oil and basil is one of the most harmonious food affinity groupings.

2 tablespoons olive oil

2 large cloves garlic, peeled and minced

**1½ pounds (about 6 small) zucchini, ends trimmed and cut
    crosswise into ¼-inch-thick slices**

**1½ pounds (about 12 to 14 small) Roma tomatoes, cut crosswise
    into ¼-inch-thick slices**

2 tablespoons olive oil

Salt and freshly ground black pepper to taste

**2 tablespoons fresh minced basil or thyme or 2 teaspoons dried
    thyme, crumbled**

Pour 2 tablespoons of the oil into the bottom of a 9-inch gratin pan, pie plate or shallow baking dish, swirling to coat the sides of the pan. Sprinkle the garlic over the bottom of the pan. Starting with the edge of the dish, alternate zucchini and tomato slices in concentric circles. Stand the slices upright and pack them in tightly. Brush the vegetables with 2 tablespoons olive oil. Season with salt and pepper. Sprinkle with basil. (This can be prepared ahead, covered and set aside at cool room temperature.)

To bake, preheat the oven to 350°F. Bake the vegetables for 1¼ hours or until tender. If the vegetables render considerable juice, remove it with a bulb baster to a very small saucepan. Boil the juices down to 2 tablespoons and spoon over the vegetables.

To serve warm, let the vegetables rest for 15 minutes, then spoon out onto 4 to 6 plates and serve immediately. To serve at room temperature, either cool to room temperature, or cool, cover and refrigerate overnight, then bring to room temperature before serving.

4 to 6 Servings

Planning Ahead

The vegetables can be prepped at any time during the day they are to be cooked. Bake the gratin just before serving to present warm or several hours or 1 day in advance to present at room temperature.

Technique Tip

For an attractive presentation, choose zucchini and tomatoes that are approximately the same diameter.

Variation

The vegetables can also be baked in 4 to 6 small gratin dishes for individual servings.

Glazed Turnip and
Fava Bean Sauté

4 Servings

Planning Ahead

The fava beans and turnips can be cooked at any time during the day they are to be served. Reheat and glaze them just before presenting.

Technique Tips

Look for little fava beans. The smaller they are, the sweeter, less starchy they will be. When fava beans are young and tender, they can be eaten raw or, when blanched, without their outer skin removed.

To prepare fava beans for cooking, snap the end and pull down the string to open the pod. Remove the beans from the pod.

I originally prepared this recipe with fava beans and salsify, but I substituted turnip here because salsify is, unfortunately, difficult to find. I chose turnip not because it was similar to salsify but to underscore an important principle of recipe development: Create interest by pairing items that don't frequently fraternize. I could have used the favas by themselves, but that would have meant peeling them all. I'm too lazy.

2 cups (about 8 ounces) shelled fava beans (about 2½ pounds unshelled)

2 medium (about 12 ounces) turnips, peeled and cut into ¼-inch dice

1 ounce (¼ stick) unsalted butter

2 teaspoons soy sauce

2 drops Oriental (toasted) sesame oil

2 tablespoons unsalted chicken stock

Salt and freshly ground black pepper to taste

Cook the favas and turnips in a large saucepan of boiling water for 5 minutes; drain. Peel off the outer fava skins; discard. Halve the beans through their natural seam, if desired, using knife tip. (This can be prepared ahead and set aside at room temperature.)

To serve, melt the butter in the same saucepan. Add the favas and turnips and stir over medium-high heat until lightly browned. Pour in the soy sauce, sesame oil and chicken stock and cook until the vegetables have absorbed the liquid, for about 2 minutes. Season with salt and pepper. Mound in a vegetable dish or spoon out onto 4 plates with an entree. Serve immediately.

Vegetable Chips

Other than an occasional *frite*, nothing was fried in the great restaurants in France until recently when a new attitude declared that anything was a go. This unspoken taboo never affected my cooking, though, for like a kid told "no," frying has always been one of my favorite techniques. My frying days started with parsley and other herbs soon followed. The next step was a chip sandwich with an herb in the middle, then on to taro chips to be used as a cracker for tuna tartar. (I thought this was a brilliant idea until I went to Hawaii and was surrounded by taro chips.) I've probably fried everything in my kitchen, including a few bad chefs, but it's root vegetables I like best, for they become the firmest and crispest fries of all.

"How do you get your chips so crisp?" I am often asked. "Easy," I respond. "Cook them slow and long. Dry them, don't fry them. If the temperature is too high, the chips brown before their water can evaporate and they become soft and soggy." The problem? Chips are flaccid and greasy. The solution? Lower the temperature of the fryer and cook longer.

People worry about eating deep-fried food today because they think it is laden with fat. I did a test to see how much oil a giant batch of chips actually absorbed by measuring the amount of oil in my pot before and after frying. The total missing was two tablespoons.

Root vegetables with higher sugar content to be cooked at 325°F, such as sweet potato, carrot and beet, peeled and thinly sliced

Root vegetables with lower sugar content to be cooked at 350°F, such as white russet potato, celery root, rutabaga, turnip and parsnip, peeled and thinly sliced

Peanut, corn or vegetable oil (about 4 cups) for deep frying

Salt, seasoned salt or herb mixture to taste

To cook, line a baking sheet (or sheets) with several layers of paper towels. Prepare as many of the chosen vegetables as desired for frying. Heat the oil to the appropriate temperature in a deep fryer, wok or large pot. Fry the vegetables in small batches until brown on both sides, for about 10 to 20 minutes, adjusting the heat as necessary so the chips dry out slowly. Transfer to the prepared baking sheet in a single layer using a slotted spatula. Season with salt. Mound in a vegetable dish. Serve immediately. (This can be prepared ahead, set aside at room temperature and refried or reheated for 5 minutes or until warm in preheated 500°F oven.)

1 Medium Vegetable per Serving

Planning Ahead
The chips can be sliced at any time during the day they are to be served and kept in a covered bowl. If preparing white potatoes in advance, they need to be rinsed until the water runs clear and kept in a bowl of cold water so they won't become brown. Drain and dry before frying.

Technique Tips
Slice the vegetables as thinly as possible, either by hand, with a mandoline or in a food processor fitted with a thin slicing blade.

With its tapered bottom, a wok enables you to fry with a minimum amount of oil.

The vegetables will be limp when removed from the fryer, but will crisp soon afterward if properly fried.

If serving chips as soon as they are fried, keep first-fried vegetables warm while cooking the remainder. To do so, preheat the oven to 150°F to 200°F. Place a baking sheet lined with parchment paper in the oven and transfer chips to the sheet as they are cooked.

Roasted Vegetable Medley

Planning Ahead

The vegetables can be prepped and marinated for at least 2 to 8 hours at any time during the day they are to be served. Although I usually cook them just before eating to serve hot, they are also delicious at room temperature.

Technique Tip

The cooking time will vary according to the size and tenderness of the vegetables and the number of layers in the pan.

Variation

Mix any leftover vegetables with pasta for a light main course.

Before Escoffier codified French recipes, a salad was something you picked in the garden from whatever was ripe, not a formula such as a *Salade Niçoise* with a specific list of ingredients that included potatoes and anchovies. This Roasted Vegetable Medley possesses the same sensibility for me as the garden salad: It is more a concept than a particular group of items. Although the vegetables I've included as an example have a pronounced Provençal cast, you can substitute cauliflower, carrots, turnips, winter squash or whatever appeals to you. I actually use the same vegetables here that are found in a ratatouille, but rather than cooking them in a skillet until melted into a compote, I've roasted them to concentrate their flavors. Olive oil, which is drained after cooking, seals the vegetables, protecting their individual shapes and flavors much as duck or goose fat preserves a confit. This is a great dish for entertaining a crowd because the numbers of vegetables can be shrunk or expanded according to the number of leaves added or subtracted from the table.

4 small (about 1 pound) zucchini, ends trimmed, halved lengthwise and cut into 1-inch-thick pieces

5 small (about 1 pound) Japanese eggplants, ends trimmed, halved lengthwise and cut into 1-inch-thick pieces

4 small (about 1 pound) yellow bell peppers, cored, seeded and cut into 1-inch squares

4 small (about 1 pound) red bell peppers, cored, seeded and cut into 1-inch squares

2 medium (about 1¾ pounds) fennel bulbs

1 bunch green onions (white and light green parts only), thinly sliced

4 large cloves garlic, peeled and minced

½ cup minced flat-leaf parsley

2 tablespoons fresh minced thyme or marjoram or 2 teaspoons dried, crumbled

1 tablespoon fresh minced tarragon or 1 teaspoon dried tarragon, crumbled

2 cups olive oil

Salt and freshly ground black pepper to taste

To marinate, combine the zucchini, eggplants and yellow and red bell peppers in an 8-quart bowl. Trim off the fennel fronds. Mince the fronds and add them to the bowl. Cut off the stalks. Peel the stalks and the fibrous exterior of the bulbs using a vegetable peeler. Cut the stalks into 1-inch pieces and add them to the bowl. Quarter the bulb lengthwise, core it and add the individual pieces to the bowl, trimming as necessary. Add the green onions, garlic, parsley, thyme, tarragon and olive oil to the bowl. Season with salt and pepper; mix well. Cover and set aside at room temperature to marinate for at least 2 hours, mixing occasionally.

To cook, preheat the oven to 350°F. Divide the vegetable mixture between 2 large baking sheets. Bake until the eggplant is very soft and tender when tasted, for about 20 to 25 minutes, mixing occasionally. Transfer to a vegetable dish with a slotted spoon. Serve immediately or set aside to cool and serve at room temperature. Strain the remaining oil and reserve it for salad dressings or for cooking vegetables.

California Ratatouille

Planning Ahead

The vegetables can be prepped and the seasonings measured at any time during the day the California Ratatouille is to be served. Cook vegetables just before serving to maintain their garden freshness.

Technique Tip

If the ingredients are not readied in advance, they can be prepped as you cook. To protect the vegetables from overcooking, turn the burner heat off when the prepping time lags behind the cooking time.

Variation

The vegetables can also be tossed with pasta and dressed with cheese for a main course. Any leftovers can be used for an omelet filling or a pita sandwich.

Based on eggplant, which must be well cooked to taste good, a traditional French ratatouille is simmered for many hours until the mixture coalesces and caramelizes. Minus an eggplant, this California version is quickly cooked until it is just al dente and crunchy with each ingredient maintaining its own identity. Side by side, these dishes would appear to have little in common other than the fact that they both contain a mixture of vegetables and are cooked with onion and olive oil. For me, though, they also share the most important aspect of a ratatouille: produce fresh from the market or, even better, from the garden. To maintain the spirit of this dish, substitute whatever herbs and vegetables are freshest in your backyard or at the local grocery.

2 tablespoons olive oil

1 medium red onion, peeled and diced

1 large ear corn, husked and kernels removed

1 large red pepper, cored, seeded and thinly sliced

1 large yellow pepper, cored, seeded and thinly sliced

1 poblano or anaheim chili, cored, seeded and minced

1 jalapeño chili, cored, seeded and minced

3 tablespoons olive oil

2 teaspoons chili powder

2 tablespoons fresh minced cilantro, marjoram or mint

1 medium zucchini, ends trimmed, quartered lengthwise and cut crosswise into ⅜-inch pieces

1 medium yellow crookneck squash, ends trimmed, top halved and bottom divided into thirds lengthwise and cut crosswise into ⅜-inch pieces

4 medium green onions (white and light green parts only), quartered lengthwise and cut into ½-inch pieces

2 medium tomatoes, halved crosswise, seeded and diced into ¼-inch pieces

½ cup tomato juice

1 tablespoon Champagne or white wine vinegar

Salt and freshly ground black pepper to taste

Heat 2 tablespoons of olive oil in a heavy large nonstick skillet over medium-low heat. Add the onion, cover and cook until translucent, for about 10 minutes, stirring occasionally. Add the corn, red pepper, yellow pepper, poblano and jalapeño; increase heat to medium and cook uncovered 5 minutes, stirring occasionally.

Add the 3 tablespoons of olive oil, chili powder and cilantro. Stir in the zucchini, yellow squash, green onion and tomatoes. Pour in the tomato juice and vinegar, increase heat to medium-high and cook until the vegetables are crisp-tender, for about 5 to 7 minutes, stirring occasionally. Season with salt and pepper. Mound in 4 bowls or a vegetable dish or ladle out onto 4 plates with an entree. Serve immediately or cool for 15 to 30 minutes to lukewarm.

Desserts

I started my career as a pastry chef. With this orientation, I incorporate classic dessert techniques almost unconsciously into whatever I make. As much as I enjoy cooking at this point in my life, desserts and pastries continue to hold a special fascination. When puff pastry rises like a soufflé, it is mystical. So, too, a golden brioche that floats cloudlike, its topknot bobbing, from the oven.

Desserts have a magical power also in the delight and smile they bring. I get so sad on Sunday afternoons when my children are watching TV and not speaking to each other. "Papa is going to make a cake," I announce. "Who wants to help?" Immediately the mood shifts. "Me," says Christophe, jumping around. "Me, too," says Chloe, jumping after him. Magic without a magician.

I want to distinguish between simple desserts and a pastry chef's complex time-consuming constructions. To prepare these fancy celebration cakes, there is a recipe for the layers, another for ganache or buttercream, and myriad formulas for soaking, layering, weighting and decorating that can go on for days and may be just for show, not even affecting the ultimate flavor. To undertake this assemblage at home, you have to remove everything else from your refrigerator and station a guard to protect the cake from poachers. As hard as you work, you will have no idea what your masterpiece tastes like until you cut into it. Then it may be too late.

I'm not trying to discourage you from tackling a sophisticated cake. I just want to point out that the rewards for cooking a good meal come much easier than those from a fussy dessert.

There is another issue, too. Rich heavy cakes are no longer fashionable today. Can you imagine how you would feel if you spent four days on a spectacular pastry and your guests said, "No thank you, I don't care for any. I'm watching my weight." I know. It hurts.

At any rate, what I have included in this chapter are good simple desserts that finish a meal splendidly without overworking the pastry bag or the pastry bag puppeteer. If you bring a bowl of strawberries in red wine to the table, it will be a winner. Who is going to say no to a strawberry?

Although these desserts are simple, they should be made from only the finest ingredients you can afford: unsalted butter, imported bittersweet chocolate, heavy cream that has not been cooked and ultrapasteurized and pure vanilla extract or vanilla beans. I use seven vanilla beans for one small custard recipe, an indulgence that borders on lunacy. I have restrained myself calling for two here, and will more than understand if you buy only one. Speaking of nuts, I buy only those that are freshly harvested. Before using, I always toast them to a rich medium brown to intensify their flavors.

Techniques never waver. When I measure flour, I dip the measuring cup into a mound, then run a knife across the top to level it off. When I beat egg whites to gossamer peaks, they have to be just right: neither so soft that they collapse nor so firm that they taste like cotton. When folding them into a dessert base, the motions must be gentle so it doesn't deflate. A small portion is folded into the mixture initially to aerate, lighten and better absorb the remainder. I never present desserts (or any food, for that matter) directly from the refrigerator. If I did, the textures and flavors I have strived so hard to achieve would be masked. This philosophy is also directed toward homemade ice creams and frozen desserts, whose unctuous creaminess comes only with a slight warming.

I find frozen desserts refreshing, particularly after a heavy meal, so you will find many licks in this collection to go along with the strawberries. Some, such as the Chocolate Port Sorbet (page 303) and the Frozen Apricot and Chocolate Dot Terrine (page 308), can even be made without an ice cream machine. I suspect I'm making up for lost time here because when I was growing up in France, ice cream was only a summer tradition.

With a scoop on ice cream and frozen dessert recipes, cookies and confections can't be far behind. I love this type of dessert that can be served all day long or whenever you feel like a munch. I also like those particular to tea time or brunch, such as the Rum Spice Cake (page 344), Banana Colada Soup (page 310), Apple Rum Risotto (page 314) and Couscous with Orange and Pistachios (page 312).

Desserts, unlike other dishes, are deposited in a memory bank to charge you emotionally throughout life. This chapter contains many recipes that have nurtured me since I was a small boy. Among them are the Raisin Tart with Hot Buttered Rum Sauce (page 322), Apple Crêpes Flambées (page 340) and Basque Custard Cookie Cake (page 347).

As much as I looked forward to summer fruit as a boy, there are, perhaps surprisingly, few desserts that call for them here. Since their season is so short, I prefer to eat them out of hand or to present them simply. Bushels of apples make up for their absence. This fruit appears in so many manifestations, it borders on the embarrassing. You know how some flavors resonate so perfectly they become an inner mantra? You'll be repeating mine whenever apples, caramel and almonds appear on your countertop.

Amazingly, the one thing I haven't used apples in is a pie. I'm not sure which is more American: to love pies or to be afraid of making them. Whether you call them pies or tarts as I do—because I bake them in a metal pan with a removable bottom—there are merely two main points to remember:

First of all, handle the dough gently. If making it in the food processor, remove it when all the ingredients are just moistened; before it forms a ball. When a crust with my formula tastes like cardboard run over by a truck, you can guess with almost 100 percent certainty that it has been overprocessed. Roll out the dough as thinly as possible between two pieces of plastic wrap. This way it won't be necessary to add additional flour which can toughen it.

The second trick is to prebake the crust until it is golden brown and crisp before adding a filling. Even a crust that is too thick will taste delicious if it is browned well. If the edges start burning, just cover them with aluminum foil.

In seeming contrast to my criteria for this chapter, this collection also includes several of Citrus's more intricate desserts: Filo Apple Crowns with Cinnamon Custard (page 338), Crème Brûlée Napoleon with Hazelnuts (page 335) and Blackberry Fig Tartlets with Orange Caramel Sauce (page 332). Although they are elaborate enough to qualify for a special occasion, there is a major difference between these fantasies and the cakes I was describing above: These are doable at home without a 500-year apprenticeship to a master pastry chef.

A restaurant dessert, historically, was an event that took a good pastry chef an entire night to produce. If he was not there, no one else had the skill to fabricate the decoration. My goal has been to make my restaurant desserts as stylish as those of yore, but also doable by the home cook. The elements are basic and familiar, just combined in new ways. As you handle the components, you will be creating your own magic on the plate.

Sesame Crisps

Prepare the batter and bake the cookies at any time during the day they are to be served. Once baked, the cookies will keep for about 1 week.

Technique Tip
The batter used to make these cookies is the same used for Basque Custard Cookie Cake (page 347). To make both desserts simultaneously, prepare the batter with the amount of ingredients listed for Sesame Crisps, minus the sesame oil. Divide the batter in half. Add ½ teaspoon sesame oil to the cookie batter and proceed with the recipe as described above. Use the other half of the batter for Basque Custard Cookie Cake.

A French chef depends on almonds for flavoring in much the same way a Chinese chef turns to sesame seeds as the accent of choice. As a French chef who has spent considerable time in China, I use *both* almonds and sesame seeds. The first time I tasted sesame seeds, it was neither in Asia nor in Europe, however, but in America. Living in New York and quite broke, I ate many a meal at McDonald's, where I encountered them atop a hamburger bun. I liked the bite of these little seeds between my teeth and started mixing them with caramel for an Oriental nougatine. Since then, sesame seeds have become a regular in my repertoire, along with toasted sesame oil, which must be used sparingly as a little can go a long way. Sesame seeds are like salt and pepper in that they can be sprinkled over many different foods. Sometimes I mix black and white seeds for fun. The joy of cooking, you know, is in having fun.

3 tablespoons sesame seeds

4 ounces (1 stick) unsalted butter, room temperature

2¼ cups powdered sugar, sifted

6 egg whites, at room temperature

1 cup all-purpose flour

1 teaspoon Oriental (toasted) sesame oil

Preheat 1 or 2 ovens to 350°F. Line 2 large baking sheets with parchment paper. Stir the sesame seeds in a heavy small dry skillet over medium heat until lightly browned.

Beat the butter and sugar using an electric mixer on medium speed until fluffy. Beat in the egg whites a bit at a time until well blended. Mix in the flour until just incorporated. Stir in the sesame oil. Place ½ of the batter in a pastry bag fitted with a ½-inch plain tip (or use a spoon). Pipe out as many 1½-inch disks as will fit, spacing them 1½ inches apart (the cookies will spread), on the prepared sheets. Gently push down each tip and sprinkle with toasted sesame seeds. Bake until medium brown around the edges, about 15 minutes, exchanging the position of the baking sheets in the oven halfway through baking.

Meanwhile, pipe out the second batch of cookies on parchment paper. Transfer the second batch to the baking sheets and bake as above.

Cool the cookies completely on a rack, then store in an airtight container.

Pistachio Lace Cookies

T he most fun part of working in a restaurant is being creative and doing something out of the ordinary. When I got tired of bringing *tuiles* out at the end of each and every dinner, I just made a different cookie. The only criterion was that it had to be crunchy. For this crunch, I turned first to pistachios and then combined this nut with orange because the two ingredients are often seen together in the Middle East. When you mix components, it is important to respect their heritage.

> **3 ounces (¾ stick) unsalted butter**
>
> **1¼ cups shelled pistachios**
>
> **⅞ cup (¾ cup plus 2 tablespoons) sugar**
>
> **6 tablespoons all-purpose flour**
>
> **¼ cup orange juice**
>
> **2 tablespoons Grand Marnier or other orange liqueur**

For the cookie dough, melt the butter and cool until tepid or barely warm to the touch, for about 40 minutes.

Grind the pistachios and sugar in a food processor, pulsing on/off until the nuts are coarsely chopped, or chop the nuts by hand and mix them with the sugar. Blend the flour and the pistachio/sugar mixture using an electric mixer. Add the tepid butter, orange juice and Grand Marnier and mix just until evenly moistened. The dough will be wet and sticky. Spread the dough out into a 1-inch-wide log on a sheet of plastic wrap. Using the wrap as an aid, roll the dough up in plastic. Refrigerate or freeze until firm, for about 6 hours. (This can be prepared ahead and refrigerated 1 week or wrapped in freezer paper and frozen several months. Defrost in the refrigerator before continuing with the recipe.)

To bake, preheat the oven to 325°F. Line 2 large baking sheets with parchment paper. Slice the dough into ⅛-inch-thick coins. Arrange as many as will fit on the prepared sheets, leaving 2 inches between the cookies. Dip a fork in water, shake dry and use it to flatten the cookies. Bake the cookies until well browned, for about 12 minutes, exchanging the position of the baking sheets in the oven halfway. Let the cookies cool on parchment until firm enough to dislodge with a spatula, for about 5 minutes. Gently transfer to racks in a single layer. Arrange and bake the remaining coins in the same manner. Cool the cookies completely on racks. Store in an airtight container at room temperature.

Makes About 8 Dozen

Planning Ahead

The cookie dough can be mixed and frozen several months before baking. If baking the same day the dough is prepared, allow at least 4 to 6 hours for it to chill. Although the cookies keep several days after baking, they tend to pick up moisture when it is humid. For best results, bake on the day they are to be served.

Technique Tips

The cookies can also be spooned out and baked as soon as they are mixed, but their shape will be more uniform if they are refrigerated or frozen first.

Freeze or refrigerate the cookie dough in several smaller logs to bake as needed.

Hazelnut Graham Cracker Cookies

**Makes About 5½
Dozen 2-inch Disks**

Planning Ahead

The graham crackers can be crushed and the hazelnuts roasted and husked a few days before making the cookie dough. The dough can be prepared several months in advance. If baking the dough the same day it is prepared, allow at least 4 to 6 hours for it to firm. Once baked, the cookies will keep a week or two.

Technique Tip

Freeze or refrigerate the cookie dough in several smaller logs to bake as needed.

When I first moved to this country, I didn't think cheesecake would taste very good, and I was too much of a snob to try it. When I finally snuck a sample, I sure saw what I had missed. Not only did I love it as a cake, but I was wild about each of its components.

Its ground graham cracker crumb crust reminds me of *pâté sablée*, the short sweet pie crust with such a delectable sandy texture. Since this crust is often cut up and baked as cookies, I thought the same approach would work with a cheesecake crust. Being French, I must try to improve on something that is already perfect, so I added hazelnuts as well. Besides, these nuts are very dear to my heart. As children, we used to pick them fresh off the tree and stuff the inside of our shirts with enough to snack on all day long. We cracked them in school and, boy, did our teachers love us.

½ cup hazelnuts, toasted and husked

16 graham crackers, broken (2 crushed cups)

½ pound (2 sticks) unsalted room temperature butter, chopped

½ cup packed dark brown sugar

1 large egg, at room temperature

For the dough, grind the hazelnuts and graham crackers together in a food processor into a fine powder, pulsing on/off.

Beat the butter and brown sugar just to blend (without aerating), using an electric mixer on low speed. Add the egg and mix in just until incorporated. With the mixer running, gradually add the graham cracker mixture. Cover the bowl with plastic and refrigerate until the dough is firm enough to shape, for about 15 to 30 minutes.

Divide the dough into 2 or more parts. Place each part on a 12-inch length of plastic wrap and form into a log with a 1½- to 2-inch diameter using the plastic as an aid. Roll up the logs in the plastic, folding in the ends. Refrigerate at least 4 hours or until firm. (This can be refrigerated for several days or wrapped in freezer paper and frozen for several months. Defrost in the refrigerator before continuing with the recipe.)

To bake, preheat 1 or 2 ovens to 350°F. Line 2 large baking sheets with parchment paper. Slice the dough into ¼-inch-thick coins. Arrange as many as will fit on the prepared sheets, leaving ¾ inch between cookies. Bake the cookies until the rims darken, for about 10 to 12 minutes, exchanging the position of the baking sheets in the oven halfway. Let sit on the parchment until firm enough to dislodge with a spatula, for 3 to 5 minutes. Carefully transfer to racks in a single layer. Arrange and bake the remaining coins in the same manner. Cool the cookies completely on racks. Store in an airtight container at room temperature.

French *Brownies*

The macaroon is probably the most popular cookie in France, where there are frequent competitions to determine the *best*. Good pastry chefs take pride in mastering the macaroon, often staking their reputations on this ability. They will order the finest almonds from Italy's Piedmont region and shell them at the last minute to be sure they are smooth and fresh.

Unlike the hard, typically coconut-flavored American copy, the French-style sweet has a crisp shell, moist interior and an almond, sometimes-chocolate, base. When I first served the cookie this way in the States, my customers said, "That's not a macaroon." This response was so discouraging, I changed its name to French *Brownie*. Since then, it's been a great hit.

These French *Brownies* can be served individually or stuck together as a sandwich. In either case, the cookie tastes as if it has a creamy filling. This impression is the result of a strange technique based on steam, which is created by pouring water onto paper towel —yes, paper towel-lined cookie sheets immediately after baking.

1½ cups whole blanched almonds, toasted and cooled completely

Generous 1 cup confectioners' sugar

4 large (about ½ cup) egg whites, at room temperature

½ cup granulated sugar

Preheat the oven to 400°F. Line 2 large baking sheets with paper towels. Process the almonds in a food processor with the confectioners' sugar until very finely ground, pulsing on/off.

Beat the egg whites using an electric mixer until soft peaks form. Beat in the granulated sugar, 1 tablespoon at a time, and continue beating until the whites are stiff, but not dry. Gently fold the almond mixture into the whites.

Place the egg white mixture in a pastry bag fitted with a ½-inch plain tip. Pipe out 1½-inch rounds on the prepared baking sheets, leaving about ½ inch between the rounds. Bake until golden brown, for about 12 minutes, exchanging the position of the baking sheets in the oven halfway. Holding the tray at a slight angle, immediately lift up the paper towel and carefully pour enough cold water down one long side of the pan to just cover the bottom. Gently tilt the pan until the water covers the bottom completely. Repeat with the second tray. Let sit for 10 minutes. Lift 2 cookies off the towel with a spatula. Press the bottoms together to sandwich, sealing the edges well. Transfer to racks in a single layer and air-dry several hours. Store in an airtight container.

Makes About 2½ Dozen Sandwiches

Planning Ahead

The nuts can be toasted and ground several days in advance. Prepare the batter and bake the cookies at any time during the day they are to be served. Once baked, they will keep beautifully for about 1 week. I guess. They have never lasted that long.

Technique Tips

Pipe the cookies the same size so their edges will meet, tracing a template if necessary.

The cookies can also be spooned onto the baking sheets, but it will be harder to keep them the same size.

Pour sufficient water onto the baking sheet to dampen the paper towel and cookie bottoms, but not enough to come up the sides of the cookies and make them soggy.

Variation

For Chocolate French *Brownies*, add ⅓ cup cocoa powder to the food processor with the almonds and confectioners' sugar.

Old-Fashioned
Apricot Oatmeal Bars

Makes About 21 Bars

Planning Ahead

The apricots must be soaked for at least 2 hours or overnight and the batter mixed at least a half hour before baking. The bars are best eaten several days after baking.

Technique Tip

By refrigerating the bottom layer of the batter until it is firm, the apricot layer is easily spread over it. Do not chill much longer than 30 minutes or the baking powder will begin to activate in the batter and lose its power.

W hen I was trying to lose weight on the Jenny Craig program, I did not find the food to be exactly the dream of a gourmet chef. The only thing I could tolerate was a chewy oatmeal bar with dried fruit. I have lots of this rabbit food left over (get in touch with me if you would like some), but the bars are all gone. Unfortunately, so is my willpower for dieting.

To make it seem as if I'm still watching my weight, I've started baking some of my own homey bar cookies. This particular one is modeled after my diet delight. Half-cookie, half-fruitcake, it is unlike anything I've ever baked before. *Tuiles, Palets de Dames, sablés, palmiers* and other French cookies are small, crisp and refined. They are a part of an elegant dessert presentation, not a heavy substantial treat for a child's lunchbox. I will always look forward to my platter of *friandises*, but both my children and I are happy I have also added these toothsome grandmother-style treats to our cookie jar. Particularly mid-morning.

¼ pound (about 1 cup) or 22 small dried apricots

½ cup water

2 tablespoons sugar

½ pound (2 sticks) unsalted butter

¾ cup whole blanched almonds

2 tablespoons sugar

2 cups all-purpose flour

½ cup old-fashioned oats

1 teaspoon baking powder

¾ cup packed dark brown sugar

6 tablespoons light corn syrup

¾ cup half-and-half

Confectioners' sugar

Soak the apricots in a small bowl with the water and 2 tablespoons sugar for at least 2 hours or overnight.

Melt the butter and cool it to room temperature, for about 30 to 40 minutes.

Grind the almonds with 2 tablespoons sugar in a food processor, pulsing on/off until they are the texture of fine meal.

Mix the flour, oats and baking powder using an electric mixer until well blended. Add the brown sugar and ground almond meal and mix until blended. Mix the corn syrup and cooled melted butter into the half-and-half. Gradually pour into the dry ingredients in the mixer and stir just until the batter is evenly moistened.

Line the bottom of an 8- × 10-inch baking dish with parchment paper. Butter the dish and paper lightly. Turn half of the batter into the baking dish and spread it evenly over the bottom with a spatula. Cover with plastic wrap and chill until firm, for about 30 minutes.

Meanwhile, preheat the oven to 325°F. Process the apricot mixture in the same processor bowl used for the almonds until pureed and smooth, for about 5 minutes, stopping to scrape down the sides of the container.

Spread the pureed apricot mixture evenly over the firm batter layer in the baking dish. Spread the remaining batter evenly over the apricot layer, smoothing the top. Bake until slightly puffed and browned and the bar cake has started to pull away from the sides of the pan, for about 30 minutes. Cool the baking dish completely on a rack.

To serve, slice the apricot cake into 1½- × 2⅔-inch bars by cutting it lengthwise into seven 1½-inch-wide bands and crosswise into thirds. Dust with confectioners' sugar. Carefully free the bottom of the bars and remove them from the pan using a flexible spatula. Arrange on a serving platter. The cake can also be cut into large rectangles and served on individual dessert plates. Serve immediately.

Store the remaining bars in a covered container at room temperature or in the refrigerator. Bring to room temperature before serving.

Chocolate Coconut *Tuiles*

**Makes About
4½ Dozen Disks**

Planning Ahead

Once the candies are prepared, they will keep indefinitely.

Technique Tips

The candies should be about ⅛ inch thick—thin enough to be elegant but not so thin as to melt or crumble when eaten.

If you do not have enough trays for the disks, set parchment paper to fit trays on a work surface and form disks on the parchment. When a tray becomes available, transfer the parchment to the tray and refrigerate to firm the candies.

If the chocolate is very warm and too runny to form the disks, let it sit several minutes to firm before shaping.

Variation

To form curved *tuiles*, I form the disks and let them sit at room temperature long enough so they no longer run. Then I gently roll up the parchment paper loosely like a jelly-roll cake, set it on a baking sheet and refrigerate until very firm.

I had, surprisingly, never toasted coconut until quite recently when I was searching for a handsome finish to a piña colada cake. The shreds stuck together like praline and exploded in the mouth like a firecracker. Definitely a sensation I wanted to repeat. One day I had both leftover chocolate and coconut at the restaurant. I mixed these two ingredients together and molded them into *tuiles*, a whimsical roof tile shape, to serve while customers waited for dessert. Today I don't even bother forming *tuiles*. I merely spread the molten chocolate and toasted coconut into spiky disks. With only two major ingredients, these confections are a cinch to make. Yet when you serve them to friends, they will think they have been fashioned by a professional candy maker.

½ pound sweetened shredded coconut

1 tablespoon light corn syrup

½ ounce (⅛ stick) unsalted butter, chopped

½ teaspoon vanilla extract

1 pound bittersweet or semisweet chocolate, finely chopped

Preheat the oven to 350°F. Place the coconut in a 9- or 10-inch baking pan. Add the corn syrup, butter and vanilla; mix well. Bake until medium brown, for about 15 to 20 minutes, stirring occasionally. (This can be prepared several days ahead, cooled, covered and set aside at room temperature.)

Melt the chocolate in the top of a double boiler above gently simmering water and stir until smooth. Mix in the toasted coconut.

Line 4 or 5 large baking sheets with parchment paper. Place a 2-inch-round cookie cutter on the parchment, spoon a scant tablespoon of the chocolate mixture into the cutter and spread it to the edges of the cutter with a small flexible spatula. Gently lift the cutter and repeat, spacing the disks about ½ inch apart, until all the chocolate mixture is used. Refrigerate the trays as space allows until the disks harden. The time will vary according to the temperature of the chocolate when the candy is refrigerated.

Run a long narrow spatula under the disks to free them from the paper. Carefully peel the disks off the paper. Store in a large airtight container in the refrigerator or freezer until 30 minutes to 1 hour before serving. The *tuiles* can also be stored in a cool dark spot. Arrange in a candy dish or on a dessert platter. Serve immediately.

Chocolate Port Sorbet

I am possessed by chocolate ice cream. But since I love food too much, I am on a diet at least five months of every year, and this treasure is all too rarely on my list of allowables. As a substitute for the ice cream during periods of deprivation, I often depend on this chocolate sorbet. It is low in fat, almost rich from the port, as well as clean and refreshing, particularly after a rich meal. A nice addition to a plate of sorbets and a multicomponent dessert, it can be mixed in literally less than two minutes. And I only feel a little bit bad that it's not chocolate ice cream.

1/3 cup sugar

4 tablespoons unsweetened cocoa

2 cups warm water

1/4 cup port

Mix the sugar and cocoa together in a medium bowl. Whisk in several tablespoons of water, or enough to form a thick paste. Whisk in the remaining water, a little at a time, until well mixed and smooth. Stir in the port. If time allows, refrigerate at least several hours or overnight.

Process the cocoa mixture in an ice cream machine according to the manufacturer's instructions. Transfer the sorbet to a covered container and freeze at least 1 hour to mellow. If frozen solid, soften in the refrigerator or at room temperature for about 15 to 30 minutes until creamy. Scoop into 4 dessert dishes. Serve immediately.

Makes About 1 1/2 Pints to Serve 4

Planning Ahead

The sorbet can be mixed the day before it is processed. Process the sorbet several hours before serving so it has time to set and mellow.

Technique Tip

If an ice cream machine is not available, freeze the mixture in trays and then process in a food processor until smooth. Refreeze until it is the desired consistency.

Malted Milk Ice Cream
with Strawberry Cassis Sauce

**Makes About 1½
Pints to Serve 4**

Planning Ahead

The ice cream base can be prepared 1 day before the ice cream is processed. The ice cream can be processed about 6 hours before serving. Allow at least 2 to 3 hours for it to mellow.

Technique Tips

Store cleaned used vanilla beans in several cups of sugar to make vanilla sugar.

Adjust the heat as necessary to keep the ice cream base below a simmer. If the mixture boils, it can curdle.

This ice cream is like a spider. As soon as it emerges from the machine, it entraps my spoon. We've had all kinds of exotic flavors at the restaurant—cardamom, rosemary, nutmeg, passion fruit and so on—but soon after we go off on a tangent, we return to the simple pleasure of vanilla. Although this ice cream also contains a bit of malt, it counts as vanilla bean.

The Malted Milk Ice Cream is fabulous by itself. Nevertheless, I've included the Strawberry Cassis Sauce to serve alongside because it is so nice with it. The French serve this country compote frequently during the summer. The alcohol dissipates after a few hours, and all that is left is a fruity refresher. If I find it lurking in the refrigerator when I am thirsty, I am likely to drink it straight up. Other good toppings for this ice cream include the Chocolate Sauce (page 308) and Orange Caramel Sauce (page 334). These, however, are strictly sauces, not drinks. I have some pride.

2 cups milk

1 to 2 vanilla beans, slit lengthwise

5 egg yolks, at room temperature

½ cup sugar

¼ cup malted milk powder

Strawberry Cassis Sauce (page 305)

Place the milk in a heavy large saucepan. Scrape the seeds from the vanilla beans into the milk, add the beans and bring to a boil over medium heat. Remove from the heat and let the beans steep for at least 1 hour or until the mixture cools to room temperature. Discard the beans (or wash, dry and reserve them for another use).

Beat the egg yolks with the sugar using an electric mixer until thick and pale lemon in color. Meanwhile, reheat the milk mixture, then gradually whisk it into the yolks. Return the mixture to the saucepan. Whisk over medium-low heat until thickened enough to leave a path on a wooden spatula when a finger is drawn across it. Remove from heat. Stir in the malted milk powder. Strain through a fine sieve. Cool to room temperature. Refrigerate overnight if time allows.

Process the mixture in an ice cream machine according to the manufacturer's instructions. Freeze in a covered container several hours to mellow flavors. If frozen solid, let soften in the refrigerator or at room temperature until creamy, for about 15 to 30 minutes. Scoop into 4 dessert dishes. Spoon on Strawberry Cassis Sauce, if desired. Serve immediately.

Strawberry Cassis Sauce

½ cup Beaujolais or other fruity red wine

3 tablespoons honey

2 tablespoons crème de cassis

1 pint strawberries, hulled

Whisk the wine and honey together in a medium bowl. Stir in the crème de cassis. Halve the strawberries lengthwise and add to the wine mixture. Cover and refrigerate for at least 30 minutes. Serve in individual bowls as soup or spoon over Malted Milk Ice Cream (page 304).

Planning Ahead

The sauce should be made at least ½ hour in advance. If possible, allow 4 to 6 hours for the flavors to deepen.

Prune and Armagnac Ice Cream

Makes About I Pint
to Serve 3 to 4

Planning Ahead

The custard base for the ice cream can be prepared several days in advance. The prunes should be marinated for at least one hour. Like most homemade ice creams, this one is best churned about 4 hours before serving. It does, however, keep nicely for several days.

Technique Tips

Store cleaned used vanilla beans in several cups of sugar to make vanilla sugar.

Adjust the heat as necessary to keep the ice cream base below a simmer. If the mixture boils, it can curdle.

P eople make such a big deal about sun-drying fruits today, you would think it was a new discovery. Yet, when I was growing up, my mother did this as automatically as the seasons changed. Of all the fruit she dried, my favorite was the prune from the plum tree in our backyard. Our plums may not have been as famous as those from the Agenais, an area in southwest France near Armagnac country, but they were delicious. We did not use Armagnac with our prunes as they do in Gascony, but I've used it here in honor of France's prize crop. I've pureed the marinated prunes, but they can also be chopped for an ice cream similar in style to Rum Raisin. Dark, delicious and mysterious, this ice cream is an intriguing counterpart to a fruit salad or fresh apple or pear tart.

9 to 10 large (3 ounces) pitted prunes, coarsely chopped

2 tablespoons Armagnac, Cognac or rum

Water (optional)

1½ cups milk

½ cup heavy cream

1 to 2 vanilla beans, slit lengthwise

4 egg yolks, at room temperature

½ cup sugar

Marinate the prunes with the Armagnac in a small bowl for at least 1 hour, stirring occasionally. Puree the prunes and Armagnac in a food processor or blender into a smooth thick paste, adding 1 tablespoon of water at a time as necessary.

Place the milk and cream in a heavy large saucepan. Scrape the seeds from the vanilla beans into the mixture, add the beans and bring to a boil over medium heat. Remove from heat and let the beans steep for at least 1 hour or until the mixture cools to room temperature. Discard the beans (or wash, dry and reserve them for another use).

Beat the egg yolks with the sugar using an electric mixer until thick and pale lemon in color. Meanwhile, reheat the milk mixture, then gradually whisk it into the yolks. Return the mixture to the saucepan. Whisk over medium-low heat until thickened enough to leave a path on a wooden spatula when a finger is drawn across it. Remove from heat. Stir in the prune puree. Strain through a fine sieve, if desired. Cool to room temperature. Refrigerate overnight if time allows.

Process in an ice cream machine according to the manufacturer's instructions. Freeze in a covered container several hours to mellow flavors. If frozen solid, let soften in the refrigerator or at room temperature until creamy, for about 15 to 30 minutes before serving. Scoop into 3 or 4 dessert dishes or on top of or next to a slice of tart or cake. Serve immediately.

Frozen Lemon Cheesecake

As soon as I joined the ranks of cheesecake addicts, I became very particular about the flavor of my cheesecake and the temperature at which it was served. I found I liked it best very, very cold. And what is colder than the freezer? Cheesecake is quite refreshing when it has the texture of ice cream and, for some reason, it doesn't seem as rich this way. In other words, I can eat a container at one sitting. To complete the cheesecake effect, I like to serve this frozen dessert with the Hazelnut Graham Cracker Cookies (page 298). These stay crisp, unlike a cheesecake crust, which can become damp and pasty.

1 cup milk

2 tablespoons freshly squeezed lemon juice

⅔ cup sugar

8 ounces room temperature cream cheese, chopped

Mix all of the ingredients in a blender until very smooth, pulsing on/off and stopping to scrape down the sides of the container, for about 4 minutes. (This can be prepared 1 day ahead and refrigerated overnight.)

Process the mixture in an ice cream machine according to the manufacturer's instructions. Transfer to a covered container and freeze at least several hours to mellow. (This can be prepared 1 day ahead.)

To serve, if frozen solid, soften in the refrigerator or at room temperature until creamy, for about 15 to 30 minutes. Scoop into 3 to 4 dessert dishes or form into ovals using 2 spoons and present on small plates.

Planning Ahead

The mixture can be prepared 1 day before processing and processed 1 day before serving.

Frozen Apricot and Chocolate Dot Terrine

8 to 12 Servings

Planning Ahead

The sauce can be prepared several days before serving and reheated before ladling. The terrine can be prepared 1 day in advance. If preparing the day it is served, allow at least 6 hours for it to set.

Technique Tips

To avoid hard chunks of frozen chocolate in the terrine, I melt the chocolate, spread it into a paper-thin sheet and firm it up before chopping coarsely into bits. This is a good routine to follow whenever you use chocolate in a frozen mixture.

To slice the terrine neatly, dip a large sharp knife into hot water and dry it between each slice.

This rich, frozen mousse is what we call a parfait in France. Made without an ice cream machine, it depends on beaten egg whites to keep the mixture creamy and to prevent ice crystals from forming. Its primary flavorings, chocolate and apricot, were not an item when I was a young chef. Chocolate with praline, chocolate with orange, chocolate with rum, yes, but not chocolate with apricot. Nor with raspberry. At that time, we laughed at the popular American mint chocolate duo and now all the fancy restaurants in France are mixing these two flavors together. I think American food has influenced French food much more than the other way around.

TERRINE

> 3 ounces bittersweet or semisweet chocolate, finely chopped
>
> ¾ pound (about 3 cups) or 66 dried apricots
>
> 1 tablespoon fresh peeled minced gingerroot
>
> 2 egg whites, at room temperature
>
> Pinch of cream of tartar
>
> 4 tablespoons sugar
>
> 1 cup heavy cream
>
> ½ cup sugar

CHOCOLATE SAUCE

> ¾ pound bittersweet or semisweet chocolate, finely chopped
>
> 1 cup heavy cream
>
> 2 tablespoons apricot liqueur, Amaretto or rum

For the terrine, line a large baking sheet with parchment paper. Melt the chocolate in the top of a double boiler above gently simmering water and stir until smooth. Turn the chocolate out onto the prepared sheet and spread into a paper-thin layer using a metal spatula. Refrigerate until firm, for about 10 to 15 minutes. Remove the chocolate from the parchment, breaking it up with your fingers; chop coarsely. Return the chopped chocolate to the refrigerator.

Meanwhile, cover the apricots with warm water in a bowl and soak for 15 minutes, stirring occasionally. Place the apricots and ginger in a blender with ½ cup of the soaking liquid. Process, pulsing on/off, until the apricots are almost pureed, but small bits remain. Transfer the mixture to a large bowl.

Beat the egg whites with the cream of tartar using an electric mixer until soft peaks form. Add 4 tablespoons of sugar, 1 at a time, and continue beating until stiff, but not dry. Gently fold ¼ of the egg whites into the apricot puree to lighten it, then gently fold in the remaining whites.

Meanwhile, beat the cream with ½ cup sugar using the same beater until soft peaks form. Gently fold into the apricot mixture with the chopped chocolate pieces.

Line a 9- × 5-inch loaf pan with plastic wrap, leaving several inches of overhang. Turn the apricot mixture into the loaf pan, smooth the top with a spatula and tap it lightly on a work surface to eliminate any air pockets. Fold the plastic over to cover. Freeze the terrine for at least 6 hours or until firm.

For the Chocolate Sauce, combine the chocolate, cream and apricot liqueur in the top of a double boiler above gently simmering water. Melt until smooth, stirring occasionally. If serving within an hour, let it sit above the gently simmering water. (This can be prepared ahead and set aside in a widemouthed thermos, at room temperature or in the refrigerator in a covered container.)

To serve, if the terrine is frozen solid, let it sit in the refrigerator for 15 to 30 minutes. Unmold the terrine on a cutting board. Cut eight to twelve ¾- to 1-inch-thick slices. Transfer the slices to the top half of large plates using a large broad spatula. Let sit at room temperature several minutes, if necessary, until creamy. Rewrap and refreeze any remaining terrine.

Meanwhile, reheat the Chocolate Sauce, if necessary, in the top of a double boiler above gently simmering water, and stir until smooth. Ladle a puddle of sauce below each terrine slice. Dip a fork in the remaining sauce and drizzle zigzags of chocolate over each slice. Serve immediately.

Banana Colada Soup

4 Servings

Planning Ahead

The coconut can be toasted several days in advance. The soup can be made at any time during the day it is to be served. Allow at least 4 to 6 hours to chill completely. Prepare it the night before if you are offering it at an early brunch.

T he *piña colada* was the first American-style cocktail I ever tasted, and I thought it was great from the first sip. Coming from a cold region, I gravitate toward food that reminds me of the sun. With its frothy, lighthearted disposition, the *piña colada* makes me think of the beach and puts me in a terrific mood.

This soup serves as a particularly nice first course or dessert at brunch as well as a refreshing dessert for a spring or summer dinner. Don't worry if the bananas turn a bit gray; they'll be hidden under the toasted coconut. To further perk them up, scoop pineapple, coconut or banana sorbet or ice cream on top. If you've just come back from the Caribbean, you may want to ladle each serving into a pineapple shell that has been hollowed out and frozen. I won't tell if you stick a paper parasol in it.

¾ cup sweetened shredded coconut

2 tablespoons freshly squeezed lemon juice

3 large ripe (but firm) bananas, cut crosswise into ¼-inch-thick slices

1 cup water

8 ounces coconut milk or cream

4 fresh mint sprigs for garnish (optional)

For the coconut, preheat the oven to 350°F. Arrange the coconut on a small baking sheet and bake until medium brown, for about 10 minutes, stirring occasionally. (This can be prepared several days ahead and stored at room temperature in an airtight container.)

Gently mix the lemon juice with the bananas to coat in a small bowl. Stir the water and coconut milk together in a large skillet until blended. Bring to a gentle simmer over medium heat, add the bananas and cook until they are just tender when pierced with a knife, for about 2 minutes. Cool completely. Cover and refrigerate until well chilled, for about 4 to 6 hours.

To serve, gently remove the bananas from the soup using a slotted spoon and overlap them in a circle in the center of 4 large soup plates. Gently ladle the soup through a fine strainer over and around the bananas. Mound the toasted coconut over the bananas. Place a mint sprig in each bowl and serve immediately.

Chocolate Red Wine Soup
with Strawberries

When I was working as an apprentice, one of my main jobs was to dip strawberries in chocolate. I would dip the fruit in the chocolate and then hold up the dipping fork and catch the chocolate on my tongue as it dripped off the fruit. Every once in a while I would eat a strawberry along with the chocolate, and just swoon at what was happening in my mouth. One day I ate so much chocolate it made me violently ill. For the next 15 years, I couldn't even stand the smell of it. Then my old desire crept up on me, and here I am, a relapsed chocoholic.

Chocolate is sometimes too heavy after a multicourse meal, so I am more likely to respond to my cravings for it late in the afternoon during teatime. This light refreshing soup is, however, an exception that works well any time of day. If I ever serve my fantasy six-course chocolate dinner at Citrus, you can be sure I will be the first guest to sit down.

4 to 6 Servings

Planning Ahead

The soup can be completely prepared at any time during the day it is to be served. Allow 2 hours for the strawberries to marinate and 4 to 6 hours for the soup to chill.

½ cup sugar

1 cup Cabernet Sauvignon, Pinot Noir, Zinfandel or other dry red wine

1 tablespoon vanilla extract

1 pint strawberries, hulled and thinly sliced lengthwise

2 ounces bittersweet chocolate, finely chopped

4 to 6 large strawberries, preferably long-stemmed for garnish

Mix the sugar with the red wine and vanilla in a large bowl. Add the strawberries. Marinate for 2 hours at room temperature.

Melt the chocolate in the top of a double boiler above gently simmering water and stir until smooth. Strain the strawberry mixture, reserving the strawberries. Heat the marinating liquid in a medium saucepan to the same temperature as the chocolate. Whisk several tablespoons of the marinating liquid into the chocolate and stir until smooth, then gradually whisk in the remaining liquid. Strain back into the bowl through a fine sieve. Cool to room temperature. Add the reserved strawberries. Refrigerate until well chilled, for about 4 to 6 hours.

To serve, ladle the soup into 4 soup plates. Garnish each with a long-stemmed strawberry.

Couscous with
Orange and Pistachios

Planning Ahead

The couscous can be completely prepared 1 to 2 days before serving. If not preparing in advance, allow at least 4 to 6 hours for the couscous to chill.

Technique Tip

Heating the cake pan before pouring in the caramel allows the caramel to be evenly distributed before hardening.

When sweetened and chilled, couscous resembles a firm rice pudding that can be served either for dessert or for a main course at brunch. The idea to present it this way came to me one afternoon when I was yearning for the sweet semolina pudding my mother often made when I was a small boy. As is always the case when you are in the mood for a particular food, there was no semolina in the house. The coarser grained couscous, my substitute, was very nurturing, nonetheless. With a Middle Eastern grain, my flavorings—honey, orange and pistachios— were, accordingly, Mediterranean.

1½ cups sieved orange juice (about 5 to 8 large oranges)

½ cup honey

1½ cups couscous

3 ounces (¾ stick) unsalted butter, chopped

¼ cup Grand Marnier or other orange liqueur

½ cup sugar

⅓ cup pistachios, coarsely chopped

Bring the orange juice and honey to a boil in a heavy large saucepan. Remove from heat and stir in the couscous and butter. Cover and set aside for 15 minutes, stirring once after 2 minutes. Mix in the Grand Marnier.

Place a 9-inch-round cake pan in a 250°F oven. Place the sugar in a heavy medium saucepan with water to cover. Cook over low heat until the sugar dissolves, swirling the pan occasionally. Increase the heat and boil until the sugar caramelizes and turns a deep mahogany brown, watching carefully so the mixture doesn't burn. Using hot pads, immediately pour the caramel into the heated cake pan, tilting the pan to spread the caramel over the bottom and up the sides. Sprinkle the pistachios over the caramel. Spread the couscous evenly over the caramel. Cover with plastic wrap and refrigerate for at least 4 hours or overnight.

Remove the couscous from the refrigerator 1 hour before serving. Unmold immediately while still cold by running a knife around the rim of the pan and inverting onto a serving platter. If the caramel is too firm to unmold, stir briefly over medium-low heat until it dissolves and spread it over the couscous. Let sit at room temperature for 1 hour. To serve, slice 6 wedges and transfer to dessert plates. Serve immediately.

Coffee Chocolate Mousse

Chocolate is my favorite flavor and chocolate mousse one of my favorite desserts. When I went to a restaurant with my friend André, he would call beforehand to check if they had it. "Do you have a good chocolate mousse?" he would ask. "A good chocolate cake? Terrific," he would say. "Michel will be happy."

Chocolate mousse could always be found in small restaurants in France. It was also the dessert most frequently made at home. Yet, as difficult as this may be to believe today, you could not buy it in a pastry shop until refrigeration was introduced commercially in the early 1970s.

When I heighten a chocolate mousse with coffee, my chocolate of choice is usually white chocolate. Less intense than bittersweet, it allows the true taste of strong coffee to shine, while giving this dessert the buoyant texture of chocolate. Coffee was an impossible flavor to sell ten years ago, but since Italian food has had such a profound impact on our diet, it has become à la mode. Since good quality white chocolate is hard to come by and, admittedly, a bit stubborn to work with, I've called for either milk chocolate or white chocolate here. If the mousse is not hedonistic enough by itself, spoon it alongside a deep, dense chocolate cake.

8 ounces milk or white chocolate, finely chopped

1½ cups heavy cream

3 tablespoons instant espresso powder dissolved in 1 to 2 tablespoons hot water

4 large (½ cup) egg whites, at room temperature

Large pinch of cream of tartar

4 tablespoons sugar

3 to 4 tablespoons crushed amaretti cookies (optional)

Melt the chocolate in the top of a double boiler above gently simmering water and stir until smooth. Let cool to tepid room temperature. Whip the cream with the dissolved coffee powder until soft peaks form. Using clean, dry beaters in a separate bowl, beat the egg whites with the cream of tartar until soft peaks form. Add the sugar, 1 tablespoon at a time, and continue beating until the whites are stiff but not dry. Gently fold ¼ of the whites into the chocolate to lighten it. Return to bowl with remaining whites, add whipped cream and gently fold the entire mixture together. Cover and refrigerate until well chilled, about 4 hours or overnight.

To serve, spoon egg-shaped mounds of the mousse into 6 to 8 crystal glasses. Let sit at room temperature until creamy, for about 15 to 30 minutes before serving. Top with amaretti cookies, if desired.

Planning Ahead

The mousse is even better when prepared 1 day in advance so its flavors can deepen and mellow. If making the mousse the day it is to be served, allow at least 4 to 6 hours for it to chill.

Technique Tips

If liquid coffee is added to melted chocolate, the chocolate will seize. Add it to the cream instead before whipping.

Beat the cream just until soft peaks form and the egg whites only until just stiff, but not dry. If either one is overbeaten, the mousse's texture will be unpleasantly cottony.

When folding the egg whites or cream into the mixture, cut a plastic spatula down to the bottom of the bowl as if slicing a cake, turn it over and pull the mixture in the bottom of the bowl up over the whites or cream in the top of the bowl. Give the bowl a ¼ turn and repeat. Repeat these movements until the ingredients are completely blended. Work gently and carefully so as not to deflate the beaten whites or cream.

Apple Rum Risotto

4 Servings

Planning Ahead

Risotto is best served as soon as it is cooked. The apples can simmer while the rice mixture is cooking, so there is no need to do anything in advance except, perhaps, ready ingredients. If you want to be able to focus on conversation, the apples can be prepared at any time during the day the risotto is to be served.

Technique Tip

Arborio rice, an Italian import that maintains a toothsome quality, gives this dish its special texture. Look for this rice at Italian grocers, specialty food stores and well-stocked supermarkets.

I n France, we have two *pommes: pommes en l'air* (apple) and *pommes de terre* (potato). I have always enjoyed playing with these words and exchanging recipes traditionally used with apples for those with potatoes and vice versa. Since we make a potato dish that looks like risotto (page 260) at the restaurant, I thought it would be fun to have an apple risotto as well. Although this rice dish is traditionally served as a savory first course in Italy, I've found that a sweet rendition works wonderfully for dessert or for brunch. It could be the new hot cereal for the nineties. Since apples and rice are staples in most homes, this is a great recipe to pull out when guests drop by unexpectedly. Welcome these interlopers with a wooden spoon, and let them stir the risotto while you work on something else.

APPLES

1 ounce (¼ stick) unsalted butter

2 small (10 to 12 ounces) Pippin or Granny Smith apples, peeled, cored and cut into ¼-inch dice

2½ tablespoons sugar

1 tablespoon rum

1½ tablespoons vanilla extract

RISOTTO

4½ to 5 cups unsweetened apple juice

1 ounce (¼ stick) unsalted butter

1½ cups Arborio rice

Rum-sweetened whipped cream or vanilla ice cream (optional)

Scant ¼ cup almonds or walnuts, toasted and coarsely chopped

For the apples, melt the butter in a heavy small nonstick skillet over medium heat. Add the apples and sugar and cook until the apples are just tender, for 6 to 7 minutes. Pour the rum into the corner of the skillet. Heat briefly, ignite carefully and shake the skillet until the flame goes out. Stir in the vanilla. (This can be prepared ahead, covered and set aside at room temperature.)

For the risotto, meanwhile, bring the apple juice to a simmer in a medium saucepan. Melt the butter in a heavy large nonstick saucepan over medium-low heat. Add the rice and stir for 2 minutes. Pour in about ¾ cup apple juice and bring to a boil, stirring. Lower the heat to the point where the liquid is simmering gently. Stir continually until the liquid is completely absorbed. Stir in the cooked apple mixture and ½ cup apple juice. Stir until the liquid is absorbed. Add the remaining apple juice ½ cup at a time (¼ cup toward the end of cooking), stirring until each addition is absorbed. Continue cooking, adjusting the heat as necessary so the liquid simmers gently, until the rice is tender, but not mushy, for about 20 to 25 minutes total.

To serve, divide the risotto among 4 soup plates. Top with whipped cream or ice cream, if desired. Sprinkle with nuts. Serve immediately.

Chocolate-Vanilla
Double-Dip Crème Brûlée

6 Servings

Planning Ahead

Both the custard and chocolate mousse can be prepared and assembled 1 day in advance. If preparing the day the dessert is to be served, allow at least 4 to 6 hours for it to chill. Sprinkle with sugar and caramelize just before presenting.

Technique Tips

The chocolate should be cooled just to tepid or barely warm before folding into the egg yolks. If not cooled enough, the yolks will curdle. If cooled too much, chocolate flakes will form.

When folding a light mixture such as beaten egg whites into a heavier mixture such as chocolate, fold a small part or half of the lighter mixture in first to lighten the heavier mixture. If everything is folded in at once, the lighter mixture will deflate.

T his double-dip crème brûlée brings hot and cold and soft and crisp together in one dish. Built in layers like a sandwich, it requires the expertise of a cook who has apprenticed to a Dagwood maker or spent lots of time glopping peanut butter and jelly on bread for kids. Unlike a cake whose individual rows are immediately visible, the layers here are unveiled slowly as the spoon descends into the dessert's mysterious depths. With its surprise ending, it is the perfect detective story plotted by a pastry chef.

CUSTARD

½ cup milk

2 cups heavy cream

½ cup sugar

1 to 2 vanilla beans, slit lengthwise

9 egg yolks, at room temperature, blended with fork

CHOCOLATE MOUSSE

5 ounces bittersweet or semisweet chocolate, coarsely chopped

4 ounces (1 stick) unsalted butter, chopped

4 large eggs, separated, at room temperature

4 tablespoons sugar

¼ teaspoon cream of tartar

6 tablespoons sugar

For the custard, place the milk, cream and sugar in a heavy medium saucepan. Scrape the seeds from the vanilla beans into the milk mixture. Add the beans and bring to a boil over medium heat. Remove from heat and let the beans steep for at least 1 hour or until the mixture cools to room temperature. Discard the beans (or wash, dry and reserve them for another use).

Preheat the oven to 300°F. Place six 4- × 2-inch soufflé or baking dishes in a large baking pan. Pour enough water into the pan to come ¾ of the way up the sides of the dishes. Remove the dishes and place the baking pan with water in the oven to preheat for about 15 minutes.

Whisk the egg yolks into the cooled milk mixture. Strain through a fine sieve into soufflé dishes. Place the soufflé dishes in the baking pan and bake until set and a knife inserted into the custard comes out almost dry, for about 30 minutes. Remove from the water bath and cool to room temperature.

For the Chocolate Mousse, melt the chocolate and butter in the top of a double boiler over gently simmering water until smooth, stirring occasionally. Cool until tepid, for about 25 minutes.

Beat the egg yolks with 2 tablespoons of the sugar using an electric mixer until a slowly dissolving ribbon forms when the beaters are lifted. Fold the tepid chocolate into the yolks. Using a clean dry beater and bowl, beat the egg whites with the cream of tartar until soft peaks form. Add the remaining 2 tablespoons sugar, 1 at a time, and continue beating until barely stiff. Gently fold ½ of the whites into the chocolate mixture; fold in the remaining whites.

Spoon the chocolate mousse over the cooled baked custard, smoothing the top with a spatula. Cover with plastic wrap and refrigerate at least 4 to 6 hours or overnight. Remove from the refrigerator for 30 minutes before serving.

To serve, preheat the broiler. Sprinkle 1 tablespoon sugar over each dessert. Place about 2 inches below the heat source and broil until the sugar is melted and caramelized, for about 2 minutes, watching carefully. Serve immediately.

Blackberry Cobblettes

The fruit can be prepared and the crust ingredients measured several hours before the Cobblettes are to be served. Mix the crust and bake for 15 to 30 minutes before presenting.

Variations
Crème fraîche can be substituted for the half-and-half and sour cream, or an additional tablespoon of half-and-half can be substituted for the sour cream.

For a quick fix for overripe berries, sugar the fruit and let it sit several hours or overnight to form a sauce to spoon over ice cream.

Fruit looks so luscious in the summer that I always buy more than my family—and the families on either side of us and on either side of them—can possibly eat. Ever. Rather than throwing my bounty away, I just make a cobbler with whatever is on the verge of overripening according to the formula below. Since much of the fruit is pureed and all is hidden under the crust, less-than-perfect-looking berries can be used. A brief baking time preserves fresh flavors.

I made minicobblers here, rather than one large tray, as a way to justify my purchase of individual soufflé dishes that have been gathering dust while taking valuable space in my cupboard. (Plus I think they are cute.) If you prefer, make one large cobbler in an 8- or 9-inch soufflé dish or pie plate.

BLACKBERRIES

    12 ounces (three ½-pint baskets) blackberries

    2 tablespoons sugar or to taste

COBBLETTE CRUST

    1 cup all-purpose flour

    ¼ cup sugar

    1½ teaspoons baking powder

    ¼ teaspoon baking soda

    Pinch of salt

    2 ounces (½ stick) chilled unsalted butter, chopped

    ¾ cup half-and-half

    1 tablespoon sour cream

    Sweetened whipped cream or vanilla ice cream

For the blackberries, puree 1 cup of the fruit with 2 tablespoons sugar in a blender, pulsing on/off. Taste and add additional sugar as necessary if mixture is too tart. Divide the remaining berries among four 1-cup or six ½-cup soufflé dishes or custard cups. Divide the puree among the cups. Mix the puree and whole berries using a knife or small spatula. (This can be prepared ahead and set aside at room temperature.)

For the crust, place the flour, sugar, baking powder, baking soda, salt and butter in the bowl of an electric mixer. (This can be prepared ahead to this point and set aside at room temperature.)

To bake and serve, preheat the oven to 350°F. Mix the crust ingredients in an electric mixer until the butter is the size of small peas. Add the half-and-half and sour cream and mix on low speed until just blended, for about 30 seconds. Divide the topping among the soufflé dishes. Spread to the edges and seal using a small spatula. Bake until the topping is golden brown, for about 12 to 15 minutes. Cool for 15 to 30 minutes. Place on 4 to 6 small plates. Serve warm with whipped cream or ice cream.

Summer Apricot Pastries

T he fresh apricot season is so short that I never get enough of this fruit. On the too few occasions I have apricots, I like to cook them simply as they are in these tartlets without many other ingredients to mask their ripe, sweet fruitiness. The apricot is the star here, with the almonds playing a practical, support-ing role. Layered between the fruit and the pastry, they become a delicious sponge, soaking up the juices and preventing the crust from becoming soggy.

ALMOND FILLING

⅓ cup whole blanched almonds, toasted

1 tablespoon sugar

1 ounce (¼ stick) unsalted room temperature butter, chopped

1 tablespoon cream cheese, at room temperature

1 egg, blended with fork

PASTRY

1 8-ounce frozen puff pastry sheet, defrosted 20 minutes at room temperature

About 1 cup coarse sugar (see Technique Tips)

6 to 8 medium apricots, halved and pitted

Confectioners' sugar

For the almond filling, grind the almonds and sugar in a food processor until the mixture is the texture of fine meal, pulsing on/off. Add the butter and cream cheese to the processor. Measure 1 tablespoon of egg and add it to the processor. Reserve the remaining egg for another use. Process until the filling is well mixed and creamy. (This can be prepared ahead, transferred to a covered bowl and set aside at room temperature for several hours or refrigerated for several days. Bring to room tem-perature before using.)
(continued)

Planning Ahead

The almond filling can be prepared several days in advance. The pastry can be rolled and cut at any time during the day the tartlets are to be served. The apricots can be cut several hours in advance. Assemble and bake the tartlets no more than 1 hour before presenting.

Technique Tips

Coarse sugar can often be begged or purchased from a local bakery or market selling Scandinavian prod-ucts. If not available, sub-stitute regular granulated sugar or omit completely. Coarse sugar can also be ordered from Maid of Scandinavia, 3244 Raleigh Avenue, Minneapolis, MN 55416 (1/800/328-6722).

Sometimes apricots that taste sweet when eaten out of hand become quite astringent as they cook and their acid concentrates. To

Desserts

balance the sweetness, taste the cooked fruit to determine how much confectioners' sugar to sprinkle on top before serving.

For the pastry, line a large baking sheet with parchment paper. Roll the pastry out into a 12½- × 12½-inch square on a lightly floured surface. Roll the pastry up on a rolling pin, brush off excess flour and sprinkle the work surface with the coarse sugar. Roll the pastry out over the sugar, pressing the pastry into the sugar. Cut out four 5-inch circles. Arrange the circles on the baking sheet. Cover with plastic wrap and refrigerate for at least 30 minutes.

To bake, preheat the oven to 350°F. Divide the almond filling among the centers of the pastry circles, spreading into approximately 2-inch circles. Quarter each apricot half lengthwise. Arrange the apricot quarters over the filling in a daisy shape with tips toward the center. Bake until the pastry is cooked and browned and puffs into a rim around the filling, for about 25 to 30 minutes. Slide a spatula under the tartlets to loosen them. Transfer to 4 dessert plates. Sprinkle with confectioners' sugar. Serve immediately.

Lemon Meringue Tart

6 Servings

Planning Ahead

The Lemon Curd can be made 2 days in advance. If preparing the day it is to be used, allow at least 4 to 6 hours for it to chill. The tart crust can be mixed 1 day in advance and both rolled and completely baked at any time during the day it is to be served. Fill the tart and bake the meringue just before presenting.

I can't imagine writing a cookbook to be published in America that does not include a recipe for lemon meringue pie, which—along with apple and chocolate—appears to be the country's favorite. I have departed from classic conventions by making the lemon curd without cornstarch, spreading the meringue on smoothly instead of swirling it in peaks and baking it in a tart pan rather than in a sloped pie dish. These variations are the clues that this is a Frenchman's recipe. At the restaurant, I bake my lemon tart in a bottomless rectangular form which gives it a handsome tailored look and makes slicing neatly as easy as . . . pie. If you have this tart form, use it by all means.

LEMON CURD

⅔ cup (about 4 to 5 large lemons) freshly squeezed, strained lemon juice

8 egg yolks, at room temperature

1 cup sugar

5 tablespoons (2½ ounces) unsalted room temperature butter, chopped

Desserts

ALMOND TART CRUST

¼ cup whole blanched almonds

¼ cup sugar

Pinch of salt

4 ounces (1 stick) unsalted room temperature butter, chopped

1 egg

1¼ cups all-purpose flour

4 egg whites, at room temperature

Pinch of salt

Pinch of cream of tartar

6 tablespoons sugar

Technique Tips

Placing plastic directly on top of the cooked curd prevents a crust from forming.

If the dough is too firm to roll, let it sit about 15 minutes at room temperature.

For 2 large sheets of plastic to roll the dough between, cut open 2 plastic produce bags.

Variations

Either orange juice or a mixture of lemon and orange can be substituted for the lemon juice.

My Basic Tart Crust (page 322) can be substituted for the Almond Tart Crust.

Instead of 1 large tart, bake individual tartlets.

For the Lemon Curd, fill a large pot with several inches of water and bring to a simmer. Whisk the lemon juice, egg yolks and sugar together in a medium heatproof bowl. Set the bowl into the pot of simmering water and continue whisking until the mixture thickens to the consistency of thick hollandaise sauce, for about 5 minutes. Add the butter and stir until the sauce is smooth. Remove from the water bath. Press a piece of plastic wrap onto the sauce. Cool, then refrigerate until chilled, for about 6 hours. (This can be prepared 2 days ahead.)

For the Almond Tart Crust dough, grind the almonds with the sugar and salt in a food processor until finely chopped. Add the butter and process until smooth. Add the egg and process until incorporated. Add ⅓ of flour and mix just until incorporated. Add remaining flour in 2 batches, processing just until barely incorporated. (Dough will be soft.) Scrape the dough out onto a piece of plastic wrap. Shape into a disk. Wrap and refrigerate for at least 1 hour. (This can be prepared 1 day ahead.)

To form the crust, butter a 9-inch tart pan with a removable bottom. Roll the dough out between 2 large sheets of plastic wrap into a 10-inch circle. Remove the top sheet of plastic. Invert into the prepared pan. Trim and finish the edges. Cover and refrigerate for at least 1 hour.

To bake the crust, preheat the oven to 350°F. Line the tart with parchment paper or aluminum foil and fill with beans or pie weights. Bake until the crust is firm and set, for about 15 minutes. Remove the beans and paper. Prick the bottom of the crust so it does not puff. Continue baking until golden brown for 10 to 15 minutes. (This can be prepared ahead and set aside on a rack.)

To serve, preheat the broiler. Fill the tart with the chilled Lemon Curd. Beat the egg whites with salt and cream of tartar using an electric mixer until soft peaks form. Beat in the sugar, 1 tablespoon at a time, and continue beating until the meringue is stiff but not dry. Spoon the meringue on top of the Lemon Curd, then spread it in a flat smooth layer with a spatula, covering completely and sealing the edges of the crust. Broil the tart about 4 inches below the heat source until the meringue browns, for about 3 minutes, watching carefully. Remove the tart ring, cut 6 wedges and transfer to dessert plates. Serve immediately.

Desserts

Raisin Tart with Hot Buttered Rum Sauce

6 to 8 Servings

Planning Ahead

The raisins should be marinated for at least 4 hours or, preferably, overnight. The Raisin Custard and Hot Buttered Rum Sauce can be completely prepared the day before. The crust can be mixed 1 day in advance and rolled out at any time during the day it is to be served. Bake and fill several hours before presenting.

Technique Tips

If the dough is too firm to roll, let it sit for about 15 minutes at room temperature.

For 2 large sheets of plastic to roll the dough between, cut open 2 plastic produce bags.

If it is more convenient, bake the crust completely earlier in the day and set it aside on a rack. Fill and bake it 3 to 4 hours before serving.

Brushing the custard with the egg before baking gives it a deep rich brown color.

L ike the Basque Custard Cookie Cake (page 347) and *pain au chocolat*, the flan (baked pastry cream) filling in this tart was a big favorite of French children during the sixties. When school was out, the kids would race to our pastry shop, and within half an hour we had sold 50 of these desserts. The children claimed the bakery for their own in the late afternoons just as their mothers reserved the mornings. On Sundays, though, the patisserie belonged to the entire family. As well-dressed parishioners stopped by on their way home from church to buy the cake of the day, it became the bustling center of village life. France had finally recovered from the war, and there was money to be made once again. It was a charming time.

Though children ate their flan plain, I've added rum and raisins along with a sauce to give this old-fashioned dessert a modern look and a bit of sophistication. Besides, I thought it was time for it to become an adult and grow old like me.

RAISIN CUSTARD

¾ cup raisins

1½ tablespoons dark rum

3 cups half-and-half or milk

Pinch of salt

¼ cup sugar

1 to 2 vanilla beans, slit lengthwise

6 egg yolks, at room temperature

½ cup sugar

½ cup all-purpose flour

HOT BUTTERED RUM SAUCE

1 cup brown sugar

½ cup dark rum

½ cup heavy cream

2 ounces (¼ stick) chilled unsalted butter, chopped

BASIC TART CRUST

4 ounces (1 stick) room temperature unsalted butter, chopped

Pinch of salt

2 tablespoons sugar

¼ cup heavy cream, half-and-half or milk

1¼ cups all-purpose flour

1 egg, blended with fork

Variation

My Almond Tart Crust (page 324) can be substituted for the Basic Tart Crust.

For the Raisin Custard, soak the raisins in the rum in a small bowl at room temperature for at least 4 hours or overnight, stirring occasionally.

Place the milk, salt and ¼ cup sugar in a heavy, large saucepan. Scrape the seeds from the vanilla beans into the mixture, add the beans and bring to a boil over medium-high heat. Remove from the heat and let the vanilla beans steep for at least 1 hour or until the mixture cools to room temperature. Discard the beans (or wash, dry and reserve them for another use).

Beat the yolks and ½ cup sugar using an electric mixer until thick and pale lemon in color. Mix in the flour. Reheat the milk mixture and gradually beat it into the yolks. Return the mixture to the saucepan. Whisk over medium-high heat until the mixture comes to a boil and becomes very lumpy. Reduce heat to medium-low and whisk until smooth, for about 2 to 3 minutes. Stir in the raisins with the rum. Press a sheet of plastic wrap onto the custard so a crust doesn't form. (This can be prepared ahead, cooled, covered and set aside at cool room temperature for several hours or refrigerated overnight. Bring to room temperature before filling tart.)

For the Hot Buttered Rum Sauce, stir the brown sugar in a heavy small saucepan over medium heat until melted and smooth. Pour in the rum and cream and simmer, stirring until the sauce is smooth, thickened and reduced to about ¾ cup. Whisk in the butter until melted. (This can be prepared ahead, cooled, covered and set aside at cool room temperature for several hours or refrigerated overnight.)

For the Basic Tart Crust dough, cream the butter using an electric mixer. Beat in the salt and sugar. Stir in the cream and ⅕ of the flour. Add the remaining flour, mixing with your fingertips or a fork until the ingredients are combined. Turn the dough out onto a piece of plastic wrap and shape into a flat disk. Wrap and refrigerate for at least 1 hour. (This can be prepared 1 day ahead.)

To form the crust, butter a 10-inch tart pan with a removable bottom. Roll the dough out between 2 large sheets of plastic wrap into an 11-inch circle. Remove the top sheet of plastic. Invert into the prepared pan. Trim and finish the edges. Cover and refrigerate for at least 1 hour.

To bake, preheat the oven to 350°F. Line the tart with parchment paper or aluminum foil and fill with beans or pie weights. Bake until the crust is firm and set, for about 15 minutes. Remove the beans and paper. Prick the bottom of the crust so it does not puff. Continue baking until well browned, for 10 to 15 minutes. Fill the tart with the custard and smooth the top with a spatula. Brush with the egg.

(continued)

Desserts

Return to the oven and bake until the custard is well browned, for 20 to 25 minutes. Cool in the tart pan on a rack for 3 to 4 hours.

To serve, remove the outer ring of the tart pan. Cut 6 to 8 wedges and transfer them to dessert plates. Stir the rum sauce over medium-high heat to rewarm. Ladle over tarts. Serve immediately.

Prune Tart with Almonds and Tea

6 to 8 Servings

Planning Ahead

The Prune Almond Filling can be completely prepared 1 day in advance. The crust can be mixed 1 day in advance and rolled out at any time during the day it is to be served. Bake and fill several hours before presenting.

Technique Tips

If the dough is too firm to roll, let it sit for about 15 minutes at room temperature.

For 2 large sheets of plastic to roll the dough between, cut open 2 plastic produce bags.

If more convenient, bake the crust completely earlier in the day and set aside on a rack. Fill and bake 3 to 4 hours before serving.

This recipe is dedicated to my friend Jean-Louis Palladin, the chef of Jean-Louis at Watergate in Washington, D.C., who grew up in southwest France where both prunes and Armagnac are produced. Many chefs know about food, but not about wine or spirits. Jean-Louis knows about everything. Extremely creative, he is the chef who has impressed me most throughout my life. But there is one thing I hate about him: He is tall and skinny.

For most people, the greatest alcoholic beverage is one that is freshly poured, holding promises of wondrous tastes. Not for Jean-Louis. He looks to a just-emptied glass to reveal its glory as imprisoned aromas of vanilla and cedar are released. Fiercely proud of Armagnac, Jean-Louis will never be seen with a glass of Cognac, the brandy's competitor that is distilled north of his region. To evaluate an Armagnac, he rubs several drops on his arm, where the alcohol evaporates, leaving its essence for examination. There is probably no better way to learn about Armagnac . . . as long as you've taken a shower beforehand.

PRUNE ALMOND FILLING

3 tea bags

2 cups boiling water

39 (about ¾ pound) pitted prunes

1 cup slivered almonds, toasted

1 cup confectioners' sugar

2 eggs, at room temperature

4 ounces (1 stick) unsalted butter, at room temperature

ALMOND TART CRUST

¼ cup whole blanched almonds

¼ cup sugar

Pinch of salt

4 ounces (1 stick) unsalted room temperature butter, chopped

1 egg

1¼ cups all-purpose flour

2 tablespoons Armagnac or other brandy

Confectioners' sugar

Lightly sweetened whipped cream or vanilla ice cream

Variation
My Basic Tart Crust (page 322) can be substituted for the Almond Tart Crust.

For the Prune Almond Filling, place the tea bags in a medium bowl. Add the boiling water and steep for 5 minutes. Add the prunes and soak until plump and tender, for about 1½ hours, stirring occasionally; drain.

Finely grind the almonds with the sugar in a processor, pulsing on/off. Add 14 drained prunes and the eggs and process, pulsing on/off until the prunes are finely chopped. Add the butter and process until smooth. (This can be prepared ahead and set aside at room temperature for several hours or refrigerated. Bring to room temperature before baking. Place the remaining whole prunes in a covered container and set aside at room temperature.)

For the Almond Tart Crust dough, grind the almonds with the sugar and salt in a food processor until finely chopped. Add the butter and process until smooth. Add the egg and process until incorporated. Add ⅓ of the flour and mix just until incorporated. Add the remaining flour in 2 batches, processing just until barely incorporated. (Dough will be soft.) Scrape the dough out onto a piece of plastic wrap. Shape into a disk. Wrap and refrigerate for at least 1 hour. (This can be prepared 1 day ahead.)

To form the crust, butter a 10-inch tart pan with a removable bottom. Roll the dough out between 2 large sheets of plastic wrap into an 11-inch circle. Remove the top sheet of plastic. Invert into the prepared pan. Trim and finish the edges. Cover and refrigerate for at least 1 hour.

To bake the crust, preheat the oven to 350°F. Line the tart with parchment paper or aluminum foil and fill with beans or pie weights. Bake until the crust is firm and set, for about 15 minutes. Remove the beans and paper. Prick the bottom of the crust so it does not puff. Continue baking until well browned, for 10 to 15 minutes. Fill the tart with the Prune Almond Filling and smooth the top with a spatula. Arrange the remaining 25 whole prunes evenly in concentric circles, pressing gently into the filling. Return the tart to the oven and bake until the filling is puffed and set, for about 50 minutes. Immediately drizzle the Armagnac over the tart. Cool in the tart pan on a rack for 3 to 4 hours.

To serve, remove the tart ring. Dust the tart with confectioners' sugar and cut 6 to 8 wedges. Transfer to dessert plates. Accompany with whipped cream or ice cream. Serve immediately.

Macadamia Nut Pie

6 to 8 Servings

Planning Ahead

The filling can be completely prepared 1 day in advance. The crust can be mixed 1 day in advance and rolled out at any time during the day it is to be served. Bake and fill several hours before presenting.

Technique Tips

If the dough is too firm to roll, let sit for about 15 minutes at room temperature.

For 2 large sheets of plastic to roll the dough between, cut open 2 plastic produce bags.

If more convenient, bake the crust completely earlier in the day and set aside on a rack. Fill and bake 3 to 4 hours before serving.

Delicate and refined, the macadamia is the ultimate, perfect nut. If only it wasn't so expensive. I know Americans love gooey pecan tarts, so I replaced the pecans with macadamias for this special treat. Like a quiche, this tart filling is a formula in which one ingredient—in this case, one nut—can be replaced with another. The recipe is the same, but the result is quite different. Since macadamias are crunchier than pecans, this filling is more candylike.

Every time I make a good tart or pie like this, I remember my mother's sad attempts. Her tarts were so bad no one took more than a bite. We used to call them *Tart de Plomb* (lead) because they were so heavy. The fillings were fine. The problem was the crust, and this was simply a matter of economics: My mother could not afford to use enough butter to make a short, tender crust. Better that she had made a cake.

MACADAMIA FILLING

3 tablespoons (1½ ounces) unsalted butter

2 tablespoons all-purpose flour

2 tablespoons sugar

⅓ cup dark brown sugar

¾ cup dark corn syrup

2 tablespoons molasses

1 tablespoon vanilla extract

2 eggs, at room temperature

2 cups macadamias or other nut, preferably unsalted

BASIC TART CRUST

4 ounces (1 stick) unsalted butter, at room temperature

Pinch of salt

2 tablespoons sugar

¼ cup heavy cream, half-and-half or milk

1¼ cups all-purpose flour

For the Macadamia Filling, melt the butter and cool. Whisk the flour, sugar and brown sugar together in a large bowl or use an electric mixer. Add the corn syrup, molasses, vanilla and melted butter; mix well. Whisk in the eggs until incorporated. Stir in the nuts. (This can be prepared ahead and set aside at cool room temperature for several hours or refrigerated. Bring to room temperature before using.)

For the Basic Tart Crust dough, cream the butter using an electric mixer. Beat in the salt and sugar. Stir in the cream and ⅕ of the flour. Add the remaining flour and mix it in with your fingertips or a fork until ingredients are combined. Turn the dough out onto a piece of plastic wrap and shape into a flat disk. Wrap and refrigerate for at least 1 hour. (This can be prepared 1 day ahead.)

To form the crust, butter a 10-inch tart pan with a removable bottom. Roll the dough out between 2 large sheets of plastic wrap into an 11-inch circle. Remove the top sheet of plastic. Invert into the prepared pan. Trim and finish the edges. Cover and refrigerate for at least 1 hour.

To bake, preheat the oven to 350°F. Line the tart with parchment paper or aluminum foil and fill with beans or pie weights. Bake until the crust is firm and set, for about 15 minutes. Remove the beans and paper. Prick the bottom of the crust so it does not puff. Continue baking until well browned, for 10 to 15 minutes. Fill the tart with the Macadamia Filling, smoothing the top. Return to the oven and bake until the tart is set and cracks, for about 30 minutes. Cool completely in the tart pan on a rack.

To serve, remove the tart ring. Cut 6 to 8 wedges and transfer to dessert plates. Serve immediately.

Orange Spice Tart

Planning Ahead

The Cinnamon Crust can be mixed up to 2 days in advance. The crust can be rolled out and prebaked and the Orange Filling prepared at any time during the day the tart is to be served. Fill the tart and bake completely several hours before presenting.

Technique Tips

If the dough is too firm to roll, let sit for about 15 minutes at room temperature.

For 2 large sheets of plastic to roll the dough between, cut open 2 plastic produce bags.

If more convenient, bake the crust completely earlier in the day and set aside on a rack. Fill and bake 3 to 4 hours before serving. If the tart is filled and baked more than several hours ahead, it will become soggy.

If the oranges are not very sweet, add to the filling additional sugar to taste.

This is the second recipe I developed for the book using oranges with a cinnamony linzer-style dough. My reasons for doing so are twofold: First, the freshness and harmony of the Orange Caramel Sauce was so extraordinary in contrast to the Blackberry Fig Tartlets, my first combo (page 332), that I wanted to repeat this success. Second, I think there is no better way to learn about the subtle nuances and possibilities of ingredients than to experience the same ones differently.

In the tartlets, the crust is more like a cookie and the orange the flavoring base of a pureed sauce, whereas here I have used both items in a more conventional preparation that allows the fruit to shine: a tart. Being a perfectionist, I segmented the oranges to remove all trace of membrane. If, however, you want to trade speed for perfection, just slice the oranges into rounds.

CINNAMON CRUST

6 tablespoons sugar

⅓ cup pistachios

1¼ teaspoons ground cinnamon

1¼ cups all-purpose flour

5 ounces (1¼ sticks) chilled unsalted butter, coarsely chopped

3 tablespoons water

ORANGE FILLING

7 large oranges

1 cup orange juice

2 tablespoons freshly squeezed lemon juice

¼ cup heavy cream

½ cup sugar

2 tablespoons Grand Marnier or other orange liqueur

3 large eggs

For the Cinnamon Crust, mix the sugar, pistachios, cinnamon and flour in a food processor until the nuts are finely ground, pulsing on/off. Add the butter and process until it is the texture of coarse meal. Add the water and process until the mixture is just crumbly and moistened, but has not formed a ball. Turn the dough out onto a piece of plastic wrap, shape into a flat disk, wrap and refrigerate for at least 1 hour. (This can be prepared up to 2 days ahead.)

Butter a 10-inch tart pan with a removable bottom. Roll the dough out between 2 large sheets of plastic wrap into an 11-inch circle. Remove the top sheet of plastic. Invert into the prepared pan. Trim and finish the edges. Cover and refrigerate for at least 1 hour.

For the Orange Filling, holding the oranges over a bowl 1 at a time, cut off the peel and white pith in 1 large corkscrew strip by starting at the top of the orange and cutting down and around using a small sharp knife. Cut between the coarse whitish membranes to remove each segment, letting the segments fall into the bowl. Squeeze the juice from the membranes into the bowl; discard membranes. (This can be prepared ahead and set aside at room temperature.)

Whisk the orange juice, lemon juice, sugar, Grand Marnier and eggs together in a second medium bowl until blended. (This can be prepared ahead, covered and set aside at cool room temperature for several hours or refrigerated until 2 hours before baking.)

To bake, preheat the oven to 350°F. Prick the tart all over with a fork and bake until well browned, for about 40 minutes. Check the oven occasionally while baking and prick the crust as necessary if it puffs; push edges up if they fall. Remove tart from the oven.

Drain the orange segments well and arrange them in concentric circles in the crust. Pour over the orange juice mixture. Return to a 350°F oven. Bake until the filling is almost set and barely moves when the pan is shaken, for about 25 to 30 minutes. Transfer to a rack and cool several hours until tepid.

To serve, remove the tart ring and cut 6 to 8 wedges. Transfer to dessert plates. Serve immediately.

Variation

To glaze the tart, preheat the broiler and sprinkle the tart generously with confectioners' sugar as soon as it is baked. Broil as close to the heat source as possible until the sugar melts and caramelizes, watching carefully.

Chocolate Chestnut Tart

6 Servings

Planning Ahead

The Chestnut Filling can be prepared 1 or 2 days in advance. The Chocolate Crust can be mixed several hours before baking. Bake the tart several hours before serving.

Technique Tips

If the dough is too firm to roll, let sit for about 15 minutes at room temperature.

For 2 large sheets of plastic to roll the dough between, cut open 2 plastic produce bags.

If more convenient, bake the crust completely earlier in the day and set aside on a rack. Fill and bake 3 to 4 hours before serving.

Although fresh chestnuts are not used for this tart, I will give you an invaluable tip for working with whole chestnuts so you won't have to fight with peeling them any longer. Simply deep fry the unpeeled chestnuts in a pot of oil heated to 350°F until they pucker and their shells practically fall off by themselves, for about 3 minutes.

Crème de marrons (cream of chestnuts) can be found in the baking or gourmet section of many supermarkets and specialty grocers.

I still remember the aroma of chestnuts roasting on the corner near my schoolyard. It was cold and dark by five o'clock when I departed for home, and the fabulous smell of the chestnuts warmed me up and made me feel good. Every day I stopped by the brazier to hold my hands in front of the sparkling fire, but I never bought any chestnuts because the old man roasting them had burned, scary fingers.

I roast whole chestnuts at home today in my fireplace for a snack or to mix with sausage to stuff my turkey. I braise them, too, as a side dish to accompany game and poultry. My family likes them any way they can get them, but guests aren't always so enthusiastic. Perhaps they find them too rustic and heavy. Their reaction changes completely, though, when I combine the tinned chestnut cream with chocolate for a flavor and texture similar to that of *gianduja*, the Italian chocolate-hazelnut paste.

CHESTNUT FILLING

4 ounces bittersweet or semisweet chocolate

5 ounces *crème de marrons* (cream of chestnuts)

1 tablespoon rum

1 teaspoon vanilla

¼ cup sugar

¾ cup milk

2 eggs

CHOCOLATE CRUST

½ cup (1 stick) unsalted butter, at room temperature

⅓ cup sugar

1 small egg

Pinch of salt

1¼ cups all-purpose flour

2 tablespoons cocoa powder

2 teaspoons baking powder

Lightly sweetened whipped cream with rum

Whole candied chestnuts (optional)

For the Chestnut Filling, melt the chocolate in the top of a double boiler above gently simmering water. Cool until tepid.

Process the melted chocolate with the *crème de marrons* in a food processor until mixed and smooth, pulsing on/off. Add the rum, vanilla and sugar. Process until well mixed. Mix the milk and eggs in a 2-cup glass measure. With the machine running, gradually pour in the milk mixture. Continue processing until well mixed, stopping to scrape down the sides of the container. (This can be prepared ahead and set aside at cool room temperature for several hours or refrigerated for several days. Bring to room temperature before using.)

For the Chocolate Crust, cream the butter and sugar using an electric mixer on medium speed until smooth. Beat in the egg and salt. Sift the flour, cocoa and baking powder together. Add ⅓ of the flour mixture and stir until barely incorporated. Add the remaining flour mixture and stir on low speed until just incorporated. (Dough will be soft and sticky.) Scrape the dough out onto a piece of plastic wrap. Flour hands lightly and shape into a flat disk. Wrap in plastic. Refrigerate for about 1 hour.

Lightly butter a 9-inch tart pan with a removable bottom. Roll the dough out between 2 large sheets of plastic wrap ⅛ inch thick. Remove the top sheet of plastic. Invert into the tart pan. Trim and finish the edges. Cover and refrigerate for 1 hour.

To bake, preheat the oven to 350°F. Prick the tart with a fork and bake for 20 minutes to firm the crust, pushing up edges if they fall. Pour the filling into the tart; smooth the top. Bake until puffed and a knife tip inserted into the center comes out clean, for about 35 to 40 minutes. Cool completely on a rack.

To serve, decorate with whipped cream and candied chestnuts. Cut 6 wedges and transfer to dessert plates. Serve immediately.

Blackberry Fig Tartlets
with Orange Caramel Sauce

6 Servings

Planning Ahead

The Orange Caramel Sauce, Fig Puree and dough for Cinnamon Cookies can be prepared 2 to 3 days in advance. The cookies can be rolled and cut 1 day in advance of baking and baked at any time during the day the dessert is to be served. Assemble just before presenting.

Technique Tip

If the dough is too firm to roll, let sit for about 15 minutes at room temperature.

Variation

This tartlet dough (or any scraps of dough from cutting circles) can also be used to make cookies. Roll the dough up into a 1- to 1½-inch diameter log, wrap in plastic and refrigerate for at least 1 hour or up to 2 days. Cut the cookies ¼ inch thick and arrange on parchment-lined baking sheets, leaving about 1½ inches between each cookie. Sprinkle with confectioners' sugar. Bake and cool as directed above. Store in an airtight container.

If you have some fig puree left over, use it for your breakfast toast.

T he idea for this dessert started with a Linzer Torte. I have always liked its spicy crust, but the edges are too thick for me and its raspberry jam filling too sweet. For my tartlets, I've fashioned a rimless crust or cookies. Made much more simply, they contain less cinnamon so as not to overwhelm other flavors. On top, I've spread a dried fig puree to contrast with the fresh berries arranged above it. My Orange Caramel Sauce replaces the ubiquitous raspberry puree being poured indiscriminately over everything.

You have it in a pistachio shell: Individual tartlets that more or less taste like a Linzer Torte but look like a California sunset. A finale for the most spectacular occasion that takes little time to produce. If you're thinking of adding a scoop of vanilla ice cream to this glamorous kaleidoscope of taste and texture, don't hesitate for one moment.

Orange Caramel Sauce (page 334)

FIG PUREE

7 (about 3 ounces) dried figs, stemmed

About 3 tablespoons water

CINNAMON COOKIES

⅔ cup sugar

½ cup pistachios

2 teaspoons ground cinnamon

2 cups all-purpose flour

8 ounces (2 sticks) chilled unsalted butter, chopped

1 chilled egg, blended with fork

3 (½ pint each) baskets blackberries or raspberries

8 fresh figs, quartered

Confectioners' sugar

Prepare the Orange Caramel Sauce. Refrigerate until 30 minutes before serving. (This can be prepared 2 days ahead.)

For the Fig Puree, process the figs in a food processor until minced, pulsing on/off. With the machine running, pour in the water 1 tablespoon at a time, until the puree is a smooth paste and of spreading consistency, stopping to scrape down the sides of the container. Transfer to a covered container. (This can be prepared ahead and set aside at cool room temperature for 1 day or refrigerated for several days. Bring to room temperature before using.)

For the Cinnamon Cookies, process the sugar, pistachios, cinnamon and flour in a food processor until the nuts are finely ground, pulsing on/off. Add the butter and process until mixture is the texture of coarse meal. Add the egg and process until just crumbly and moistened, but not yet a ball. If too dry, add water as necessary, 1 tablespoon at a time. Turn out onto a piece of plastic wrap and form into a flat rectangle. Wrap and refrigerate for at least 1 hour. (This can be prepared 2 days ahead.)

To form the cookies, line 2 large baking sheets with parchment paper. Roll the dough out into a 12- × 16-inch rectangle about ¼ inch thick between 2 large pieces of plastic wrap. Cut out six 5-inch circles using a sharp floured cutter. Transfer the cookies to 1 baking sheet using a large spatula. Cover with plastic wrap. Refrigerate for at least 1 hour. (This can be prepared to this point 1 day ahead.)

To bake the cookies, preheat the oven to 350°F with 1 rack in the upper part of the oven and 1 rack in the lower part. Transfer half of the cookies to the second prepared baking sheet, spacing evenly. Bake until golden brown, for 15 to 20 minutes, switching positions of the baking sheets in the oven halfway. Cool completely on baking sheets. Gently slide a spatula under the cookies to loosen them and transfer to racks in a single layer.

To serve, gently spread cookies with Fig Puree. Transfer to 6 large plates. Arrange berries and figs on top of the cookies. Sprinkle confectioners' sugar on top of the berries. Ladle Orange Caramel Sauce around cookies. Serve immediately.

Orange Caramel Sauce

Makes About 2 Cups

Planning Ahead

The sauce can be prepared several days in advance. If preparing the day of serving, allow at least 4 to 6 hours for it to chill.

Technique Tip

When caramelizing sugar, cook it over low heat until sugar dissolves or the mixture may crystallize.

his zesty sauce is also good over ice cream sundaes, cream puffs, soufflés or fruit. Use it as well as a base for a fruit soup.

I orange

½ cup sugar

2 cups (about 6 to 9 large oranges) orange juice

2 tablespoons freshly squeezed lemon juice

I tablespoon cornstarch

2 tablespoons Grand Marnier or other orange liqueur or brandy

Remove the orange part of the peel only using a vegetable peeler. Fill a heavy medium saucepan with water and bring to a boil. Add the peel. Simmer for 5 minutes. Transfer the peel with ¼ cup cooking water to a blender. Discard the remaining cooking water. Process until the peel is minced, pulsing on/off.

Return the minced peel mixture to the saucepan. Add the sugar. Cook over low heat until the sugar dissolves, swirling the pan occasionally. Increase heat and boil until the mixture caramelizes and turns deep brown. Standing back to avoid splatter, pour in the orange and lemon juices. Bring to a simmer and stir until sugar crystals dissolve and the sauce is smooth. Mix the cornstarch with the Grand Marnier, add to the sauce and boil for I minute. Cool. Strain into a container through a fine sieve. Cover and refrigerate until well chilled, for about 4 to 6 hours. (This can be prepared 2 days ahead. Remove from the refrigerator 30 minutes to I hour before serving.)

Crème Brûlée Napoleon
with Hazelnuts

8 Servings

This is the most popular dessert at Citrus. Its success does not come as a total surprise to me, for it is the ultimate napoleon. Made without flour, its Crème Brûlée filling is lighter and more refined than the pastry cream classically used. Studded with chopped caramelized hazelnuts, its filo dough layers are even crisper and crunchier than the puff pastry traditionally sandwiching the creamy interior. Unlike puff pastry, filo dough doesn't shrink.

I've used Caramel Sauce here, but the vanilla base of the filling lends itself to any flavoring or fruit accompaniment. This spectacular dessert offers an advantage to the home cook as well in that it does not require a *Grande Diplôme de Pâtisserie* to execute. Though its multiple components may make it appear complicated, steps are simple. Everything except assembling the layers can be completed in advance.

Crème Brûlée (page 336)

Caramel Sauce (page 337)

1 cup hazelnuts

¾ cup sugar

8 sheets filo dough, defrosted overnight in refrigerator if frozen

½ cup (1 stick) unsalted butter, melted

About ½ cup confectioners' sugar

Prepare the Crème Brûlée and Caramel Sauce up to 2 days in advance and refrigerate.

For the hazelnuts, preheat the oven to 350°F. Place the hazelnuts on a small baking sheet and toast until brown, for about 15 minutes. Rub the nuts in a sieve or towel to remove their husks. Grind the nuts coarsely with the sugar in a food processor, pulsing on/off. (This can be prepared ahead, transferred to an airtight container and set aside at room temperature.)

For the pastry, preheat the oven to 300°F. Line 2 large baking sheets with parchment paper. Remove filo from its package and unroll. Remove 1 sheet and cover the remaining filo with plastic and a damp towel. Brush the sheet with melted butter and sprinkle generously with the hazelnut-sugar mixture. Top with the second sheet of filo, pressing to seal. Brush with butter and sprinkle with the nut mixture. Repeat with the third and fourth sheets.

(continued)

Planning Ahead
The Crème Brûlée, Caramel Sauce and hazelnut-sugar mixture can be prepared 2 days in advance. The filo dough squares can be baked at any time during the day the dessert is to be served. Assemble the napoleons just before presenting.

Filo dough is less brittle and likely to tear if it has not been frozen. Though harder to find, unfrozen filo dough can often be purchased at a Middle Eastern market.

When working with filo dough, keep unused pieces wrapped in plastic and covered with a damp towel so they don't dry out.

Using a ruler as a guide, trim the edges with a knife or pastry wheel to form a 12- × 16-inch rectangle. Cut the pastry into 3 strips lengthwise and 4 strips crosswise, forming twelve 4-inch squares. Transfer the squares to the prepared baking sheets in a single layer using a large spatula. Bake until brown, for about 10 minutes.

Make and bake 12 additional 4-inch squares using 4 more sheets of filo and the remaining butter and nut mixture. Rewrap the remaining filo and refrigerate or freeze for another use.

Preheat the broiler. Place as many filo squares as will fit under the broiler at one time on a baking sheet. Sieve confectioners' sugar generously over the squares and broil several inches below the heat source until golden brown, for about 1 minute, watching carefully. Transfer to racks in a single layer. Repeat with remaining squares. (This can be prepared ahead.)

To serve, divide the Crème Brûlée among 16 pastry squares, nut side up, spreading evenly. Make 8 napoleons by stacking 2 Crème Brûlée-filled squares and topping with 1 unfilled square, nut side up. Place the napoleons in the centers of 8 large plates. Reheat the Caramel Sauce and ladle around the napoleons. Serve immediately.

Makes About 2½ Cups

CRÈME BRÛLÉE

½ cup milk

2 cups heavy cream

½ cup sugar

1 to 2 vanilla beans, slit lengthwise

9 room temperature egg yolks, blended with fork

Technique Tip

Adjust the heat so the water bath does not go above a gentle simmer. If the water boils, the custard can curdle.

Place the milk, cream and sugar in a heavy medium saucepan. Scrape the seeds from the vanilla beans into the milk mixture. Add the beans and bring to a boil over medium-high heat. Remove from heat and let beans steep for at least 1 hour or until the mixture cools to room temperature. Discard beans (or wash, dry and reserve them for another use).

Preheat the oven to 300°F. Place a 9- × 13-inch baking dish in a larger baking pan. Pour enough water into the larger pan to come ¾ of the way up the sides of the baking dish. Remove the baking dish and place the baking pan with water in the oven to preheat for about 15 minutes.

Whisk the egg yolks into the cooled custard mixture. Strain through a fine sieve into the baking dish. Place the dish in the baking pan with water and bake until the custard is set and a knife inserted into the center comes out dry, for about 45 minutes to 1 hour. Remove the baking dish from the water bath. Cool, cover and refrigerate until 15 minutes before assembling the napoleons. (This can be prepared 2 days ahead.)

CARAMEL SAUCE

1½ cups sugar

Water

1¼ cups heavy cream

Place the sugar in a heavy medium saucepan. Cover with water and cook over low heat until the sugar dissolves, swirling the pan occasionally. Increase the heat and boil until the sugar caramelizes and turns a deep mahogany brown, watching carefully so the mixture doesn't burn. Standing back to avoid splatter, gradually pour in the cream. Simmer the sauce, stirring occasionally, until the caramel dissolves and the sauce is smooth and thick, for about 3 minutes. Cool, cover and refrigerate. (This can be prepared 2 days ahead.)

To serve, stir over medium heat until melted and warm, thinning with additional cream or milk as desired.

Variation

This sauce can also be served cold. Thin it with additional cream or milk.

Filo Apple Crowns
with Cinnamon Custard

4 Servings

Planning Ahead

The Cinnamon Custard can be made 1 day in advance. If preparing the day it is to be served, allow at least 4 to 6 hours for it to chill. The filo can be baked and the apples caramelized at any time during the day the dessert is to be consumed. Assemble the Crowns just before presenting.

Technique Tips

When cooking the Cinnamon Custard, adjust heat to keep it below a simmer. If the mixture boils, it can curdle.

Filo dough is less brittle and likely to tear if it has not been frozen. Though harder to find, unfrozen filo dough can often be purchased at a Middle Eastern market.

When working with filo dough, keep unused pieces wrapped in plastic and covered with a damp towel so they don't dry out.

When caramelizing sugar, cook it over low heat until the sugar dissolves or the mixture may crystallize.

Pastry, caramel and apples are the most compatible of bedfellows. The key to their alliance in this ménage à trois—two crunchy filo crowns sandwiching caramelized fruit—is a crisp crust. The typical French fruit tart, soggy from juices and an uncooked doughy center, has never worked for me. It is, instead, the toothsome crust of a tarte Tatin or deep dish pie, hovering smugly above the fruit, that I seek. Additional texture and bite are achieved here by scrunching the filo dough so it looks somewhat like a moon crater. This dessert's overall effect is other-worldly, too. The comments I hear most frequently are ''awesome'' and ''spectacular.'' The best news is it's no trouble or fuss to get it this way.

CINNAMON CUSTARD

> 1 cup heavy cream
>
> 2 tablespoons sugar
>
> 2-inch cinnamon stick
>
> 2 room temperature egg yolks, blended with fork
>
> 2 tablespoons dark rum

FILO PASTRY

> 5 ounces (1¼ sticks) unsalted butter, melted
>
> 5 tablespoons sugar
>
> 4 sheets filo dough, defrosted overnight in refrigerator if frozen

CARAMELIZED APPLES

> 3 ounces (¾ stick) unsalted butter
>
> ⅓ cup sugar
>
> 1 pound (4 medium) Pippin or Granny Smith apples, peeled, quartered, cored and cut into ⅜-inch-thick slices

For the Cinnamon Custard, mix the cream with the sugar in a heavy small saucepan. Add the cinnamon stick and bring to a boil. Remove from heat and let sit for 1 hour. Slowly whisk the yolks into the cream mixture. Add the rum. Stir over medium-low heat using a wooden spatula until the sauce has thickened enough to leave a path when a finger is drawn across the spatula. Strain the sauce through a fine sieve into a bowl. Discard the cinnamon stick. Cool to room temperature, then cover and refrigerate until chilled, for about 4 to 6 hours. (This can be prepared 1 day ahead.)

For the Filo Pastry, preheat the oven to 350°F. Line 2 large baking sheets with parchment paper. Trace four 4-inch circles in heavy ink on each sheet. Invert the parchment paper. If the circles are not visible, redraw them so they are. Brush inside of the circles lightly with melted butter and sprinkle with about 1 tablespoon sugar total. Remove filo from the package and unroll it. Remove 1 sheet and cover the remaining filo with plastic and a damp towel. Brush the sheet with melted butter and sprinkle with 1 tablespoon sugar. Cut the sheet in half crosswise. Turn one of the ½ filo sheets over (buttered sugared side down) and crumple it until it conforms to the contours of one 4-inch circle on the parchment. Place on a circle. Crumple the second half of filo sheet and place on another circle in the same manner. Repeat the process with the remaining 3 filo sheets. Rewrap the remaining filo dough and refrigerate or freeze for another use. Press the filo circles down gently to flatten them. Bake until golden brown, for about 15 minutes. Transfer to a rack sugar side up. (This can be prepared ahead and set aside at room temperature.)

For the Caramelized Apples, melt the butter in a heavy large nonstick skillet over low heat. Add the sugar and stir until dissolved. Add the apples, increase heat to medium-high and cook until just tender and caramelized, for about 15 minutes. (This can be prepared ahead, cooled, covered and set aside at room temperature.)

To serve, place 1 round of pastry, sugar side down, on each plate. Overlap ¼ of the apples on top of the pastry. Top with another round of pastry, sugar side up. Ladle Cinnamon Custard around the pastry. Serve immediately.

Apple Crêpes Flambées

4 to 6 Servings

Planning Ahead

The crêpes can be completely prepared and frozen several months in advance. The apple mixture can be cooked, the sauce prepared and the crêpes filled 1 day before serving. Bake crêpes just before presenting.

Technique Tip

Although it is not dangerous, it can be frightening to flame a dish on top of the stove. To do it more comfortably, hold the lit match with tongs and stand back.

O n Mardi Gras, crêpes are traditionally prepared in France according to this ritual: You hold a golden coin in one hand and make a wish. With the other hand, you flip the crêpe by tilting the skillet and jerking the wrist. If you flip your crêpe perfectly, your wish will come true.

In our household, it was a very special fiesta day whenever my mother tackled crêpes. We would take turns flipping, so there were crêpes flying all over and sticking to the ceiling. We worked at this for hours, yet the plate was always empty. With five hungry, sneaky children, it took forever to accumulate a stack. When we finally finished a pile of crêpes, my mother put them on the table with a variety of jams, fresh fruits, ice creams and toppings and everyone chose his favorite filling. It was a big family celebration and the ambiance was great. In France, we really love to cook for family and friends.

You can fill your crêpes as my family did or prepare the apple filling below that is typical of Brittany. As far as flipping goes, it is perfectly acceptable to turn the crêpes with your fingers. Just don't make a wish beforehand.

12 Crêpes (page 342)

APPLES

> 2 ounces (½ stick) unsalted butter
>
> 3½ to 3¾ pounds (about 10 large) Pippin or Granny Smith apples, peeled, quartered, cored and cut into ⅜-inch-thick slices
>
> ½ cup sugar
>
> 3 tablespoons dark rum

APPLESAUCE

> 1¼ cups (about) unsweetened hard or soft apple cider or unsweetened apple juice
>
> 3 tablespoons (1½ ounces) unsalted butter, melted
>
> 2 tablespoons sugar
>
> ½ cup heavy cream, whipped (optional garnish)

Prepare the crêpes. (This can be prepared ahead, covered and set aside at room temperature for several hours, refrigerated for several days or wrapped in freezer paper and frozen for several months. Defrost in the refrigerator before continuing.)

For the apples, melt the butter in a heavy large nonstick skillet over medium heat. Add the apples, sprinkle with sugar and cook until tender when pierced with a knife, for about 15 to 17 minutes, stirring frequently. Increase heat at the end to evaporate any liquid. Pour rum into the corner of the pan, heat briefly and carefully ignite. Stir to distribute the flame.

To assemble the crêpes, butter a large baking dish. Using ½ of the cooked apples, form a log down 1 side of 12 crêpes, ½ inch in from the bottom edge. Fold bottom crêpe edge over the apples and roll up like a jelly roll, folding in sides. Place the crêpes seam side down in a single layer in the prepared dish. (This can be prepared ahead, covered with aluminum foil and set aside at cool room temperature for several hours or refrigerated overnight. Bring to room temperature before baking.)

For the applesauce, transfer the remaining ½ of the cooked apples to a food processor with the cider. Process until completely smooth, pulsing on/off and stopping to scrape down the sides of the container. Add more cider as necessary for a saucelike consistency. Taste and adjust sweetness and rum as desired. Strain the sauce through a fine sieve if desired. (The applesauce can be prepared ahead and set aside at room temperature or refrigerated. Remove from refrigerator several hours ahead to serve at room temperature or 1 hour ahead to serve slightly chilled.)

To serve, preheat the oven to 425°F and preheat the broiler. Brush the crêpes with butter and sprinkle with sugar. Re-cover and bake until heated through, for 5 to 7 minutes. Turn the oven up to broil. Uncover and brown slightly under broiler, watching carefully. Ladle the applesauce into the center of 6 plates, tilting the plate so the sauce spreads evenly. Transfer 2 crêpes seam side down to the center of each plate using a large spatula.

To decorate the plates, place whipped cream in a pastry bag fitted with a ½-inch plain tip. Pipe decorative dots of cream in a circle around the crêpes. Drag a knife tip through each circle, forming a tail that connects 1 circle with the next.

Crêpes

Makes About 16
7-inch Crêpes

1 cup all-purpose flour

1 tablespoon sugar

1⅓ cups milk, at room temperature

2 eggs, at room temperature

2 ounces (½ stick) unsalted butter

Planning Ahead

The batter can be prepared 2 days in advance of making the crêpes. The crêpes can be cooked 2 to 3 days before serving and refrigerated for several months before serving and frozen.

Technique Tips

Fruit juice can be substituted for some of the liquid in the batter.

The heat for cooking crêpes must be hot enough for the crêpes to cook in 1 to 2 minutes per side and for the bottom of the first side to come out mottled and brown with pronounced ridges before flipping, but not so hot that the crêpes burn. Adjust the heat as necessary between medium-high and high. A lower heat will not brown the crêpe properly.

Many recipes call for stacking crêpes with a piece of plastic wrap, waxed paper or parchment paper in between. I've never found this necessary—even when making crêpes ahead—as long as I carefully peel each crêpe off the pile one at a time.

For the crêpe batter, mix the flour and sugar in a large bowl. Whisk in about ⅓ cup milk or enough to make a thick, smooth paste. Gradually whisk in the remaining milk. Whisk in the eggs and stir until smooth. Strain through a fine sieve if any lumps remain. Let rest at room temperature for at least 1 hour. (This can be prepared 2 days ahead, covered and refrigerated. Bring to room temperature before cooking.)

To cook the crêpes, melt the butter in a 6- or 7-inch crêpe pan or nonstick skillet. Pour into a small glass and let cool to tepid. Spoon off the surface foam. Whisk 1 tablespoon of the butter into the batter.

Heat the crêpe pan over medium-high heat. Remove from heat and brush lightly with melted butter. Working quickly, ladle about 3 tablespoons of batter into the corner of the pan. Tilt the pan until the bottom is covered with a thin layer of batter; pour any excess batter back into the bowl.

Return the crêpe pan to medium-high heat. Cook several seconds or until the bottom is brown, releasing the crêpe from the pan with a small metal spatula. Flip the crêpe or turn it over using your fingers or a spatula. Cook until the second side is brown. Slide out onto a plate. Repeat with the remaining batter, stacking the crêpes. Stir the batter occasionally and brush the pan with butter between every 1 or 2 crêpes as necessary. (This can be prepared ahead, cooled, covered and set aside at room temperature for several hours, refrigerated for several days or wrapped in freezer paper and frozen for several months.)

To serve unfilled, preheat the oven to 350°F. Wrap the crêpes in aluminum foil and bake for 10 to 15 minutes or until warm.

Cherry Almond Financier

6 to 8 Servings

In France, the topping for this fruit dessert is baked into tiny cakes called *financiers*. These were very inexpensive in olden days when I was young—particularly if they were day-old—so I could often be found nibbling on one after school. I always liked the flavor of these almond sweets, but I thought they were a bit too dry, which is why I added cherries here. This fruit is so delicious fresh and its season so short that I am always on the lookout for new ways to use it.

This Cherry Almond Financier reminds me of a *clafouti*, the crêpe batter studded with fruit and baked into a pancake. Like a *clafouti*, this mixture makes a delicious main-course brunch dish as well as a rustic dessert or tea cake.

Planning Ahead

The nuts, flour and sugar can be mixed and ground and the cherries pitted at any time during the day the Cherry Almond Financier is to be served. Bake just before presenting.

5 ounces (1¼ sticks) unsalted butter

1½ to 1¾ pounds fresh cherries, pitted

1 cup whole blanched almonds

½ cup all-purpose flour

1⅓ cups confectioners' sugar

5 (scant ⅔ cup) egg whites, at room temperature

¼ teaspoon cream of tartar

¼ cup sugar

About 2 tablespoons kirsch (optional)

Confectioners' sugar

Lightly sweetened whipped cream or vanilla ice cream (optional)

For brown butter, melt the butter over low heat in a small skillet until brown, stirring occasionally. Cool to room temperature.

Preheat the oven to 350°F. Butter a 9- × 12-inch or 10-inch-round gratin dish. Arrange the cherries over the bottom of the dish in a single snug layer. Grind the almonds with the flour and confectioners' sugar in a food processor until reduced to a fine powder, pulsing on/off and stopping to scrape down the sides of the container. Transfer to a large bowl.

Beat the egg whites with the cream of tartar using an electric mixer until soft peaks form. Beat in ¼ cup sugar, 1 tablespoon at a time. Continue beating until stiff but not dry. Gently fold ½ of the whites into the nut mixture to lighten, then fold in the remaining whites. Fold in the cooled butter. Gently spread the mixture over the cherries, covering completely. Bake until puffed and brown, for about 15 to 20 minutes. Immediately spoon the optional kirsch over the dessert. Cool to tepid, for about 15 minutes. Sprinkle with confectioners' sugar. Cut 6 to 8 wedges and transfer to dessert plates. Serve immediately with whipped cream or ice cream, if desired.

Rum Spice Cake

Makes 1 Small Loaf Cake

Planning Ahead

This cake can be baked anytime during the day it is to be served. Once baked, it will keep nicely for several days.

Technique Tip

To cut a parchment or waxed paper liner for a loaf pan, tear off a piece of paper slightly larger than the bottom of the pan. Turn the pan over, place the paper over the bottom of the pan and cut the paper even with the bottom by brushing a knife edge around the bottom of the pan.

French fruit cakes contain very little fruit—and alcohol—compared with the dense, solid loaves Americans give each other at Christmastime (and often save until the following Christmas to pass on to someone else). When I had my bakery in Santa Fe, I sold a *gateaux aux fruits*, a sweet bread with raisins similar to panettone, that was frequently returned with the complaint that it didn't have enough fruit. Finally, I just stopped making it.

This Rum Spice Cake is based on the French cake made from spices and dried fruit called *pain d'épices*. Be forewarned, for it, too, is a lightweight when it comes to proportion of fruit. Its texture is light as well with the pleasing airiness of a soufflé or soft meringue. This gossamer quality may just be more popular in California than in New Mexico, for this cake has found great favor at Citronelle, where it is gobbled up at both breakfast and tea time.

¼ cup minced mixed dried fruits, such as apricots, raisins and figs

2 tablespoons almonds, toasted

2 tablespoons packed dark brown sugar

⅓ cup all-purpose flour

1 tablespoon baking powder

½ teaspoon ground cinnamon

1 ounce (¼ stick) unsalted butter, at room temperature

1 generous tablespoon honey

1 tablespoon dark rum

About 1 tablespoon orange juice

4 egg whites, at room temperature

¼ teaspoon cream of tartar

2 tablespoons confectioners' sugar

Confectioners' sugar

Cover the fruit with warm water in a small bowl and soak for 1 hour, stirring occasionally; drain.

Preheat the oven to 325°F. Line an 8- × 4-inch loaf pan with parchment or waxed paper. Process the almonds in a food processor with the brown sugar until finely ground, pulsing on/off. Add the drained fruit and process until finely minced, pulsing on/off. Add the flour, baking powder, cinnamon, butter, honey, rum and orange juice. Process until mixture is a smooth puree, pulsing on/off and stopping to scrape down the sides of the container, for about 3 minutes. If the mixture is too thick to puree, add additional orange juice, 1 tablespoon at a time. Transfer to a large bowl.

Beat the egg whites with the cream of tartar using an electric mixer until soft peaks form. Add confectioners' sugar, 1 tablespoon at a time, and beat until stiff but not dry. Gently fold ¼ of the beaten whites into the fruit mixture to lighten it, then fold in the remaining whites. Turn into the prepared loaf pan, smoothing the top. Bang lightly on a work surface to eliminate air bubbles. Bake until a toothpick inserted into the center comes out clean, for about 45 minutes. Cool completely on a rack.

To serve, run a knife around the edge of the pan to loosen the cake. Unmold onto a cake platter, dust with confectioners' sugar and cut into thin slices. Serve immediately. Wrap any leftover cake airtight and store at room temperature.

Apple Almond Upside-Down Cake

6 Servings

Planning Ahead

This cake can be completely baked several hours before serving. It is crisper if served the day it is baked, but it keeps nicely for several days thereafter.

Technique Tip

The cake must be unmolded 5 to 7 minutes after removing from the oven or the caramel will become too hard to unmold. If caramel remains in the pan, return to the oven to soften and then pour over the cake.

A t the risk of becoming boring, I must say again how much I like apples and caramel together. Initially, I wanted to use a sponge cake for the base here, but I found the almond paste contributed a terrific taste as well as a lighter, more pleasing texture. It is also less likely to become soggy. I use Pippin or Granny Smith apples because they not only hold their shape as Golden Delicious do, but they also pack a piquant, more complex flavor.

2 ounces (½ stick) chilled unsalted butter

½ cup sugar

1 pound (3 medium-large) Pippin or Granny Smith apples, peeled, quartered, cored and thinly sliced

2 ounces (½ stick) unsalted butter, at room temperature

4 ounces almond paste

2 large eggs, at room temperature

1 tablespoon Calvados or apple brandy (optional)

Vanilla ice cream or slightly sweetened whipped cream with Calvados (optional)

Preheat the oven to 375°F. Shave the chilled butter in very thin slices and distribute evenly over the bottom of a 9-inch-round tart pan with a removable bottom. Sprinkle the sugar over the butter. Starting at the outer edge of the pan, closely overlap the apples in concentric circles, forming a single layer. Bake 1 hour or until the apples are golden and the sugar starts to caramelize.

Meanwhile, beat the room temperature butter using an electric mixer until creamy. Add the almond paste and beat until smooth. Mix in the eggs just until blended; do not overbeat.

Spread the almond paste mixture evenly over the apples using a broad spatula. Bake until the almond mixture is golden brown, for about 30 more minutes. Drizzle with optional Calvados. Let rest for 5 minutes. Run a long narrow spatula around the rim of the pan. Remove the bottom of the pan. Run a spatula under the apples to free them. Invert onto a serving dish. Remove the pan. Remove any stuck apples or caramel with a knife and spread them on the cake. Serve warm or at room temperature.

To serve, cut 6 wedges with a serrated knife. Transfer to dessert plates with a spatula. Spoon vanilla ice cream or whipped cream next to the cake, if desired. Serve immediately.

Cover and store any leftover cake in the refrigerator, but bring to room temperature before serving.

Basque Custard Cookie Cake

E ating this cake is like listening to a few notes of an old song where a short refrain—or one bite—unleashes the floodgates of memory. From the time we were little kids through our teen-age years, this was the very dessert we would order at the pastry shop with a glass of orange juice. It's not much of a looker, but its rich gooey pastry cream and crunchy crust often bring tears to the eyes of one middle-aged man I know who is still a boy inside. The instructions for this assemblage, in actuality, a pastry cream wrapped in a crisp cookie that looks like a cake, may sound a little strange, but have faith, for it is very easy to do.

6 Servings

Planning Ahead

The pastry cream can be prepared a day in advance. Bake the cake several hours before serving. It is crisper if served the day it is baked, but it keeps nicely for several days thereafter.

PASTRY CREAM

> 2 cups milk
>
> Pinch of salt
>
> ¼ cup sugar
>
> 1 to 2 vanilla beans, slit lengthwise
>
> 4 egg yolks, at room temperature
>
> ¼ cup sugar
>
> ⅓ cup all-purpose flour

COOKIE DOUGH

> 2 ounces (¼ stick) unsalted butter, at room temperature
>
> 1 cup confectioners' sugar, sifted
>
> 3 (scant ⅓ cup) egg whites, at room temperature
>
> Generous ½ cup flour

For the pastry cream, place the milk, salt and sugar in a heavy medium saucepan. Scrape the seeds from the vanilla beans into the milk mixture. Add the beans and bring to a boil over medium-high heat. Remove from heat and let beans steep for at least 1 hour or until the mixture cools to room temperature. Discard the beans (or wash, dry and reserve them for another use).

Beat the yolks and ¼ cup sugar using an electric mixer until thick and pale lemon in color. Mix in the flour. Reheat the milk mixture and gradually beat it into the yolks. Return the mixture to the saucepan. Whisk over medium-high heat until the mixture comes to a boil and becomes very lumpy. Reduce heat to medium-low and whisk until smooth, for about 2 to 3 minutes. Press a sheet of plastic wrap onto the cream and place in the freezer while preparing the cookie dough. (This can be cooled and refrigerated overnight.)

(continued)

The batter used to make this cake is the same as the one used for Sesame Crisps (page 296). If you want to make both desserts simultaneously, double the dough here and use half for Basque Cake as described above and half for a half-recipe of Sesame Crisps. Add ½ teaspoon Oriental (toasted) sesame oil to the batter for the Crisps and proceed with both recipes.

Pressing plastic directly on top of the custard prevents a crust from forming.

For the cookie dough, preheat the oven to 350°F. Butter and flour a 9-inch-round tart pan with a removable bottom, shaking out the excess. Blend the butter and sugar using an electric mixer. With the machine running at medium speed, pour in the whites a little at a time until incorporated. Mix in the flour to form a soft dough. Spoon enough of the dough into the bottom of the prepared pan to form a ⅛-inch-thick layer, pressing with your fingers. Bake for 10 minutes.

Spread the pastry cream evenly over the baked layer, leaving a ½-inch border around the outside edge. Spoon the remaining cookie dough over the chilled pastry cream and border, spreading evenly to the edge of the pan. Bake until golden brown, for about 25 to 35 minutes. Cool completely on a rack.

To serve, remove the cake from the pan and slice 6 wedges. Transfer to dessert plates. Serve immediately. Wrap and store any leftover cake in the refrigerator. Remove from the refrigerator at least 1 hour before serving.

Chocolate Peanut Crunch Bar Cake

8 Servings

Planning Ahead

The bars can be completely made several days in advance. If the cake is prepared the day it is to be served, allow at least 6 to 8 hours for it to set before presenting.

T his Chocolate Peanut Crunch Bar is really 70 percent confection and 30 percent cake, but no matter whether you consider it a candy or a dessert, it adds up to be 100 percent *formidable*. Composed of two intense layers, a bittersweet chocolate mousse astride a crunchy milk chocolate nut paste, this rich, bichocolate bar is deceptively tailored in appearance, but dramatic enough for the most magnificent occasion. I always worry about satisfying my guests, so on days I don't think two types of chocolate, peanut butter, cigarette cookies and cream are enough, I ladle a pool of Crème Anglaise, Cinnamon Custard (page 338) or Caramel Sauce (page 337) or Orange Caramel Sauce (page 334) around each serving.

The nut paste must be creamy to ensure that the milk chocolate layer doesn't become too hard. At the restaurant, we generally select a commercial hazelnut or praline product, but I've substituted peanut butter here because it is more readily available. I suspect that *crème de marrons*, Nutella or any smooth nut paste would work well, too.

MILK CHOCOLATE LAYER

7 ounces milk chocolate, coarsely chopped

6 ounces creamy peanut butter

2 tablespoons peanut oil

1¼ cups (about 3 ounces) purchased rolled cigarette or gaufrette cookies, coarsely crushed with hands or rolling pin

BITTERSWEET CHOCOLATE LAYER

5 ounces bittersweet chocolate, coarsely chopped

1¼ cups heavy cream

Cocoa powder

For the milk chocolate layer, line an 8-inch square pan with plastic wrap, leaving an overhang. Melt milk chocolate in the top of a double boiler above gently simmering water and whisk until smooth.

Beat the peanut butter and oil using an electric mixer until smooth. Mix in the milk chocolate and cookies until well blended. Pour into the prepared pan, smoothing the top with a spatula. Bang the pan on a work surface to even contents. Cover with plastic wrap and refrigerate until firm, for about 2 hours.

For the bittersweet chocolate layer, melt the bittersweet chocolate in the top of a double boiler above gently simmering water and whisk until smooth. Cool to tepid. Meanwhile, whip cream to soft peaks. Quickly fold ½ of whipped cream into the chocolate, then fold in the remainder. Pour over the firm, chilled milk chocolate layer. Spread with a spatula until smooth. Bang on a work surface to eliminate air bubbles. Cover with plastic wrap and refrigerate until firm, for about 4 to 6 hours. (This can be prepared several days ahead.)

To serve, remove from the refrigerator at least 1 hour before serving. Immediately lift the chocolate dessert out of the pan. Cut lengthwise into 1-inch-wide strips using a knife rinsed in hot water and dried, then cut each strip in half crosswise to form two 4- × 1-inch bars. Sieve cocoa powder over the tops of the bars. Place 2 bars on 8 plates, resting 1 edge of 1 bar dramatically atop the second bar. Let sit at room temperature about 1 hour before serving.

Technique Tips

The bittersweet chocolate should be neither too hot (or it will deflate the cream) nor too cold (or it will set into hard chips). *Just right* in this case is warm room temperature or tepid to the touch.

Whip the cream only to very soft peaks. If over-whipped, the texture of the mousse will be cottony. If time allows, try to make the cake 2 days in advance so the ingredients mellow; the key to optimum taste whenever the flavor is chocolate.

Variation

This confection can also be molded in a rectangular pastry form (about 14 × 4 inches) that is placed on a parchment-lined baking sheet. To free the chocolate confection when it is set, cut around the rim of form with a knife dipped in hot water and lift the ring off.

Desserts

Sauce Exchange

T hroughout the book, there are many salad dressings or vinaigrettes and sauces for main courses and desserts that have been paired with a particular dish that could be just as happily partnered with another offering. Sauces that can be most readily adapted to another preparation are listed here for easy reference.

Sauces for Salads and Cold Preparations

Sauces for Hot Foods

Dessert Sauces

Menu Suggestions

One-dish Meals

 little salad, a little bread . . . these are essentially one-dish meals and are substantial enough to be satisfying on their own.

Brunch

These simple brunches can be prepared either ahead or at the last minute, so you don't have to spend the entire morning in the kitchen. Also included is a brunch buffet for special occasions.

Smoked Fish and Mushroom Salad *(page 105)*
Scrambled Eggs and Oysters on the Half-shell
    (page 68)
Apple Rum Risotto *(page 314)*

Corn Pancakes *(page 273)*
Thousand-Layer Smoked Salmon Terrine with Caviar
    Sauce *(page 60)*
Brioche and Turkey Corn Dogs *(pages 80 and 194)*
Rum Spice Cake *(page 344)*

Brunch Buffet

Asparagus Frittata Terrine *(page 71)*
Thousand-Layer Smoked Salmon Terrine with Caviar
    Sauce *(page 60)*
Duck Salad with Citrus and Spice *(page 116)*
Eggs in a Hole *(page 70)*

Brioche Pillows with Basil Goat Cheese Filling
    (page 82)
Cherry Almond Financier *(page 343)*
Macadamia Nut Pie *(page 326)*

Meatless Menus

St. Tropez–Santa Fe Black Bean Soup with Basil
    (page 32)
Limestone Lettuce with Goat/Cheese/Cake, Croutons
    and Tomatoes *(page 92)*
Parmesan Génoise *(page 78)*
Chocolate-Vanilla Double-Dip Crème Brûlée *(page 316)*

Eggplant-Tomato Terrine with Parsley-Cilantro Sauce
    (page 46)
Brioche Pillows with Basil Goat Cheese Filling
    (page 82)
Coffee Chocolate Mousse *(page 313)*

Onion and Olive Tartlets *(page 53)*
Cream Cheese Gnocchi with Corn Spinach *(page 72)*
Chocolate Red Wine Soup with Strawberries
    (page 311)

Vine-Ripened Tomato Soup *(page 18)*
White Bean Belly Dancer Rolls and Avocado Salsa
    (pages 274 and 140)
Fresh Corn Polenta *(page 276)*
Apple Rum Risotto *(page 314)*

Sweet and Sour Corn Soup with Glazed Red Pepper
    (page 20)
Baked Brie Filo Bars with Mesclun and Hazelnuts
    (page 94)

Ratatouille Bisque *(page 24)*
Corn Pancakes *(page 273)*
Summer Tomato Tart with Basil Crust *(page 58)*
Malted Milk Ice Cream with Strawberry Cassis Sauce
    (page 304)

Cocktail Buffet

Make sure to invite good conversationalists so your guests don't spend the entire evening clustered around this irresistibly lavish buffet table.

Short Rib Terrine with Mustard Dressing *(page 206)*
Shrimp Porcupines *(page 130)*
Eggplant-Tomato Terrine with Parsley-Cilantro Sauce
    (page 46)
Summer Tomato Tart with Basil Crust *(page 58)*
Brioche Pillows with Basil Goat Cheese Filling *(page 82)*

Cream Puff Kisses *(page 77)*
Tuna Tartare Salad *(page 104)*
Chocolate Coconut *Tuiles*, Frozen Lemon Cheesecake,
    Hazelnut Graham Cracker Cookies, Macadamia
    Nut Pie, Chocolate Peanut Crunch Bar Cake,
    Orange Spice Tart *(pages 302, 307, 298, 326,
    348, and 328)*

Three-course Menus

Sunday suppers, outdoor summer luncheons, birthday dinners, entertaining-the-boss dinners—there's a menu here for every occasion, simple or fancy.

Duck *Ham* with Muscat and Farm Apples *(page 75)*
Leek and Potato Soup with Clams/Green Salad
   (page 26)
Chocolate Port Sorbet and Pistachio Lace Cookies
   (pages 303 and 297)

Lacy Cheese Chips *(page 76)*
Avocado Soup with Snapper Seviche *(page 22)*
Summer Apricot Pastries *(page 319)*

Artichokes Citronette *(page 43)*
Laurence's Fish Soup *(page 128)*
Macadamia Nut Pie *(page 326)*

Onion and Olive Tartlets *(page 53)*
Chicken, Mushroom and Barley Soup/Green Salad
   (page 35)
Apple Almond Upside-Down Cake *(page 346)*

Egg Roll Cups with Cheese Chive Filling *(page 52)*
Short Rib Stick-to-the-Rib Soup with Corn and Parsley
   Puree *(page 36)*
Old-Fashioned Apricot Oatmeal Bars or Apple Rum
   Risotto *(page 300 or 314)*

Goat/Cheese/Cake *(page 56)*
Super *Pistou* with Beef *(page 210)*
Blackberry Cobblettes *(page 318)*

Field Greens with Shrimp, Corn and Ginger *(page 96)*
Michel-Michel Shabu-Shabu *(page 208)*
Frozen Lemon Cheesecake and Hazelnut Graham
   Cracker Cookies *(pages 307 and 298)*

Ratatouille Bisque *(page 24)*
Baked Brie Filo Bars with Mesclun and Hazelnuts
   (page 94)
Cherry Almond Financier *(page 343)*

Lemon Soup with Mint and Couscous *(page 23)*
Crab Coleslaw *(page 98)*
Coffee Chocolate Mousse *(page 313)*

Corn Pancakes *(page 273)*
Smoked Salmon Soup with Eggs in a Hole
   (pages 28 and 70)
Rum Spice Cake *(page 344)*

Asparagus Frittata Terrine *(page 71)*
Marinated Salmon Trout with Warm Potato Salad
   (page 102)
Chocolate Red Wine Soup with Strawberries
   (page 311)

Spicy Thai Clams *(page 63)*
Chicken Medallions with Toasted Sesame Slaw
   (page 108)
Lemon Meringue Tart *(page 320)*

Summer Tomato Tart with Basil Crust *(page 58)*
Chicken and Green Bean Salad *(page 110)*
Coffee Chocolate Mousse *(page 313)*

Baked Brie Filo Bars with Mesclun and Hazelnuts
   (page 94)
Stir-fried Chicken and Vegetable Salad *(page 114)*
Orange Spice Tart *(page 328)*

Red Onion Upside-Down Tart *(page 54)*
Pepper-Pork Salad with Blood Oranges and Avocado
   (page 120)
Banana Colada Soup *(page 310)*

Ratatouille Bisque *(page 24)*
Lamb Salad with Watercress and New Potatoes
   (page 122)
Malted Milk Ice Cream with Strawberry Cassis Sauce
   and French *Brownies* *(pages 304 and 299)*

St. Tropez–Santa Fe Black Bean Soup with Basil
   (page 32)
Shrimp Porcupines *(page 130)*
Chayote with Mustard Mayonnaise *(page 42)*
Lemon Meringue Tart *(page 320)*

Lemon Soup with Mint and Couscous *(page 23)*
Scallop Asparagus Lollipops *(page 135)*
Potato Pancakes A.K.A. Latkes *(page 265)*
Frozen Apricot and Chocolate Dot Terrine *(page 308)*

Sweet and Sour Corn Soup with Glazed Red Pepper
    (page 20)
Rex and Lily Solewiches *(page 136)*
B.L.T. Potato Salad *(page 252)*
Cherry Almond Financier *(page 343)*

Quiche-in-a-Potato *(page 259)*
Sole with Avocado Salsa *(page 140)*
Macadamia Nut Pie *(page 326)*

Cream Cheese Gnocchi with Corn Spinach *(page 72)*
Steamed Red Snapper with Tomato Herb Sauce
    (page 138)
Mini Potatoes Alex Humbert *(page 261)*
Lemon Meringue Tart *(page 322)*

Baked Brie Filo Bars with Mesclun and Hazelnuts
    (page 94)
Mahi Mahi Rice Box *(page 144)*
Blackberry Fig Tartlets with Orange Caramel Sauce
    (page 332)

Corn Pancakes *(page 273)*
Salmon Steak 'n Eggs and Basolivaise Sauce
    (pages 146 and 64)
Potato Fettuccine with Tomato and Basil *(page 254)*
Rum Spice Cake and Fresh Fruit *(page 344)*

Onion and Olive Tartlets *(page 53)*
Salmon with Red Wine Shiitake Sauce *(page 148)*
Potato Pancakes A.K.A. Latkes *(page 265)*
Celery Crunch with Anise *(page 279)*
Chocolate Peanut Crunch Bar Cake *(page 348)*

Brioche Pillows with Basil Goat Cheese Filling
    (page 82)
Salmon with Onion Ringlets *(page 152)*
Baked Zucchini and Tomato Arènes de Nîmes
    (page
Macadamia Nut Pie *(page 326)*

Warm Asparagus with Tomato and Tarragon Sauce
    (page 44)
Tunaburgers *(page 156)*
Potato Gold Bricks *(page 269)*
Frozen Lemon Cheesecake *(page 307)*

Crab Coleslaw *(page 98)*
Tangy Chicken with Shiitake Crust *(page 172)*
Fresh Corn Polenta *(page 276)*
Crème Brûlée Napoleon with Hazelnuts *(page 335)*

Limestone Lettuce with Goat/Cheese/Cake, Croutons
    and Tomatoes *(page 92)*
Chicken Kataifi with Purple Sauce *(page 178)*
Parsnip Potato Puree *(page 255)*
Raisin Tart with Hot Buttered Rum Sauce *(page 322)*

Tuna Tartare Salad *(page 104)*
Chicken Vichyssoise *(page 174)*
Chocolate Peanut Crunch Bar Cake *(page 348)*

Asparagus Vichyssoise *(page 19)*
Coq au California *(page 182)*
Garlic Crème Brûlée *(page 282)*
Prune Tart with Almonds and Tea *(page 324)*

Brioche Rolls with Ratatouille *(page 84)*
Tuna with Broccoli and Anchovy Butter *(page 158)*
Baker's Memory Potatoes *(page 262)*
Frozen Lemon Cheesecake and Hazelnut Graham
    Cracker Cookies *(pages 307 and 298)*

Eggplant and Arugula Salad *(page 48)*
Tunados with White Bean Chili Sauce *(page 159)*
White Bean Belly Dancer Rolls *(page 274)*
Blackberry Fig Tartlets with Orange Caramel Sauce
    (page 332)

Shrimp Pastry Triangles with Garlic Butter *(page 55)*
Grilled Swordfish with Crispy Tomato Onion Relish
    (page 162)
Roasted Vegetable Medley *(page 288)*
Chocolate-Vanilla Double-Dip Crème Brûlée *(page 316)*

Field Greens with Shrimp, Corn and Ginger *(page 96)*
Chicken and Sweet Pea Ravioli *(page 168)*
Frozen Apricot and Chocolate Dot Terrine *(page 308)*

Menu Suggestions

Red Onion Upside-Down Tart *(page 54)*
Nonfried Fried Chicken Breasts with Mustard and
    Tarragon *(page 167)*
Bouillabaisse of Fennel *(page 284)*
Apple Rum Risotto *(page 314)*

Scallop and Celery Root Soup *(page 29)*
Chicken Mushroom Trilogy *(page 170)*
Mellow Spinach *(page 281)*
Apple Crêpes Flambées *(page 340)*

Mushroom Tarts with Garlic Cream *(page 50)*
A Chicken in Every Teapot with Vegetables
    (page 188)
Apple Almond Upside-down Cake *(page 346)*

Crab Brandade *(page 132)*
Roast Chicken with Garlic, Shallot and Potato
    (page 190)
Roasted Vegetable Medley *(page 288)*
Chocolate Chestnut Tart *(page 330)*

Beet and Cabbage Borscht *(page 31)*
Turkey Corn Dogs *(page 194)*
Frites *(page 264)*
Pistachio Lace Cookies and fresh fruit *(page 297)*

Asparagus Vichyssoise *(page 19)*
Roast Turkey Breast with Lemon and Thyme
    (page 196)
Fresh Corn Polenta *(page 276)*
Forest Mushrooms with Hazelnuts and Parsley
    (page 280)
Prune and Armagnac Ice Cream *(page 306)*

St. Tropez–Santa Fe Black Bean Soup with Basil
    (page 32)
Turkey à l'Orange *(page 195)*
Sweet Potato Puree with Prunes *(page 267)*
Chocolate Chestnut Tart *(page 330)*

Red Onion Upside-Down Tart *(page 54)*
Duck Crapaudine with Dried Cherries *(page 198)*
Celery Crunch with Anise *(page 279)*
Sweet Potatoes with Rosemary *(page 266)*
Basque Custard Cookie Cake *(page 347)*

Scallop Seviche with Carrots and Cumin *(page 66)*
Stuffed Napa Cabbage with Pork and Tomato Sauce
    (page 226)
Garlic Mashed Potatoes Ali-Bab *(page 256)*
Raisin Tart with Hot Buttered Rum Sauce *(page 322)*

Mussels with Basolivaise Sauce *(page 64)*
Rack of Lamb with Tomato Crust *(page 231)*
Glazed Turnip and Fava Bean Sauté *(page 286)*
Baker's Memory Potatoes *(page 262)*
Orange Spice Tart *(page 328)*

Moussaka with Scallops and Goat Cheese *(page 133)*
Farmhouse Leg of Lamb *(page 236)*
Red Square Potato Puree *(page 257)*
Baked Zucchini and Tomato Arènes de Nîmes
    (page 285)
Chocolate Peanut Crunch Bar Cake *(page 348)*

Summer Tomato Tart with Basil Crust *(page 58)*
Veal Chops Italian-style with Garlic, Rosemary and
    Parmesan *(page 242)*
Artichokes Citronette *(page 43)*
Mini Potatoes Alex Humbert *(page 261)*
Blackberry Fig Tartlets with Orange Caramel Sauce
    (page 332)

Tuna Tomato Tart *(page 154)*
Limestone Lettuce with Goat/Cheese/Cake, Croutons
    and Tomatoes *(page 92)*
Lamb Chops with Sweet Pea and Spinach *(page 230)*
Potato Risotto with Mushrooms *(page 260)*
Chocolate Peanut Crunch Bar Cake *(page 348)*

Shrimp Pastry Triangles with Garlic Butter *(page 55)*
Rabbit with Endive and Sage *(page 247)*
Cauliflower Cheese Gratin *(page 283)*
Macadamia Nut Pie *(page 326)*

Beet and Cabbage Borscht *(page 31)*
Meat Loaf with Brown Lentils *(page 212)*
Garlic Mashed Potatoes Ali-Bab *(page 256)*
Prune Tart with Almonds and Tea *(page 324)*

Menu Suggestions

Mushroom Tarts with Garlic Cream *(page 50)*
Steak/*Frites* with Shallot Glaze *(page 216)*
Corn Spinach *(page 72)*
Chocolate Peanut Crunch Bar Cake *(page 348)*

Artichokes Citronette *(page 43)*
Black Olive Tuxedo Steak *(page 217)*
Potato Fettuccine with Tomato and Basil *(page 254)*
Chocolate-Vanilla Double-Dip Crème Brûlée *(page 316)*

Citrus Non-Caesar Salad with Oysters *(page 100)*
Prime Rib with Blue Cheese Dressing *(page 222)*
Potato Gold Bricks *(page 269)*
Filo Apple Crowns with Cinnamon Custard *(page 338)*

Field Greens with Shrimp, Corn and Ginger *(page 96)*
Steak Bourguignon *(page 219)*
Garlic Rigatoni Gratin *(page 272)*
Celery Crunch with Anise *(page 279)*
Chocolate Peanut Crunch Bar Cake *(page 348)*

Menu Suggestions

Index

Index

Index

Index

Index

Index